Parliament Great Britain.

Collection of British Parliamentary Bills

1774-1818

Parliament Great Britain.

Collection of British Parliamentary Bills
1774-1818

ISBN/EAN: 9783337155155

Printed in Europe, USA, Canada, Australia, Japan

Cover: Foto ©ninafisch / pixelio.de

More available books at **www.hansebooks.com**

A

BILL

For regulating MADHOUSES.

N. B. *The Figures in the Margin denote the Number of the Folios in the written Copy.*

WHEREAS many great and dangerous Abuses frequently arise from the present State of Houses kept for the Reception of Lunatics, for want of Regulations with respect to the Persons keeping such Houses, the Admission of Patients into them, and the Visitation, by proper Persons, of the said Houses and Patients:

And whereas the Law, as it now stands, is insufficient for preventing or discovering such Abuses:

[2]

May it therefore pleafe Your MAJESTY,

That it may be Enacted; And be it Enacted by the King's Moft Excellent Majesty, by and with the Advice and Confent of the Lords Spiritual and Temporal, and Commons, in this prefent Parliament affembled, and by the Authority of the fame, That from and after   if any Perfon or Perfons, in that Part of *Great Britain* called *England*, the Dominion of *Wales*, or Town of *Berwick upon Tweed*, fhall, upon any Pretence whatfoever, conceal, harbour, entertain, or confine, in any Houfe or Place kept for the Reception of Lunatics, more than One Lunatic at any one Time, without having fuch Licence for that Purpofe as is hereinafter directed (except fuch Lunatics as are committed by the Lord High Chancellor of *Great Britain*, or Lord Keeper, or Commiffioners for the Cuftody of the Great Seal, for the Time being) every fuch Perfon fhall for every fuch Offence forfeit and pay the Sum of

And, in order that proper Perfons may be appointed for vifiting fuch Houfes as fhall be licenfed and kept for the Reception of Lunatics, within the Cities of *London* and *Weftminfter*, and within   Miles of the fame, and within the County of *Middlefex*; Be it further Enacted by the Authority aforefaid, That the Prefident and Fellows of the Royal College of Phyficians in *London*, for the Time being, at a general Meeting of the faid College, to be held upon the   Day of *September*, or, if that Day falls upon *Sunday*, then upon the   Day of *October*, in every Year, fhall elect   Fellows of the faid College, for granting fuch Licences as aforefaid, within the faid Cities of *London* and *Weftminfter*, and within   Miles of the fame, and within the faid County of *Middlefex*, according to the Directions of this Act; and the faid   Fellows, fo elected, fhall be, and are hereby declared to be Commiffioners for granting fuch Licences within the Limits aforefaid, for the Year then next enfuing: Provided that   at leaft of the faid Fellows to be fo elected, fhall be Perfons who have not acted as Commiffioners for the preceding Year; and that no Perfon whatfoever fhall be capable of being elected, or of acting as a Commiffioner, for more than   Years fucceffively.

And

And be it further Enacted, That in case at any Time of Election there shall not be found a sufficient Number of Fellows qualified, or willing to act as Commissioners, the said President and Fellows are hereby required, upon every such Deficiency, to elect   or more from among the Licentiates, to supply the same.

And be it further Enacted by the Authority aforesaid, That as often as any of the Commissioners, to be elected as aforesaid, shall die, or refuse to act, the said President is hereby required to call a Meeting of the said Fellows, within   Days next after such Death or Refusal shall be known to the said President, in order to elect a Commissioner in the room of every Commissioner who shall so die or refuse to act; and every Commissioner so to be elected, shall be, and is hereby vested with the same Power and Authority, in all Respects whatsoever, as the Commissioner in whose Place he shall be chosen was vested with.

And be it further Enacted, That every Person who shall be elected a Commissioner to act within the Cities of *London* and *Westminster*, and within   Miles of the same, and within the County of *Middlesex* as aforesaid, shall, within   Days after such Election, take the following Oath; (that is to say)

" I *A. B.* do swear, That I will faithfully and impar-
" tially execute all the Trusts committed unto me, by
" virtue of an Act of Parliament made in the Four-
" teenth Year of the Reign of King *George* the Third,
" intituled, 'An Act for regulating Madhouses;' and
" that I will not, directly or indirectly, give Notice,
" or cause Notice to be given, to the Keeper, or Person
" having the Care of any House or Place licensed for
" the Reception of Lunatics, of the Time of Visita-
" tion of such House or Place.
" So help me GOD."

Which Oath it shall and may be lawful for the President of the College of Physicians, for the Time being, to administer to every such Commissioner so to be elected as aforesaid, upon the Day he shall be so elected, or within   Days afterwards; and in case any Person, who shall be elected a Commissioner as aforesaid, and who shall be summoned by the
President

Prefident of the faid College, to attend the faid Prefident, to take the faid Oath, at fuch Time as fhall be mentioned in fuch Summons, fhall refufe or neglect to attend, or, attending, fhall refufe to take the faid Oath, he fhall forfeit and pay the Sum of   to be applied to the Ufe of the faid College.

6 And be it further Enacted by the Authority aforefaid, That the faid Commiffioners, fo to be elected as aforefaid, or any or more of them, fhall meet in the Hall, or fome other convenient Place in the faid College, as often as they fhall think fit; fo as fuch Meetings do not interfere with the Meetings of the Board of Cenfors, nor with any other General Meeting of the College of Phyficians, and that at all Meetings of the faid Commiffioners, to be holden for the Purpofes of this Act, the Commiffioner who is of the longeft Standing in the College fhall be the Chairman.

7 And be it further Enacted, That the Treafurer of the faid College, for the Time being, fhall be the Treafurer for the Purpofes of this Act; and that the faid Commiffioners, or any   or more of them, fhall, at fome Meeting to be holden within   Days next after they fhall be elected as aforefaid, chufe and appoint a proper Perfon to be their Secretary for the Year then enfuing; and fuch Secretary fhall be paid fuch Salary or Gratuity, for his Trouble and Attendance in the Execution of his Office, by the faid Treafurer, as the faid Commiffioners, or any   or more of them, fhall order and direct; and every fuch Secretary fhall, at the next Meeting of the faid Commiffioners after he fhall be fo appointed, take the following Oath:

" I *A. B.* do fwear, That I will faithfully execute all
" fuch Trufts as fhall be committed to my Charge, as
" Secretary to the Commiffioners for executing an Act
" of Parliament, made in the Fourteenth Year of the
" Reign of King *George* the Third, intituled, ' An Act
" for regulating Madhoufes;' and that I will keep fe-
" cret all fuch Matters as fhall come to my Knowledge
" in the Execution of my Office (except when re-
" quired to divulge the fame by legal Authority.)
                    " So help me G O D."

And be it further Enacted, That the faid Commiffioners,
or

or any   or more of them, shall meet annually, on or within   Days afterwards, in order to grant Licences to Persons for keeping Houses for the Reception of Lunatics, for One Year from   then next ensuing, within the said Cities of *London* and *Westminster*, and within   Miles of the same, and within the said County of *Middlesex*; but Notice of the Place, and of the Day and Hour, of every Meeting for granting such Licences, shall always be published   several Times in the *London Gazette*, before the Day of Meeting for granting any such Licences (which Licences they are hereby required to grant to all Persons who shall desire the same;) and all Licences to be granted by the said Commissioners shall be duly stamped with a   Stamp, and shall be under the Hands and Seals of   or more of the said Commissioners; for each of which Licences there shall be paid to the said Secretary, by the Person applying to take out the same, the Sums following; (that is to say) For each and every House wherein there shall be kept any Number of Lunatics not exceeding   the Sum of   and for each and every House wherein there shall be kept above   Lunatics, the Sum of   and no more, over and above what shall have been paid for the said Stamp; which Money shall be paid over by the said Secretary to the said Treasurer; and the further Sum of   and no more, shall be paid on every such Licence, to the said Secretary, for his Fee.

Provided always, That no one Licence shall authorise any Person or Persons to keep more Houses than One, for the Reception of Lunatics; nor shall any Licence, to be granted by virtue of this Act, continue in Force for any longer Time than for

And be it further Enacted by the Authority aforesaid, That no Commissioner, to be appointed as aforesaid, shall, directly or indirectly, during the Time he shall be a Commissioner, be interested in keeping any House for the Reception of Lunatics, upon Pain of forfeiting for such Offence the Sum of

And be it further Enacted, That the President of the said College of Physicians, for the Time being, shall, and is hereby required to cause Summons to be sent to the said several Commissioners, requiring them to attend at the First Meeting after they shall be appointed Commissioners as aforesaid; all which Summons shall be sent to the Beadle, or such other Person, belonging to the said College, as the said President shall think proper, and shall be left at the respective Houses or usual Places of Abode of each Commissioner.

Provided nevertheless, That in Case any   Commissioners shall at any Time or Times think proper to call a Meeting of the said Commissioners, such   Commissioners may themselves cause the like Notice to be given, and to be sent in Manner aforesaid to the other Commissioners, requiring their Attendance, at such Time and Place as shall be expressed in such Notice.

Provided always, That at all Meetings of the said Commissioners, in the Execution of this Act, in case of an Equality of Votes, the Chairman shall have the casting Vote.

And be it further Enacted, That the said Commissioners, or any   or more of them, either by themselves, or with their Secretary, as they shall think fit, shall and they are hereby required,   at least in every Year, and whenever required by the Lord High Chancellor, or Lord Keeper, or Commissioners for the Custody of the Great Seal, or by the Lord Chief Justice of the Court of King's Bench, or by the Lord Chief Justice of the Court of Common Pleas, for the Time being, to visit and inspect all such Houses as shall have been licensed by them as aforesaid, between the Hours of   and   in the Day-time; and may in like manner, at any other Time or Times, within the Hours aforesaid, visit and inspect all such Houses, as often as they, or any   or more of them, shall think necessary; and shall have, at all such Times, Liberty and Power to continue in such House, and to examine the Persons confined as Lunatics therein, for such Time as they shall think proper.

And be it further Enacted, That the said Commissioners, or their Secretary, shall, at every such Visitation, make Minutes in Writing of the State and Condition of all such Houses which they shall so visit, as to the Care of the Patients therein, and all such other Particulars as they shall think deserve their Notice, together with their Observations thereupon; all which Minutes shall, within   next after such Visitation, be by the said Secretary entered, by Way of Report, in a Register to be kept by him in the said College of Physicians for that Purpose, and the same shall be read to, and signed by, the said Commissioners, or any   or more of them, at their next Meeting; but no Minute, which tends to impeach the Character of any House, shall be so entered, unless such Minute shall have been previously signed by   or more of the said Commissioners who shall have been present at such Visitation; and in case the Commissioners, upon their Visitations, shall discover any Thing that, in their Opinion, shall deserve Censure or Animadversion, they shall in that Case report the same; and such Part of their Report, and no more, shall be hung up in the Censor's Room of the College, to be perused and inspected by any Person who shall apply for that Purpose.

𝕬𝖓𝖉 𝖇𝖊 𝖎𝖙 𝖋𝖚𝖗𝖙𝖍𝖊𝖗 𝕰𝖓𝖆𝖈𝖙𝖊𝖉, That in Case the Keeper of any House or Place for the Reception of Lunatics, within the Cities of *London* or *Westminster*, or within   Miles Distance thereof, or within the County of *Middlesex*, shall refuse all or any of the said Commissioners, at the Time of their Visitation, Admittance into such House or Place as aforesaid, with or without their Secretary, the Master or Keeper of such House or Place shall for such Offence forfeit his Licence.

𝕬𝖓𝖉 𝖇𝖊 𝖎𝖙 𝖋𝖚𝖗𝖙𝖍𝖊𝖗 𝕰𝖓𝖆𝖈𝖙𝖊𝖉, That the said Commissioners, or any   of them, shall from Time to Time cause an exact Account to be kept of all their Proceedings; and all such Accounts shall be entered in the same Register as the Minutes taken at their Visitations are directed to be entered as aforesaid; and the said Register shall be lodged in the College of Physicians, in a strong Chest or Box; which said Chest or Box shall be under the Care of the Beadle or Housekeeper belonging to the said College, and shall be carefully locked up, from Time to Time, by the Secretary and the said Commissioners, and the Key thereof kept by such Secretary; which said Register shall be deemed to belong to the said Commissioners; and the Key of the said Chest or Box shall be delivered over to every succeeding Secretary, whenever the former Secretary shall go out of the Office, and be kept by such succeeding Secretary, in manner aforesaid, for the Use of the said Commissioners.

𝕻𝖗𝖔𝖛𝖎𝖉𝖊𝖉 𝖆𝖑𝖜𝖆𝖞𝖘, That the President of the said College shall have Liberty to inspect the said Register, from Time to Time, as often as he shall think proper; provided such Inspection

tion be made at the College, and in the Presence of the Secretary to the said Commissioners.

And be it further Enacted, That the said Treasurer shall, and is hereby required to pay to each of the said Commissioners, for every Time they shall, in Obedience to this Act, or any Requisition therein contained, visit and inspect any such licensed House or Place as aforesaid, within the Limits aforesaid, the Sum of   and shall also pay and discharge all such reasonable Expences of the said Commissioners as they shall from Time to Time incur in the Execution of this Act; and the said Treasurer is hereby required, from Time to Time, to keep an exact and true Account of all Monies by him received and disbursed in relation to this Act, and shall enter such Account in a Book to be kept for that Purpose, which Book shall be lodged in the Box or Chest where the Register of the Proceedings of the said Commissioners is directed to be kept as aforesaid; which Accounts shall be produced to the President of the said College, when required by the said President and Elects, to be examined and settled by them; and if, upon such Examination, the said Account shall appear to be just and reasonable, the same shall be allowed and signed by the said President, and at least of the Elects, and shall be by the said President reported, together with the other Accounts, at the next general Meeting of the said College; and the said Account, being so allowed, signed, and reported, shall be a full Discharge to the said Treasurer for so much Money as shall in such Account appear to have been disbursed by him, on Account of the Execution of this Act.

And, in order that the said Commissioners may know when any Patient is received into any such licensed House or Place as aforesaid, **Be it further Enacted** by the Authority aforesaid, That the Keeper of every such licensed House or Place, within the said Cities of *London* and *Westminster*, and within   Miles of the same, and within the said County of *Middlesex*, is hereby required, within the Space of 16 Days after any Patient shall be received into any such licensed House or Place (except such Pauper Lunatics as shall happen to be sent there by Parish Officers) to cause Notice thereof to be given to the Secretary to the said Commissioners; which Notice shall contain the Name of every such Person received as a Lunatic into such House or Place, the Name or Names, and Place or Places of Abode, of the Person or Persons by whose Direction such Lunatic was sent to such House or Place, and also the Name and Place of Abode of the Physician, Surgeon, or Apothecary, by whose Advice such Direction was given; all which Notices shall be sent sealed up, directed "To the Secretary to the Commissioners for licensing Houses for the Reception of Lunatics, to be left with the Beadle of the College of Physicians in *London*." All which Notices the said Beadle is hereby directed to receive, and to deliver to the said Secretary, within   Days after the same shall come to his Hands; and the Secretary is hereby required to file and preserve all such Notices, and also to enter or cause a Copy or Extract thereof to be entered in the Register, within   Days after the Receipt of such Notices; and every Keeper of any such licensed House or Place, who shall admit, harbour, entertain, or confine any Person as a Lunatic, without having an Order in Writing, under the Hand and Seal of some Physician, Surgeon, or Apothecary, that such Person is proper to be received into such House or Place as a Lunatic, or shall receive any Lunatic into any such House or Place, having such Order, and shall not give Notice thereof to the Secretary of the said Commissioners, within the Time and in the Manner aforesaid, shall forfeit and pay the Sum of

17

And, in order that such Houses or Places for the Reception of Lunatics, as are not situated within the Limits aforesaid, may be put under some Regulation, Be it further Enacted, That no House, which is not within the said City of *London*, or within   Miles of the same, or within the said County of *Middlesex*, shall be kept for the Reception of more than   unless such House or Place shall be licensed by the Justices of the Peace, at some Quarter Sessions of the Peace to be holden for the County or Place wherein such House or Place shall be situated.

18

And be it further Enacted, That the Justices of the Peace, at any General Quarter Sessions of the Peace to be holden for any such County or Place, are hereby authorized and required to grant Licences to such Person and Persons as shall apply for that Purpose, such Person or Persons paying for each Licence the Sums following; (that is to say) For each and every House wherein there shall be kept any Number of Lunatics not exceeding Ten, the Sum of   and no more; and for each

each and every House wherein there shall be kept above the Number of Ten Lunatics, the Sum of   and no more; and that no One Licence shall authorize any Person or Persons to keep more Houses than One for the Reception of Lunatics, nor shall any such Licence be granted for any longer Term than for   and the said Justices shall, at the Time of granting such Licences as aforesaid, nominate and appoint   Justices of the Peace for the said County, and also One Physician, to visit and inspect all such Houses as shall be licensed by such Justices as aforesaid; and the said Justices and Physician so nominated and appointed, or any   of them, whereof the Physician to be One, may and are hereby authorized and impowered to visit, in the Day-time, every House so licensed, within the County where such House or Place shall be so licensed, as often as they shall think fit.

And be it further Enacted, That the said Justices and Physician so nominated, or such of them as shall visit any licensed House as aforesaid, may at every such Visitation, if they think necessary, make, or cause to be made, Minutes in Writing of the State and Condition of every House which they shall visit, as to the Care of the Patients therein, and all such other Particulars as they shall think deserve their Notice, together with their Observations thereupon; all which Minutes shall be entered by way of Report in a Register to be kept for that Purpose by the Clerk of the Peace for the County where such House or Houses shall be licensed as aforesaid; a Copy whereof shall from Time to Time be sent by the said Clerk of the Peace to the Secretary to the said Commissioners, to be by him inserted in a separate Register; which Register shall be kept in the same Box, and in the same Manner, as the Register belonging to the said Commissioners is hereinbefore directed to be kept; and the said Clerk of the Peace shall be paid such Sum and Sums of Money, for his Trouble in the Execution of this Act, as the said Justices shall order and direct; and all Money to be paid for such Licences as shall be granted by the said Justices of the Peace as aforesaid, shall be paid to the Clerk of the Peace as aforesaid, who shall keep an Account thereof in a Book or Books to be kept for that Purpose, and shall account for the same to the said Justices as often as he shall be required so to do; and all Expences attending the Execution of this Act (except within the Cities of *London* and *Westminster*, and within   Miles thereof, and also except within the said County of *Middlesex*) shall be defrayed out of such Money as aforesaid,

is

in such Manner as the said Justices shall from Time to Time, within their respective Counties, order and direct.

And be it further Enacted, That at such General Quarter Session, when such Justices and Physician shall be appointed as aforesaid, the Clerk of the Peace shall take the like Oath as is appointed by this Act to be taken by the Secretary of the Commissioners.

And be it further Enacted, That in case the Keeper of any House or Place for the Reception of Lunatics, not being within the said City of *London* or *Westminster*, or within Miles of the same, or within the said County of *Middlesex*, shall, in the Day-time, refuse the said Justices and Physician, on such Visitation, Admittance, at any Time or Times, into such House or Place as aforesaid, the Master or Keeper of such House or Place shall, for such Offence, forfeit

And be it further Enacted by the Authority aforesaid, That the Keeper of any House or Place for the Reception of Lunatics, not being within the said City of *London* or *Westminster*, or within Miles of the same, or within the said County of *Middlesex*, shall, and is hereby required to give such Notice as aforesaid, of the Receipt of every such Lunatic (except such Pauper Lunatics as shall happen to be sent there by Parish Officers) to the Secretary to the Commissioners, at the College of Physicians aforesaid, within the Space of Days from the Time of such Lunatic's being received into any such House or Place ; and every Keeper of any such licensed House or Place, who shall admit, harbour, entertain, or confine, any Person as a Lunatic, without having an Order in Writing, under the Hand and Seal of some Physician, Surgeon, or Apothecary, that such Person is proper to be received into such House or Place as a Lunatic, or shall receive any Lunatic into any such House or Place, having such Order, and shall not give Notice thereof to the Secretary of the said Commissioners, within the Time and in the Manner aforesaid, shall forfeit and pay the Sum of

And be it further Enacted, That no such Licence shall be granted as aforesaid, either by the said Commissioners or Justices of the Peace as aforesaid, unless, upon granting such Licence, the Person to whom such Licence is granted shall

D enter

enter into Recognizance to the King's Majefty, His Heirs and Succeffors, in the Sum of   with fufficient Securities, each in the Sum of or One fufficient Surety, in the Sum of under the ufual Conditions, for the good Behaviour of fuch Perfon during the Time for which fuch Licence fhall be granted.

And be it further Enacted by the Authority aforefaid, That the Lord High Chancellor of *Great Britain*, or Lord Keeper, or the Commiffioners for the Cuftody of the Great Seal, or the Lord Chief Juftice of the Court of King's Bench, or the Lord Chief Juftice of the Court of Common Pleas, for the Time being, may, at any Time or Times, by any written Order, directed to the Commiffioners appointed by this Act, or to the Juftices of the Peace, and Phyfician, appointed Vifitors at any General Quarter Seffion, require the faid Commiffioners, or any   or more of them, or the faid Vifitors, or any   of them, to vifit or infpect any Houfe or Houfes fo licenfed, and alfo to make a Report to him or them, touching fuch Matters as they fhall in fuch Orders be directed to inquire into, or as they fhall think deferving his or their Lordfhips Notice; and the faid Lord High Chancellor, or Lord Keeper, or Commiffioners for the Cuftody of the Great Seal, or Lord Chief Juftice of the Court of King's Bench, or the Lord Chief Juftice of the Court of Common Pleas, may alfo, at any Time or Times, by a like Order, fend for and infpect the Regifter or Regifters fo to be kept as aforefaid, and may fummon and examine all or any of the Perfons concerned in the Execution of the faid Act, as often as fhall be thought neceffary and proper; and in cafe they or any of them fhall not obey all fuch Orders as aforefaid, within   Days after the Receipt of the fame, and fhall not fhew fufficient Caufe to the contrary, every Perfon fo offending fhall be deemed guilty of

Provided always, and it is hereby Declared, That nothing in this Act contained fhall extend, or be conftrued to extend, to any of the public Hofpitals within this Kingdom.

And be it further Enacted by the Authority aforefaid, That all Penalties and Forfeitures which fhall be incurred
within

[13]

within the said Cities of *London* or *Westminster*, or within   Miles of the same, or within the said County of *Middlesex*, for Offences against this Act, shall and may be sued for and recovered in any of the Courts of Record at *Westminster*, by Action of Debt, Bill, Plaint, or Information, by the President of the said College, for the Time being, in the Name of the Treasurer belonging to the said College, at any Time within   Calendar Months after the Offence committed; and all such Penalties and Forfeitures, when recovered, shall, and are hereby directed to be paid to the said Treasurer, and shall be applied (except such Penalties and Forfeitures as are otherwise directed to be applied by this Act) in Manner following; (that is to say)   of all such Penalties and Forfeitures shall go to the Informer, and the   towards defraying the Expences attending the Execution of this Act; and all Penalties and Forfeitures which shall be incurred for Offences against this Act, not within the said Cities of *London* or *Westminster*, or within   Miles of the same, or within the said County of *Middlesex*, shall and may be sued for and recovered by Action of Debt, Bill, Plaint, or Information, by and in the Name of the Clerk of the Peace for the County where any such Offence shall be committed; and all such Penalties and Forfeitures, when recovered, shall be applied   to the Informer, and   for defraying the Expences attending the Execution of this Act within such County.

And be it further Enacted, That if any Action or Suit shall be commenced or brought against any Person or Persons, for any Thing done in pursuance of this Act, the same shall be commenced within   Calendar Months next after the Fact committed, and shall be laid or brought in the County, City, or Place, where the Cause of Action shall have arisen, and not elsewhere; and the Defendant or Defendants, in every such Action or Suit, shall and may, at his Election, plead specially, or the General Issue, Not Guilty, and give this Act, and the special Matter in Evidence, at any Trial to be had thereupon, and that the same was done in pursuance and by the Authority of this Act; and if the same shall appear to be so done, or that such Action or Suit shall be brought in any other County, City, or Place, or shall not have been commenced within the Time before limited for bringing the same, that then the Jury shall find a Verdict for the Defendant or Defendants; and upon a Verdict being so found, or

if

if the Plaintiff or Plaintiffs shall be nonsuited, or discontinue his, her, or their Action or Suit, after the Defendant or Defendants shall have appeared, or if, upon Demurrer, Judgment shall be given against the Plaintiff or Plaintiffs, then the Defendant or Defendants shall recover   Costs, and have such Remedy for recovering the same, as any Defendant or Defendants hath or have in any other Cases by Law.

28   And be it further Enacted, That this Act shall be deemed and taken to be a Public Act, and be judicially taken Notice of as such, by all Judges, Justices, and other Persons whomsoever, without specially pleading the same.

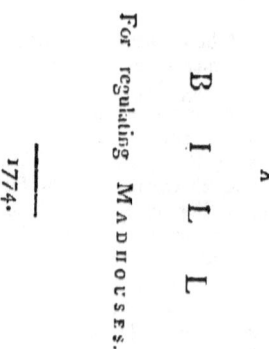

A BILL For regulating Madhouses.

1774.

AN
EPITOME
OF THE
BILL

Now depending in Parliament, the better to prevent the Illicit Exportation of Live Sheep, Wool, Woolfels, Mortlings, Shortlings, Yarn and Worsted Cruels, Coverlets, Waddings, and other Manufactures, or pretended Manufactures, slightly wrought up, or otherwise put together, so as the same may be reduced to, and made use of as, Wool again; Mattrasses or Beds stuffed with Combed Wool, or Wool fit for combing; Fullers Earth, Fulling Clay, and Tobocco-Pipe Clay: And for reducing into One Act several Laws now in being relating thereto; and also for rendering more effectual an Act passed in the Twenty-third Year of the Reign of King Henry the Eighth, intituled, " An Act for the Winding of Wool;" wherein is shewn from what Laws the Clauses contained in such Bill have been selected and taken, or are grounded upon.

[The Figures in the Margin denote the Page of the Printed Bill where each Clause may be found.]

THE Preamble sets forth the necessity that the present Wool Laws should be amended and consolidated [*];
and then it is enacted as follows:

That

---

[*] The propriety of reducing the laws now in being against the Exportation of Wool, &c. into one, will scarcely be disputed, when it is known that

A   the

[2]

2   That all Acts now in force, or so much thereof as relate to the carrying coastwise, or to prevent the Exportation of, the above-mentioned articles (except so much of the 9th and 10th W. III. c. xl. which relates to the counties of Kent and Sussex *), shall be repealed.

3   That all Exporters of Live Sheep shall forfeit   for every such Sheep, for the first offence, and be imprisoned for the space of   , and until the forfeiture shall be paid; and that all such Sheep, and the vessel on which the same shall be on board, shall be forfeited. And that for a second, and every subsequent offence, the penalty, and also the time of the imprisonment, shall be increased with the like forfeitures†. *(New Clause.)*

Provided the regulations to prevent so great a mischief are dilated into about twenty Acts of Parliament, many of which are now unnecessary.

* The 9th and 10th W. III. (after reciting that it was a common practice, in Romney Marsh, for persons *not resident upon the place* to buy up great quantities of Wool, and to export the same, enacts) That no persons residing within fifteen miles of the sea, in the counties of Kent and Sussex, shall presume to buy any Wool, before they enter into bond, with sureties, that all the Wool they buy shall not *be sold by them to any person or persons within fifteen miles of the sea*; and in case *any* Wool be found carried towards the sea side in the counties aforesaid, unless such Wool be first entered, and security given, the same shall be forfeited, and the person offending shall forfeit three shillings for every pound weight.

The same Statute also enacts, That no Wool removed from the place where it was first laid after sheering, within ten miles of the sea, shall be lodged, after the first removing, *within fifteen miles of the sea* in the said counties, upon pain of forfeiting such Wool, and three shillings for every pound weight.

The great inconvenience which the Wool Growers and Wool Dealers in the counties of Kent and Sussex would be put to by a strict attention to the execution of this law is sufficiently obvious: and would it not therefore be advisable for them to endeavour to have it repealed, and what must have been the real intent of the then Legislature re-enacted and enforced?

† The Exportation of Live Sheep is prohibited by the 8th Eliz. chap. iii. upon pain that the offender shall for the first offence forfeit and lose all

his

Provided that Live Wether Sheep may be put on board any ship as food for the crew, &c. C. II. c. xxxii. f. 11.

Provided that such Wether Sheep shall be put on board with the consent of the Comptroller of the port where the same are intended to be shipped. *(New Clause.)*

That all Exporters of Wool, &c. their aiders and abettors, shall forfeit 3*s*. for every pound weight of Wool, &c. which shall be exported; and shall, for the first offence, suffer imprisonment for the space of , and until the penalty shall be paid. And for every second and subsequent offence, such Exporter shall be subject to the same penalty, and be imprisoned for a longer time, and until such penalty shall be paid. All ships, vessels, carts, carriages, and horses employed in the Exportation of any of the said articles, and also the articles themselves, shall be forfeited. 12th C. II. c. xxxii. f. 1. 13th and 14th C. II. c. xviii. f. 3. 12th G. II. c. xxi. f. 9*.

That his goods for ever; and further, that he shall suffer imprisonment for one whole year, and at the year's end shall have his left hand cut off. And further, that if he eftsoons offend against this Statute, he shall be adjudged a felon, and shall suffer death as in cases of felony.

It is to be noted, that this prohibition is not confined to sheep the breed of this kingdom.—Vide also the following note:

* The Exportation of Thrums and Woollen Yarn was prohibited by the 8th Hen. VI.

The Exportation of Worsted Yarn is prohibited under the forfeiture of 40*s*. *per* pound by the 33d Hen. VIII. So early was it discovered that such a practice was prejudicial to the interest of this kingdom: and the enormity of the penalty shews the great anxiety of the Legislature to remedy that mischief; and it is fair to infer, that the then desire of foreigners to obtain Worsted Yarn, was as great as the anxiety to prevent it.

The Exportation of Sheep and Wool the breed and growth of the kingdom of England, and also of all Woolfels, Mortlings, Shortlings, Yarn made

6 That all Wool, &c. intended to be carried coaftwife, fhall be entered at the port from whence the fame is intended to be

made of Wool, Wool Flocks, Fullers Earth, and Fulling Clay, is prohibited by 12th C. II. c. xxxii. under the penalty that all fuch articles fhall be forfeited, and of the forfeiture of 20 s. for every fuch Sheep, and of 3 s. for every pound weight of fuch other of the aforefaid articles; and of all fhips and veffels wherein the fame fhall be loaden or laid on board, and of the forfeiture of all the goods and chattels of the mafter and mariners of fuch fhip or veffels, knowing fuch offence; who alfo are to be imprifoned for the fpace of three months. And every perfon who fhall be convicted, fhall be difabled to require any debt or account of any factor or others, for or concerning any debt or eftate properly belonging to fuch offenders.— And it is by this Act provided, that nothing therein contained fhall be conftrued to take away any greater pains or penalties for any of the offences aforefaid.

The Exportation of Tobacco-Pipe Clay is prohibited by the 13th and 14th C. II. c. xviii. under the forfeiture of 3 s. per pound.

By the 7th & 8th W. III. c. xxviii. no fhip or veffel fhall export any of the commodities in this Act mentioned, under the penalty and forfeiture of the faid commodities, fhip, and veffel, and treble the value thereof, with treble cofts of fuit; and the inhabitants of the hundred next adjoining to the fea through which fuch commodities fhall be carried, are fubject to treble the value thereof; and all perfons who fhall be aiding in fuch Exportation, fhall fuffer three years imprifonment.

The Exportation of Fullers Earth, and Scouring Clay, is alfo prohibited by the 9th & 10th W. III. c. xl. under the forfeiture of 1 s. for every pound weight.

By the 9th & 10th W. III. c. x. in actions brought for any penalty incurred by the laws againft the Exportation of Wool, &c. the defendants are required to give bail.

By the 4th Geo. I. c. xi. in cafe the perfons againft whom judgment fhall be obtained for any penalty incurred for the unlawful Exportation of Wool, &c. fhall not pay the fum recovered within the fpace of three months after the entering up of fuch judgment, fuch perfons may by order of court be tranfported for the term of feven years. By the 12th G. II. c. xxi. the laft-mentioned Act is extended to aiders and abetters of fuch Exportation.

By the 5th G. I. c. xi. it is recited, that in the coaft regulation of 1ft W. & M. Wool was only mentioned; and therefore the fame provifion is extended to
Woolfels,

be shipped, before the same shall be brought within five miles of such port. 1 W. & M. c. xxxii. f. 2. 5 G. 1. c. xi. f. 14.

Provided Woolfelts, Mortlings, Shortlings, Yarn made of Wool, Wool Flocks, Fullers Earth, Fulling Clay, and Tobacco-Pipe Clay.

By the 12th Geo. II. c. xxi. the Exportation of Coverlets, Waddings, and other Manufactures, or pretended Manufactures, made of Wool slightly stitched, worked, or otherwise put together, so as the same might be reduced to, and made use of as, Wool again; or Mattrasses or Beds stuffed with Combed Wool, or Wool fit for combing, is prohibited under the like penalties and forfeitures as the Exportation of Wool.

Such has been the systematic attention of former Legislatures to prevent the Exportation of our Wool; and it has been reserved for later times, and the wisdom of a few modern politicians, to condemn that system; the beneficial effects whereof in Yorkshire, and all other manufacturing parts of the kingdom, will oppose every speculative opinion. To be consistent, the opposers of the present Bill ought to endeavour to obtain the repeal of the laws now in being (to the making whereof, it is presumed, some of them have in a legislative capacity consented) against the enticing our Manufacturers in Wool to go out of the kingdom; and the Exportation of Tools or Utensils made use of in the working up of Wool. The poor Manufacturer, and the ingenious inventor of these tools, submit to this restriction without murmuring. But, how absurd must it appear to retain the hands and instruments, and permit to be sent away, either openly or clandestinely, the material which Providence has given in so eminent a degree to this Nation for their employment.

By the evidence adduced before the Committee of the House of Commons, it appears that about 600,000 Packs of Wool are annually grown in this kingdom: of this, one half may upon the best enquiry be supposed to be pulled from Sheep Skins, the remaining half therefore will be shorn Wool; of which it is presumed, upon the same ground, that one third is Short Wool, and the remaining two-thirds, or 200,000 Packs, are Long Combing Wool. Of these 200,000 Packs, 13,000 Packs may be deemed, from evidence as positive as the nature of the fact will admit of, to have been yearly smuggled to France[*]; and that this Wool will enable the French to manufacture 39,000 Packs of their own Wool, into articles which in a great degree would be supplied from England.

To mark the magnitude of this evil, it is necessary to shew the very great advantages which this kingdom derives by the working up of our Long Combing Wool. Two hundred thousand Packs of such Wool, will upon

[*] See the Report of the Committee of the House of Commons.

a moderate

7 Provided that nothing in the foregoing Clause shall hinder any person from carrying his Wool from the place of sheering to his dwelling house or outhouses, though the same be within five miles or less of the sea; notice of removal being first given to the officers of the customs at the adjacent port. 1 W. & M. c. xxxii. s. 3.

8 That Wool, &c. lying near the sea, or any navigable river, with intent to be exported, may be seized, and shall be forfeited. 12 C. II. c. xxxii. s. 7.

Provided that a limited quantity of Wool may be shipped, under certain regulations, to the islands of Jersey, Guernsey, Alderney, and Sark. 12 C. II. c. xxxii. s. 12. 1 W. & M. c. xxxii. s. 14.

10 That the governors of such islands shall take for a licence to bring Wool to the said islands. 12 C. II. c. xxxii. s. 14.

a moderate computation, when manufactured, make ten millions of money; and the manufacturing of it will employ upwards of two millions of persons annually: these considerations sufficiently evince the propriety of keeping our Wool at home. But when it is considered that the Smuggling of 13,000 Packs of Wool is the loss of 520,000 *l.** annually to this nation, in the first instance; and will enable the French to meet us at the foreign market (to which market our Worsteds are chiefly sent) with manufactured goods the same as our own, of the value of two millions and an half, or one-fourth of the English stock at such market (supposing all the English Worsteds were exported, which is not the case)—the effects of preventing such a mischief are obvious: the Manufacturer would have no longer reason to complain that Wool was advanced almost double, and that he was now obliged by necessity to sell the manufactured articles at losing prices †; and the Grower would find the demand for his Wool increased, and consequently the price kept up; inasmuch as there would be an end to the rivalship of 30,000 Packs of French Wool, and of course an additional demand of the products of the English.

* The Wool is estimated at £.40 per Pack. That addition by labour, in Yorkshire Worsteds, is five times the value of the Wool; in Norwich, &c. the £.520,000 are taken from the Yorkshire increase only.

† See Mr. Clayton's evidence, as reported by the Committee of the House of Commons.

That

That no Wool, &c. shall be put on board alien ships, except Lamb Skins prepared for Fur or Linings. 12 C. II. c. xxxii. f. 9 & 10.

The third section of 9 & 10 W. III. c. xl. which relates to the practice on Romney Marsh, being recited, it is enacted, That the certificate mentioned in such section, shall be returned to the officer who granted it. *(New Clause.)*

That every person who shall alter a certificate or licence, 12 shall forfeit the sum of . *(New Clause).*

That no Wool shall be carried between sun setting and sun rising. 7 & 8 W. III. c. xxxviii. f. 8.

That all Wool, Woollen, and Worsted Articles, shall be packed in leather or canvas, and marked " Wool" on the outside. 12 Geo. II. c. xxi. f. 10.

That persons who shall pack Wool, or any such arti- 13 cles, in any box or barrel, or shall cause the same to be pressed by any engine into any butt or pipe, shall forfeit per pound, and also such articles. 13th and 14th C. II. c. xviii. f. 7.

That all such persons shall also be punished as Exporters of Wool. *Ibid.*

That persons who shall have assisted in such package, and 14 shall discover the master packer, shall not be liable to any penalty. *(New Clause.)*

· That if the master packer shall discover the person who employed him to make such illegal package, he shall not be liable to such pains and penalties. *(New Clause.)*

That

That no cafk shall be put on board any veffel till the fame shall have been fearched, and a fufferance obtained. *(New Claufe.)*

15 That wharfingers shall give bond that they will give a regular account of Wool by them received and delivered. *(New Claufe.)*

16 That wharfingers shall give notice of the Wool by them received to the cuftomer at the port where fuch wharf shall be kept. *(New Claufe.)*

That no Wool, &c. shall be shipped to be carried coaft-wife before notice be given at the port from whence the fame is intended to be shipped, and bond given for the due landing thereof. 12 G. II. c. xxi. f. 11.

18 That the cuftomer at the port from whence Wool, &c. shall be shipped, shall tranfmit an account thereof to the cuftomer at the port to which the fame is intended to be conveyed; and before any bond shall be difcharged, a certificate shall be produced of fuch Wool, &c. being duly landed. *Ibid.*

19 That no Wool, &c. shall be put on board veffels bound to foreign parts, under the penalty of fuch Wool, &c. and ship, being forfeited, and the mafter being punifhed as an Exporter, unlefs fuch mafter difcover the fhipper. 12 G. II. c. xxi. f. 23.

20 Provided that the mafters of veffels not regularly cleared out, shall not have any benefit or exemption from fuch difcovery. *Ibid.*

Provided that where it shall appear from the fmallnefs of the quantity of any Wool, &c. which shall be found on board

any

any ship regularly cleared out, or in any waggon, that the same might be there without the knowledge of the owner or master, no punishment or forfeiture in any such case shall ensue. *(New Clause.)*

That a register of all Wool, &c. sent coastwise shall be kept, and a copy thereof transmitted to the Custom House in London. 1 W. & M. c. xxxii. f. 11.

That no Wool, which shall be on board any vessel to be carried coastwise, shall be unpacked. *(New Clause).*

That all Wool, &c. shall be shipped and landed in the presence of the proper officer, and at lawful quays. 12 G. II. c. xxi. f. 13.

That all cockets shall be wrote upon paper, and shall not be erased or interlined. 1 W. & M. c. xxxii. f. 4.

That persons insuring Wool, &c. to be delivered in foreign parts, shall be deemed Exporters, and so punished. 12 G. II. c. xxi. f. 29.

That the insured shall be subject to the like penalty. *Ibid.* sect. 30.

That the persons insuring, or becoming the insured, who shall first discover the offence, shall be acquitted. *Ibid.* sect. 31.

That all insurances on Wool, &c. shall be void. *Ibid.* sect. 33.

That the Lord High Admiral shall appoint cruizers, with orders to seize all ships bound to foreign parts, having Wool, &c. on board. 10th & 11th W. III. c. x. f. 16. 5th Geo. II. c. xxi. f. 1.

B That

26   That the mafter of any cruizer may fearch any fhip within his ftation.   5 G. II. c. xxi. f. 5.

That Ships, Wool, &c. which fhall be feized by any cruizer, fhall be fold to the beft bidder.   *Ibid.* f. 3.

27   That the commander of any fuch cruizer, who fhall neglect his duty, fhall be punifhed.   10 & 11 W. III. c. 10. f. 18.

That revenue officers by themfelves, and all other perfons in company of a conftable only, or other peace officer, may examine and feize the articles prohibited from being exported.   12 C. II. c. xxxii. f. 7.   1 W. & M. c. xxxii. f. 9. and 12 G. II. c. xxi. f. 14.

28   That officers of the revenue, and peace officers, who fhall neglect their duty, fhall be punifhed.   12 G. II. c. xxi. f. 16.

That perfons acting under any deputation from Commiffioners of the Cuftoms, Excife, or Salt, fhall be deemed officers to execute this Act.   12 G. II. c. xxi. f. 24.

That all perfons who fhall make collufive feizures, fhall be deemed and punifhed as Exporters of Wool, except fuch as fhall turn Informers.   12 G. II. c. xxi. f. 16.

29   That all perfons who fhall prevent or hinder the execution of this Act, or fhall wound or beat any one who fhall be in the execution thereof, fhall be tranfported.   12 G. II. c. xxi. f. 26.

30   That perfons offering to bribe any officer, or other perfon, to connive at the Exportation of Wool, &c. fhall forfeit the fum of £   12 G. II. c. xxi. f. 25.

That

That officers of the revenue who shall neglect their duty, shall be punished as Exporters of Wool. 1 W. & M. c. xxxii. f. 5.

That bonds which shall be taken in pursuance of this Act, shall not be chargeable with any stamp. 12 G. II. c. xxi. f. 28.

That in all questions upon this Act, the proof of the breed of Sheep or growth of Wool to be of this kingdom, shall not be upon the seizer or prosecutor. *(New Clause.)*

That all seizures and penalties not exceeding may be determined in a summary way. 13 & 14. c. ii. c. xviii. f. 12.—12 G. II. c. xxi. f. 18. 31

That penalties not before appropriated shall go and be paid between the informer and the officer of the revenue who shall assist in making any seizure. 12 G. II. c. xxi. f. 19 & 21. 32

That officers of the revenue, and officers of the peace, may seize upon and arrest persons offending against this Act, and convey them before a magistrate. *(New Clause.)*

That officers making the arrest shall be bound over to prosecute. *(New Clause.)* 33

That in case it shall appear to the magistrate that the penalty incurred cannot be levied from the goods of the offender, every such offender may be immediately committed. *(New Clause.)*

That until the warrant for levying the penalty incurred shall be returnable, the offender may be kept in custody. *(New Clause.)*

34 That if the offender give security, to the satisfaction of the magistrate, for the payment of the penalty incurred by him, that then every such offender may be set at liberty. *(New Clause.)*

That all persons who shall think themselves aggrieved, may, upon entering into recognizance, appeal to the sessions. (*New Clause.*)

35 That appellants who shall pay the penalty by way of deposit, may appeal, upon their entering into recognizance, without sureties. (*New Clause.*)

That all persons who shall appear to be necessary witnesses, in any complaint or information, may be compelled to appear and give their evidence. (*New Clause.*)

36 That persons taking greater fees than allowed by this Act, shall forfeit   for every Penny that shall be taken, over and above the fee allowed. 12 C. II. c. xxxii. f. 14.

That all actions which shall be brought for the recovery of any penalty not herein before directed to be recovered in a summary way; and also such penalties as are herein before directed to be so recovered in a summary way, may, if the party claiming the same shall so think proper, be prosecuted in any of his Majesty's Courts of Record at Westminster, or in the Court of Exchequer at Edinburgh. 12 G. II. c. xxi. f. 32.

That persons who shall be prosecuted for any penalty incurred by this Act, shall be obliged to give bail. 10 & 11 W. III. c. x. f. 20.

37 That all actions that shall be prosecuted by virtue of this Act, shall be tried by a jury to be summoned out of any other

other county than that wherein the fact shall be committed. 7 & 8 W. III. c. xxviii. f. 11.

That judgment by default may be entered against any person who shall be in prison, and who shall refuse to plead. 4 G. I. c. xi. f. 6.

That where no seizure shall happen to be made whereby the informer can be rewarded, a reward shall be paid to him by the Commissioners of the Customs. 12 G. II. c. 21. f. 22.

Provided that no person shall be prosecuted for any offence done contrary to this Act, unless such prosecution shall be commenced within the space of   next after the offence committed. 9 & 10 W. III. c. xl. f. 9.

That the first three persons who shall be aiding in the exporting of any of the said articles, and who shall give information thereof, shall not suffer any of the penalties or punishments herein before mentioned. 7 & 8 W. III. c. xxviii. f. 11.

38

Provided that the owner or master of any ship, who shall give the first information, within a limited time, of the Exportation of any of the said articles, and enter into recognizance to give evidence of the same, shall not be liable to any of the penalties contained in this Act. 13 & 14 C. II. c. xviii. f. 11. and 1 W. & M. c. xxxii. f. 8.

That Abstracts of this Act shall be delivered at every Easter Sessions to the High Constables, and that they shall cause one of the said Abstracts to be fixed upon the church and chapel door of every parish church and chapel within their respective liberties, within a certain distance of the sea. *(New Clause.)*

The

39   The said Bill also, after reciting the Act passed in the twenty-third year of King Henry the Eighth, whereby the seller of deceitful Wool is to forfeit, for every fleece deceitfully wound, six-pence (one moiety to the King, and the other to the finder or prover of the said deceit, to be recovered by Action of Debt); and also, after reciting that the said Law had not now the good effects thereby proposed, by reason of the said penalty being so small *, and one moiety thereof being directed to be paid to the King, and the great expence attending the recovery of the same—enacts, That, in lieu of Six-pence, the penalty shall be Two Shillings and Six-pence, and shall be recovered in a summary way. *(New Clause.)*

40   That where the penalty shall not be paid, the same may be levied by warrant of distress and sale. *(New Clause.)*

That all persons convicted, shall have liberty to appeal, upon entering into recognizance to try such appeal. *(New Clause.)*

41   That no conviction shall be set aside through want of form, nor shall the same be removed into any of his Majesty's Courts of Record. *(New Clause.)*

42   That all actions which shall be brought against any person for any thing done by virtue of this Act, shall be brought within a limited time, &c. &c.   19 G. II. c. xxxii. s.

---

* Among a number of witnesses who were ready to be adduced to prove the great deceits in the Winding of Wool, and the inadequacy of the present penalty to prevent it—an eminent Woolstapler was only examined; when he proved that he was defrauded in an instance, where the offender, after paying to him the whole of the penalty, was a gainer of 3*d.* *per* Fleece.

AN
EPITOME
OF THE
BILL

To prevent the Exportation of WOOL, &c. *being the Variations of such Bill from the present Laws.*

[1]

A

BILL

To prevent Abuses in the Packing or Bagging of Hops.

WHEREAS divers Abuses are practised in the Packing or Bagging of Hops: For Remedy whereof,

May it please Your MAJESTY,

That it may be Enacted, **and be it Enacted** by the King's most Excellent Majesty, by and with the Advice and Consent of the Lords Spiritual and Temporal, and Commons, in this present Parliament assembled, and by the Authority of the same, That from and after the   all Planters, Growers, and Owners of Hops, shall, before the Duty is charged thereon, mark or cause to be marked, with Ink or Paint, in plain and legible Characters, upon the Outside of every Bag or Pocket in which any Hops shall be packed, the Weight or Tare of every such Bag or Pocket, with the Planter or Planters Name or Names at full Length, or the Initial Letters thereof, together with the Date of the Year in which such Hops were grown: And if any Planter, Grower or Owner of Hops, shall not mark all such Bags or Pockets, within the Time and in the Manner aforesaid, or shall not mark or cause to be marked the exact and true Weight of all

A   such

such Bags or Pockets, every such Planter, Grower or Owner of Hops, shall, for every such Offence, forfeit the Sum of

And be it further Enacted by the Authority aforesaid, That all and every Person and Persons, who shall sell any Hops which shall be grown after the said
shall make an Allowance to the Buyer of such Hops for the Tare of every Bag or Pocket, according to the Weight so marked thereon; and so in Proportion for a Part of any Bag or Pocket which shall be cut and sold in any less Quantity than a whole Bag or Pocket; which Allowance shall be deducted from the gross Weight of all such Hops before Payment shall be demanded for the same.

Provided always, That every Person who shall sell a whole Bag or Pocket of Hops, shall be allowed to charge for every Bag or Pocket wherein such Hops shall be contained, such Sum as any such Planter or Seller shall have actually paid for the same, not exceeding   for any One Bag, and   for any One Pocket.

And be it further Enacted by the Authority aforesaid, That all Penalties and Forfeitures for Offences against this Act shall, upon Information and Proof of the Offences respectively before any One Justice of the Peace for the County or Place where the Offence shall be discovered, or wherein the Offender shall be or reside, either by the Confession of the Party or Parties offending, or by the Oath of One or more Witness or Witnesses (which Oath such Justice of the Peace is hereby impowered and required to administer without Fee or Reward) be levied by
of the Goods and Chattels of the Party or Parties offending, by Warrant or Warrants under the Hand and Seal of such Justice (which Warrant or Warrants such Justice is hereby impowered to grant); and the Overplus, after such Penalties and Forfeitures, and the Charges of such   are recovered and deducted, shall be returned upon Demand unto the Owner or Owners of such Goods and Chattels; and the Penalties and Forfeitures, when so paid or levied, shall from time to time be paid to the Person who shall give Information of any such Offence.

Provided always, That nothing herein contained shall extend to subject any such Planter, Grower or Owner of Hops, to the
said

said Penalty in Cases where an Increase of Weight shall appear to such Justice to have arisen by the Flour or Dust of the Hops, or other Dust, Dirt or Thing that may have unavoidably adhered to such Bag or Pocket; such Increase not exceeding   Pounds Weight for any one Bag, or   Pounds Weight for any one Pocket.

Provided always, and it is hereby Declared, That no Person shall be liable to be prosecuted for any Penalty for any Offence against this Act, unless Complaint shall be made thereof to some Justice of the Peace for the County or Place where the Cause of Complaint shall arise or be discovered, within   Months next after the Sale of any such Hops; any Thing herein before contained to the contrary hereof notwithstanding.

And be it further Enacted by the Authority aforesaid, That this Act shall be deemed and taken to be a Public Act, and shall be judicially taken Notice of as such by all Judges, Justices, and other Persons whomsoever, without specially pleading the same.

BILL

To prevent Abuses in the Packing or Bagging of Hops.

[1774.]

This Clause
Proposed to be inserted
to the purchasers of making
By this Bill
the Consumer is Subject
pays for the bagging
of the pores of Hops

the Penalty
is to allow the Weight of the
Bag as is Usual to the Buyer
is found the Value of the
Bag is the less

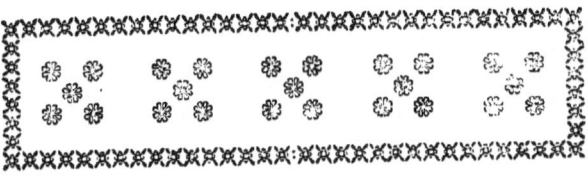

A

BILL

FOR

Altering, explaining, and amending, several Acts of the Parliament of *Scotland*, respecting Colliers, Coalbearers, and Salters.

Note.—*The Figures in the Margin denote the Number of the Folio in the written Copy.*

WHEREAS by the Statute Law of *Scotland*, as explained by the Judges of the Courts of Law there, Colliers and Coalbearers, and Salters, are in a State of Slavery, bound to the Collieries and Salt Works, where they work for Life, transferrable, with these Collieries and Salt Works, when their original Masters have no further Use for them:

A And

1

And whereas Persons are discouraged and prevented from learning the Art or Business of Colliers, or Coalbearers, and Salters, by their becoming bound to the Collieries and Salt Works for Life, where they shall work for the Space of One Year, by Means whereof there are not a sufficient Number of Colliers, Coalbearers, and Salters, in *Scotland*, for working the Quantity of Coal and Salt necessarily wanted, and many new discovered Coals remain unwrought, and many are not sufficiently wrought; nor are there a sufficient Number of Salters for the Salt Works, to the great Loss of the Owners, and Disadvantage to the Public:

And whereas the emancipating the Colliers, Coalbearers, and Salters, now in being in *Scotland*, gradually, upon reasonable Conditions, and the preventing others from coming into such a State of Servitude, would be the Means of increasing the Number of Colliers, Coalbearers, and Salters, to the great Benefit of the Public, without doing any Injury to the present Masters, and would remove the Reproach of allowing such a State of Servitude to exist in a free Country:

May it therefore please Your MAJESTY,

That it may be Enacted; And be it Enacted by the King's Most Excellent MAJESTY, by and with the Advice and Consent of the Lords Spiritual and Temporal, and Commons, in this present Parliament assembled, and by the Authority of the same, That from and after

no Person working as a Collier, Coalbearer, or Salter, or in any other Way, in a Colliery or Salt Work in *Scotland*, shall be bound to such Colliery or Salt Work, or to the Owner thereof, in any Way or Manner different from what is permitted by the Law of *Scotland* with regard to Servants and Labourers; and that they shall be deemed free, and shall enjoy the same Privileges, Rights, and Immunities with the rest of His Majesty's Subjects, any Law or Usage in *Scotland* to the contrary notwithstanding.

Provided always, That it shall be lawful for all Owners and Lessees of Collieries and Salt Works, and for Colliers, Coalbearers, and Salters, to take Persons, bound by Contract

tract or Indenture, as Apprentices, to learn the Art or Business of Coalhewing, Coalbearing, or making Salt, for any Term of Years permitted by the Law of *Scotland* with regard to Apprentices in other Arts and Mysteries.

And be it further Enacted by the Authority aforesaid, That all Persons under the Age of   at the Commencement of this Act, employed as Colliers, Coalbearers, or Salters, in *Scotland*, shall, after   Service from and after the Commencement of this Act, be free from their Service and Servitude, and at Liberty to engage themselves as Servants or Labourers in any other Colliery or Salt Work, or in any other Kind of Labour whatever.

And be it further Enacted by the Authority aforesaid, That all Colliers and Salters in *Scotland*, above the Age of
            and under the Age of   at the Commencement of this Act, after a Service of   and all Colliers and Salters above the Age of   but under the Age of   at the Commencement of this Act, after a Service of   and all Colliers and Salters above the Age of   at the Commencement of this Act, after a Service of   after their having respectively sufficiently instructed a Person as an Apprentice in the Art or Mystery of Coalhewing, or making of Salt, of the Age of   at least, when such Instruction shall be perfected, shall be free from any other Servitude or Bondage to the Colliery or Salt Work to which they were bound.

Provided always, That every Collier or Salter claiming Liberty under the Authority of this Act, shall, prior to his being freed from his Servitude or Bondage, obtain a Decree of the Sheriff Court of the County in which he resides, finding and declaring that he is intitled to his Freedom under the Authority of this Act.

And be it Enacted by the Authority aforesaid, That for the Purpose of obtaining such Decree, it shall and may be lawful for the Collier or Salter claiming his Freedom, to present a Petition to the Sheriff Depute or Substitute of the County where he resides, stating his Claim of Freedom, and offering to prove the Facts which entitle him to it; and the Sheriff Depute or Substitute is hereby authorized and required to

B   order

order the Petition to be served upon the Owner, Leſſee, or Overſeer of the Colliery or Salt Works to which the Petitioner is bound, and to order an Anſwer to be put in to the Petition in   Days after Service, ſtating the Objection or Objections to the Freedom claimed, if any ſuch are intended to be made; and the Sheriff ſhall thereafter proceed in a ſummary Way in taking the Proofs, and all other Procedure neceſſary, until a Decree ſhall be pronounced; and if the Decree of the Sheriff ſhall be againſt the Petitioner, finding him not intitled to Freedom, it ſhall nevertheleſs be competent to ſuch Petitioner, at any Period after the Expiration of   to preſent a Second Petition, ſtating his Claim of Liberty of new, and which ſhall be proceeded upon in the ſame Manner as the former; and if the Petitioner fails in obtaining a Decree for him on the Second Petition, he may, after the Expiration of
from the Date of the Second Decree, preſent a Third Petition, which ſhall likewiſe be proceeded upon in the ſame Manner; and if he fails in obtaining Decree upon his Third Petition, he may preſent a Fourth; and ſo on till he obtains a Decree declaring his Freedom;   at leaſt being expired after a Decree upon one Petition, before it ſhall be competent to preſent another.

Provided always, and be it Enacted, That a Collier or Salter claiming his Liberty under the Authority of this Act, his not having inſtructed an Apprentice in Manner before directed ſhall afford no Objection to ſuch Collier or Salter obtaining a Decree of his Freedom, if he ſhall produce to the Sheriff a Writing under the Hand of the Owner or Leſſee of the Colliery or Salt Work to which he is bound, or of the Steward or Factor of the Owner, diſcharging the Obligation upon ſuch Collier or Salter to have inſtructed an Apprentice in Manner before directed.

And be it further Enacted by the Authority aforeſaid, That it ſhall not be competent for either of the Parties to remove the Proceedings upon any ſuch Petition into the Court of Seſſion in *Scotland*, by Advocation, or to complain of any Decree, by Appeal or Suſpenſion, or to ſue for Reduction of any ſuch Decree; and that every Decree upon ſuch Petition, finding and declaring the Freedom of the Petitioner, ſhall be final and concluſive againſt the Perſon to whom the Petitioner was bound.

And

And be it further Enacted by the Authority aforesaid, That when Colliers or Salters obtain their Freedom under the Authority of this Act, their Wives and Children, and all others who make Part of their Family, and are Coalbearers, or otherwise affiftant to them, fhall likewife be free.

And be it further Enacted by the Authority aforesaid, That all Coalbearers, Salters, and other Labourers in Collieries or Salt Works, who are bound to any Colliery or Salt Work in *Scotland*, and do not belong to the Family of any particular Collier or Salter, fhall, after   Service from the Commencement of this Act, be free from their Service and Servitude, and at Liberty to engage themfelves as Servants or Labourers in any other Colliery or Salt Work, or in any other kind of Work whatfoever.

And be it further Enacted by the Authority aforesaid, That from and after   all Colliers and Salters then free, and all Perfons that may thereafter become Colliers and Salters, and all Colliers and Salters bound to any Colliery or Salt Work upon the faid   from the Time of obtaining their Freedom under the Authority of this Act, fhall be entitled to the Benefit of an Act, made in the Parliament of *Scotland*, in the Year One thoufand Seven hundred and One, intituled, " Act for preventing wrongous Imprifonment, and " againft undue Delays in Trials," any thing in the faid Act to the contrary notwithftanding.

A

BILL

FOR

Altering, explaining, and amending, several Acts of the Parliament of *Scotland*, respecting Colliers, Coalbearers, and Salters.

———

1774.

A

B   I   L   L

FOR

The more eafy Attendance of Freeholders at Elections of Knights of the Shire for certain Counties.

Note.—*The Figures in the Margin denote the Number of the Folios in the written Copy.*

WHEREAS several Counties in this Kingdom are of fo large an Extent, that the Freeholders thereof cannot, without great Expence and Fatigue, be affembled together, at any One Place within the fame, to make their Elections of Knights of the Shire to ferve in Parliament for the faid Counties :

And whereas the County Towns, or Places where fuch Elections have been ufually and by Law ought to be made, are

A in

[2]

in some other Counties so inconveniently situated, as to subject the Freeholders to the same Inconveniencies:

And whereas the giving Money by the Candidates to the Freeholders, under Pretence of paying their Charges to and from such Places of Election, hath given Occasion to much Bribery and Corruption; In order, therefore, that such Elections may be made in a less expensive and more convenient Manner, and that such Bribery and Corruption may be effectually prevented,

May it please Your MAJESTY,

That it may be Enacted; And be it Enacted by the KING's Most Excellent Majesty, by and with the Advice and Consent of the Lords Spiritual and Temporal, and Commons, in this present Parliament assembled, and by the Authority of the same, That from and after the Dissolution or other Determination of this present Parliament, when and as often as any Writ for the Election of a Knight or Knights of the Shire for the County of   shall be proclaimed, and a Poll shall be demanded by any Candidate, or by any or more Persons having a Right to vote at such Election, such Poll shall be taken at   for the
            within the said County, and at
for the   and at   for
the   within the same.

And be it further Enacted by the Authority aforesaid, That when a Poll shall be demanded at the Proclamation of any such Writ, the same shall proceed in the Manner as by Law is directed, in the City, Town, or Place where such Writ shall be proclaimed, for the District, Division, or Part of such County in which such City, Town, or Place is situated; and that the Poll for all the other Districts, Divisions, and Parts of the said County shall commence on the   Day after the Proclamation of such Writ, if it be not a *Sunday*, and if it be a *Sunday*, then on the Day following; and that in the Computation of such   Day, the Day of the Proclamation of the Writ shall be One; and that in all Cases where Notice of the Time and Place of such Election is required by Law to be given, Notice of the Commencement of
            such

such Poll at the Cities, Towns, and Places, other than that in which the Writ shall be proclaimed, shall be likewise given.

𝔄𝔫𝔡 𝔟𝔢 𝔦𝔱 𝔣𝔲𝔯𝔱𝔥𝔢𝔯 𝔈𝔫𝔞𝔠𝔱𝔢𝔡, That every Freeholder shall give his Vote and Poll, at such Election, at the City, Town, or Place of the District, Division, or Part of the County hereby appointed, in which such Freehold is situated, and not in any other District, Division, or Part of the said County; and if any Freeholder shall poll, or give his Vote, in any other District, Division, or Part of such County, than that wherein his Freehold is situated, his Vote, so given contrary hereto, shall be void and of no Effect.

𝔄𝔫𝔡 𝔟𝔢 𝔦𝔱 𝔣𝔲𝔯𝔱𝔥𝔢𝔯 𝔈𝔫𝔞𝔠𝔱𝔢𝔡, That if any Person shall give his Vote or Poll more than Once, or in more than One District, Division, or Part of such County, the Vote of every such Person shall be void and of no Effect in such Election, and such Person shall for every such Offence forfeit and pay   and be

𝔄𝔫𝔡 𝔟𝔢 𝔦𝔱 𝔣𝔲𝔯𝔱𝔥𝔢𝔯 𝔈𝔫𝔞𝔠𝔱𝔢𝔡, That in order to carry this Act into Execution, it shall and may be lawful for the Sheriff, or, in case of his Death or Absence, for the Under Sheriff, and such Sheriff or Under Sheriff is hereby empowered and required, by Writing under his Hand and Seal, to authorize and appoint One or more proper Person or Persons to take the Poll at such Place or Places, other than the Place in which such Writ shall be proclaimed; and that every such Person, so authorized and appointed, shall, at the Time and Place appointed for taking the said Poll, and before he shall proceed to take the same, openly read, or cause to be read, an Act, made in the Second Year of the late King *George* the Second, intituled, " An Act for the more effectually preventing Bribery " and Corruption," and shall take and subscribe the following Oath:

" I *A. B.* do solemnly swear, That I have not, directly
" nor indirectly, received any Sum or Sums of Money,
" Office, Place, or Employment, Gratuity or Re-
" ward, or any Bond, Bill, or Note, or any Promise
" or Gratuity whatsoever, either by myself, or any
" other

" other Perſon to my Uſe, or Benefit or Advantage,
" for or concerning the taking or returning the Poll
" now about to be taken; and that I will admit
" every Perſon's Name to be inſerted in the ſaid
" Poll, who ſhall appear to me to be qualified by
" Law to give his Vote thereat, and alſo the Name
" or Names of the Perſon or Perſons for whom he
" ſhall vote; and that I will not admit the Name
" of any Perſon to be inſerted therein, unleſs he ſhall
" appear to me to be ſo qualified; and that I will
" take the ſaid Poll honeſtly, uprightly, and impar-
" tially, to the beſt of my Skill and Knowledge; and
" that I will not ſtrike the Name of any Perſon out
" of the ſaid Poll, after the Name of ſuch Perſon ſhall
" be inſerted therein, and he hath been permitted to
" give his Vote; and that I will not alter the ori-
" ginal Poll by me taken, nor cauſe, ſuffer, nor
" permit the ſame to be altered by any other Per-
" ſon or Perſons whatſoever; and that I will return
" the ſame unaltered to the High Sheriff, or his
" Under Sheriff, within   Days after I ſhall have
" compleatly taken the ſame."

Which Oath any Juſtice or Juſtices of the Peace of the ſaid County, City, Corporation, or Borough, where ſuch Election ſhall be made, or, in his or their Abſence, any Three of the Electors, are hereby required and authorized to adminiſter; and ſuch Oath, ſo taken, ſhall be entered among the Records of the Seſſions of ſuch County, City, Corporation, and Borough as aforeſaid.

And be it further Enacted, That the ſaid Perſon or Perſons ſo authorized and appointed, ſhall duly and orderly proceed in the taking of the Poll for ſuch Diſtrict, Diviſion, or Part of the ſaid County, from Day to Day, without any further or other Adjournment, until all the Freeholders then and there preſent ſhall be polled, and no longer; and when the ſaid Poll ſhall be ended in Manner aforeſaid, ſuch Perſon or Perſons ſo authorized and appointed ſhall, within   Days, return the ſame to the Sheriff of the County, or the Under Sheriff, as the Caſe may happen, with an Oath thereunder written, to be taken before any One Juſtice of the Peace, in the following Words:

" I *A. B.*

" I *A. B.*" (infert the Names of the Perfon or Perfons authorized to take the faid Poll) " do fwear, That " the foregoing Poll is the original Poll by me" (or by us, as the Cafe may happen) " taken at " for the" (naming the Diftrict, Divifion, or Part of the County) " within the Coun- " ty of and that I" (or we, as the Cafe may be) " have not altered the fame fince the " fame was taken.
" So help me" (or us) " G O D."

And that when the Sheriff, or Under Sheriff, fhall have finifhed the Poll taken before him, and have received all the Polls taken in the Manner aforefaid, by virtue of this Act, then, and not before, he fhall make his Return of Perfon or Perfons chofen Knight or Knights of the Shire to ferve in Parliament for the faid County.

And be it further Enacted, That the Perfon or Perfons authorized and appointed, by virtue of this Act, to take the Poll, are hereby authorized and required to do all and every Act, Matter, and Thing, that the Sheriff or Under Sheriff might lawfully do at the taking of any Poll, or is required by Law to do, was he perfonally prefent, other than that of adminiftering the Oath of Qualification appointed to be taken by Candidates, by an Act, intituled, " An Act for fecuring the Freedoms of Parliaments, by the " further qualifying the Members to fit in the Houfe of " Commons," made in the Ninth Year of Queen *Anne*; and fuch Perfon and Perfons fo authorized and appointed, fhall be liable to the fame Pains and Penalties, for all and every Omiffion and Breach of his or their Duty in relation to the fame, as any Sheriff or Under Sheriff would have been liable to, in Cafe fuch Sheriff or Under Sheriff, or either of them, had been perfonally prefent, and omitted or committed fame.

And whereas there may be Perfons who hold Freeholds in Right of their Offices, refpecting the County at large, and others may have Freeholds not within any particular Diftrict, Divifion, or Part of a County mentioned in this Act; *Be it further Enacted,* That Perfons having fuch Offices or Freeholds may poll at the Place where the Writ fhall be proclaimed, or at any other Place hereby
B appointed

appointed for taking such Poll, provided such Person give no more than One Vote at such Election; and if any Person, having such Office or Freehold, shall give his Vote more than Once at such Election, every Vote he shall so give shall be void and of none Effect, and he shall incur the Penalties, Incapacities, and Forfeitures, hereby imposed upon Persons who give their Vote more than Once at such Elections.

And be it further Enacted, That every Person who shall give his Vote or Poll, before the Person or Persons authorized and appointed by virtue of this Act to take the same, shall, and is hereby required, before he shall be admitted to give his Vote or Poll thereat, to take all and every Oath and Oaths, and to do every other Act, Matter, or Thing, as by Law he is required to do before the Sheriff or Under Sheriff, in Case the said Sheriff or Under Sheriff had been present at the said Poll, and taken the same; and such Person omitting to take the said Oath or Oaths, or swearing falsly, or neglecting to do any Matter or Thing required by Law to be done by him, before he be admitted to give his Vote at any Election of a Knight or Knights of the Shire, such Person so omitting to take the said Oaths, or swearing falsly, or neglecting to do any Matter or Thing required by Law to be done by him, shall incur the same Forfeitures, Penalties, and Incapacities, as he would have incurred in Case the Sheriff or Under Sheriff had been present at taking the said Poll, and had taken the same.

Provided always, and be it further Enacted, That in Case no Poll shall be demanded in the Manner aforesaid, at the Proclamation of any Writ for the Election of a Knight or Knights of the Shire for any County hereinbefore mentioned, then and in such Case this Act shall not take place.

A BILL

FOR

The more easy Attendance of Freeholders at Elections of Knights of the Shire for certain Counties.

1774.

A

BILL

FOR

The better securing the Rights of Voters at County Elections.

Note.—*The Figures in the Margin denote the Number of the Folios in the written Copy.*

WHEREAS the Laws now in being, for ascertaining the Rights of Persons claiming to vote at the Elections of Knights of the Shire to serve in Parliament for that Part of Great Britain called England, and for the Dominion of Wales, have by Experience been found inadequate:

And whereas it is highly expedient to prevent, in such Elections, Disputes, Delays, Uncertainty, and Expence:

Be it therefore Enacted, and it is hereby Enacted, by the KING's Most Excellent MAJESTY, by and with the Advice and Consent of the Lords Spiritual and Temporal, and Commons,

2 mons, in this present Parliament assembled, and by the Authority of the same, That from and after the   Day of One thousand Seven hundred and   no Person (except as is hereinafter excepted) shall vote at any Election of any Knight or Knights of the Shire to serve in Parliament for any County in that Part of Great Britain called England, or in the Dominion of Wales, without having had his Name enrolled, as hereinafter mentioned, in the Register of some Parish within such County, at least Twelve Calendar Months before the Day on which such Person shall tender his Vote at such Election; and such Register shall be called "*The Register of Freeholders*" for such Parish; and every Person (except as is hereinafter excepted) who shall, after the said Day, tender his Vote at any such Election as aforesaid, shall, before he
3 be permitted to vote at such Election, take the following Oath; videlicet:

" I do solemnly swear" [*or, being one of the People called Quakers,* " I do solemnly affirm] That my Name is A. B. " and that I am   " [*specifying the Addition, Profession, or Trade of such Person*] " and that the usual " Place of my Abode is at   " [*and if it be in a Town consisting of more Streets than one, specifying in what Street*] " in the County of   and that I " have been enrolled at least Twelve Calendar Months " in the Register of Freeholders for the Parish of "   in the County of   and that " I am in the actual Possession of the Estate for which " I was so enrolled, or of a Part thereof of the clear " Yearly Value of Forty Shillings, over and above the
4 " Yearly Interest of any Money on any Mortgage, or on " any other Security affecting such Estate, and also over " and above all Rents and Charges payable out of or in " respect of the same, other than Parliamentary, Public, " or Parochial Taxes; and that the said Estate consists of   " [*specifying whether the same consist of Lands or Messuage, or of both, or of Great Tythes or Small Tythes, or of both, or of an Office, or of an Annuity or Rent Charge, and describing the same, and specifying the Name of some Occupier of the Lands or Messuage out of which the Rents and Profits shall issue*] " and that I do not hold the said Estate in Trust, " or for or on the Behalf of any other Person or Persons, " whomsoever; and that the Rents and Profits of the " same are, and have been for at least Twelve Calendar " Months

" Months laſt paſt, received for my own Uſe, by my-
" ſelf, or others; and that the ſaid Eſtate was not
" granted to me fraudulently; and that my Intereſt in
" the ſame is not nominal or fictitious; and that, to the
" beſt of my Knowledge and Belief, the ſaid Eſtate is a
" Freehold Eſtate, and my Intereſt in the ſame really and
" truly a Freehold Intereſt; and that I am, to the beſt
" of my Knowledge and Belief, of the full Age of Twenty-
" one Years; and that I have not been polled before at
" this Election."

Provided always, and be it further Enacted by the Authority aforeſaid, That if any Perſon (without having had his Name enrolled as aforeſaid) ſhall claim a Right to vote in virtue of a Freehold Eſtate, which ſhall have come to him either by the Death of any Perſon, or by Preſentation to a Benefice in a Church, or by Marriage, it ſhall and may be lawful for him to vote for ſuch Eſtate, any Thing hereinbefore contained to the contrary notwithſtanding, provided that the ſaid Freehold Eſtate ſhall have come to him within Two Years before the Day on which he ſhall tender his Vote; and provided ſuch Eſtate ſhall have been regiſtered in the Regiſter of Freeholders for ſome Pariſh within the County, at leaſt Twelve Calendar Months before the ſaid Day, and ſhall have been regiſtered in ſuch Regiſter in the Name of ſome Perſon who ſhall have been his Predeceſſor within Two Years previous to the ſaid Day; and every ſuch Perſon who ſhall, after the ſaid   Day of
One thouſand Seven hundred, and   tender his Vote at any ſuch Election as aforeſaid, ſhall, before he be permitted to vote at ſuch Election, take (inſtead of the Oath abovementioned) the following Oath; videlicet:

" I do ſolemnly ſwear" [*or, being one of the People called Quakers,* " I do ſolemnly affirm] That my Name is A. B.
" and that I am   " [*ſpecifying the Addition, Profeſſion, or Trade of ſuch Perſon*] " and that the
" uſual Place of my Abode is at   " [*and if it be in a Town conſiſting of more Streets than one, ſpecifying in what Street*] " in the County of   and that
" I am in the actual Poſſeſſion of an Eſtate which has
" been regiſtered at leaſt Twelve Calendar Months in the
" Regiſter of Freeholders for the Pariſh of
" in the County of   or of a Part thereof,
" of the clear Yearly Value of Forty Shillings, over and
" above

[4]

8
" above the Yearly Intereſt of any Money on any Mort-
" gage, or on any other Security affecting ſuch Eſtate, and
" alſo over and above all Rents and Charges payable out
" of or in reſpect of the ſame, other than Parliamentary,
" Public, or Parochial Taxes ; and that the ſaid Eſtate
" was regiſtered in ſuch Regiſter of Freeholders, in the
" Name of   " [ſpecifying the Chriſtian
Name and the Surname of the Perſon] " and that ſuch
" Perſon was within Two Years laſt paſt my Predeceſſor
" in ſuch Eſtate; and that the ſaid Eſtate came to me
" within Two Years laſt paſt, [by the Death of ſuch
" Perſon," or " by the Death of   " ſpecifying the Chriſtian Name and the Surname of the Perſon by
whoſe Death the Perſon claiming to vote ſhall have acquired
ſuch Eſtate, or " by Preſentation to a Benefice in the
" Church of   " or " by Marriage," as the Caſe may

9
be] " and that the ſaid Eſtate conſiſts of   "
[ſpecifying whether the ſame conſiſt of Lands or Meſſuage, or
of both, or of Great Tythes or Small Tythes, or of both, or of
an Office, or of an Annuity or Rent Charge, and deſcribing the
ſame, and ſpecifying the Name of ſome Occupier of the Lands
or Meſſuage out of which the Rents and Profits ſhall iſſue]
" and that I do not hold the ſaid Eſtate in Truſt, or for
" or on the Behalf of any other Perſon or Perſons whom-
" ſoever; and that I am in the Receipt of the Rents and
" Profits of the ſame for my own Uſe; and that the
" ſaid Eſtate was not granted to me fraudulently; and
" that my Intereſt in the ſame is not nominal or ficti-
" tious ; and that, to the beſt of my Knowledge and

f
" Belief, the ſaid Eſtate is a Freehold Eſtate, and my In-
" tereſt in the ſame really and truly a Freehold Intereſt ;
" and that I am, to the beſt of my Knowledge and Belief,
" of the full Age of Twenty-one Years ; and that I have
" not been polled before at this Election.

10
 𝐀𝐧𝐝 𝐛𝐞 𝐢𝐭 𝐟𝐮𝐫𝐭𝐡𝐞𝐫 𝐄𝐧𝐚𝐜𝐭𝐞𝐝 by the Authority aforeſaid, That
the Sheriff for every County in that Part of Great Britain called
England, and in the Dominion of Wales, ſhall provide a Regiſter
(or Regiſters) for each Pariſh within ſuch County, and each Folio
of every ſuch Regiſter ſhall be of the Form ſpecified in the Schedule hereunto annexed, N° 1 ; and to each and every ſuch Regiſter
ſhall be annexed a Copy of this Act, printed by the King's Printer,
in the Roman Letter, or in the Roman and *Italic :* And every ſuch
Sheriff ſhall, on or before the   Day of   One
                                                        thouſand

thousand Seven hundred and   deliver such Register (or Registers) or cause the same to be safely delivered, to the Register-keeper of each such respective Parish; and such Register-keeper shall and is hereby required to sign a Receipt for the same, of the Form specified in the Schedule hereunto annexed, N° 2.

𝕬𝖓𝖉, for the better promulgating this Act, 𝕭𝖊 𝖎𝖙 𝖋𝖚𝖗𝖙𝖍𝖊𝖗 11 𝕰𝖓𝖆𝖈𝖙𝖊𝖉 by the Authority aforesaid, That on some One or more of the Sundays in the Month of   One thousand Seven hundred and   Notice shall be publicly given by the Parish Clerk (or by the Person who shall act as such) in the Parish Church or Chapel of every Parish in every County in that Part of Great Britain called England, and in the Dominion of Wales, immediately before Morning or Evening Service, in the following Words; (that is to say) " By an Act made and passed
" in the Twenty-sixth Year of the Reign of His Majesty King
" George the Third, intituled, " *An Act for the better securing*
" *the Rights of Voters at County Elections,*" it is Enacted, That no
" Person (except as is therein excepted) shall vote at any Election
" of any Knight or Knights of the Shire to serve in Parliament
" for any County in that Part of Great Britain called England, 12
" or in the Dominion of Wales, without having had his Name
" enrolled in the Register of Freeholders for some Parish within
" such County, at least Twelve Calendar Months before the
" Day on which such Person shall tender his Vote at such Elec-
" tion: All Freeholders, therefore, are to take Notice of the
" same, and to cause their Names to be enrolled accordingly, in
" pursuance of the said Act, on any Day from and after the
"   Day of   One thousand Seven hundred
" and   ;" and the said Notice (omitting the Words, " on any Day from and after the   Day of
"   One thousand Seven hundred and   ") shall afterwards be given by the Parish Clerk (or by the Person who shall act as such) in every Parish Church or Chapel as aforesaid, at least on some One Sunday in each of the respective Months of January, April, July, and October, in every Year.

𝕬𝖓𝖉 𝖇𝖊 𝖎𝖙 𝖋𝖚𝖗𝖙𝖍𝖊𝖗 𝕰𝖓𝖆𝖈𝖙𝖊𝖉 by the Authority aforesaid, That 13 from and after the   Day of   One thousand Seven hundred and   it shall and may be lawful for any Freeholder of any County aforesaid, being in the actual Possession of a Freehold Estate within the true Intent and Meaning of this Act, to cause his Name to be enrolled for the said Estate, in the Register of Freeholders for the Parish
B   within

within which such Estate (or any Part thereof) shall lie, or out of which such Estate (or any Part thereof) shall issue, upon making personal Application for that Purpose to the Register-keeper of such Parish; but if the Whole of the said Estate shall lie in or shall issue out of an Extra-parochial Place, or any Two or more Extra-parochial Places, then and in such Case it shall and may be lawful for the Freeholder to cause his Name to be enrolled for such Estate in the Register of Freeholders for any Parish within the said County, which Parish shall adjoin to any such Extra-parochial Place, or (in case no such Parish shall adjoin) shall be adjacent to any such Extra-parochial Place.

14 *Provided always, and be it further Enacted* by the Authority aforesaid, That if the Freehold Estate, in virtue of which any Freeholder claiming a Right to be enrolled as aforesaid shall be an Annuity or Rent Charge issuing out of Freehold Lands or Tenements, then and in such Case no Enrolment as aforesaid shall be made, unless the Freeholder making as aforesaid personal Application to be enrolled shall produce to the Register-keeper of such Parish as aforesaid an Attestation, of the Form specified in the Schedule hereunto annexed, N° 3, which shall have been sworn to and subscribed by such Freeholder before any Justice of the Peace for the County within which shall be situate the Freehold Estate out of which such Annuity or Rent Charge shall issue; and such Justice is hereby empowered and required, upon Request being made to him by such Freeholder, to administer the Oath contained in the said Attestation, and to sign the Jurat at the Foot thereof; and such Attestation shall be left with the said Register-keeper, who is hereby required to demand the same.

15 *And whereas* it would be expedient that Freeholders residing at a Distance from the Parish or Extra-parochial Place within which their Freeholds shall lie, or out of which the same shall issue, should be enabled to cause their Names to be enrolled in the Register of Freeholders for such Parish as aforesaid, without their being obliged to travel to such Parish; *Be it therefore further Enacted* by the Authority aforesaid, That it shall and may be lawful for any Freeholder of any County aforesaid, who shall reside (or shall be) within such County, or within any other County of Great Britain, to cause his Name to be enrolled in the Register of Freeholders for such Parish as aforesaid, in the following Manner; that is to say, such Freeholder (whether his Freehold shall consist of an Annuity or Rent Charge, or other Estate) shall produce to any Justice
of

of the Peace for the County where such Freeholder shall reside (or shall then be) an Attestation, of the Form specified in the Schedule hereunto annexed, Nº 3, which Attestation shall be sworn to and subscribed by such Freeholder before such Justice; and such Justice is hereby empowered and required, upon Request being made to him by such Freeholder, to administer such Oath, and to sign the Jurat at the Foot thereof; and an Oath of the Form specified in the Schedule hereunto annexed, Nº 4, shall be written or printed at the End of the said Attestation; and the said Attestation shall be produced to some Justice of the Peace for the County in which the Estate of such Freeholder shall lie, or out of which the same shall issue; and the Person producing such Attestation to such Justice shall, before such Justice, take and subscribe the said last-mentioned Oath; and such Justice is hereby empowered and required, upon Request being made to him by such Person, to administer such Oath, and to sign the Jurat at the Foot thereof; and such Attestation being afterwards produced by the said Person to the Register-keeper of the Parish aforesaid, the Freeholder whose Estate is described in the said Attestation shall be as fully entitled to have his Name enrolled in such Register of Freeholders, as if such Freeholder were personally to apply as aforesaid to such Register-keeper for that Purpose; and such Attestation shall be left with such Register-keeper, who is hereby required to demand the same. 16

And be it further Enacted and Declared by the Authority aforesaid, That no Register-keeper authorized to make Enrolments in pursuance of this Act, shall have any judicial Power or Authority whatsoever with respect to any Question which may arise relative to the Right of any Person to any Freehold Estate which such Person shall claim to be in the actual Possession of, within the true Intent and Meaning of this Act; but every such Register-keeper shall and is hereby required to enrol, or in his Presence to cause to be enrolled, the Name of every such Person as shall in pursuance of this Act (in any Manner aforesaid) request to be enrolled in the Register of Freeholders for any such Parish as aforesaid; and every Freeholder or other Person as aforesaid who shall in any Manner aforesaid make Application for any such Enrolment to be made, shall have the Right to be present, and to examine that the same be correctly entered in the Register of Freeholders, and shall likewise have the Right to require that the said Register-keeper should sign the said Enrolment forthwith in the Presence of the Person making such Application. 17

18. **And whereas** great Inconvenience might arise, if Persons not being in Possession of any Freehold Estate, within the true Intent and Meaning of this Act, were to cause their Names to be enrolled in any Register of Freeholders as aforesaid; **Be it therefore further Enacted** by the Authority aforesaid, That if any Person shall (in any Manner aforesaid) cause his Name to be enrolled in any Register of Freeholders which shall be kept in pursuance of this Act, without such Person being, at the Time of such Enrolment, in the actual Possession of the Estate which he shall cause to be registered in his Enrolment, or if the said Estate shall not be a Freehold Estate, or if such Person shall not actually have in such Estate (at the Time of such Enrolment) a Freehold Interest, or if the said Estate shall not be of the clear Yearly Value of Forty Shillings, over and above the

19. Yearly Interest of any Money on any Mortgage, or on any other Security affecting such Estate, and also over and above all Rents and Charges payable out of or in respect of the same, other than Parliamentary, Public, or Parochial Taxes, or if the Rents and Profits of such Estate shall not be (at the Time of such Enrolment) received for such Person's own Use, by himself or others, or if any Person, who shall cause his Name to be enrolled in any such Register of Freeholders shall register any Estate which shall have been granted to him fraudulently, or in which his Interest shall be nominal or fictitious, or shall (by Attestation or otherwise) wilfully misstate any of the Particulars directed by this Act to be specified in his Enrolment, every Person who shall be found guilty of any of the said Offences shall forfeit the Sum of   of lawful Money of Great Britain, to any Person or Persons who shall sue for the same.

20. **Provided always, and be it further Enacted and Declared** by the Authority aforesaid, That no Public or Parliamentary Tax, or County, Church, or Parish Rate, Cess, or Duty, or any other Tax, Rate, or Assessment whatsoever, which is or at any Time hereafter shall or may be assessed or levied upon any County, Riding, Rape, Lathe, Wapentake, Ward, Hundred, Parish, District, or Division, is, or shall be deemed or construed to be, any Charge payable out of or in respect of any Freehold Estate within the true Intent and Meaning of this Act.

21. **And provided also, and be it further Enacted and Declared** by the Authority aforesaid, That if any Estate, which shall be registered in any Register of Freeholders in pursuance of this Act,

Act, shall, jointly with any other Estate or Estates, be affected by any Mortgage or other Security; and if the clear Yearly Value of such Estate so registered shall exceed, by Forty Shillings or more, that Part of the Yearly Interest of the Money on such Mortgage, or on such other Security, which shall be payable out of the Estate so registered according to the Proportion which such registered Estate shall bear to the other Estate or Estates affected by the said Mortgage or other Security, then and in such Case the Estate so registered shall not be deemed to be affected by such Mortgage or other Security, within the true Intent and Meaning of this Act.

And whereas great Inconvenience might arise, if the same 22 Freeholders were to cause different Enrolments to be made within the same County, without any Notice being taken of the said different Enrolments; Be it therefore further Enacted by the Authority aforesaid, That if any Person, whose Name shall be enrolled in any Register of Freeholders as aforesaid, and who shall not have sold or otherwise have alienated the Whole of the Estate or Estates so enrolled, shall (by Attestation or otherwise) cause his Name to be inrolled in the Register of Freeholders for any other Parish in the same County, or shall cause any other Enrolment to be made in the Register of Freeholders for the same Parish, then and in such Case there shall be written, immediately under the said Person's Name in the last Enrolment, Words to the following Effect; videlicet:

" Already enrolled in the Register of Freeholders for the 23
" Parish of   N°.   " [*specifying the
said Parish or Parishes, and the progressive Number or progressive Numbers of the former Enrolment or Enrolments.*]

And if any Person who shall (by Attestation or otherwise) cause his Name to be enrolled in any Register of Freeholders shall in any Case act contrary hereunto, he shall forfeit the Sum of   of lawful Money of *Great Britain*, to any Person or Persons who shall sue for the same; but the Validity of any or either of the said Enrolments shall not be affected hereby.

And be it further Enacted by the Authority aforesaid, That 24 the Registers of Freeholders aforesaid (of the Form specified in the Schedule hereunto annexed, N° 1) shall be kept in the following Manner (that is to say): The Name of the Parish to

C   which

which any such Register of Freeholders shall belong, and also the Name of the County within which such Parish shall lie, shall be written or printed at the Head of each Folio of such Register, together with the progressive Number of such Folio; and there shall be a progressive Number opposite to each Enrolment entered in such Register; and the Register-keeper shall take down, or in his Presence cause to be taken down, the Christian Name or Christian Names, and the Surname or Surnames, of the Person requesting to be enrolled, together with his Addition, Profession, or Trade, and his usual Place of Abode, and if it be in a Town consisting of more Streets than One, specifying in what Street, and specifying whether such Person be "*present*" or "*absent*" at the Time of his Enrolment being made, and specifying the Nature of his Freehold Estate, that is to say, specifying whether his Freehold Estate consist of Lands or Messuage, or of both, or of Great Tythes or Small Tythes, or of both, or of an Office, or of an Annuity or Rent Charge; and if the said Freehold Estate be on any Life or Lives, then specifying whether the same be on his own Life, or on the Life of C. D. or on the longest of the Lives of E. F. and G. H. &c. or on the shortest of the Lives of K. L. and M. N. &c.; and if the Freehold Estate consist of Lands or Messuage, or of both, then describing the said Lands or Messuage, or such Part or Parts thereof as shall be of the clear Yearly Value of Forty Shillings as aforesaid, and specifying the Name of some Occupier of the said Lands or Messuage; or if the Freehold Estate consist of Great Tythes or Small Tythes, or of both, then specifying some of the Lands out of which such Tythes shall issue, and specifying the Name of some Occupier of such Lands; or if the Freehold Estate consist of an Office, then specifying the said Office, and specifying some Lands or Messuage out of which the Profits of such Office shall issue, and specifying the Name of some Occupier of the said Lands or Messuage; but if the Freehold Estate consist of an Annuity or Rent Charge, or if any Person shall apply by Attestation as aforesaid to have his Name enrolled in any Register of Freeholders, then the Name and Description of the Person requesting to be enrolled, and the Description of the said Annuity or Rent Charge, or other Freehold Estate (as the Case may be) shall be taken from the Attestation aforesaid; and the Year, Month, and Day on which any Enrolment shall be made shall in all Cases be specified; and the Register-keeper who shall, in pursuance of this Act, make any Enrolment as aforesaid, or who shall cause the same in his Presence to be made, shall and is hereby required to sign such Enrolment.

And, in order to facilitate the Means of preventing fraudulent Votes in such Elections as aforesaid, Be it further Enacted by the Authority aforesaid, That every Register-keeper aforesaid shall, previous to every General Quarter Sessions of the Peace, make, or cause to be made, an exact and correct Copy, fairly written, of every Enrolment which shall, since the last preceding General Quarter Sessions of the Peace, have been made as aforesaid, in the Register of Freeholders for the Parish; and every such Copy shall be of the Form specified in the Schedule hereunto annexed, N° 1; and the said Register-keeper shall carefully examine the said Copy, and shall, at the End of each Page or Folio of such Copy, certify that the same is "*a true Copy*," and shall sign each Page or Folio of such Copy; and whenever any Enrolment shall have been copied as aforesaid (in order to be delivered to the Clerk of the Peace as hereinafter is directed) the said Register-keeper shall, upon the original Register, write, or in his Presence cause to be written, the Word "*copied*," immediately under the progressive Number that shall be opposite to the Enrolment so copied; and such Register-keeper shall deliver (or safely transmit, sealed up) unto the Clerk of the Peace, at the First General Quarter Sessions of the Peace for the County, or for the Riding or Division of the same to which such Parish shall belong, every such Copy which shall have been made as aforesaid; and such Register-keeper shall, at the same Time, deliver (or safely transmit, sealed up) unto such Clerk of the Peace, every Attestation which shall have been left with such Register-keeper as aforesaid, and if no Enrolment shall have been made in any Register of Freeholders as aforesaid, since the last Copy which shall have been sent to the Clerk of the Peace as aforesaid, then and in such Case such Register-keeper shall deliver (or safely transmit, sealed up) unto such Clerk of the Peace as aforesaid a Notice, of the Form specified in the Schedule hereunto annexed, N° 5, which Notice shall be signed by such Register-keeper.

Provided always, and be it further Enacted by the Authority aforesaid, That it shall and may be lawful for every such Register-keeper as aforesaid to deliver or safely transmit any such Papers as aforesaid unto any Constable within such County, or within such Riding or Division as aforesaid (as the Case may be) and the same shall be sealed up, and shall be directed to "*the Clerk of the Peace*," and the Name of the Parish to which such Papers shall belong shall be also specified on the Direction; and such Constable shall and is hereby required safely to deliver such Papers (without breaking the Seal) unto such Clerk of the Peace at such General Quarter Sessions as aforesaid.

32. **And be it further Enacted** by the Authority aforesaid, That every Clerk of the Peace aforesaid shall provide, for each Parish within the County, Riding, or Division, a Register, of the Form specified in the Schedule hereunto annexed, N° 1; and such Clerk of the Peace, on receiving any Copy of any Enrolment or Enrolments as aforesaid, shall forthwith enter, or cause to be entered, an exact and correct Copy of the same in the said Register, which shall be kept by him for the Parish to which such Enrolment or Enrolments shall belong; and such Clerk of the Peace shall carefully examine each such Copy so entered, and shall (on such Register) certify that the same is "*a true Copy*," and shall sign each Register on which any such Copy shall be entered; and every such Clerk of the Peace shall care-

33. fully examine all the Copies of Enrolments which he shall have received as aforesaid; and if it should appear (from the progressive Numbers opposite to the same) that the Number of such Enrolments sent from any Parish be incomplete, or if it should appear that any of the said Enrolments be not dated, or be not made or copied in the proper Form as aforesaid, or if it should appear (from the Copy of any Enrolment or Enrolments) that any Attestation be missing, or if such Clerk of the Peace shall not have received from each and every Parish either a Copy of some Enrolment or Enrolments, or else a Notice as aforesaid, then and in every such Case the said Clerk of the Peace shall give written Notice thereof unto the Register-keeper hereby directed to deliver or safely transmit such respective Paper

34. or Papers to such Clerk of the Peace, and the said Clerk of the Peace shall repeat such Notice as aforesaid, if the Case shall require it; and every Clerk of the Peace aforesaid shall and is hereby required carefully to preserve all such Registers as aforesaid, and also carefully to preserve all Copies of any Enrolment or Enrolments, and likewise all Attestations and Notices which shall or may have been delivered to him, or to any other Clerk of the Peace, in pursuance of this Act; and such Clerk of the Peace shall keep the Copies of Enrolments which he shall have received (and which he shall have entered as aforesaid) in a Place separate and apart from the said Registers, in order to preserve the One, in case any Accident, by Fire or otherwise, should damage or destroy the other; and all such Registers, Copies,

Attestations,

[13]

Attestations, and Notices as aforesaid, shall be safely delivered to the Successor in Office of such Clerk of the Peace.

And be it further Enacted by the Authority aforesaid, That at every Election of any Knight or Knights of the Shire to serve in Parliament for any County aforesaid, the Clerk of the Peace aforesaid shall, on the Day of the Election (and before the Hour of proceeding to the said Election) safely deliver unto the Sheriff for such County (at the Place of Election) the Registers of Freeholders for all the Parishes within such County, which shall be kept, in pursuance of this Act, by such Clerk of the Peace as aforesaid; which Registers the said Sheriff is hereby required carefully to preserve, and safely to deliver back unto the said Clerk of the Peace, at the Place of Election, after the said Election shall be over. 35

And, for the more effectually preventing fraudulent Votes being given at any Election of any Knight or Knights of the Shire to serve in Parliament for any County aforesaid, Be it further Enacted by the Authority aforesaid, That at every such Election the Sheriff of such County shall, for the taking of the Poll, provide, or cause to be provided, for each Parish within such County, a separate Book (or separate Paper) or separate Books (or separate Papers) of the Form specified in the Schedule hereunto annexed, N° 6; and at every such Election every Freeholder shall give his Vote at some Poll Book (or Paper) provided for the Parish to which shall belong the Register of Freeholders wherein the Estate, in virtue of which such Freeholder shall claim a Right to vote, shall have been registered as aforesaid. 36

And be it further Enacted by the Authority aforesaid, That from and after the said   Day of   One thousand Seven hundred and   no Sheriff, or other Person, who shall by Law be authorized to take the Poll at any such Election as aforesaid, shall have any judicial Power or Authority whatsoever, to determine the Right of voting of any Person, who shall tender his Vote at such Election; but every such Sheriff or other Person authorized to take the Poll at any such Election as aforesaid, shall, from and after the said Day, act merely officially (or ministerially) in the taking of such Poll, that is to say, he shall and is hereby required to receive the Vote of every Person who shall tender his Vote at the proper Poll Book (or Paper) as aforesaid, and who shall take either of the respective Oaths above directed to be administered at such County Election, and who shall 37

38

shall also take any other such respective Oath or Oaths as shall, by any Act or Acts of Parliament then in Force, be directed to be administered at such Election, and no Scrutiny shall be granted at any such Election; but every Sheriff or other Person authorized to take the Poll at such Election as aforesaid shall forthwith (upon the Conclusion of the said Poll) return such Person or Persons as a Knight or Knights of the Shire to serve in Parliament, as shall have been elected by the Majority of Votes taken at such Poll as aforesaid; and every Person who shall by Law be authorized to take, or to assist in taking, the Poll at any such Election as aforesaid, is hereby empowered and required to administer the said respective Oaths.

39. And be it further Enacted by the Authority aforesaid, That if any Person shall vote, at any Election of any Knight or Knights of the Shire to serve in Parliament for any County aforesaid, in virtue of any Estate which shall not be a Freehold Estate, or without actually having in such Estate a Freehold Interest, or without being of the full Age of Twenty-one Years, such Person shall forfeit the Sum of   of lawful Money of Great Britain to any Candidate for whom such Person shall not have voted at the said Election, and who shall first sue for the said Forfeiture; but if no such Candidate shall sue for the said Forfeiture within   Calendar Months after the Offence shall have been committed, then the said Forfeiture shall go to any Person or Persons who shall sue for the same.

40. And be it further Enacted by the Authority aforesaid, That from and after the said   Day of   One thousand Seven hundred and   the Oath commonly called The Returning Officer's Oath, prescribed by an Act made and passed in the Second Year of his late Majesty King George the Second, intituled "*An Act for the more effectual preventing Bribery and Corruption in the Elections of Members to serve in Parliament,*" shall not be administered at any Election of any Knight or Knights of the Shire to serve in Parliament for any County aforesaid.

41. And be it further Enacted by the Authority aforesaid, That from and after the said   Day of   One thousand Seven hundred and   the Oath commonly called The Freeholder's Oath, prescribed by an Act made and passed in the Eighteenth Year of his late Majesty King George the Second, intituled " *An Act to explain and amend*
" *the*

" the Laws touching the Elections of Knights of the Shire to serve in
" Parliament for that Part of Great Britain called England," shall
not be administered at any Election of any Knight or Knights
of the Shire to serve in Parliament for any County aforesaid.

And be it further Enacted by the Authority aforesaid, That 42
from and after the said   Day of   One thousand Seven hundred and   the Act made and passed in
the Third Year of His present Majesty King George the Third,
intituled, " *An Act to prevent fraudulent and occasional Votes in the*
" *Elections of Knights of the Shire, and of Members for Cities and*
" *Towns which are Counties of themselves, so far as relates to the*
" *Right of voting by virtue of an Annuity or Rent Charge,*" shall
be and is hereby repealed, as far as the said Act relates to the
Election of any Knight or Knights of the Shire to serve in Parliament for any County aforesaid.

And be it further Enacted by the Authority aforesaid, That 43
from and after the said   Day of   One thousand Seven hundred and   the Act made and passed
in the Twentieth Year of His present Majesty King George the
Third, intituled, " *An Act to remove certain Difficulties relative to*
" *Voters at County Elections,*" shall be and is hereby repealed, as
far as the said Act relates to the Election of any Knight or
Knights of the Shire to serve in Parliament for any County
aforesaid.

And be it further Enacted by the Authority aforesaid, That 44
from and after the said   Day of   One thousand Seven hundred and   all such Parts of the
above recited Act made and passed in the Eighteenth Year of his
late Majesty King *George* the Second (and all such Parts of any
other Act or Acts of Parliament) as do disable any Person to
vote at any Election of any Knight or Knights of the Shire to
serve in Parliament for any County aforesaid, in respect or in
Right of any Messuages, Lands, or Tenements, which shall not
have been charged or assessed towards a Land Tax, shall be and
the same are hereby repealed.

And be it further Enacted by the Authority aforesaid, That 45
where any Woman, the Widow of any Person Tenant in Fee,
or in Tail, shall be entitled to Dower or Thirds by the Common
Law, out of the Freehold Estate of which her Husband died
seised or possessed, and shall intermarry with a Second Husband,

such

such Second Heir, and shall be entitled to vote in respect of such Lower or Thirds, if such Dower or Thirds shall be of the clear Yearly Value of Forty shillings as aforesaid, although the same shall not have been assigned or set out by Metes or Bounds; provided always, that such Second Husband shall pursue, as aforesaid, the Directions of this Act.

46   And, in order that no Objection may be made to the Validity of the Enrolment of any Freeholder as aforesaid, by Reason of any immaterial Defect in or relative unto such Enrolment, or on Account of any Neglect, Negligence, or Error of any Clerk of the Peace as aforesaid, or of any Register-keeper authorized to make Enrolments in pursuance of this Act, 𝕭e it further Enacted and Declared by the Authority aforesaid, That no Enrolment aforesaid, which shall not be essentially or materially defective, shall be considered as void on Account of mere Want of Form, or on Account of any Want of Form in the Description of the Freehold Estate contained in any Attestation as aforesaid (if the Case shall so happen); and in any Cause or Proceeding touching the Validity of any Enrolment which shall have been entered in any Register

47 of Freeholders aforesaid, and which shall have been signed by the Register-keeper aforesaid, no Evidence shall be received to prove that the said Enrolment was not entered in such Register in the Presence of such Register-keeper; and nothing in this Act contained shall extend, or be construed to extend, to affect the Validity of any Enrolment or Enrolments entered in any original Register of Freeholders as aforesaid, by Reason or on Account of any Neglect, Omission, or Error of any such Register-keeper as aforesaid, in or relative unto the making of any Copy of such Enrolment or Enrolments, or in or relative unto the sending of the same to any Clerk of the Peace aforesaid, or by Reason or on Account of any Neglect, Omission, or Error of any Clerk of the Peace aforesaid, relative unto or in respect of any Register or Registers by this Act directed to be provided or kept by such Clerk of the Peace, or relative unto or in respect of the delivering of any such Register or Registers to the Sheriff, at the Place or at the Time of Election.

48   And be it further Enacted by the Authority aforesaid, That it shall and may be lawful for any Person, at all seasonable Times, to resort to and inspect any Register of Freeholders which shall or may be kept for any Parish in pursuance of this Act, such Person, previous to such Inspection, paying to the Register-keeper

[17]

keeper aforesaid the Sum of   for each Inspection
of every such Register.

And be it further Enacted by the Authority aforesaid, That 49
it shall and may be lawful for any Person, on any Day (except on
a Sunday, a Good Friday, or a Christmas Day) between the
Hours of   in the Forenoon and   in the
Afternoon, to resort to and inspect the Register of Freeholders
for any Parish, which shall or may, in pursuance of this Act, be
kept by any Clerk of the Peace as aforesaid, such Person, previous to such Inspection, paying to such Clerk of the Peace the
Sum of   for each Inspection of every such Register
of Freeholders; and it shall and may be lawful for any Person
(on any Day and Hour as aforesaid) to resort to and inspect the
Copy of any Enrolment or Enrolments, or any Attestation or
other Paper as aforesaid, which by this Act is directed to be sent
to the Clerk of the Peace, such Person giving not less than
         Notice in Writing to such Clerk of the Peace, to produce such Copy or Attestation, or other Paper as aforesaid, and
paying to such Clerk of the Peace (at the Time of giving such
Notice) the Sum of   for every such Copy or Attestation, or other Paper so requested to be produced.

And be it further Enacted by the Authority aforesaid, That 50
every Register-keeper authorized to make Enrolments in pursuance of this Act in the Register of Freeholders for any Parish,
shall, and is hereby required, to deliver a true Copy of all or any
Part or Parts of any such Register in his Custody, unto any
Person who shall, in Writing, demand the same, and such Copy
shall be of the Form specified in the Schedule hereunto annexed, N° 1; and such Copy shall be stated to be "*a true Copy*,"
and each Page or Folio thereof shall be signed by such Register-keeper as aforesaid, and such Copy shall be delivered within a
reasonable Time after the same shall have been demanded; and
such Register-keeper shall be paid for every such Copy (at the
Time the same shall be demanded) at and after the Rate of
         and no more, for every   Words or Figures, and
so in Proportion for any greater or smaller Number of Words or
Figures, but shall not be paid for any Words or Figures in the
Title of such Copy, or in the Title of the respective Columns
contained in the same.

And be it further Enacted by the Authority aforesaid, That 51
every Clerk of the Peace as aforesaid shall and is hereby required
E

-quired to deliver a true Copy, or a true Abſtract, of all or any Part or Parts of the Regiſter of Freeholders for any Pariſh, which ſhall or may be kept by ſuch Clerk of the Peace, in purſuance of this Act, unto any Perſon who ſhall in Writing demand the ſame; and every ſuch Copy as aforeſaid ſhall be of the Form ſpecified in the Schedule hereunto annexed, N° 1; and every ſuch Abſtract as aforeſaid ſhall be of the Form ſpecified in the Schedule hereunto annexed, N° 7; and every ſuch Copy or Abſtract as aforeſaid ſhall be ſtated to be "*a true Copy,*" or "*a true Abſtract*" (as the Caſe may be); and each Page or Folio of ſuch Copy or Abſtract ſhall be ſigned by ſuch 52 Clerk of the Peace; and ſuch Copy or Abſtract ſhall be delivered within a reaſonable Time after the ſame ſhall have been demanded; and ſuch Clerk of the Peace ſhall be paid for every ſuch Copy, or ſuch Abſtract (at the Time the ſame ſhall be demanded) at and after the Rate of   and no more, for every Words or Figures, and ſo in Proportion for any greater or ſmaller Number of Words or Figures, but ſhall not be paid for any Words or Figures in the Title of ſuch Copy, or of ſuch Abſtract, or in the Title of the reſpective Columns contained in the ſame; and every ſuch Clerk of the Peace as aforeſaid ſhall at all Times be provided with a ſufficient Number of Blank Certificates, printed in the Form ſpecified in the Schedule hereunto annexed, N° 1; and alſo with a ſufficient Number of Blank Certificates, printed in the Form ſpecified in the Schedule hereunto annexed, N° 7.

53   And, for the better carrying of this Act into Execution, Be it further Enacted by the Authority aforeſaid, That it ſhall and may be lawful for every Regiſter-keeper, authorized to make Enrolments in any Regiſter of Freeholders, in purſuance of this Act, to provide, or to cauſe to be provided, a ſufficient Number of Blank Certificates, printed in the Form ſpecified in the Schedule hereunto annexed, N° 1, for Copies of Enrolments to be made thereon; and likewiſe a ſufficient Number of Blank Notices, printed in the Form ſpecified in the Schedule hereunto annexed, N° 5, and the Expence of the ſame ſhall be defrayed by the Overſeer or Overſeers of the Poor for the Pariſh, and ſhall be charged in the Overſeer's Accounts.

54   And be it further Enacted by the Authority aforeſaid, That if any Regiſter of Freeholders for any Pariſh as aforeſaid ſhall be materially damaged, or if but few Blank Folios of any ſuch Regiſter ſhall be left unfilled, then and in ſuch Caſe the Regiſter-keeper, authorized by this Act to make Enrolments in ſuch Regiſter,

[19]

gifter, shall and is hereby required to give early Notice thereof in Writing to the Clerk of the Peace for such County (or for the Riding or Division of the same to which such Parish shall belong) and such Clerk of the Peace, upon receiving any such Application, shall and is hereby required forthwith to deliver or safely transmit to such Register-keeper as aforesaid another Register, to which shall be annexed a Copy of this Act (printed as above directed) and such Register shall be in all Respects similar to the Registers above directed to be provided by the Sheriff; and if at any Time any more than One Register shall have been received for any Parish by any Register-keeper aforesaid, One such Register only shall be in Use at the same Time; and when any other such Register shall be opened to receive Enrolments, the progressive Numbers opposite to the Enrolments in such Register shall be a Continuation of the progressive Numbers in the former Register, and the Numbers at the Head of the Folios of the one shall in like Manner be a Continuation of the Numbers at the Head of the Folios of the other. 55

And be it further Enacted by the Authority aforesaid, That every Register-keeper aforesaid, who shall, in pursuance of this Act, have signed any Enrolment or Enrolments made as aforesaid in the Register of Freeholders for any Parish, shall, for each and every Enrolment so made and signed, be entitled to receive, from the Freeholder or other Person making Application for the said Enrolment to be made, the Sum of   but if any such Enrolment shall exceed the Number of
    Words or Figures, then and in such Case the said Register-keeper shall and may receive, from the Freeholder or other Person applying for such Enrolment to be made, the further Sum of   for every   Words or Figures above
    which such Enrolment shall contain; and the Copy of all Enrolments to be sent to the Clerk of the Peace as aforesaid, shall be made and sent " *gratis.*" 56

And be it further Enacted by the Authority aforesaid, That in case of the Illness or Absence of any such Clerk of the Peace as aforesaid, the lawful Deputy of such Clerk of the Peace is hereby empowered and required to act as such with respect to all Matters and Things by this Act directed to be done. 57

And be it further Enacted by the Authority aforesaid, That all such necessary Expences as shall or may be incurred by the Sheriff of any County aforesaid, or by any such Clerk of the 58

Peace

Peace as aforesaid, in or by the carrying of this Act into Execution, shall be borne and defrayed by such respective County out of the County Rate, as also all other reasonable Charges which shall be made by any such Clerk of the Peace, on account of the Trouble which he shall or may have had in the carrying of this Act into Execution, and the Amount of such Expences or Charges shall be settled and allowed by the Justices at any General Quarter Sessions of the Peace; and in such of the Counties aforesaid in which there are or shall hereafter be separate and distinct Rates for different Ridings or other Divisions of such Counties respectively, the said Expences or Charges shall be borne and defrayed out of such respective Rates, in such respective Shares and Proportions as such respective Ridings or other Divisions of such County shall then pay (or shall then last have paid) towards the Land Tax of such County.

59 **And be it further Enacted** by the Authority aforesaid, That all Forfeitures aforesaid, by this Act to be incurred, shall and may be sued for and recovered by Action of Debt, Bill, Plaint, or Information, in any of His Majesty's Courts of Record at Westminster, wherein no Essoign, Protection, Wager of Law, or more than One Imparlance, shall be allowed, and in every such Action the Party against whom Judgment shall be given (whether Plaintiff or Defendant) shall pay the   of Suit; and every such Action or Prosecution as aforesaid shall be brought or commenced within Three Years after the Offence committed, and not afterwards; and the Person against whom any such Action or Prosecution shall be brought or commenced shall be

60 legally served, within the Time aforesaid, with the Writ or Process by which such Action or Prosecution shall be intended to be commenced, unless the Service of such Writ or Process shall have been prevented by such Person's absconding or withdrawing out of this Kingdom; and every Action or Prosecution which shall be brought or commenced as aforesaid shall be carried on without wilful Delay.

61 **And be it further Enacted** by the Authority aforesaid, That if any Register-keeper, authorized and required by this Act to make Enrolments in any Register of Freeholders for any Parish, shall wilfully refuse to enrol therein as aforesaid the Name of any Person who shall (in any of the Ways hereinbefore prescribed) make Application to have his Name so enrolled, then and in such Case, on Oath being made before some Justice of the Peace for the County in which such Parish shall lie (who shall

reside

reside in, or near unto, or next unto, such Parish) that Application (in One of the Ways before prescribed) had been made to such Register-keeper as aforesaid, to make such Enrolment, and that such Register-keeper had refused so to do, it shall be lawful for such Justice, and he is hereby required, to summon such Register-keeper to appear before him, and to shew Cause why he did so refuse to make such Enrolment; and if such Register-keeper shall not shew to such Justice that such Refusal did proceed from Illness, sudden Accident, or other Cause justifiable by this Act, or if such Register-keeper, being duly summoned as aforesaid, shall refuse or neglect to obey such Summons, such Justice shall, by Warrant under his Hand and Seal, cause the Sum of   of lawful Money of Great Britain to be levied on the Goods and Chattels of the said Register-keeper; and in case such Justice shall grant such Warrant as aforesaid, it shall moreover be lawful for such Justice, and he is hereby required, to order such Register-keeper forthwith to make such Enrolment, or to cause the same to be made as aforesaid; and if such Register-keeper shall not obey such Order, such Justice, or any other Justice of the Peace for such County (upon such Fact being proved to him upon the Oath of any Two or more credible Witnesses) shall, by Warrant under his Hand and Seal, cause the further Sum of   of lawful Money of Great Britain to be levied by Distress on the Goods and Chattels of such Register-keeper so disobeying such Order; and the said Sum or Sums so levied (the reasonable Costs and Charges of levying the same being thereout first paid and satisfied) shall respectively go and be paid to the Person who shall have been refused to be enrolled as aforesaid: Provided always, that if the Person making such Application to such Justice, or if the said Register-keeper shall think himself aggrieved by any Determination of such Justice, it shall and may be lawful for the Person so thinking himself aggrieved to appeal to the next General Quarter Sessions of the Peace to be holden for such County, or for that Riding or Division of such County in which such Parish shall lie, by giving Fourteen Days Notice in Writing to such Justice, and to the other Person concerned in such Determination, of such his Intention to appeal, if there shall be sufficient Time for that Purpose, and if there shall not be sufficient Time, then, by giving the like Notice of his Intention to appeal to the next subsequent General Quarter Sessions of the Peace to be holden as aforesaid, and from the Time of giving such Notice all Proceedings relative to the Execution of the said Warrant or Warrants (if the Case shall so be) shall stop; and the Determination of the Justices at the said General

neral Quarter Seſſions to which ſuch Appeal ſhall be made as aforeſaid, ſhall be final and concluſive; and ſuch Juſtices may order ſuch Coſts to be paid by either of the ſaid Parties to the other, as the ſaid Juſtices ſhall think proper; but no Determination of the ſaid Juſtices on any ſuch Appeal ſhall extend, or be conſtrued to extend, to preclude any Perſon who ſhall have been ſo refuſed to be enrolled, from making a freſh Application to have his Name enrolled as aforeſaid, or from having the like Remedy in caſe of a freſh Refuſal.

66 And be it further Enacted and Declared by the Authority aforeſaid, That nothing in this Act contained ſhall extend, or be conſtrued to extend, to prevent any Freeholder under the Age of Twenty-one Years, and above the Age of Eighteen Years, or to prevent any unmarried Woman or Widow, from being enrolled in any Regiſter of Freeholders aforeſaid, provided ſuch Perſon ſhall have a Freehold Eſtate within the true Intent and Meaning of this Act, and provided ſuch Perſon ſhall (in any of the Ways above-mentioned) make Application for the Enrolment to be made; but every ſuch Perſon ſhall be as fully entitled to be enrolled, and ſhall, in caſe of a Refuſal as aforeſaid, have the ſame Remedy or Remedies as any other Freeholder.

67 And be it further Enacted by the Authority aforeſaid, That if any Perſon taking any Oath or Affirmation, by this Act authorized or required to be taken or made, ſhall thereby commit wilful Perjury, or be guilty of falſe Affirmation, or if any Perſon ſhall unlawfully procure or ſuborn any Perſon to take any Oath or Affirmation, by this Act authorized or required to be taken or made, whereby ſuch Perſon ſhall commit wilful Perjury, or be guilty of falſe Affirmation, every ſuch Perſon, on being duly convicted of any ſuch Offence, ſhall

68 And be it further Enacted by the Authority aforeſaid, That if any Perſon, from and after the paſſing of this Act, ſhall wilfully deſtroy, or cauſe or procure to be deſtroyed, or ſhall aid or aſſiſt in deſtroying, any Regiſter of Freeholders for any Pariſh, or any Copy of any Enrolment or Enrolments, which Copy ſhall have been received as aforeſaid by any Clerk of the Peace, or any Regiſter of Freeholders, which ſhall in purſuance of this Act be kept by any Clerk of the Peace, or any Part of any ſuch Copy, or of any ſuch Regiſter as aforeſaid; or ſhall wilfully eraſe or falſely alter, or cauſe or procure to be eraſed or falſely altered, any Enrolment or Enrolments, or any Part of any Enrolment

or

or Enrolments, in any such Copy, or in any such Register as aforesaid; or shall wilfully insert, or cause or procure to be inserted, in any such Copy, or in any such Register as aforesaid, any counterfeit or fictitious Enrolment or Enrolments; or shall forge or counterfeit any such Copy, or any such Register as aforesaid, or any Part of any such Copy or of any such Register; or shall forge or counterfeit any Notice, Receipt, Oath, or Attestation, aforesaid, or shall forge or counterfeit the Name of any Person, which shall or which may, in pursuance of this Act, be signed to any Enrolment or Enrolments, or to any Copy, Register, Notice, Receipt, Oath, or Attestation aforesaid, every Person so offending, and being thereof lawfully convicted, shall

69

And whereas it would be expedient that every Register of Freeholders, which shall be kept in pursuance of this Act for any Parish, should at all seasonable Times be accessible to every Freeholder as aforesaid, who may apply to have his Name enrolled in such Register of Freeholders, **Be it therefore further Enacted** by the Authority aforesaid, That every such Register of Freeholders shall always remain in or near the Parish to which the same shall belong, and shall be in the Custody of the Register-keeper of the Parish for the Time being; and every Copy of any Enrolment or Enrolments in any such original Register of Freeholders as aforesaid, which shall be proved upon Oath to be a true and correct Copy, by any Person who shall have carefully examined the same, shall be deemed legal Evidence of such Enrolment or Enrolments, without such original Register of Freeholders as aforesaid being produced; and if in any Case no such Copy, examined with the original Register of Freeholders, and proved upon Oath to be a true and correct Copy as aforesaid, shall be produced, then and in such Case the Copy of any Enrolment or Enrolments which shall have been received by any Clerk of the Peace as aforesaid, shall be deemed the next best Evidence of any such Enrolment or Enrolments; and if no such Copy so received by the Clerk of the Peace as aforesaid shall be produced, then and in such Case the Register of Freeholders (of the Form specified in the Schedule hereunto annexed, N° 1) which shall be kept by such Clerk of the Peace in pursuance of this Act, shall be deemed the next best Evidence of any such Enrolment or Enrolments as aforesaid: Provided always, that nothing herein contained shall extend, or be construed to extend, to prohibit the producing of any original Register of Freeholders, upon a Charge being brought of any

70

71

undue

undue Practice or Practices in refpect of fuch original Regifter itfelf.

72 And whereas Doubts may arife, whether certain Diftricts ought or ought not to be deemed and confidered as feparate and diftinct Parifhes, within the true Intent and Meaning of this Act: And whereas it is expedient to prevent fuch Uncertainty: Be it therefore further Enacted by the Authority aforefaid, That the Commiffioners of the Land Tax within every County in that Part of Great Britain called England, and in the Dominion of Wales, fhall, on the   Day of   One thoufand Seven hundred and   (and between the Hours of Ten and Eleven in the Forenoon) and they are hereby required to meet within each County refpectively, at the Place where the Election of the Knight or Knights of the Shire to ferve in Parliament for the County was held at the laft General Election; and the Sheriff for each County refpectively fhall, at

73 leaft Fourteen Days previous to the Day of the faid Meeting, fend written or printed Summons to the faid Commiffioners, to attend fuch Meeting, fpecifying in fuch Summons the Time, Place, and Purpofe of fuch Meeting; and the faid Sheriff fhall attend the faid Meeting, and fhall prepare and produce to the faid Meeting a complete Lift or Lifts of all the Parifhes within fuch County; and the Clerk of the Peace for the faid County, or for any Riding or Divifion of the fame, fhall alfo attend the faid Meeting, and fhall likewife prepare and produce to the faid Meeting a complete Lift or Lifts of all the Parifhes within fuch County, Riding, or Divifion; and it fhall and may be lawful for the faid Commiffioners, or the Majority of them, who fhall be prefent at fuch Meeting, and they are hereby required, to fet-

74 tle and finally to determine any Queftion that may arife, whether any particular Diftrict is or is not a feparate and diftinct Parifh, within the true Intent and Meaning of this Act; and the faid Commiffioners are hereby required to make out, or in their Prefence to caufe to be made out, a complete Lift of all the feparate and diftinct Parifhes within the County; and the faid Lift fhall be figned by the Sheriff of the County, in the Prefence of the faid Commiffioners; and the faid Lift fhall be kept and preferved amongft the Records of the County; and the faid Sheriff fhall caufe the faid Lift of Parifhes to be publifhed in the " *London Gazette* :" Provided always, that if any Parifh, in any County aforefaid, fhall be divided into different Townfhips, Parochial Chapelries, or other Diftricts, having feparate Church-

75 wardens, or having other feparate Officers to execute the Duty

of

of Churchwarden, then and in such Case it shall and may be lawful for the said Commissioners, at such General Meeting as aforesaid (if they shall judge that it will be more convenient to the Freeholders of the said Townships, Parochial Chapelries, or other Districts) to appoint the said Townships, Parochial Chapelries, or other Districts, or any of them, to be separate and distinct Parishes, within the true Intent and Meaning of this Act, but for no other Purpose; and in case of such Appointment being made by the said Commissioners, the said Commissioners shall, and are hereby required, to cause the Names of the said Townships, Parochial Chapelries, or other Districts, to be inserted in the List of Parishes aforesaid.

And whereas it is highly expedient that the said Register-keeper should always be one of the sufficient Inhabitants of the Parish, and a Person well qualified to execute the Duty which by this Act he is directed to perform: And whereas it is expedient that the said Register of Freeholders should not pass frequently into the Hands of different Persons, but should remain in the Custody of the same Register-keeper: Be it therefore further Enacted by the Authority aforesaid, That as soon as the complete List of Parishes shall (in each of the said Counties respectively) have been made out by the Commissioners of the Land Tax, at such General Meeting as aforesaid, the said Commissioners shall and are hereby required to determine whether they shall proceed forthwith (at such General Meeting) to make the Appointments hereinafter mentioned, or whether they shall proceed forthwith to divide the said List of Parishes into different Lists, for different Parts or Divisions of the County; and if the said Commissioners should determine to form different Lists of Parishes as aforesaid, the said Commissioners shall then decide what shall be the Number of such Lists, and shall make out, or in their Presence cause to be made out, the said respective Lists of Parishes in the Manner that they shall judge the most expedient, and the said different Lists (if such there be) shall be signed by the Sheriff of the County, in the Presence of the said Commissioners; and the said Lists shall be kept and preserved amongst the Records of the County; and the said Sheriff shall cause the said respective Lists of Parishes (instead of the List of Parishes aforesaid) to be published in the " *London Gazette*;" and each and every of the aforesaid Determinations of the said Commissioners respectively shall be final and conclusive; and in those Counties wherein different Lists of Parishes shall be made out as aforesaid,

76

77

78

the said Commissioners shall hold separate Meetings for the separate Districts comprized in the respective Lists of Parishes aforesaid; and the said Commissioners shall appoint the Times and Places when and where the said respective Meetings shall forthwith be holden, and shall adjourn themselves to the same respectively; and it shall and may be lawful for the said Commissioners (at such General Meeting or other Meetings as aforesaid, as the Case may be) and they are hereby required to nominate and appoint, for each Parish contained in the List of Parishes afore-

79 said, or in the respective Lists of Parishes aforesaid (as the Case may be) a proper Person as a Register-keeper, who shall be willing to be so appointed, and likewise a proper Person as Register-keeper-elect, who shall be willing to be so appointed; and every Person who shall, as aforesaid, be appointed Register-keeper by the said Commissioners is hereby required to act as such; and every Person who shall, as aforesaid, be appointed Register-keeper-elect by the said Commissioners is hereby empowered and required to act as Register-keeper, in case of the Death, Illness, or Absence of the Register-keeper himself; and the said Commissioners are hereby required, in the appointing of any Person as the Register-keeper (or as the Register-keeper-elect) of any Parish, to attend that the Person so to be appointed do not reside any Part of the Year at an inconvenient Distance from such Parish, and that such Person be duly qualified to execute the Office of Register-keeper in pursuance of this Act.

80 And whereas there may be Parishes so small, so situate, or so circumstanced, as to render it inexpedient for a separate and distinct Register-keeper (or Register-keeper-elect) to be appointed for each and every such Parish; Be it therefore further Enacted and Declared by the Authority aforesaid, That it shall and may be lawful for the said Commissioners of the Land Tax to appoint the same Person as the Register-keeper (or as the Register-keeper-elect) for any Two or more adjoining or adjacent Parishes, if the said Commissioners shall judge that it be expedient so to do: Provided always, that both a Register-keeper and a Register-keeper-elect shall be appointed for each and every Parish aforesaid.

81 And be it further Enacted by the Authority aforesaid, That the said Commissioners of the Land Tax, or (if at any Time there be no Land Tax granted and assessable) the Persons who shall last have been Commissioners of the Land Tax in each County

County refpectively, fhall and are hereby required to affemble at fuch General Meeting, or at fuch other Meetings as aforefaid (as the Cafe may be) Twice in every Year, videlicet, on the Day of and on the Day of in each Year, if fuch Day be not a Sunday, and if any fuch Day be a Sunday, then on the Day following: And the faid Commiffioners are hereby required, at fuch refpective Meetings as aforefaid, to nominate and appoint other Regifter-keepers (or other Regifter-keepers-elect) in the Room of thofe who may have died, or who may be defirous to refign their Office, or whom the faid Commiffioners may think proper to difmifs; but the faid Commiffioners are hereby required not to change the faid Regifter-keeper (or the faid Regifter-keeper-elect) without fufficient Caufe, of which the faid Commiffioners are hereby fully and finally empowered to judge; and the faid Commiffioners, at every General or other Meeting as aforefaid (as the Cafe may be) fhall appoint One of the Commiffioners prefent to prefide at the faid Meeting; and in cafe of Equality of Voices on fuch Queftion, the fame fhall be determined by Lot; and the Commiffioner who fhall be appointed to prefide at any fuch Meeting, fhall have, in any Cafe of Equality of Voices, a double (or the cafting) Voice; and all Appointments made, or Refolutions come to, by the faid Commiffioners, in purfuance of this Act, fhall be entered in a Book, and fhall be figned by the Commiffioner who fhall prefide at fuch General or other Meeting as aforefaid; and it fhall and may be lawful for the faid Commiffioners to adjourn any fuch General or other Meeting as aforefaid, from Place to Place, as they fhall judge moft expedient; and if (from there being no Commiffioners or Commiffioner prefent, or from Want of Time, or other Caufe) the faid Commiffioners at any fuch Meeting as aforefaid fhall not do or complete all the Bufinefs which is by this Act directed to be done, the faid Meeting fhall be adjourned to fome Day not later than the Eighth Day from the Day of fuch Meeting: And it fhall and may be lawful for the faid Commiffioners, at any fuch General or other Meeting as aforefaid, to direct their Precept to fuch Parifh Officers, or other Inhabitants of any Parifh or Parifhes within their refpective Jurifdictions as aforefaid, as they fhall think proper, directing fuch Perfon or Perfons to appear before the faid Commiffioners at any Meeting to be holden at any Time, not later than the Day after the Date of fuch Precept; and if any fuch Parifh Officer, or other Perfon as aforefaid, fhall refufe or neglect to attend fuch Meeting, without lawful Excufe, to be

proved

proved on the Oath of Two Witnesses (which Oaths the said Commissioners are hereby authorized to administer) such Person shall forfeit to the Overseer or Overseers of the Poor for the Parish, and for the Relief of the said Poor, any Sum that the said Commissioners shall think fit, not exceeding
and the said Commissioners (at the said Meeting, or at the next subsequent Meeting) shall determine whether the Excuse (if any) be sufficient, and if not sufficient, then what such Forfeiture shall be; and the said Commissioners, at the said Half Yearly Meetings, are hereby required to make strict Enquiry, whether any Register-keeper (or Register-keeper-elect) shall reside at an inconvenient Distance from his respective Parish, or shall be dead, or shall have become incapable of executing the Duty of his Office: And the said Commissioners shall cause the

85 Name of every Person who shall be by them appointed the Register-keeper (or the Register-keeper-elect) of any Parish (together with the Addition, Profession, or Trade, and the usual Place of Abode of such Person) to be forthwith notified in Writing unto the Clerk of the Peace for the County, or for the Riding or Division of the same to which such Parish shall belong (as the Case may be) and also unto the Churchwarden or Churchwardens of such Parish : Provided always, that in case of the Death, Illness, or Absence, both of the Register-keeper and of the Register-keeper-elect of any Parish, or in case (from any Omission or Neglect of the said Commissioners, or from any other Cause) there shall be no Person who shall have been appointed either Register-keeper or Register-keeper-elect, for any particular Parish contained in the List or Lists of Parishes aforesaid, then the Churchwarden or Churchwardens of such Parish is or are hereby empowered to act as the Register-keeper of the said Parish, and such Churchwarden or Churchwardens is or are hereby required to act as such, until there shall be a Register-keeper or a Register-keeper-elect to act as aforesaid.

86 **And be it further Enacted and Declared** by the Authority aforesaid, That nothing in this Act contained shall extend, or be construed to extend, to repeal or to alter the Act made and passed in the Twentieth Year of His present Majesty King George the Third, intituled, " *An Act to remove certain Difficulties relative to* " *Voters at County Elections,*" so far as the same relates to the Election of any Member or Members to serve in Parliament for the Borough of *Cricklade*, in the County of *Wilts*, or to repeal or to alter any of the Laws now in Force, or any Part thereof, so far as the same relate to the Election of any Member or Members

bers to serve in Parliament, either for the Borough of *New Shoreham*, in the County of *Sussex*, or for the Borough of *Cricklade*, in the County of *Wilts*; but that all and every of the said Laws, and every Part thereof, so far as the same relate to the Qualification of Voters for the said Boroughs, or for either of them, shall remain and continue in Force, to all Intents and Purposes, as if this Act had not been made.

N° 1.

S C H E D U L E

Referred to by this Act, stating the Form of the "REGISTER OF FREEHOLDERS."

Folio   of the Register of Freeholders for the Parish   in the County of

Note.—Whenever any Enrolment shall have been copied (in order to be delivered unto the Clerk of the Peace) the Register-keeper shall upon this Register write, or in his Presence cause to be written, the Word "*copied*," immediately under the progressive Number that shall be opposite to the Enrolment so copied.

Progressive Number of the Freeholder's Enrolment.	Freeholder's Christian Name and Surname.	Freeholder's Addition, Profession, or Trade.	Freeholder's usual Place of Abode.—And if it be in a Town consisting of more Streets than one, (specifying in what Street.	Freeholder "*present*" or "*absent*" at the Time of Enrolment.	Nature and Description of the Freehold Estate.—And if it be on any Life or Lives, then (specifying whether it be on his own Life, or on the Life of C.D. or on the longest of the Lives of E.F. and G.H. &c. or on the shortest of the Lives of K.L. and M.N. &c.	Name of some Occupier of the Freehold Lands or Messuage.	Year, Month, and Day of the Enrolment.	Enrolment made by or in the Presence of me

[*Note for the Stationer.*]

[*The Register of Freeholders is to be of the above Form, and is to be made of large and durable Folio Paper.—The above Columns are to be ruled across with Lines at proper and equal Distances from each other, or as nearly so as may be, in order that all Enrolments may be written upon or near unto such ruled Lines, which ruled Lines are to run lengthwise of the Paper.—And to each and every such Register of Freeholders shall be annexed a Copy of this Act, printed by the King's Printer, on durable Paper, of the same Size as the said Register, and in the Roman Letter, or in the Roman and Italic.*]

N° 2.

SCHEDULE.

Referred to by this Act, stating the Form of the "RECEIPT."

" I A. B. the Regifter-keeper of the Parifh of
"   in the County of   do
" hereby acknowledge to have received from C. D. the Sheriff of
" the faid County, and by the Hands of E. F. a Regifter for the
" faid Parifh, to which Regifter is annexed a printed Copy of an
" Act, intituled " *An Act for the better fecuring the Rights of*
" *Voters at County Elections,*" made and paffed in the Twenty-fixth
" Year of the Reign of His Majefty King George the Third.
" Witnefs my Hand, this   Day of
" One thoufand Seven hundred and
                                        " A. B."

N° 3.

SCHEDULE

Referred to by this Act, stating the Form of the
"ATTESTATION."

"I Request to be enrolled in the Register of Freeholders for the
" Parish of   in the County of   and I do
" solemnly swear" [*or, being one of the People called Quakers,* "I do
" solemnly affirm*]* That my Name is A. B.; and that I am
[*specifying the Addition, Profession, or Trade of such Person*] " and
" that the usual Place of my Abode is at   "
[*and if it be in a Town consisting of more Streets than one, specifying
in what Street*] " in the County of   and that I am
" in the actual Possession of an Estate of the clear Yearly Value
" of Forty Shillings, over and above the Yearly Interest of any
" Money on any Mortgage or on any other Security affecting
" such Estate, and also over and above all Rents and Charges
" payable out of or in respect of the same, other than Parliamen-
" tary, Public, or Parochial Taxes; and that I do not hold the
" said Estate in Trust, or for or on the Behalf of any other Person
" or Persons whomsoever; and that the Rents and Profits of the
" same are received for my own Use, by myself or others; and
" that the said Estate was not granted to me fraudulently; and
" that my Interest in the same is not nominal or fictitious;
" and that, to the best of my Knowledge and Belief, the said
" Estate is a Freehold Estate, and my Interest in the same really
" and truly a Freehold Interest; and that the following is a true
" Description of the same (that is to say)" [*if the said Freehold
Estate consist of Lands or Messuage, or of both, the Description of the
same shall be as follows; videlicet*] " Lands," *or* " Messuage," *or*
"   Messuages," *or* " Lands and Messuage," *or* " Lands and
"   Messuages," [*and if the said Freehold Estate be on any Life or
Lives, then specifying whether the same be on his own Life, or on the
Life of C. D. or on the longest of the Lives of E. F. and G. H. &c.
or on the shortest of the Lives of K. L. and M. N. &c.*] [*here
describing the said Lands or Messuage, or such Part or Parts thereof
as*

as shall be of the clear Yearly Value of Forty Shillings as aforesaid]
" in the Occupation of   " [*specifying the Name
of some Occupier of the said Lands or Messuage.*] " Witness my
" Hand, this   Day of   One thousand
" hundred and
                                           " A. B."

" Already enrolled in the Register of Freeholders for the Parish
" of   Nº   " [*specifying the said Parish or
Parishes, and the progressive Number or progressive Numbers of such* 93
former Enrolment or Enrolments, if the Case shall so be.]

" The said Oath was taken and subscribed, on the Day ⎫
" and Year aforesaid, before me, P. Q. one of the ⎬ P. Q."
" Justices of the Peace for the County of   ⎭

[*or, if the Freehold Estate consist of Great Tythes or Small Tythes, or
of both, then the Description of the same shall be as follows; videlicet*]
" Great Tythes," *or* " Small Tythes," *or* " Great and Small
" Tythes;" [*and if the said Tythes be on any Life or Lives, then
specifying whether the same be on his own Life, or on the Life of
C. D. or on the longest of the Lives of E. F. and G. H. &c. or on
the shortest of the Lives of K. L. and M. N. &c.*] " issuing out of
"   " [*specifying some of the Lands out of which such
Tythes shall issue*] " in the Occupation of   " [*specifying the* 94
Name of some Occupier of such Lands.] " Witness my Hand, this
"   Day of   One thousand
" hundred and
                                           " A. B."

" Already enrolled in the Register of Freeholders for the Parish
" of   Nº   " [*specifying the said Parish or Parishes,
and the progressive Number or progressive Numbers of such former Enrolment or Enrolments, if the Case shall so be.*]

" The said Oath was taken and subscribed, on the Day ⎫
" and Year aforesaid, before me, P. Q. one of the ⎬ P. Q."
" Justices of the Peace for the County of   ⎭

[*or, if the Freehold Estate consist of an Office, then the Description of
the same shall be as follows; videlicet*] " Office of   "
[*specifying the said Office; and if the said Office shall be on any Life
or Lives, then specifying whether the same be on his own Life, or on* 95
*the Life of C. D. or on the longest of the Lives of E. F. and G. H.
&c. or on the shortest of the Lives of K. L. and M. N. &c.*] " the
" Profits of which issue (wholly or in Part) out of   "
                          I   [*specifying*

"[*specifying some Lands or Messuage out of which the Profits of such Office shall issue*] " in the Occupation of "
[*specifying the Name of some Occupier of the said Lands or Messuage*]
" Witness my Hand, this   Day of
" One thousand   hundred and
                                        " A. B."

" Already enrolled in the Register of Freeholders for the Parish
" of   N°   " [*specifying the said Parish or Parishes, and the progressive Number or progressive Numbers of such former Enrolment or Enrolments, if the Case shall so be.*]

" The said Oath was taken and subscribed, on the Day ⎫
" and Year aforesaid, before me, P. Q. One of the ⎬ P. Q."
" Justices of the Peace for the County of   ⎭

96 [*or, if the Freehold Estate consist of an Annuity or Rent Charge, then the Description of the same shall be as follows; videlicet*] " an Annuity or Rent Charge;" [*and if the said Annuity or Rent Charge be on any Life or Lives, then specifying whether the same be on his own Life, or on the Life of C. D. or on the longest of the Lives of E. F. and G. H. &c. or on the shortest of the Lives of K. L. and M. N. &c.*] " issuing entirely out of a Free-
" hold Estate, consisting of   " [*describing all the Lands and Tenements out of which such Annuity or Rent Charge shall issue*] " situate wholly in   " [*specifying the Parish or Place, Parishes or Places*] " in the County of
" belonging to   " [*specifying the Name of some Owner of such Lands or Tenements*] " whose usual Place of
" Abode is at   " [*and if it be in a Town consisting of more Streets than one, specifying in what Street*] " in the County of
97 "   and in the Occupation of   " [*specifying the Name of some Occupier of such Lands or Tenements.*] " Witness my Hand, this   Day of
One thousand   hundred and
                                        " A. B."

" Already enrolled in the Register of Freeholders for the Parish
" of   N°   " [*specifying the said Parish or Parishes, and the progressive Number or progressive Numbers of such former Enrolment or Enrolments, if the Case shall so be*]

" The said Oath was taken and subscribed, on the Day ⎫
" and Year aforesaid, before me, P. Q. one of the ⎬ P. Q."
" Justices of the Peace for the County of   ⎭

N° 4.

SCHEDULE

Referred to by this Act, stating the Form of the "OATH" *to be written (or printed) at the End of the Attestation,* N° 3, *in certain Cases mentioned in the said Act.*

" I Do solemnly swear," [*or, being one of the People called Quakers,*
" I do solemnly affirm] " That my Name is R. S. and that I am
"   " [*specifying the Addition, Profession, or
Trade of such Person*] " and that the usual Place of my Abode is at
"   " [*and if it be in a Town consisting of more Streets
than one, specifying in what Street*] " in the County of
"   and that the above Attestation does, to the
" best of my Knowledge and Belief, come from A. B. the Person
" therein mentioned. Witness my Hand, this   Day of
" One thousand   hundred and

" R. S."

" The said Oath was taken and subscribed,
" on the Day and Year aforesaid, be-
" fore me, T. U. one of the Justices of   } T. U."
" the Peace for the County of

N° 5.

N° 5.

SCHEDULE

Referred to by this Act, stating the Form of the "NOTICE."

"I A. B. the Regifter-keeper of the Regifter of Freeholders
" for the Parish of   in the County of
"   do hereby give Notice to the
" Clerk of the Peace for the County of
" that the progreffive Number oppofite to the laft Enrolment
" entered in the faid Regifter of Freeholders is   "
[*fpecifying the faid Number*] " and that the   Day
" of   17.. is the Date of the faid laft Enrolment.
" Witnefs my Hand, this   Day of   One
" thoufand   hundred and

"A. B."

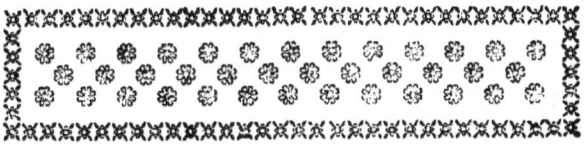

A

BILL

FOR

Making the Estates of such Persons as are Bankers only, within the Cities of *London* and *Westminster*, and within a certain Distance thereof, liable to the Payment of their own and Partnership Debts; and for preventing certain Bankers from dealing in Goods, Wares, and Merchandize; and for regulating the Manner of issuing Bankers Promissory Notes; and for inflicting further Punishment on Clerks to Bankers, who shall embezzle Money or Effects.

Note.—*The Figures in the Margin denote the Number of the Folios in the Written Copy.*

WHEREAS the Support of Credit in a commercial Country is an Object of great National Concernment; and it is apprehended that the State of Credit in this Kingdom would be benefited, in Case the Freehold and Customary or Copyhold Estates of Persons dealing as Bankers were, under due Regulations and Restrictions, made liable to the Payment of their Debts of every Denomination; and inasmuch as

A   Debts

Debts due from or contracted by them, in their Way of Business as Bankers, do not by Law create such an express Lien or Charge upon Freehold Estates as will bind the Heir for the Debt of the Ancestor; nor are Customary or Copyhold Estates liable at Law, or in Equity, to the Payment of such Debts:

And whereas the Business of Bankers is frequently carried on in Partnership, and the Persons engaged in such Partnership are only at Law jointly liable to the Payment of the Debts contracted in their Business of Bankers; and in case of the Death of any of them, the Remedy which the Creditors of such Bankers have at Law, to inforce the Payment of the Debts due to them, is against the Survivors or Survivor of such Partner, and not against the Representatives of such Partners or Partner:

And in regard that it is highly reasonable and expedient that those Persons who, by intrusting Money in the Hands of Persons dealing as Bankers, contribute to the Improvement of their Fortune and Estates, should have the most effectual Security for the Sums so intrusted, upon or out of the real as well as personal Assets of such Banker or Bankers respectively;

May it therefore please Your MAJESTY,

That it may be Enacted; And be it Enacted by the KING's most Excellent Majesty, by and with the Advice and Consent of the Lords Spiritual and Temporal, and Commons, in this present Parliament assembled, and by the Authority of the same, That from and immediately after

each and every Person and Persons engaged in any Partnership, in the issuing of Notes, and keeping open Shops, as Bankers, and following the Business of a Banker only, within the Cities of *London* and *Westminster*, or within thereof, his her, and their Heirs, Executors, and Administrators, shall be liable to the Payment of all Debts contracted by such Partnership in the Course of their dealing as Bankers, and to the same Remedies for the Recovery thereof, as if each and every such Person had severally engaged for the Payment of such Debts.

And

And be it further Enacted by the Authority aforesaid, That from and after all the Manors, Messuages, Lands, Tenements, and Hereditaments, as well Customary or Copyhold as Freehold, whereof any Person or Persons now dealing, or who shall or may at any Time hereafter deal as a Banker, in Manner aforesaid, shall respectively die seised, or whereto he, she, or they shall be intitled at Law or in Equity, of or for any Estate of Freehold, which shall not determine by the Death of such Person respectively, so dealing as a Banker, or of or for any Estate of Inheritance in Fee Tail, General or Special, or of or for an absolute Estate in Fee Simple; shall be, and the same are hereby from henceforth made subject and liable to the Payment of all such Debts and Sums of Money as shall at the Time of the Decease of such Banker be due and owing from him or her alone, or from him or her jointly with any Person or Persons whomsoever, in such Manner and Form as if such Person dealing as a Banker had, at the Time of his Decease, an absolute Power to dispose of such Estates by his Will, and had by his last Will and Testament in Writing, duly executed by him, and attested as by Law is required to pass real Estates and Lands of Inheritance, devised all such Estates, Freehold, Copyhold, or Customaryhold, for the Payment of his Debts.

Provided always, and it is hereby Declared and Enacted, That all the Personal and Real Assets and Estates of such Person dealing as a Banker, shall be first applied in the Satisfaction of his Debts, and the Estates of which he died seised in Fee Tail, General or Special, shall only be liable to make good the Deficiency.

And, to the End that it may be publicly known who are and shall be deemed Bankers, within the true Intent and Meaning of this Act; **Be it further Enacted** by the Authority aforesaid, That all such Persons respectively, who do or shall, at any Time hereafter, deal as Bankers as aforesaid, within the Limits aforesaid, either alone or in Partnership, shall cause and procure their respective Names to be registered in the Public Register Office for the County of *Middlesex*, by the Register of the said Office, or his Deputy, for the Time being, and who is hereby required to register the same alphabetically, in a Book to be kept for that Purpose, expressing the Day of the Month, and Year, and Hour of the Day, when

[4]

when such Registry is made; and a true Copy of such Registry, signed by the Register, or his Deputy, for the Time being, shall be allowed in all Courts of Law and Equity as Evidence of the same; and the said Register, or his Deputy, shall be intitled for every such Registry to the Sum of   and shall permit and suffer any Person or Persons, at all Times within the Office Hours of Attendance, to peruse and inspect the said Book, on being paid for every such Perusal and Inspection   and no more; and that such Persons only whose Names shall be registered as aforesaid, shall, during so long Time as their Names shall continue to be registered, be deemed, construed, and taken to be Bankers, within the true Intent and Meaning of this Act.

7

𝕻𝖗𝖔𝖛𝖎𝖉𝖊𝖉 𝖆𝖑𝖜𝖆𝖞𝖘 𝖓𝖊𝖛𝖊𝖗𝖙𝖍𝖊𝖑𝖊𝖘𝖘, That nothing herein contained shall extend to hinder such Person or Persons, who shall discontinue the Trade or Business of a Banker, from having his, her, or their Name or Names struck out of such Register, upon Application made to the said Register, or his Deputy, for that Purpose; who shall immediately upon such Application strike his, her, or their Name or Names out of such Register, and sign and deliver to the Person applying, a Memorial, containing the Name of the Banker desiring to be struck off the List, together with the Day of the Month, and Year, and Hour of the Day, when the said Register shall strike off the same; which Memorial so signed shall be allowed in all Courts of Law and Equity as Evidence, that the Person or Persons, whose Name and Names shall be therein inserted, is or are struck off the List of Bankers; and the said Register, or his Deputy, shall be intitled for every such Memorial to the Sum of

8

𝕻𝖗𝖔𝖛𝖎𝖉𝖊𝖉 𝖆𝖑𝖜𝖆𝖞𝖘 𝖓𝖊𝖛𝖊𝖗𝖙𝖍𝖊𝖑𝖊𝖘𝖘, That the Real Estates, Freehold, Copyhold, or Customaryhold, of all and every such Banker or Bankers, who shall either die, or whose Name or Names shall be struck out of such Register as aforesaid, shall not, by virtue of this Act, be liable to answer or satisfy any Debt or Debts contracted during the Time his, her, or their Name or Names continued upon such Register, unless a Claim shall be made, and some Suit or Action commenced for the Recovery of such Debt or Debts, within   Calendar Months next after such Banker or Bankers shall die, or his, her, or their Name or Names shall be struck out of such Register as aforesaid.

9

And

And to the Intent His Majesty's Subjects may not be oppressed by such Person or Persons, who now do, or shall at any Time hereafter, deal as Bankers, within the Limits aforesaid, either alone or in Partnership, by their monopolizing or ingrossing any Sort of Goods, Wares, or Merchandizes; **Be it further Enacted** by the Authority aforesaid, That such Person or Persons, who now do, or shall at any Time or Times hereafter, deal as Bankers, within the Limits aforesaid, either alone or in Partnership, whose respective Name or Names shall be registered in Manner aforesaid, shall not, at any Time or Times hereafter, deal or trade, or permit or suffer any Person or Persons whatsoever, either in Trust or otherwise, to deal or trade, with any of the Stock, Monies, or Effects of, or any Way belonging to such Banker or Bankers, in the buying or selling of any Goods, Wares, or Merchandizes whatsoever; and every Person or Persons who shall so deal or trade, or by whose Order or Directions such Dealing or Trading shall be made, prosecuted, or managed, shall forfeit for every such Dealing or Trading the Value of the Goods and Merchandizes so traded for, to such Person or Persons who shall sue for the same, by Action of Debt, Bill, Plaint, or Information, in any of His Majesty's Courts of Record at *Westminster*; wherein no Essoign, Protection, nor other Privilege whatsoever, nor any Injunction, Order, or Restraint, nor Wager of Law, shall be allowed, nor any more than One Imparlance.

Provided always, That nothing herein contained shall be any Ways construed to extend to hinder such Person or Persons, who now do, or shall at any Time or Times hereafter, deal as Bankers, either alone or in Partnership, whose respective Name or Names shall be duly registered as aforesaid, from dealing in Bills of Exchange, or in buying or selling Bullion, Gold, or Silver, or in selling any Goods, Wares, or Merchandize whatsoever, which shall really and *bona fide* be left or deposited with such Banker or Bankers, for Money lent and advanced thereon, and which shall not be redeemed at the Time agreed on, or within Calendar Months after; or from selling such Goods as shall or may be the Produce of Lands purchased or hired by such Banker or Bankers.

[6]

And be it further Enacted by the Authority aforesaid, That the Name of every Person, who, after
shall alone, or jointly with any other Person or Persons, carry on the Business of a Banker or Bankers, within the Limits aforesaid, shall be mentioned in or subscribed to all Promissory Notes issued or given by him or them respectively, under the Penalty of
for every such Promissory Note as shall be issued or given contrary to this Act, to be recovered by and to the Use of any Person who shall sue for the same, by Action of Debt, Bill, Suit, or Information, in any of His Majesty's Courts of Record at *Westminster*.

13 **And be it further Enacted** by the Authority aforesaid, That if any Clerk or Servant to any Person or Persons dealing as a Banker or Bankers, being intrusted with any Note, Bill, Dividend, Warrant, Bond, Deed, or any Security, Money, or other Effects, to the Amount of
or upwards, belonging to such Banker or Bankers, or having any Note, Bill, Dividend, Warrant, Bond, Deed, or any Security, Money, or Effects, to the Amount of
or upwards, of any other Person or Persons, lodged or deposited with such Banker or Bankers, or with him as a Clerk or Servant to such Banker or Bankers, shall secrete, embezzle, or run away with any such Note, Bill, Dividend, Warrant, Bond, Deed, Security, Money, or Effects, to the Amount or Value of
14 or upwards; or in case any such Clerk or Servant shall issue any Note, or give any Receipt for any Sum of Money, to the Amount of
or upwards, other than and except such Sum of Money, to the Amount of
or upwards, as he shall actually have received from or on Account of the Person or Persons respectively to whom he shall issue any such Note, or give any such Receipt as aforesaid; or in case any such Clerk, having received such Sum or Sums of Money, to the Amount of
or upwards, for which such Note was issued, or Receipt given as aforesaid, shall not bring the same to account, but shall withhold or keep, or otherwise secrete, embezzle, or apply the same to his own Use, with Intent to defraud; every Clerk or Servant so offending, and being thereof convicted in due Form of Law, shall be deemed

And

And be it further Enacted by the Authority aforesaid, That this Act shall be deemed, adjudged, and taken to be a Public Act, and be judicially taken Notice of as such by all Judges, Justices, and other Persons whomsoever, without specially pleading the same.

A

BILL

FOR

Making the Estates of such Persons as are Bankers only, within the Cities of *London* and *Westminster*, and within a certain Distance thereof, liable to the Payment of their own and Partnership Debts; and for preventing certain Bankers from dealing in Goods, Wares, and Merchandize; and for regulating the Manner of issuing Bankers Promissory Notes; and for inflicting further Punishment on Clerks to Bankers, who shall embezzle Money or Effects.

1774.

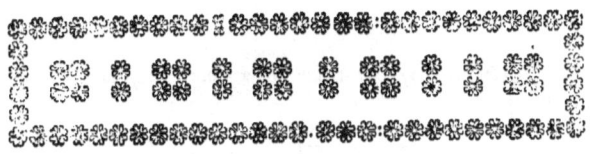

A

B I L L

FOR

The more easy Attendance of Freeholders at Elections of Knights of Shires.

Note.—*The Figures in the Margin denote the Number of the Folios in the written Copy.*

WHEREAS the Freeholders of the several Counties within this Kingdom cannot, without great Expence, Loss of Time, and Fatigue, attend at any One Place to give their Votes at Elections of Knights of the Shire to serve in Parliament for the said Counties, in Cases wherein such Elections shall be contested, and Polls shall be necessary to determine the same: In order therefore that

A such

[2]

such Elections may be made in a more easy and convenient Manner;

May it please Your MAJESTY,

That it may be Enacted; 𝕬𝖓𝖉 𝖇𝖊 𝖎𝖙 𝕰𝖓𝖆𝖈𝖙𝖊𝖉 by the KING's Most Excellent MAJESTY, by and with the Advice and Consent of the Lords Spiritual and Temporal, and Commons, in this present Parliament assembled, and by the Authority of the same, That from and after the   Day of   in the   if, at the Publication or Proclamation of the Writ of Election of a Knight or Knights of the Shire, a Poll shall be demanded by any Candidate, or any   of the Electors there present, and any   or more of the Candidates shall, on the same Day, and not afterwards, desire and request that the said Poll may be taken at Places other than the City, Town, or Place, where such Writ shall be published or proclaimed, the Poll for the Election of such Knight or Knights of the Shire for the several and respective Counties hereinafter named, shall and may be taken at the several and respective Places herein mentioned; (that is to say)

  For the County of *Bedford*, at
  For the County of *Berks*, at
  For the County of *Bucks*, at
  For the County of *Cambridge*, at
  For the County of *Cheshire*, at
  For the County of *Cornwall*, at
  For the County of *Cumberland*, at
  For the County of *Derby*, at
  For the County of *Devon*, at
  For the County of *Dorset*, at
  For the County of *Durham*, at
  For the County of *Ebor* or *York*, at
  For the County of *Essex*, at
  For the County of *Gloucester*, at
  For the County of *Hereford*, at
  For the County of *Herts*, at
  For the County of *Huntingdon*, at
  For the County of *Kent*, at
  For the County of *Lancaster*, at
  For the County of *Leicester*, at
  For the County of *Lincoln*, at

For the County of *Middlesex*, at
For the County of *Monmouth*, at
For the County of *Norfolk*, at
For the County of *Northampton*, at
For the County of *Northumberland*, at
For the County of *Nottingham*, at
For the County of *Oxon*, at
For the County of *Rutland*, at
For the County of *Salop* or *Shrop*, at
For the County of *Somerset*, at
For the County of *Southampton* or *Hamps*, at
For the County of *Stafford*, at
For the County of *Suffolk*, at
For the County of *Surry*, at
For the County of *Sussex*, at
For the County of *Warwick*, at
For the County of *Westmorland*, at
For the County of *Worcester*, at
For the County of *Wilts*, at
For the County of *Anglesey*, at
For the County of *Brecon*, at
For the County of *Cardigan*, at
For the County of *Caermarthen*, at
For the County of *Caernarvon*, at
For the County of *Denbigh*, at
For the County of *Flint*, at
For the County of *Glamorgan*, at
For the County of *Merioneth*, at
For the County of *Montgomery*, at
For the County of *Pembroke*, at
For the County of *Radnor*, at

And be it further Enacted by the Authority aforesaid, That when a Poll shall be demanded, at the Publication or Proclamation of the Writ of Election of a Knight or Knights of the Shire, the same shall proceed in the Manner as by Law is directed, in the City, Town, or Place, where such Writ shall be published and proclaimed; and that the Poll in all and every other City, Borough, Town, or Place within such County, shall commence on the
Day after the Publication or Proclamation of such Writ, if it be not a *Sunday*, and if it be a *Sunday*, then on the Day following, and that in the Computation of such

Day,

Day, the Day of the Publication or Proclamation of the Writ shall be one.

And be it further Enacted, That it shall and may be lawful for every Freeholder to give his Vote and Poll, at such Election for the County in which his Freehold is situated, at any City, Town, or Place of such County, hereby appointed for taking such Poll.

And be it further Enacted, That in order to carry this Act into Execution, it shall and may be lawful for the Sheriff, or in case of his Death or Absence, for the Under Sheriff, and such Sheriff or Under Sheriff is hereby impowered and required, by Writing under his Hand and Seal, to authorize and appoint One or more proper Person or Persons to take the Poll at such City, Town, or County hereby appointed, other than the Place in which such Writ shall be published and proclaimed; and that every such Person so authorized and appointed shall, at the Time and Place appointed for taking the said Poll, and before he shall proceed to take the same, openly read, or cause to be read, an Act, made in the Second Year of the late King *George* the Second, intituled, " An Act for the more effectually pre- " venting Bribery and Corruption," and shall take and subscribe the following Oath:

" I *A. B.* do solemnly swear, That I have not, directly
" nor indirectly, received any Sum or Sums of Money,
" Office, Place, or Employment, Gratuity or Reward,
" or any Bond, Bill, or Note, or any Promise or
" Gratuity whatsoever, either by myself or any
" other Person to my Use, or Benefit, or Advan-
" tage, for or concerning the taking or returning the
" Poll now about to be taken; and that I will admit
" every Person's Name to be inserted in the said
" Poll, who shall appear to me to be qualified by
" Law to give his Vote thereat, and also the Name
" or Names of the Person or Persons for whom
" he shall vote; and that I will not admit the Name
" of any Person to be inserted therein, unless he shall
" appear to me to be so qualified; and that I will
" take the said Poll honestly, uprightly, and impar-
" tially, to the best of my Skill and Knowledge;
" and that I will not strike the Name of any Per-
" son

" son out of the said Poll, after the Name of such
" Person shall be inserted therein, and he hath been
" permitted to give his Vote; and that I will not
" alter the original Poll by me taken, nor cause,
" suffer, nor permit the same to be altered by any
" other Person or Persons whatsoever; and that I will
" return the same unaltered to the High Sheriff or
" his Under Sheriff, within   Days after I
" shall have completely taken the same."

Which Oath any Justice or Justices of the Peace of the said County, City, Corporation, or Borough, where such Election shall be made, or, in his or their Absence, any   of the Electors, are hereby required and authorized to administer; and such Oath so taken, shall be entered among the Records of the Sessions of such County, City, Corporation, and Borough, as aforesaid.

And be it further Enacted, That the said Person or Persons, so authorized and appointed, shall duly and orderly proceed in the Taking of the Poll, without any further or other Adjournment, than from Day to Day, (*Sunday* excepted) until all the Freeholders then and there present shall be polled, and no longer.

Provided always, That such Poll shall not continue, at any City, Town, or Place, at which the Writ shall be published and proclaimed, or at any other City, Town, or Place, hereby appointed for taking such Poll, more than   Days in the Whole; and when the said Poll shall be ended in Manner aforesaid, such Person or Persons so authorized and appointed shall, within   Days, return the same to the Sheriff of the County, or the Under Sheriff, as the Case may happen, with an Oath thereunder written, to be subscribed by him or them, and to be taken before any One Justice of the Peace, or Two of the Electors, in the following Words:

" I *A. B.*" (insert the Names of the Person or Persons, authorized to take the said Poll) " do swear, That
" the foregoing Poll is the original Poll by me"
(or by us, as the Case may happen) " taken at
"   for the" (naming the City, Town, or Place, at which such Poll shall be taken) " within
"   the

[6]

"the County of   and that I" (or we,
as the Case may be) "have not altered the same
"since the same was taken.

"So help me" (or us) "GOD."

9   And that when the Sheriff, or Under Sheriff, shall have finished the Poll taken before him, and have received all the Polls taken in the Manner aforesaid, by virtue of this Act, then, and not before, he shall make his Return of Person or Persons chosen Knight or Knights of the Shire to serve in Parliament for the said County.

And be it further Enacted, That the Person or Persons authorized and appointed, by virtue of this Act, to take the Poll, are hereby authorized and required to do all and every Act, Matter, and Thing, that the Sheriff or Under Sheriff might lawfully do at the taking of any Poll, or is required by Law to do, was he personally present, other than that of administering the Oath of Qualification, appointed to be taken by Candidates, by an Act intituled, "An Act for "securing the Freedoms of Parliaments, by the further "qualifying the Members to sit in the House of Commons," made in the Ninth Year of Queen *Anne*; and such Person and Persons, so authorized and appointed, shall be liable to the same Pains and Penalties, for all and every Omission and Breach of his or their Duty in Relation to the same, as any Sheriff or Under Sheriff would have been liable to, in Case such Sheriff or Under Sheriff, or either of them, had been personally present, and omitted, or committed the same.

10   And be it further Enacted, That every Person who shall give his Vote or Poll before the Person or Persons authorized and appointed by virtue of this Act to take the same, shall, and is hereby required, before he shall be admitted to give his Vote or Poll thereat, to take all and every Oath and Oaths, and to do every other Act, Matter, or Thing, as by Law he is required to do before the Sheriff or Under Sheriff, in case the said Sheriff or Under Sheriff had been present at the said Poll, and taken the same; and such Person omitting to take the said Oath or Oaths, or swearing falsly, or neglecting to do any Matter or Thing required by Law to be done by him before he be admitted

to

to give his Vote at any Election of a Knight or Knights of the Shire, such Person so omitting to take the said Oaths, or swearing falsly, or neglecting to do any Matter or Thing required by Law to be done by him, shall incur the same Forfeitures, Penalties, and Incapacities, as he would have incurred in case the Sheriff or Under Sheriff had been present at taking the said Poll, and had taken the same.

Provided always, and be it further Enacted, That in case no Poll shall be demanded at the Publication or Proclamation of any Writ for the Election of a Knight or Knights of the Shire for any County hereinbefore mentioned; or if such Poll shall be demanded, and no such Desire or Request as is hereinbefore mentioned shall be made by any One or more of the Candidates, within the Time limited for making the same; then, and in either of such Cases, so much of this Act as relates to taking the Poll, shall not take Place.

A
B I L L
FOR

The more easy Attendance of Freeholders at Elections of Knights
of Shires.

―――
1775.

A

BILL

FOR

The Payment of Costs to Parties, and Charges to Constables, Witnesses, and others, on Complaints determined before Justices of the Peace out of Sessions; for the Payment of the Charges of Constables in certain Cases; and for the more effectual Payment of Charges to Witnesses and Prosecutors of any Larceny, or other Felony.

Note.—*The Figures in the Margin denote the Number of the Folios in the written Copy.*

WHEREAS, by the Laws now in being, His Majesty's Justices of the Peace are not sufficiently authorized, on Complaints that come before them out of Sessions, to award Costs against either the Person or Persons complaining, or the Person or Persons against whom any Complaint is made, as to Justice may appertain:

1

A May

May it please Your MAJESTY,

That it may be Enacted; **And be it Enacted** by the KING's Most Excellent MAJESTY, by and with the Advice and Consent of the Lords Spiritual and Temporal, and Commons, in this present Parliament assembled, and by the Authority of the same, That where any Complaint shall be made before any of His Majesty's Justices of the Peace, for any County, Riding, Division, City, Town Corporate, Franchise, or Liberty, and any Warrant or Summons shall issue in Consequence of such Complaint, that then it shall and may be lawful to and for any Justice or Justices of the Peace, who shall have heard and determined the Matter of the said Complaint, to award such Costs to be paid by either of the Parties, and in Manner and Form as to him or them shall seem fit, as well to the Party injured, as also a reasonable Satisfaction for the Trouble and Loss of Time of the Constables and Persons summoned to appear, and appearing, to give their Evidence before such Justice or Justices; and in case any Person, so ordered by the said Justice or Justices of the Peace to pay such Sum or Sums of Money as aforesaid, shall not immediately pay down or give Security for the same, to the Satisfaction of the Justice or Justices, it shall and may be lawful for the said Justice or Justices, by Warrant under his Hand and Seal, or their Hands and Seals, to levy the said Sum or Sums by   of the Goods and Chattels of such Person so refusing or neglecting; and where Goods and Chattels of such Person cannot be found, to   such Person to the   for the County, Riding, Division, City, Town Corporate, Franchise, or Liberty, wherein such Person shall reside, there to be kept to hard Labour for any Time not exceeding   or until such Sum or Sums of Money, together with the Expences attending the Commitment of such Person to such House of Correction, be first paid.

Provided nevertheless, That upon the Conviction of any Person or Persons upon any Penal Statute or Statutes, where the Penalty or Penalties shall amount to or exceed the Sum of   the said Costs, and Satisfaction

for

for Charges, Trouble, and Loss of Time, shall be deducted by the said Justice or Justices, according to his or their Discretion, out of the said Penalty or Penalties, so that the said Deduction shall not exceed One   Part of the said Penalty or Penalties, and the Remainder of the said Penalty or Penalties shall be paid to or divided among the Person or Persons who would have been entitled to the Whole of the Penalty or Penalties in case this Act had not been made.

And whereas Constables, Headboroughs, and Tythingmen, are or may be at great Charge and Loss of Time in doing the Business of their Parish, Township, or Place, and in many Cases are not sufficiently indemnified by the Laws; *Be it therefore Enacted* by the Authority aforesaid, That every Constable, Headborough, or Tythingman, may yearly, within   Days after he shall go out of such Office, deliver to the Overseers of the Poor of the said Parish, Township, or Place, for the Time being, a just Account in Writing, fairly entered in a Book to be kept for that Purpose, and signed by him, of all Sums so by him expended on Account of the said Parish, Township, or Place, or so by him charged for his Trouble and Loss of Time, in all Cases not hitherto provided for by the Laws heretofore made, or by this Act, and also of all Sums received by him on the Account of the said Parish, Township, or Place; and the said Overseers of the Poor, or their Successors, shall, within the next   Days after the said Account shall be so delivered, take the Opinion of the Inhabitants of the said Parish, Township, or Place, upon the said Accounts, and shall then deliver back to the said Constable, Headborough, or Tythingman, such Book of Accounts; and it shall and may be lawful to and for the said Constable, Headborough, or Tythingman, then to produce the said Book before Two of His Majesty's Justices of the Peace in and for the County, Riding, Division, City, Town Corporate, Franchise, or Liberty, wherein such Parish or Township shall be situate, giving reasonable Notice thereof to the Overseers of the Poor of the said Parish, Township, or Place, for the Time being; which said Justices are hereby authorized to examine the same, and to hear and determine any Objection or Objections that shall be made to the said Accounts by the Overseers of the Poor of the

said

said Parish, Township, or Place, for the Time being, and to settle, according to the received Usage or Custom of such Parish, Township, or Place, the Sum which to them shall appear due on the said Account, and to enter the same in the said Account, and to sign their Names thereto; and the Overseers of the Poor of the said Parish, Township, or Place, for the Time being, are hereby authorized and required to pay the said Sum, out of the Money which shall come to their Hands by virtue of any Rate or Assessment made or to be made for the Relief of the Poor.

Provided nevertheless, That in case the Overseer or Overseers of the Poor of the said Parish, Township, or Place, for the Time being, shall find that the said Parish, Township, or Place, is aggrieved by any Neglect, Act, or Thing done, or omitted, by the said Constable, Headborough, or Tythingman, or by any of His Majesty's Justices of the Peace, or shall have any material Objection to such Account, or any Part thereof, or to such Determination as aforesaid, it shall and may be lawful for such Overseer or Overseers, in any of the Cases aforesaid, giving reasonable Notice to the said Constable, Headborough, or Tythingman, to appeal to the next General or Quarter Sessions of the Peace for the County, Riding, Division, City, Town Corporate, Franchise, or Liberty, where such Parish, Township, or Place lies; and the Justices of the Peace there assembled are hereby authorized and required to receive such Appeal, and to hear and finally determine the same; but if it shall appear to the said Justices, that reasonable Notice was not given, then they shall adjourn the said Appeal to the next Quarter Sessions, and then and there finally hear and determine the same; and the said Justices may award and order, to the Party for whom such Appeal shall be determined, reasonable Costs, in the same Manner that they are impowered to do in Case of Appeals concerning the Settlement of poor Persons, by an Act made in the Eighth and Ninth Years of King *William* the Third, intituled, " An Act for supplying some Defects in the Laws " for the Relief of the Poor of this Kingdom."

Provided always, That in all Corporations or Liberties which have not Four Justices of the Peace, it shall and may be lawful for the Overseer or Overseers of the Poor of of the Parish, Township, or Place, for the Time being, where an Appeal is given by this Act, to appeal, if he or they shall think fit, to the next General or Quarter Sessions of the Peace for the County, Riding, or Division, wherein such Corporation or Liberty is situate.

And whereas, by an Act passed in the Twenty-fifth Year of his late Majesty King *George* the Second, intituled, " An Act for the better preventing Thefts and Robberies, " and for regulating Places of public Entertainment, and " punishing Persons keeping disorderly Houses," it was recited, that " whereas many Persons are deterred from pro- " secuting Persons guilty of Felony, upon account of the " Expence attending such Prosecutions, which is a Cause " of the Encouragement of Thefts;" and it was therein, among other Things, enacted, That it should and might be in the Power of the Court before whom any Person has been tried and convicted of any Grand or Petit Larceny, or other Felony, at the Prayer of the Prosecutor, and on Consideration of his Circumstances, to order the Treasurer of the County in which the Offence shall have been committed, to pay unto such Prosecutor such Sum of Money as to the said Court shall seem reasonable, not exceeding the Expences which it shall appear to the Court the Prosecutor was put unto in carrying on such Prosecution, making him a reasonable Allowance for his Time and Trouble therein; which Order the Clerk of Assize, or Clerk of the Peace, respectively, was thereby directed and required forthwith to make out, and to deliver unto such Prosecutor, upon being paid for the same the Sum of One Shilling, and no more:

And whereas, by an Act passed in the Twenty-seventh Year of his late Majesty King *George* the Second, reciting, That the Expence, as well as Loss of Time, in attending Courts of Justice, is a Discouragement to the poorer Sort to appear as Witnesses against Offenders; who thereby escape the public Justice, and the Punishment due to their Crimes; it was Enacted, That when any poor Person shall appear on Recognizance in any Court, to give Evidence against another accused of any Grand or Petit Larceny, or other Felony, it should and might be in the Power of the Court, at the Prayer and on the Oath of such Person, and on Consideration of his Circumstances, in open Court to pay unto such Person such Sum of Money as

B to

to the said Court shall seem reasonable, for his Time, Trouble, and Expence; which Order the proper Officer of such Court is required to make out and deliver to such Person, upon being paid for the same the Sum of Six Pence, and no more:

And whereas the said recited Acts of the Twenty-fifth and Twenty-seventh Years of his late Majesty King *George* the Second, have been a great Encouragement towards bringing Offenders to Justice, in all such Cases as are within the Purview of the said Statutes; but nevertheless it has been found by Experience, that the said hereinbefore recited Statute of the Twenty-seventh Year of his said late Majesty, with regard to Persons appearing on Recognizance in any Court, to give Evidence as aforesaid, extends only to poor Persons, such Court also considering their Circumstances; and also does not extend to Persons appearing on Subpœna to give Evidence:

And whereas the said Act of the Twenty-fifth Year of his said late Majesty, with regard to Prosecutors, directs the Court to consider the Circumstances of such Prosecutor, and also gives him Relief only where the Offender is convicted:

And whereas it is just and reasonable, and may tend in future to the Prevention of Crimes, or to the due Prosecution of all Offenders against the Laws, that every Prosecutor to Conviction, and every Person so appearing on Recognizance or Subpœna to give Evidence, should be allowed his reasonable Expences, and also, in case he be poor, a reasonable Satisfaction for his Trouble and Loss of Time; and that such Allowance should be made to Prosecutors as aforesaid, even though the Person so accused be acquitted, provided it shall appear to such Court, before whom the said Prisoner shall have been tried, that there was a reasonable Ground of Prosecution, and that the Prosecutor hath *bona fide* prosecuted:

Be it further Enacted by the Authority aforesaid, That from and after the passing of this Act, it shall and may be in the Power of the Court before whom any Person has been tried and convicted of any Grand or Petit Larceny, or other Felony, or before whom any Person has been tried and acquitted of any Grand or Petit Larceny, or other Felony, in case it shall appear to the said Court that there was a reasonable Ground of Prosecution, and that the said Prosecutor hath *bona fide* prosecuted, to order, upon Prayer of the said Prosecutor, the Treasurer of the County, Riding, or Division, in which the Offence shall have been committed, or shall have been supposed to have been committed, to pay unto such Prosecutor such Sum of Money as to the said Court shall seem reasonable, not exceeding the Expences which it shall appear to the Court the Prosecutor was *bona fide* put unto in carrying on such Prosecution, making, in case the said Prosecutor shall appear to the Court to be in poor Circumstances, a reasonable Allowance to such Prosecutor for Trouble and Loss of Time; which Order the Clerk of Assize, or Clerk of the Peace, respectively, is hereby directed and required forthwith to make out and deliver unto such Prosecutor, upon being paid for the same the Sum of One Shilling, and no more; and the Treasurer of the said County, Riding, or Division, is hereby authorized and required, upon Sight of such Order, forthwith to pay to such Prosecutor, or other Person authorized to receive the same, such Sum of Money as aforesaid, and shall be allowed the same in his Accounts. [14]

And be it further Enacted by the Authority aforesaid, That it shall and may be in the Power of the Court, where any Person shall appear on Recognizance or Subpœna, to give Evidence as to any Grand or Petit Larceny or other Felony, whether any Bill of Indictment be preferred or not to any Grand Jury, provided the said Person shall, in the Opinion of the said Court, *bona fide* have attended the said Court in Obedience to such Recognizance or Subpœna, to order the Treasurer of the County, Riding, or Division, in which the Offence shall have been committed, or shall have been supposed to have been committed, to pay unto such Person such Sum of Money as to the said Court shall seem reasonable, not exceeding the Expences which it shall appear to the said Court the said Person was *bona fide* put unto by reason of the said Recognizance and Subpœna, making, in case the said Person shall appear to the Court to be in poor Circumstances, a reasonable Allowance to such Person for Trouble and Loss of Time; which Order the Clerk of Assize, or Clerk of the Peace, respectively, is hereby directed and required forthwith to make out and deliver to such Person, upon being paid for the same the Sum of Six Pence, and no more; and the Treasurer of the said County, Riding, or Division, is hereby authorized and required, upon Sight of such Order, forthwith to pay to such Person, or other Person authorized [15] [16]

[8]

to receive the fame, such Sum of Money as aforesaid, and shall be allowed the same in his Accounts.

17 **Provided nevertheless, and be it further Enacted,** That it shall and may be lawful for His Majesty's Justices of the Peace, in and for any County, Riding, Division, City, Town Corporate, Franchise, or Liberty, in Quarter Sessions assembled, to lay down, from Time to Time, such Rules and Regulations, as to any Costs and Charges thereafter to be allowed to any Person whatsoever by virtue of any Part of this Act, for the better carrying the Intent of any Part of this Act into Execution, and for the preventing any unnecessary Expence, as to them shall seem most just and reasonable; which Rules and Regulations, having received the Approbation and Signature of One or more of His Majesty's Judges of Oyer and Terminer, or General Gaol Delivery, at the Assizes for the County wherein such Rules and Regulations shall have been made, shall be binding, and not otherwise, on all Persons whatsoever; and no Person whatsoever shall be allowed any greater Sum of Money, by virtue of this Act, than according to the said Rules and Regulations so approved of as aforesaid, any thing herein contained to the contrary thereof in any wise,
18 notwithstanding.

19 **And be it further Enacted** by the Authority aforesaid, That if any Action or Suit shall be commenced against any Person or Persons, for any Thing done in pursuance of this Act, that then and in every such Case the Action or Suit shall be brought within   Calendar Months next after the Fact committed; and the Defendant or Defendants in such Action or Suit may plead the General Issue, and give this Act and the Special Matter in Evidence at any Trial to be had thereupon, and that the same was done in pursuance and by the Authority of this Act; and if it shall appear so to have been done, the Jury shall find for the Defendant or Defendants; and if the Plaintiff shall be nonsuit, or discontinue his Action after the Defendant or Defendants shall have appeared, or if Judgment shall be given, upon any Verdict or Demurrer, against the Plaintiff, the Defendant and Defendants shall and may recover   Costs, and have the like Remedy for the same as the Defendant or Defendants hath or have in other Cases by Law.

A BILL

FOR

The Payment of Costs to Parties, and Charges to Constables, Witnesses, and others, on Complaints determined before Justices of the Peace out of Sessions; for the Payment of the Charges of Constables in certain Cases; and for the more effectual Payment of Charges to Witnesses and Prosecutors of any Larceny, or other Felony.

1777.

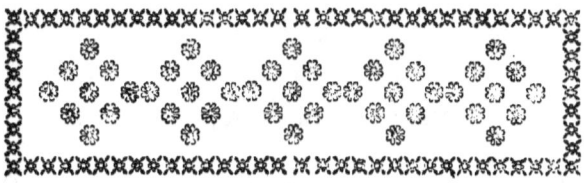

A

BILL

FOR

The Relief of Prisoners charged with Felony or other Crimes, who shall be acquitted, or discharged by Proclamation, respecting the Payment of Fees to Gaolers, and giving a Recompence for such Fees out of the County Rates; and for more effectually securing the Health of Prisoners in Gaol, during their Confinement.

Note.—*The Figures in the Margin denote the Number of the Folios in the Written Copy.*

WHEREAS Persons are frequently in Custody for Felonies or other Crimes, or on Suspicion thereof, or as Accessaries thereto, and though no Bills of Indictment are afterwards preferred or found against them, or they are acquitted on their Trials, yet they are detained for certain Fees to the Sheriffs, Gaolers, or Keepers of Prisons, in whose Custody they happen to be; which is both oppressive and unjust: For Remedy whereof,

1.

May

May it pleafe Your MAJESTY,

That it may be Enacted; **And be it Enacted** by the KING's Moft Excellent MAJESTY, by and with the Advice and Confent of the Lords Spiritual and Temporal, and Commons, in this prefent Parliament affembled, and by the Authority of the fame, That every Prifoner, who now is, or hereafter fhall be, charged with any Felony, or other Crime, or as an Acceffary thereto, in that Part of *Great Britain* called *England*, and *Wales*, againft whom no Bill of Indictment fhall be found by the Grand Jury, or who, on his or her Trial, fhall be acquitted, or who fhall be difcharged by Proclamation for want of Profecution, fhall be immediately fet at large, without the Payment of any Fee or Sum of Money to the Sheriff, Gaoler, or Keeper of the Gaol or Prifon from whence he or fhe fhall be difcharged and fet at Liberty, for or in refpect of fuch Difcharge.

And be it further Enacted by the Authority aforefaid, That all fuch Fees as have been ufually paid, or payable, to the feveral Sheriffs, Gaolers, and Keepers of Prifons, in *England* and *Wales*, in any of the Cafes aforefaid, fhall abfolutely ceafe, and the fame are hereby abolifhed and determined; and, from and after

no Gaoler or Keeper of any Gaol or Prifon fhall afk, demand, take, or receive, any Sum or Sums of Money, from any of the faid Prifoners, as Fees, upon his or her Difcharge.

And be it further Enacted by the Authority aforefaid, That, in Lieu of fuch Fees fo abolifhed as aforefaid, the Treafurers, or other proper Officers of the feveral Counties, and of fuch Cities, Towns Corporate, Cinque Ports, Liberties, Franchifes, and Places, that do not pay to the Rates of the feveral Counties in which they are refpectively fituated, fhall, on receiving a Certificate figned by One or more Judge or Juftice before whom fuch Prifoner fhall have been difcharged as aforefaid, (which Certificate the Judge or Juftice is hereby required to give) pay out of the Rates of fuch County, or out of the Public Stock of fuch City, Town Corporate, Cinque Port, Liberty, Franchife, or Place, the Sum of   to the Sheriff, Gaoler,

Gaoler, or Keeper of the Prison whence the said Prisoner shall have been discharged as aforesaid; which several Sums, so paid in pursuance of this Act, shall be respectively allowed to the said Treasurers and Officers, by the Justices before whom their Accounts shall be passed: Provided nevertheless, that it shall and may be lawful for the Justices of the Peace, in Quarter Sessions assembled, to allow a certain Annual Salary, if they think proper, to the Sheriff, Gaolers, or Keepers of Prisons, within their respective Jurisdictions, instead of the Payments herein before directed to be made to such Sheriff, Gaolers, or Keepers of Prisons.

And, for the Prevention of the Calamities attending what is commonly called the Gaol Disorder, Be it Enacted by the Authority aforesaid, That the several Justices of the Peace, within their several Jurisdictions, in Quarter Sessions assembled, are hereby authorized and required to order a Cold and Hot Bath, or commodious Bathing Tubs, to be made and provided within the several Gaols and Prisons to which Felons are usually committed, and likewise Cloaths for Prisoners to take their Trials in, at the Expence of the County or Place in which such Gaols or Prisons are respectively situated, and to which the same belong, and to order the Prisoners to be washed in such Cold or Hot Baths, or in such Bathing Tubs, according to the Condition in which they shall be at the Time, and cloathed in such Cloaths so provided as aforesaid, before they are brought out to take their respective Trials: And if any Gaoler shall offend, in disobeying the Orders of such Justices as aforesaid, he may be proceeded against in a summary Way, by Complaint to the Court where the Offence was committed; and if he be found guilty, he shall forfeit his Office, be adjudged incapable of ever holding the said Office, and moreover shall pay such Fine as the Court shall impose, and be in Case of Nonpayment.

A

BILL

FOR

The Relief of Prisoners charged with Felony, or other Crimes, who shall be acquitted, or discharged by Proclamation, respecting the Payment of Fees to Gaolers, and giving a Recompence for such Fees out of the County Rates; and for more effectually securing the Health of Prisoners in Gaol, during their Confinement.

1774.

A

B I L L

TO

Explain, amend, and enlarge the Powers of an Act of Parliament, made in the Twelfth Year of the Reign of his late Majesty King *George* the Second, intituled, "An Act for the more easy and speedy "assessing, collecting, and levying of County "Rates;" and of another Act, made in the Ninth Year of the Reign of His Majesty King *George* the Third, intituled, "An Act to enable the Justices "of the Peace, in the General Quarter Sessions of "their respective Counties and Divisions, to repair "the Shire Halls, County Halls, or other Build- "ings, wherein the Assizes or Grand Sessions are "usually held;" so far as the same relate to public Bridges, and to County Halls or Shire Houses.

Note.—*The Figures in the Margin denote the Number of the Folios in the written Copy.*

WHEREAS by an Act, made in the Ninth Year of the Reign of His present Majesty, intituled, "An Act to enable the Justices of the Peace, in "the General Quarter Sessions of their respective "Counties and Divisions, to repair the Shire Halls, "County Halls, or other Buildings, wherein the Assizes or "Grand Sessions are usually held," it is Enacted, That it shall

[2]

and may be lawful for the Justices of the Peace, in their respective General or Quarter Sessions, or the greater Part of them, then and there assembled, within the Limits of their Commissions, upon Presentment of the Grand Jury at the Assizes or Great Sessions, or General Gaol Delivery held for the said County, at their Shire Hall, or other Building usually made use of for the holding the Assizes or Great Sessions within such County, of the ill State and Condition of any such Shire Hall or other Building, and the Necessity of repairing the same, to order and direct, in pursuance of such Presentment, such Shire Hall or other Building to be repaired in Manner therein mentioned:

And whereas Doubts have arisen, in several Counties within the Kingdom of *England* and Principality of *Wales*, whether there be any lawful Authority for the pulling down and new building such Shire Halls or other Buildings wherein the Assizes or Grand Sessions within such Counties are usually held: For the removing such Doubts, and for making Provision for the pulling down and new building the same, whenever it shall be necessary,

May it please Your MAJESTY,

That it may be Enacted; And be it Enacted by the King's Most Excellent MAJESTY, by and with the Advice and Consent of the Lords Spiritual and Temporal, and Commons, in this present Parliament assembled, and by the Authority of the same, That it shall and may be lawful for the Justices of the Peace, in their respective General or Quarter Sessions, or the greater Part of them, then and there assembled, within the Limits of their Commissions, upon Presentment of the Grand Jury, at the Assizes or Great Sessions, or General Gaol Delivery, held for the said County, of the ill State and Condition of any such Shire Hall or other Building, and the Necessity of pulling down and new building the same, to order and direct, in pursuance of such Presentment, such Shire Hall or other Building to be pulled down and new built, and the old Materials to be employed or disposed of, in such Manner as they in their Discretion shall think fit; and shall assess and rate all and every Sum and Sums of Money, which shall be laid out and expended in pulling down and new building the same, upon the several Hundreds, Lathes, Wapentakes, Rapes, Cities, Towns, Parishes,

rithes, Townships, Wards, or other Divisions of the said County; and to cause and direct such Sum and Sums of Money to be collected, levied, and paid, in the same Manner, and by and to the same Officers and other Persons, and under the same Conditions, Terms, Limitations, Restrictions, Pains, Penalties, and Forfeitures, as other County Rates are ordered and directed to be assessed, rated, collected, levied, and paid, in and by an Act, made in the Twelfth Year of the Reign of his late Majesty King *George* the Second, intituled, " An Act for
" the more easy assessing, collecting, and levying of County
" Rates," and in and by a Clause in an Act, made in the Thirteenth Year of the said King, intituled, " An Act to con-
" tinue several Laws therein mentioned, for punishing such
" Persons as shall wilfully and maliciously pull down or destroy
" Turnpikes, for repairing Highways, or Locks or other
" Works erected by Authority of Parliament, for making
" Rivers navigable; for preventing Exactions of the Occupiers
" of Locks and Wears upon the River of *Thames* westward, and
" for ascertaining the Rates of Water Carriage upon the said
" River; for preventing frivolous and vexatious Arrests; and
" for the better securing the lawful Trade of his Majesty's
" Subjects to and from the *East Indies*, and for the more ef-
" fectual preventing all his Majesty's Subjects trading thither
" under foreign Commissions; and for limiting the Time for
" suing forth Writs of *Certiorari*, upon Proceedings before
" Justices of the Peace, and for regulating the Time and
" Manner of applying for the same; for the better and more
" speedy Execution of Process within particular Franchises or
" Liberties; and for extending the Powers and Authorities of
" Justices of the Peace of Counties, touching County Rates,
" to the Justices of the Peace of such Liberties and Franchises
" as have Commissions of the Peace within themselves;" any Thing in the said recited Act contained to the contrary thereof in any-wise notwithstanding.

𝔓𝔯𝔬𝔳𝔦𝔡𝔢𝔡 𝔞𝔩𝔴𝔞𝔶𝔰, 𝔞𝔫𝔡 𝔟𝔢 𝔦𝔱 𝔣𝔲𝔯𝔱𝔥𝔢𝔯 𝔈𝔫𝔞𝔠𝔱𝔢𝔡 by the Authority aforesaid, That in Cases where any Shire Hall, County Hall, or other Building usually made use of for the holding the Assizes or Great Sessions, hath for Time out of Mind been built and repaired at the Expence of any particular Person or Persons, Riding or Ridings, Division or Divisions, Part or Parts of any County or Shire, the same shall for ever hereafter be rebuilt and repaired at the Expence of such Person or Persons, or the Inhabitants of such Riding or Ridings, Division or Divisions, Part or Parts respectively, as they have heretofore been;

been; and the Sum and Sums of Money to be laid out in rebuilding and repairing the same, shall be assessed, rated on, collected, levied, and paid by such Division or Divisions, Part or Parts, of such County, in Manner before directed.

7   And whereas, by the Laws now in being, no Money can be raised for the Purpose of repairing or rebuilding public Bridges, but by the Justices of the Peace in the General or Quarter Sessions of their respective Counties and Divisions, and until a Presentment or Indictment of such Bridges is made or preferred:

And whereas it frequently happens that great Injuries are done to Bridges by Floods, and the Public put to great Inconveniencies for Want of such Bridges being immediately repaired; Therefore, Be it Enacted by the Authority aforesaid, That when and so often as any public Bridge shall be in Want of any immediate and necessary Repair, it shall and may be lawful for any Two Justices of the Peace of any County, Riding, or Division, where such Bridge shall so want to be repaired, to order such Sum or Sums of Money, as they shall judge expedient, to be laid out and expended in the immediate Repair of such Bridge, as if the same had been presented or indicted; and the Justices of the Peace in their respective General or Quarter
8   Sessions, shall assess and rate all and every such Sum and Sums of Money, which shall be so laid out and expended, upon the respective Hundreds, Lathes, Wapentakes, Rapes, Cities, Parishes, Townships, Wards, or other Divisions, where such Bridge shall be so repaired; and cause and direct such Sum and Sums of Money to be collected, levied, and paid, and the same shall be collected, levied, and paid, in the Manner hereinbefore directed.

And be it further Enacted by the Authority aforesaid, That if any Action, Plaint, Suit, or Information shall be commenced or prosecuted against any Person or Persons, for any Thing that shall be done in pursuance or in execution of this Act, such Person or Persons shall and may plead the General Issue, and give this Act and the Special Matter in Evidence; and if it shall appear so to be done, or the Plaintiff or Prosecutor shall become Nonsuit, or forbear further Prosecution, or suffer a Discontinuance, or if a Verdict or Judgment shall be given against him, the Defendant or Defendants shall recover their
Costs, and have like Remedy for the same, as any Defendant or Defendants hath or have in other Cases by Law.

A BILL

TO

Explain, amend, and enlarge the Powers of an Act of Parliament, made in the Twelfth Year of the Reign of his late Majesty King *George* the Second, intituled, " An Act for the more " easy and speedy assessing, collecting, and " levying of County Rates;" and of another Act, made in the Ninth Year of the Reign of His Majesty King *George* the Third, intituled, " An Act to enable the Justices of the Peace, " in the General Quarter Sessions of their respective Counties and Divisions, to repair " the Shire Halls, County Halls, or other " Buildings, wherein the Assizes or Grand " Sessions are usually held;" so far as the same relate to public Bridges, and to County Halls or Shire Houses.

1774.

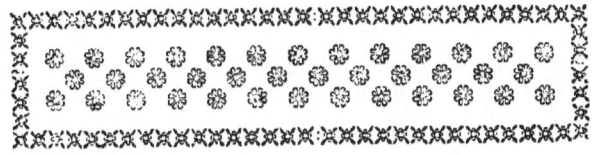

A

B I L L

More effectually to prevent the Stealing of Deer; and to repeal several former Statutes made for the like Purpose.

Note.—*The Figures in the Margin denote the Number of the Folios in the written Copy.*

WHEREAS the Statutes now in force for the Discovery and Punishment of Deer Stealers are numerous, and many of them ineffectual:

And whereas the good Purposes thereby intended might be better effected, if such of the said Statutes as are found to be defective were repealed, and such good Provisions as are therein contained, together with such further Provisions as may be expedient, were reduced into One Act; Be it therefore Enacted by the KING's Most Excellent

A MAJESTY,

MAJESTY, by and with the Advice and Consent of the Lords Spiritual and Temporal, and Commons, in this present Parliament assembled, and by the Authority of the same, That if any Person or Persons shall course, hunt, or shall take in any Slip Noose, Toyle, or Snare, or shall kill, wound, or destroy, or shall shoot at, or otherwise attempt to kill, wound, or destroy, or shall carry away, any Red or Fallow Deer, in any Forest, Chase, or Purlieu, whether inclosed or not, or in any inclosed Park, Paddock, Wood, or other inclosed Ground, where Deer are, have been, or shall be, usually kept, without the Consent of the Owner, or without being otherwise duly authorized, or shall be aiding, abetting, or assisting therein; every Person so offending, by coursing, hunting, shooting at, or otherwise attempting to kill, wound, or destroy, or by aiding therein, shall forfeit for every such Offence the Sum of   and every Person so offending, by killing, wounding, or destroying, or by taking in any Slip Noose, Toyle, or Snare, or by carrying away, or by aiding therein, respectively, shall, for every Deer so wounded, killed, destroyed, taken, or carried away, forfeit and pay the Sum of
             and if the Offender, in any of the Cases aforesaid, shall be a Keeper of, or Person in any Manner intrusted with the Custody or Care of Deer, in the Forest, Chase, Purlieu, or inclosed Park, Paddock, or Wood, or other inclosed Place, where the Offence shall be committed, every such Person shall forfeit and pay
the Penalty hereinbefore appointed to be paid by other Offenders; and if any Person or Persons, after having been convicted of either of the aforesaid Offences, shall offend a Second Time against this Act, by committing either of the aforesaid Offences, such Second Offence, whether it be the same as the First Offence, or be any other of the aforesaid Offences, shall be deemed and adjudged to be   and the Person guilty thereof, being lawfully convicted upon Indictment, shall be   in like Manner as other Offenders may be   by the Laws now, or which for the Time being shall be, in Force; and if any such Person shall return into any Part of *Great Britain* or *Ireland* within the said   every such Person shall be

And, to the Intent that the Prosecution of Persons who shall offend a Second Time in Manner aforesaid, may be carried on with as little Expence and Trouble as is possible;

fible; **Be it further Enacted,** That the Juſtice before whom any Perſon ſhall be convicted for the Firſt Time, of either of the Offences before deſcribed, ſhall tranſmit ſuch Conviction, under his Hand and Seal, to the Quarter Seſſion which, next after ſuch Conviction, ſhall be holden for the County, Riding, Diviſion, City, Town, or Place, wherein ſuch Firſt Offence ſhall be committed, there to be filed by the Clerk of the Peace, and to be kept amongſt the Records of the Peace; and ſuch Conviction ſo filed, or a true Copy thereof, certified and ſubſcribed by ſuch Clerk of the Peace, ſhall be ſufficient Evidence to prove the Conviction of ſuch Firſt Offence as aforeſaid.

And be it further Enacted, That it ſhall be lawful for any One Juſtice of the Peace, upon Complaint made to him on Oath, by any credible Perſon, that there is Reaſon to ſuſpect any Perſon or Perſons of having, in any Dwelling Houſe, Out Houſe, Yard, Garden, or Place, any Red or Fallow Deer, which ſhall have been unlawfully killed, or the Head, Skin, or other Part thereof, or any Slip Nooſe, Toyle, or Snare, for the unlawful taking of Deer, by Warrant under his Hand and Seal to cauſe ſuch Dwelling Houſe, Out Houſe, Garden, or Place, to be ſearched, in the Day Time; and if any Red or Fallow Deer, ſuſpected to have been unlawfully killed, or the Head, Skin, or other Part thereof, or any Slip Nooſe, Toyle, or Snare, ſuſpected to be uſed for the unlawful taking of Deer, ſhall be found in ſuch Dwelling Houſe, Out Houſe, Garden, or Place, to cauſe the ſame, and the Perſon or Perſons in whoſe Dwelling Houſe, Out Houſe, Garden, or other Place, the ſame ſhall be found, to be brought before any Juſtice of the Peace having Juriſdiction; and if ſuch Perſon or Perſons ſhall not ſatisfy ſuch Juſtice, that he, ſhe, or they came lawfully by ſuch Deer, or the Head, Skin, or other Part thereof, or had a lawful Occaſion for ſuch Slip Nooſe, Toyle, or Snare, or did not keep the ſame for any unlawful Purpoſe, then every ſuch Perſon, not ſo accounting to the Satisfaction of the ſaid Juſtice, ſhall, in the Caſe of the Deer, or the Head, Skin, or other Part thereof, be ſubject to the aforeſaid Penalty of   in the ſame Manner as a Perſon guilty, for the Firſt Time, of the Offence of unlawfully killing any Red or Fallow Deer, againſt the Proviſions of this Act; and in the Caſe of the Slip Nooſe, Toyle, or Snare, ſhall forfeit the Sum of

And

[4]

    And be it further Enacted, That if any Red or Fallow Deer, suspected to have been unlawfully killed, or the Head, Skin, or other Part of such Deer, shall be found in any Dwelling House, Out House, Garden, or other Place, on a Search under a Warrant from any Justice of the Peace, and the Owner or Occupier of such Dwelling House, Out House, Garden, or other Place, shall not, under the Provisions aforesaid, be liable to Conviction, then, and in every
7 such Case, for the Discovery of the Party or Parties who actually killed or stole such Deer, it shall and may be lawful to and for any Justice of the Peace having Jurisdiction, as the Evidence given, and the Circumstances of the Case, shall require, to summon before him, at his Discretion, every Person through whose Hands such Deer, or the Head, Skin, or other Part thereof, so found, shall appear to have passed; and the Person and Persons from whom such Deer, or the Head, Skin, or other Part thereof, shall appear to have been first received, or who having had Possession thereof, shall not give Proof, to the Satisfaction of such Justice, that he, she, or they, came lawfully by the same, shall be subject to the said Penalty of   in the same Manner as a Person guilty, for the First Time, of the Offence of unlawfully killing any Red or Fallow Deer against the Provisions of this Act.

    And be it further Enacted, That if any Person or Persons shall, at any Time, pull down or destroy, or cause to be pulled down or destroyed, the Pale or Pales, or any Part of the Walls, of any Forest, Chase, Purlieu, Park, Paddock, Wood, or other Ground, where any Red or Fallow Deer shall be then kept, without the Consent of the Owner or Person chiefly intrusted with the Custody thereof, or being otherwise duly authorized, every Person so offending shall be subject unto the Forfeiture and Penalty hereby inflicted for the First Offence of killing of any Deer.

8   **And be it further Enacted**, That if any Person or Persons carrying any Gun, or other Fire Arms, or any Sword, Staff, or other offensive Weapon, shall come into any Forest, Chase, or Purlieu, or in any inclosed Park, Paddock, Wood, or in any other inclosed Ground wherein Deer are usually kept, be the same inclosed or not inclosed, with an Intent unlawfully to shoot at, course, or hunt, or to take in any Slip Noose, Toyle, or Snare, or to kill, wound, destroy, or take away,

any

any Red or Fallow Deer, and shall there unlawfully beat or wound any Ranger or Keeper, or his or their Servants or Assistants, in the Execution of his or their Office or Offices, every Person so offending shall be deemed and adjudged to be   and on being lawfully convicted on Indictment, shall be   in like Manner as other Offenders may be
by the Laws now, or which for the Time being shall be, in force; and if such Person or Persons shall return into any Part of *Great Britain* or *Ireland* within the said
                                                                every such Person and Persons shall be

And be it further Enacted, That all the pecuniary Penalties of this Act shall be recoverable before One or more Justice or Justices of the Peace for the County, or other Division, in which the Offence shall be committed, on Proof of the Offence by the Oath of One or more credible Witness or Witnesses, or on Confession of the Offender; and
            of each Penalty shall belong to His Majesty, His Heirs or Successors, and the   .   thereof to the Informer or Informers prosecuting for the same; and in Case of Non-Payment thereof, with the Charges incident to the Conviction, immediately after the Conviction, or immediately afterwards giving Security, to the Satisfaction of such Justice or Justices, for paying the same within
            Days, the Offender or Offenders shall be sent by the said Justice or Justices to the   , of the County or Place where the Offence shall be committed, for the Space of   unless the said Penalty, with the Costs of Conviction, shall be sooner paid.

And, to the End that Persons convicted of any of the Offences for which pecuniary Penalties are inflicted by this Act may not, by Flight or Removal after Conviction, evade Imprisonment, where such Penalties shall not be paid on Conviction, and sufficient Distress cannot be found for raising such Penalties; **Be it further Enacted,** That it shall and may be lawful for the Justice or Justices of the Peace before whom any Offender shall be convicted of having incurred any pecuniary Penalty of this Act, immediately after such Conviction, to order him or her into Custody, in Case he or she shall not immediately pay the Penalty due on such Conviction, during such Time, not exceeding   Days, as such Justice
                                         or

or Juſtices ſhall think it proper to allow for Return of the Warrant for raiſing the Penalty by Diſtreſs.

And be it further Enacted, That it ſhall and may be lawful for any Keeper or Underkeeper of any Foreſt, Chaſe, Purlieu, Paddock, Park, or other Ground, incloſed, where Deer are, have been, or ſhall be, uſually kept, and their Servants or Aſſiſtants, to ſeize and apprehend upon the Spot any Perſon or Perſons whom they ſhall diſcover in the actual Fact of hunting, courſing, killing, wounding, ſhooting at, taking, deſtroying, or carrying away, any Red or Fallow Deer from any ſuch Foreſt, Chace, or Purlieu, whether incloſed or not, or in any incloſed Park, Paddock, Wood, or in any other incloſed Ground, or attempting ſo to do, and to carry ſuch Offender or Offenders before ſome neighbouring Juſtice of the Peace, to be dealt with according to Law.

12 **And,** for the better Diſcovery of Offenders againſt this Act; **Be it further Enacted,** That any Perſon who ſhall offend againſt this Act, and ſhall, within   next after making Diſcovery of any other Perſon or Perſons who hath or have offended againſt the ſame, ſo as he, ſhe, or they be duly convicted of ſuch Offence according to this Act, then, and in ſuch Caſe, ſuch Diſcoverer ſhall be diſcharged of all the Forfeitures and Penalties of this Act, by him, her, or them incurred previous to ſuch Diſcovery.

And, in order to prevent the Quaſhing of Convictions of Offenders againſt this Act, for Want of Form; **Be it further Enacted,** That the Conviction and Convictions of all and every Offenders againſt this Act, ſhall be certified by the Juſtice or Juſtices of the Peace before whom the ſame ſhall be made, to the next General Quarter Seſſions of the Peace, to be filed
13 amongſt the Records of the ſaid Seſſions; and that ſuch Conviction ſhall be fairly written on Parchment or Paper, in the following Form of Words, as the Caſe ſhall happen, or in any other Form of Words to the like Effect; that is to ſay (to wit)

" Be it remembered, That on the   Day
" of   in the Year
" *A. B.* was, upon the Complaint of *C. D.* convicted
" before   of the Juſtices of the
" Peace for   in Purſuance of an
" Act, paſſed in the   Year of the Reign
" of His Majeſty King *George* the Third, for

" as the Case shall be. Given under
" Hand and Seal, the Day and Year above written."

Which said Conviction shall be good and effectual in Law to all Intents and Purposes, and shall not be quashed, set aside, or adjudged void or insufficient, for Want of any Form, or Words, whatsoever.

And be it further Enacted, That no *Certiorari* shall be allowed, to remove any Conviction made, or other Proceedings, of, for, or concerning any Matter or Thing in this Act, unless the Party or Parties convicted shall, before the Allowance of such *Certiorari*, become bound to the Person or Persons prosecuting, in the Sum of   with Condition to pay unto the said Prosecutors, within after such Conviction confirmed, or a *Procedendo* granted, their full Costs and Damages, to be ascertained upon their Oaths; and shall become also bound to the Justice or Justices of the Peace before whom such Conviction was made, with such sufficient Sureties as such Justice or Justices shall approve of, in the Penalty of   for each Offence, with Condition to prosecute such Writ of *Certiorari* with Effect, and to pay such Justice or Justices the Forfeitures due by such Conviction, to be distributed as by this Act is directed, or to render the Person or Persons convicted to such Justice or Justices, within   next after such Conviction shall be confirmed, or a *Procedendo* granted; and that in Default thereof it shall be lawful to proceed to the levying of the Penalty mentioned in such Conviction, in such Manner as if no such *Certiorari* had been awarded.

And be it further Enacted, That after the Confirmation of any Conviction or Convictions upon this Act, by any of the superior Courts at *Westminster*, and delivering the Rule to the said Justice or Justices whereby such Conviction or Convictions hath or have been so confirmed, it shall and may be lawful for such Justice or Justices to proceed against the Party or Parties convicted, in the same Manner as if a *Procedendo* had been granted.

Provided always, and be it Enacted, That if any Person or Persons shall be sued or prosecuted for any Matter or Thing which he or they shall do in Pursuance of this Act, it shall and may be lawful to and for the Person or Persons so sued or prosecuted to plead the General Issue, and
give

give the fpecial Matter in Evidence; and if a Verdict fhall pafs for the Defendant, or the Plaintiff fhall become Nonfuit, or fuffer a Difcontinuance, or if upon a Demurrer Judgment fhall be given againſt the Plaintiff, the Defendant fhall have and recover his   Cofts, and have the like Remedy for the fame as any Defendant hath in any other Cafe by Law.

𝕬𝖓𝖉 𝖇𝖊 𝖎𝖙 𝖋𝖚𝖗𝖙𝖍𝖊𝖗 𝕰𝖓𝖆𝖈𝖙𝖊𝖉, That every Profecution for any Offence againſt this Act, fhall be commenced within   but not after, from the Time of the Offence committed.

𝕬𝖓𝖉 𝖇𝖊 𝖎𝖙 𝖋𝖚𝖗𝖙𝖍𝖊𝖗 𝕰𝖓𝖆𝖈𝖙𝖊𝖉, That all Actions, Writs, and Profecutions, to be commenced againſt any Perfon or Perfons, for any Thing to be done under or in purfuance of this Act, fhall be laid and tried in the County or Place where the Fact was committed, and fhall be commenced within   after the Fact committed, and not otherwife.

𝕬𝖓𝖉 𝖇𝖊 𝖎𝖙 𝖋𝖚𝖗𝖙𝖍𝖊𝖗 𝕰𝖓𝖆𝖈𝖙𝖊𝖉, That this Act fhall commence and begin to be in Force on the   and from and immediately after the Commencement thereof, fo much of the Thirteenth Chapter of the Firſt Part of the Statutes, made in the Thirteenth Year of the Reign of *Richard* the Second, as inflicts a Penalty on thofe who fhall ufe Heys, Nets, or other Engines, for deſtroying Deer; fo much of the Eleventh Chapter of the Statutes, made in the Nineteenth Year of the Reign of King *Henry* the Seventh, as relates to Deer; and alfo, fo much of an Act, made in the Fifth Year of the Reign of Queen *Elizabeth*, intituled, " An Act " for punifhing of unlawful taking Fifh, Deer, or Hawks," as relates to Deer; and alfo, fo much of an Act, made in the Third Year of the Reign of King *James* the Firſt, intituled, " An Act againſt unlawful hunting and ſtealing of " Deer and Conies," as relates to Deer, or to the unlawful breaking or entering into any Park impaled, or any other feveral Ground, inclofed with Wall, Pale, or Hedge; and alfo, fo much of an Act, made in the Seventh Year of the Reign of the faid King *James* the Firſt, intituled, " An " Act for the Explanation of One Statute, made in the Second " Seffion of this prefent Parliament, intituled, An Act againſt " unlawful hunting and ſtealing of Deer and Conies," as relates to Deer, except fuch Part thereof as repeals any Part of the Statute of the Third of *James*, before-mentioned; and

and also, an Act, made in the Thirteenth Year of the Reign of King *Charles* the Second, intituled, "An Act to prevent the unlawful coursing, hunting, or killing, of Deer;" as also, an Act, made in the Third and Fourth Years of the Reign of their late Majesties King *William* and Queen *Mary*, intituled, "An Act for the more effectual Discovery and Punishment of Deer Stealers;" and also, an Act, made in the Fifth Year of the Reign of his late Majesty King *George* the First, intituled, "An Act for making more effectual an Act of the Third and Fourth Years of the Reign of King *William* and Queen *Mary*, intituled, An Act for the more effectual Discovery and Punishment of Deer Stealers;" and also, an Act, passed in the said Fifth Year of the Reign of his late Majesty King *George* the First, intituled, "An Act for the further Punishment of such Persons as shall unlawfully kill or destroy Deer in Parks, Paddocks, or other inclosed Grounds;" and also, so much of an Act, made in the Tenth Year of the Reign of his late Majesty King *George* the Second, intituled, "An Act for continuing an Act for the more effectual punishing wicked and evil-disposed Persons going armed in Disguise, and doing Injuries and Violences to the Persons and Properties of his Majesty's Subjects, and for the more speedy bringing the Offenders to Justice; and for the continuing Two Clauses to prevent the cutting or breaking down the Bank of any River or Sea Bank, and to prevent the malicious cutting of Hopbinds, contained in an Act, passed in the Sixth Year of His present Majesty's Reign; and for the more effectual Punishment of Persons removing any Materials used for securing Marsh or Sea Walls, or Banks, and of Persons maliciously setting on Fire any Mine, Pit, or Delph, of Coal, or Cannel Coal, and of Persons unlawfully hunting or taking any Red or Fallow Deer in Forests or Chases, or beating or wounding Keepers or other Officers in Forests, Chases, or Parks; and for the more effectually securing the Breed of Wild Fowl," as relates to the Second Conviction of any Person or Persons, for unlawfully coursing, hunting, taking in Toyles, killing, wounding, or taking away, any Red or Fallow Deer in any open or uninclosed Forest or Chase, or relates to beating or wounding Keepers, or other Officers, in Forests, Chases, or Parks; shall be, and the same are hereby respectively

Provided always, and be it further Enacted, That nothing contained in this Act shall extend to that Part of *Great Britain* called *Scotland*.

A
BILL

More effectually to prevent the Stealing of Deer; and to repeal several former Statutes made for the like Purpose.

1775.

A

B I L L

[With the Amendments]

For preventing the inhuman Practice of Plundering Ships that are shipwrecked on the Coast of Great Britain; and for the further Relief of Ships in Distress on the said Coasts.

N. B. *The Words printed in Italick, and between Brackets, thus* [ ], *were inserted by the Committee.*

Note.—*The Figures in the Margin denote the Number of the Folios in the written Copy.*

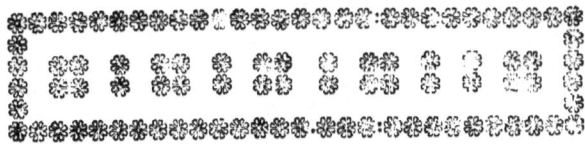WHEREAS Provisions and Regulations have been made by divers Acts of Parliament, made in the Third and Fourth Year of the Reign of King Edward the First, and in the Twelfth Year of Queen Ann, as also in the Eleventh Year of George the First, and in the Twenty-Sixth Year of George the Second, to prevent the plundering and destroying Vessels in Distress, and the felonious taking away shipwrecked or stranded Goods; which said Provisions and Regulations have not proved effectual for preventing such evil Practices: Therefore, for further Remedy of the same, Be it Enacted

Enacted by the KING's most excellent MAJESTY, by and with the Advice and Consent of the Lords Spiritual and Temporal, and Commons, in this present Parliament assembled, and by the Authority of the same, That from and after the [*First*] Day of [*August*] if any Ship or Vessel shall be wilfully destroyed or damaged upon the said Coast, or if the Cargo, or any Part thereof, be wilfully damaged and destroyed, or feloniously taken away, or by any Means detained from the Owners thereof, otherwise than by the said recited Acts is directed and authorized, in such Case the Inhabitants of the Hundred in which the Offences shall be committed, shall make full Satisfaction and Amends to such Person or Persons, their Executors and Administrators, whether His Majesty's Subjects or Foreigners, for the Damages sustained by the said Offence (provided that the Offender or Offenders as aforesaid are not discovered, and prosecuted, within the Space of [*Three Months*] after such Offence committed) the said Damages to be recovered in the same Manner as directed and authorized by an Act of the Ninth Year of his Majesty King George the First, intituled, "An Act for the more effectual punishing wicked "and evil-disposed Persons going armed in Disguise, and "doing Injuries and Violences to the Persons and Properties "of his Majesty's Subjects, and for the more speedy bringing "the Offenders to Justice;" and by several Acts, of the Twelfth Year of his Majesty King George the First, Chapter Thirty; the Tenth Year of his Majesty King George the Second, Chapter Thirty-two; the Twenty-fourth Year of the Reign of his said late Majesty, Chapter Fifty-seven; and the Thirty-first Year of his said late Majesty, Chapter Forty-two: Provided also, and it is hereby Enacted, That no more shall be recovered from the Hundred, by any Action prosecuted by the Authority of this Act, for the Damage done to any Ship or Cargo, than [*One Thousand Pounds*.]

And be it further Enacted, That any Person or Persons apprehending, and prosecuting to Conviction, any Persons whose Offences have been declared or made to be Felony without Benefit of Clergy, by the Acts of the Twelfth Year of the Reign of Queen Ann, or by the Eleventh Year of George the First, Chapter Twenty-ninth, or of the Twenty-sixth of George the Second, Chapter Nineteenth, shall be intitled to a Reward of [*Forty Pounds*] to be paid as in the Case of a Conviction for a Robbery on the Highway.

And be it further Enacted, That if any Person, attempting to to apprehend any Person guilty of the Offences against this and the aforesaid Acts, shall be killed, his Executors and Administrators shall be intitled to the said Reward.

And whereas, by a Clause in an Act of the Twentieth Year of King *George* the Second, a Subordination of Persons was established, to prevent Confusion among those who should be assembled to save any Ship or Wreck; which Order hath not been found convenient; Therefore, *Be it Enacted*, That the said Clause be, and it is hereby [*repealed*] And in Place thereof, Be it Enacted, That, to prevent Confusion amongst the Persons assembled to save any Ship, Vessel, Goods, or Effects, as aforesaid, either for Want of proper Orders, or by contradictory Orders, all Persons so assembled shall conform, in the First Place, to the Orders of the Master, or other Officers or Owners, of the Vessel; and in their Absence, or for Want of their Orders, or their not choosing to take upon them the said Direction, then to the Persons authorized by the aforesaid Act of Queen *Ann*, or of the aforesaid Act of King *George* the Second, in the following Subordination, as any of the said Persons shall happen to be present; In the First Place, to the Orders of the Sheriff of the County, or his Deputy; then to those of the Mayor or Chief Magistrate of any Corporation; then of any Justice or Justices of the Peace; then to the Coroner; then of any Officer or Officers of the Customs; then of the Excise; then of any Commissioners of the Land Tax; then of any Chief or Petty Constable, or other Peace Officers; and any Person whatsoever acting, knowingly and wilfully, contrary to such Orders, shall forfeit any Sum not exceeding [*Forty Pounds*] to be levied by Warrant of One Justice of the Peace; and in Case of Non-payment, the Offender shall be committed to the House of Correction for any Time not exceeding [*One Month*]

And whereas a wicked Practice hath prevailed, with Regard to the taking off of Buoys; for the Prevention or Punishment of which no sufficient Provision hath been made; *Be it Enacted*, That from and after the [*First*] Day of [*August*] every Person who shall maliciously take or cut off any Buoy from any Anchor or Cable, left by any Ship on any of the Coasts of this Kingdom, and being legally convicted of the same, shall be, and are hereby declared guilty of [*Felony*] and shall receive Sentence of [*Transportation*] as in Cases of [*Felony*] for which such Punishment is appointed.

A BILL

[With the Amendments]

For preventing the inhuman Practice of Plundering Ships that are shipwrecked on the Coast of Great Britain; and for the further Relief of Ships in Distress on the said Coasts.

1775.

A

B I L L

[With the Amendments]

To explain and amend an Act, made in the Thirty-second Year of his late Majesty's Reign, intituled, " An Act for Relief of Insolvent Debtors, with " respect to the Imprisonment of their Persons; " and to oblige Debtors, who shall continue in " Execution in Prison beyond a certain Time, and " for Sums not exceeding what are mentioned in " the Act, to make Discovery of, and deliver, upon " Oath, their Estates for their Creditors Benefit;" and to prevent Actions being brought upon Judgments, without Leave of the Court or Courts wherein such Judgments shall have been entered up respectively.

N. B. *The Words printed in* 𝕭𝖑𝖆𝖈𝖐 𝕷𝖊𝖙𝖙𝖊𝖗, *and between Brackets, thus* [ ], *were left out by the Committee; and the Words printed in Italic, between Brackets, and the Clauses at the End, marked A, B, C, D, (which are intended to be inserted as marked in the Bill) were added by the Committee.*

Note.—*The Figures in the Margin denote the Number of the Folios in the written Copy.*

WHEREAS the Provisions made by an Act, passed in the Thirty-second Year of his late Majesty's Reign, intituled, " An Act for the Relief of " Insolvent Debtors, with respect to the Imprison- " ment of their Persons; and to oblige Debtors, " who shall continue in Execution in Prison beyond a certain

A " Time,

" Time, and for Sums not exceeding what are mentioned
" in the Act, to make Discovery of, and deliver upon Oath,
" their Estates for their Creditors Benefit," have been found,
from Experience, to be in some Respects defective, and not
sufficiently adapted to the Circumstances and Situation of the
Persons intended thereby to be relieved; which Defect has,
in a great Measure, prevented many of the humane and lau-
dable Purposes of the said Act from operating to good
Effect:

And whereas, by an Amendment thereof, much Benefit
may arise to many Individuals, who are Objects of the greatest
Compassion; and the Purport of the said Act, with respect to
the Release of Debtors charged in Execution, may be more
fully and effectually enforced, according to the true Intent and
Meaning thereof:

May it please Your MAJESTY,

That it may be Enacted; And be it Enacted by the KING's
Most Excellent MAJESTY, by and with the Advice and
Consent of the Lords Spiritual and Temporal, and Commons,
in this present Parliament assembled, and by the Authority of
the same, That from and after the [*Twenty-fourth Day of
June One thousand Seven hundred and Seventy-five*] next after
the passing of this Act, if any Person, who is at this Time,
or may hereafter be charged in Execution, in any Gaol or
Prison within that Part of Great Britain called England, for
any Sum or Sums of Money not exceeding in the Whole the
Sum of [*Five hundred Pounds*] or on which Execution or
Executions there shall at any Time remain due, to be made
appear by Oath, a Sum or Sums of Money not amounting to
more than the Sum of [*Five hundred Pounds*] and he, she,
or they, shall desire to deliver up to his, her, or their Creditor or Creditors, who shall have so charged him, her, or
them in Execution, all his, her, or their Estate and Effects,
for and towards the Satisfaction of the Debt or Debts wherewith he, she, or they, shall so stand charged, it shall and
may be lawful for any such Prisoner, who now is, or who, on
or before the said [*Twenty-fourth Day of June*] next after the
passing of this Act, may be so charged in Execution, within
[*Six*] Months after the said [*Twenty-fourth Day of June*] and
for any such Prisoner who shall at any Time after the said
[*Twenty-*

[*Twenty-fourth Day of June*] be so charged in Execution, within [*Six*] Months after he or she shall have been so charged in Execution by his or her Creditor or Creditors, to exhibit a Petition to the next Assizes, Great Sessions, or Quarter Sessions of the Peace, which may be holden for the County, Riding, Division, City, or Liberty, within that Part of Great Britain called England, the Principality of Wales, or County Palatine of Chester, where, he, she, or they, shall be so imprisoned, in Manner and Form as is hereinafter mentioned.

And be it further Enacted, That in every such Petition so to be presented to any of the said Courts, such Prisoner shall certify the Cause or Causes of his or her Imprisonment, and shall therein set forth all Matters and Things in like Manner and Form as is directed by the before-recited Act, for exhibiting any Petition to any Court of Law from whence the Process issued upon which any such Prisoner was taken and charged in Execution.   4

And be it further Enacted, That no such Petition shall be received by any of the Courts aforesaid, unless Proof shall be made on Oath that such Petitioner did give, or did cause to be given, or left, at his, her, or their most usual Place or Places of Abode [*One Month's*] Notice in Writing at the least, before the Time of presenting such Petition, unto and for all and every the Creditor or Creditors at whose Suit such Prisoner shall stand charged in Execution, or his, her, or their Executors or Administrators, or to or for his, her, or their Agent or Attorney last employed in any such Action, Suit, Cause or Causes, in case such Creditor or Creditors cannot be met with; and such Notice shall be signed with the proper Name or Mark of every such Prisoner, and shall contain the Time when, and the Court to which, such Prisoner doth intend to present his Petition, as the Case may be; and every such Notice shall contain also a Copy of the Account or Schedule, containing the whole real and personal Estate of such Person intending so to petition, and which he or she doth intend to deliver in to any such Court as aforesaid, other than and except the necessary Wearing Apparel and Bedding of such Prisoner, and of his or her Family, with the Tools or Instruments of his or her Trade or Calling, not exceeding [*Ten*] Pounds in Value of the Whole.   5

And be it further Enacted, That an Affidavit of the due
Service

Service of every such Notice as aforesaid (which Affidavit any Justice of the Peace of any County, Riding, Division, City, or Liberty wherein such Notice shall be given, is hereby authorized and impowered to take) shall be delivered at the Time of presenting such Petition, and shall be openly read in the Court to which any such Petition shall be addressed; and if such Court shall be satisfied of the Regularity

6 of such Notice, such Petition shall be received, and such Court shall, in a summary Way, examine into the Matter of every such Petition, and hear what can or shall be alledged on either Side, for or against the Discharge of such Prisoner or Prisoners who shall so petition, as the Case may be; and upon such Examination, every such Court as aforesaid is hereby authorized and required to administer or tender to the Prisoner or Prisoners respectively the same Oath as is required to be taken by every Prisoner presenting the like Petition, in Conformity to the Directions of the before-recited Act of the Thirty second Year of King *George* the Second; and shall also, in like Manner, administer or tender another Oath, to the Effect following; that is to say,

7
" I A. B. do swear, in the Presence of Almighty God,
" That I have, neither directly nor indirectly, by myself,
" by my Order, nor with my Permission, suffered
" any Diminution to be made in my Property, real
" or personal, of which I have given an Account in
" the Schedule delivered in to this Court, whereby
" to have or accept any Benefit, Advantage, or Profit,
" to myself or my Family, or with a View, Design, or
" Intent to deceive, injure, or defraud any of my
" Creditors to whom I am indebted; nor have I
" expended, or caused to be expended, for my own
" Use or Benefit, any Part of such Property, ex-
" cepting the Sum of [*One Shilling*] per Day, from
" the Day on which I was charged in Execution,
" amounting in the Whole to the Sum of

" So help me God."

And every such Court as aforesaid is hereby respectively authorized and required to make such Order in the Premises as to such Court shall seem meet, and to proceed in the same Manner concerning the Discharge of any Prisoner or Prisoners from

from any Prisons within their respective Jurisdictions, in respect to all and every Matter and Thing thereupon required to be done, and to give the like Judgment, Relief, and Directions, relating thereto, as any Court out of which Process hath issued against any Prisoner is impowered and directed to do by the before-recited Act, so far as the same shall not have been altered or amended by this present Act; and every Order that shall be made in the Premises shall be valid and effectual to all Intents and Purposes, and the same shall be made a Record of the Proceedings at such Assizes, Great Sessions, or Quarter Sessions, as the Case may be; and a Copy thereof shall from thence be transmitted to the Court or Courts from whence the Execution or Executions against the Prisoner or Prisoners discharged shall have been issued, signed by One of the Judges of Assize, or Justices of Great Sessions, or by [*Two*] or more of the Justices of the Peace, at their Quarter Sessions, as the Case may be; which shall become a Record of such Court or Courts, to be kept as such amongst the other Records thereof, and shall be deemed and taken to be a full and perfect Satisfaction of all Judgments upon which such Prisoner shall have been so charged in Execution. 8

CLAUSES A and B to be here inserted.

And be it further Enacted, That nothing herein contained shall extend to alter or abridge any of the Provisions made by the before-recited Act, whereby any Creditor is authorized and impowered to prevent the Discharge of any Prisoner, under certain Conditions therein mentioned; provided such Creditor shall appear in Person, or by his Attorney, at the Time and Place specified in the Notice hereinbefore directed to be left with him or her, and shall then and there enter into an Agreement, according to the Directions of the before-recited Act, for Payment of a weekly Allowance [of] [*not exceeding*] [*Four Shillings*]; nor shall any Thing in this Act extend to alter the Mode of Application prescribed by the said former Act to every Prisoner, who shall thereby be entitled to his Discharge, on any Failure of Payment of such Sum or Sums of Money as shall have been agreed to be paid by any Creditor, in order to continue his Prisoner in Execution; but every Prisoner remanded to Gaol under the Authority of this Act, on such Account as aforesaid, shall, in like Manner as is by the said former Act directed [*have* 9

B *Liberty*

10 *Liberty to*] apply for his Discharge [**to the Court where the Suit, in which any such Prisoner shall be charged in Execution, was commenced**] and shall in all Things abide by the same Rules, Orders, and Regulations, as are therein given for the Conduct of any Prisoner on such an Application.

And be it further Enacted, That a Copy of the Agreement entered into by any Creditor, for the Payment of the said weekly Allowance to any Prisoner, on his being remanded to his Confinement, shall be given to every such Prisoner, signed by One Judge of Assize, One Justice of Great Sessions, or [*Two*] Justices of the Peace at their Quarter-Sessions, as the Case may be, before whom such Agreement shall have been made, and the Original shall be filed amongst the Records of the said Court wherein such Agreement shall have been entered; and such Prisoner, upon any subsequent Application for his Discharge in Manner aforesaid, shall produce to the Court or Judge to whom such Application shall be made, the Copy of such Agreement so signed and delivered to him.

11 And be it further Enacted, That every Prisoner, who intends to exhibit a Petition under the Authority of this Act, shall deliver, or cause to be delivered [**in Court,**] such Petition and Affidavit as aforesaid, to the Clerk of Assize, Clerk of Great Sessions, or Clerk of the Peace, as the Case may be (who are hereby respectively required to receive the same) on [*or before*] the first Day of holding such Assizes, Great Sessions, or Quarter Sessions; and every such Clerk respectively shall, before the Rising of the [*first*] Court [**during the Sitting of**] [*after*] which he shall have received such Petition and Affidavit) notify the Receipt thereof, and the Court shall then appoint a Time, during such Assizes, Great Sessions, or Quarter-Sessions, as the Case may be, for the Prisoner or Prisoners, and other Parties concerned, to attend the Hearing of such Petition.

And to the End that every Prisoner claiming Benefit under this Act may be brought in due Time to that Court wherein he intends to exhibit such his Petition as aforesaid, Be it further Enacted, That every such Prisoner [*Twenty-one*] Days at least before the holding of any Assizes, Great Sessions, or
12 Quarter Sessions, as the Case may be, where he or she intends to exhibit such Petition, shall deliver, or cause to be delivered,

to

to the Gaoler or Keeper of the Prison wherein he or she shall be charged in Execution, a Writing signed by himself or herself, or with his or her Mark affixed thereto, declaring the Time when, and the Court to which, he or she does intend to exhibit such Petition; and such Gaoler or Keeper shall [*Fourteen*] Days at least before the holding of any such Assizes, Great Sessions, or Quarter Sessions, as the Case may be, transmit such Writing to the Sheriff or Deputy Sheriff of the County, Riding, Division, City, or Liberty, to which such Prison shall belong; and such Sheriff or Deputy shall, on Receipt thereof, by an Order in Writing signed by himself, direct such Gaoler or Keeper to take, or cause to be taken, all such Prisoners who shall have delivered Writings in Manner aforesaid, to the Assizes, Great Sessions, or Quarter Sessions respectively, according to the Notice or Notices given in such Writings; and if by any Neglect or Refusal of such Sheriff, Deputy Sheriff, Gaoler, or Keeper, any such Prisoner shall be unable to exhibit his Petition to the Court in Manner hereinbefore directed, it shall and may be lawful for such Prisoner, in like Manner as is hereinbefore directed, to exhibit his Petition at the next ensuing Assizes, Great Sessions, or Quarter Sessions, and so toties quoties, as he shall be prevented by any such Neglect or Refusal as aforesaid; and every such Sheriff, Deputy Sheriff, Gaoler, or Keeper of any Prison, respectively, for every such Neglect or Refusal, shall each and every of them forfeit and pay the Sum of [*Fifty*] Pounds to the Party aggrieved, to be recovered by Action of Debt, Bill, or Information, in any of His Majesty's Courts of Record at Westminster, if any such Offence shall be committed out of the Principality of Wales, or County Palatine of Chester; and if within the Principality of Wales, or County Palatine of Chester, then in some Court of Record in the Principality of Wales, or County Palatine of Chester, within the Jurisdiction of which any such Offence shall have been so committed, together with [*Double*] Costs of Suit.

And be it further Enacted, That if any Prisoner or Prisoners shall cause himself, herself, or themselves, to be taken to any Assizes, Great Sessions, or Quarter Sessions, without having conformed to, and acted according to the Directions of this Act, for the due Performance of all Matters and Things that are hereby on the Part of such Prisoner or Prisoners required to be done and performed (except in Cases of unwilful Mistake)

Miſtake) or where he or ſhe ſhall refuſe to take the Oaths, or to comply with the Orders made, then every ſuch Priſoner ſhall, in Conſequence and by the Authority of this, or the before-recited Act, be immediately remanded to Priſon, and ſhall for ever loſe all Benefit and Advantage ariſing from this Act.

And be it further Enacted, That if any Priſoner as afore-ſaid ſhall deliver in any falſe or untrue Account of his or her Eſtate or Effects, or ſhall deſignedly conceal, and not inſert in the Schedule or Account he or ſhe ſhall deliver in and ſub-ſcribe as aforeſaid, any Books, Papers, Securities, or Wri-tings, relating to his or her Eſtate and Effects, with Intent to defraud his or her Creditor or Creditors, and ſhall be there-of convicted, on any Indictment found againſt him or her in reſpect thereof, he or ſhe ſhall ſuffer the Pains and Penalties which by Law are to be inflicted on any Perſon convicted of wilful Perjury.

And be it further Enacted, That the Expence of bringing any ſuch Priſoner as aforeſaid to the Aſſizes, Great Seſſions, or Quarter Seſſions, not exceeding [*One Shilling*] per Mile, ſhall be paid to the Gaoler, Keeper, or Officer, who ſhall ſo bring any ſuch Priſoner, out of his or her Eſtate and Ef-fects; but if the ſame ſhall not be ſufficient, then ſuch Ex-pence ſhall be paid by the Treaſurer of the County, Riding, Diviſion, City, or Liberty, out of the Stock of ſuch County, Riding, Diviſion, City, or Liberty, as the ſame ſhall be allowed by any ſuch Court [as aforeſaid] before which any ſuch Pri-ſoner ſhall be brought.

And be it further Enacted, That if any Creditor, after due Notice given as aforeſaid, ſhall neglect, by himſelf or herſelf, or by his or her Attorney or Agent, to attend at the Time and Place mentioned in ſuch Notice, the Court ſhall never-theleſs proceed to the hearing and determining of every ſuch Petition as aforeſaid, and ſhall give Judgment thereupon, as if ſuch Creditor was perſonally preſent.

And be it further Enacted, That in caſe any Priſoner ſhall, by any ſuch Court as aforeſaid, be remanded to Priſon on Account of any involuntary Miſtake or Error in the Pro-ceedings on the Part of ſuch Priſoner [*or for any other juſt Cauſe, ſave and except any wilful Miſtake, Neglect, Refuſal, or Fraud*] it ſhall be lawful for him or her again to deliver in

the

the like Petition to any of the said Courts at the next ensuing Assizes, Great Sessions, or Quarter Sessions, as the Case may be, and so toties quoties, under the same Restrictions and Limitations as are by this or the said former Act directed to be observed and performed.

CLAUSES C and D to be here inserted.

And be it further Enacted, That all Orders, Matters, and Things, by the before-recited Act directed to be observed and performed, and not hereby altered or amended, shall extend to every Person claiming or deriving any Benefit from, or in anywise acting under the Authority of this present Act.

And whereas [of late years] a Practice has prevailed of bringing Actions upon Judgments obtained in Courts of Law on Civil Process, to enforce the Payment of the Debts and Costs recovered by such Judgment, whereby the [Parties] Defendants [*are grievously oppressed, by the Payment of Double Costs, and*] have been frequently thrown into Prison for a Debt enlarged by the Accumulation of Costs [to more than the original Sum, which has been a grievous Oppression in many Cases] [*in Cases where by Law they could not have been imprisoned for the original Debt*] Be it therefore Enacted, That from and after the said [*Twenty-fourth Day of June One thousand Seven hundred and Seventy-five*] next after the passing of this Act, no Action or Suit at Law shall be brought on any Judgment obtained in any Court of Law within that Part of Great Britain called England, without Leave first had and obtained [in Writing] from the Court wherein any such Judgment may have been entered up, any Law, Usage, or Custom to the contrary thereof in anywise notwithstanding; and if any such Action shall, after the said [*Twenty-fourth Day of June*] be brought by any Person or Persons, contrary to the true Intent and Meaning of this Act, the Defendant or Defendants in such Action shall and may produce this Act as Evidence on his, her, or their Part; and if the Plaintiff or Plaintiffs shall not prove, to the Satisfaction of the Court wherein such Action shall have been brought, that such Leave as aforesaid was obtained prior to the Commencement of any such Action, then the Plaintiff or Plaintiffs therein shall be nonsuited, and shall pay to the Defendant or Defendants [*Double*] Costs of Suit.

17

18

C CLAUSE

Clause (A.)

And whereas it frequently happens that Perſons confined in Priſon under an Arreſt for Debt, prior to any Judgment obtained upon Proceſs of Law againſt them, are willing and deſirous to acknowledge the Debt and confeſs Judgment, in order to prevent the Delay and Expence of a Trial; Be it further Enacted by the Authority aforeſaid, That it ſhall and may be lawful for any Perſon or Perſons ſo confined as aforeſaid, and be, ſhe, or they, are hereby authorized and impowered, by Warrant of Attorney, to confeſs Judgment on any Action or Actions, and cauſe the ſame to be entered up, in any Court wherein the ſaid Action or Actions ſhall have been brought by the Plaintiff or Plaintiffs againſt any ſuch Perſon or Perſons; and when the Judgment or Judgments ſhall have been ſo entered up; every ſuch Perſon ſhall and may, after the firſt Four Days in the next Term, proceed to take the Benefit of this Act, and of the before-recited Act, in as full and ample a Manner, to all Intents and Purpoſes, as if he, ſhe, or they had been charged in Execution: Provided always, That the Creditor or Creditors bringing ſuch Action or Actions, at any Time before the Expiration of ſuch Four Days of the next Term, ſhall and may have Liberty to apply to the Court wherein any ſuch Action ſhall have been brought, to ſhew Cauſe why ſuch Judgment ſhall not be allowed; and if it ſhall appear, to the Satisfaction of ſuch Court, that ſuch Judgment was entered up with a View or Intent to defraud any ſuch Creditor or Creditors, or to prevent his, her, or their making proper Enquiries into the State and Condition of the Effects of ſuch Perſon or Perſons ſo confined as aforeſaid, then it ſhall and may be lawful for any ſuch Court to ſet aſide the ſaid Judgment or Judgments, and to render the ſame of no Effect.

Clause (B.)

Provided always, and be it further Enacted, That all Powers and Authorities, Orders and Directions, Benefits and Advantages, contained in this preſent Act, and the before-recited Act, ſhall extend and be conſtrued to extend to every Perſon claiming Benefit of the ſaid Acts after the Confeſſion and entering up of Judgment in Manner aforeſaid *(which Judgment ſhall not have been ſet aſide by the Court where ſuch Action ſhall have been brought)* in like Manner, to all Intents and Purpoſes, as they can, may, or do, extend, or ſhall be conſtrued to extend, to any Perſon claiming Benefit of the ſame after having been charged in Execution.

Clause

Clause (C.)

And be it further Enacted, That if the Court before which any such Prisoner shall be brought shall, for any of the Causes alledged in the said recited Acts, or to obtain better Information, be of Opinion that a further Time should be given for hearing the Parties concerned, it shall and may be lawful for any such Court to remand any Prisoner or Prisoners, and direct him, her, or them, and the other Parties concerned, to attend on any other Day to be appointed by such Court, some Time at furthest within the Time of holding the next subsequent Assizes, Great Sessions, or Quarter Sessions, as the Case may be.

Clause (D.)

Provided always, and be it further Enacted, That in all Cases where it shall be made appear, to the Satisfaction of any Court before whom any such Prisoner or Prisoners shall have been brought, that he, she, or they, hath or have made over his, her, or their, Estate or Effects, or any Part thereof, to any Person or Persons whatsoever, with Intent to defraud his Creditors, such Prisoner or Prisoners shall be forthwith remanded to Prison, and shall lose all Benefit and Advantage arising from this or the before recited Act.

A

B I L L

[With the Amendments]

To explain and amend an Act, made in the Thirty-second Year of his late Majesty's Reign, intituled, "An Act for Relief of Insolvent Debtors, with respect to the Imprisonment of their Persons; and to oblige Debtors, who shall continue in Execution in Prison beyond a certain Time, and for Sums not exceeding what are mentioned in the Act, to make Discovery of, and deliver, upon Oath, their Estates for their Creditors Benefit;" and to prevent Actions being brought upon Judgments, without Leave of the Court or Courts wherein such Judgments shall have been entered up respectively.

1775.

HEADS

OF A

BILL

To Relieve, upon Conditions and under Restrictions, Persons called Protesting Catholic Dissenters *from certain Penalties and Disabilities to which Papists, or Persons professing the Popish Religion, are by Law subject.*

IT RECITES, that by divers Laws now in force concerning Papists, or Persons professing the Popish Religion, diverse Penalties and Disabilities have been imposed on such Persons, on account of certain Principles attributed to them, which are dangerous to Society, and repugnant to Political and Civil Liberty:

Preamble.

And that diverse Persons, who, according to the Laws now in being, are within the Description of Papists, or Persons professing the Popish Religion, do not hold, and have protested

A against

against such Principles, although they continue to dissent in certain Points of Faith from the Church of *England*, and are therefore called PROTESTING CATHOLIC DISSENTERS; and such Persons are willing solemnly to protest against, and to declare, that they do not hold such pernicious Doctrines:

And that it is expedient that such Persons, as shall so solemnly protest and declare against their holding such Principles, although they shall continue to dissent, in certain Points of Faith, from the Church of *England*, should be relieved from the Penalties and Disabilities to which Papists, or Persons professing the Popish Religion, or their Children, or Persons educated in the Popish Religion, are by Law subject, except as thereinafter is excepted:

It is therefore Enacted, That from and after the making and passing of the Act, the Oath of Allegiance and Abjuration and of Protestation and Declaration, thereinafter expressed, may and shall be administered by any of the same Courts, and may and shall be registered in the same Manner, and shall give the same Benefits and Advantages, and shall be and operate to and for the same Intents and Purposes whatsoever, as in and by the Act passed in the Eighteenth Year of his present Majesty, is Enacted concerning the Oath therein prescribed:

And, that Lists of the Persons taking the Oath shall be returned annually to the Clerk of the Privy Council.

It is then enacted, that the Oath of Allegiance and Abjuration and of Protestation and Declaration shall be in the Words following:

" I *A. B.* do sincerely promise and swear, That I will be
" faithful and bear true Allegiance to   Majesty
"   and I do truly
" and sincerely acknowledge, profess, testify, and declare
" in my Conscience, before God and the World, that our
" Sovereign   is lawful and rightful
" of this Realm, and of all other   Majesty's Dominions
" thereunto belonging: And I do solemnly and sincerely
" declare, that I do believe, in my Conscience, that not any
" Descendants of the Person who pretended to be Prince of
" *Wales* during the Life of the late King *James* the Second,
" and, after his Decease, pretended to be, and took upon
" himself the Stile and Title of King of *England* by the
" Name of *James* the Third, or of *Scotland* by the Name of
" *James* the Eighth, or the Stile and Title of King of *Great*
" *Britain*, hath any Right or Title whatsoever to the Crown
                                                    " of

" of this Realm, or any Dominions thereunto belonging:
" And I do renounce, refuse, and abjure, any Allegiance or
" Obedience to any of them: And I do swear, that I will bear
" Faith and true Allegiance to   Majesty
"   and   will defend to the ut-
" most of my Power against all traitorous Conspiracies and
" Attempts whatsoever, which shall be made against
" Person, Crown, or Dignity: And I will do my utmost
" Endeavour to disclose and make known to   Majesty
"   and   Successors, all
" Treasons, and traitorous Conspiracies, which I shall know
" to be against   : And I do faithfully and fully pro-
" mise, to the utmost of my Power, to support, maintain,
" and defend the Succession of the Crown against the
" Descendants of the said *James*, and against all other Persons
" whatsoever; which Succession, by an Act intitled, " An
" Act for the further Limitation of the Crown, and better
" securing the Rights and Liberties of the Subject," is, and
" stands, limited to the Princess *Sophia*, Electress and
" Duchess Dowager of *Hanover*, and the Heirs of her Body
" being Protestants: And I do swear, that I do, from my
" Heart, abhor, detest, and abjure, as impious and here-
" tical, that damnable Doctrine and Position, that Princes
" excommunicated by the Pope, or by Authority of the See
" of *Rome*, may be deposed, or murdered, by their Subjects,
" or any other Persons whomsoever: And I do protest and
" declare, and do solemnly swear it to be my most firm and
" sincere Opinion, Belief, and Persuasion, That neither the
" Pope, nor any Prelate or Priest, nor any Assembly of Pre-
" lates or Priests, nor any Ecclesiastical Power whatsoever,
" can absolve the Subjects of this Realm, or any of them,
" from their Allegiance to his said Majesty: And that no
" Foreign Church, Prelate or Priest, or Assembly of Prelates
" or Priests, or Ecclesiastical Power whatsoever, hath, or
" ought to have, any Jurisdiction or Authority whatsoever
" within this Realm, that can, directly or indirectly, affect,
" or interfere with, the Independence, Sovereignty, Laws,
" Constitution, or Government thereof, or the Rights,
" Liberties, Persons, or Properties of the People of the said
" Realm, or any of them: And that no Person can be
" absolved from any Sin, nor any Sin whatever be for-
" given, at the Pleasure of any Pope, or of any Priest, or
" of any Person whomsoever; but that Sorrow for past
" Offences, Resolution to avoid future Guilt, and Atone-
" ment to GOD and the injured Neighbour, are indispensably
" requisite to obtain Forgiveness of Sin: And that no
" Breach of Faith with, or Injury to, or Hostility against,
"   any

" any Perfon whomfoever, can ever be juftified, by Reafon,
" or under Pretence, that fuch Perfon is an Heretic or an
" Infidel: And that neither the Pope, nor any Prelate,
" nor any Prieft, nor any Affembly of Prelates or Priefts,
" nor any Ecclefiaftical Power whatever, can, at any Time,
" difpenfe with, or abfolve Me from, the Obligations of
" this Oath, or of any other Oath, or of any Compact
" whatfoever: And I do alfo, in my Confcience, declare,
" and folemnly fwear, That I acknowledge no Infallibility
" in the Pope: And all thefe Things I do plainly and fin-
" cerely declare, acknowledge, and fwear, according to
" thefe exprefs Words by Me fpoken, and according to the
" plain and ordinary Senfe of the fame Words, without any
" Equivocation, mental Evafion, or fecret Refervation what-
" foever: And I do make the aforefaid Proteftation, Declara-
" tion, Recognition, Acknowledgment, Abjuration, Renun-
" ciation, Promife, and Oath, heartily, willingly, and truly,
" upon the true Faith of a Chriftian. So help me God."

And it is then Enacted, That every Perfon who fhall take and fubfcribe the Oath of Allegiance and Abjuration and of Protefta-tion and Declaration, thereinbefore appointed to be taken and fubfcribed, fhall thenceforth be deemed and taken in Law to be a "*PROTESTING CATHOLIC DISSENTER*;" and that none of the Laws now in force againft or concerning Papifts or Perfons profeffing the Popifh Religion;—or againft or concern-ing Popifh Recufants;—or againft or concerning Popifh Recu-fants Convict;—or againft or concerning Perfons educated in the Popifh Religion;—or againft or concerning Perfons reconciled to or holding a Communion with the See of Rome;—or againft or concerning Popifh Bifhops, Priefts, or Deacons, or Perfons entering into or belonging to any Ecclefiaftical Order, or Com-munity of the Church of Rome;—or againft or concerning Perfons hearing or faying Mafs, or being prefent at, or con-forming to or performing any Rite, Ceremony, Practice, or Obfervance of the Church of Rome;—or againft or concerning Perfons not reforting or repairing to his or her Parifh-Church or Chapel, or fome other ufual place of Common Prayer, to hear Divine Service, and join in Public Worfhip, according to the Forms and Rites of the Church of England, as by Law eftablifhed;—or againft or concerning Perfons keeping or having any Ser-vant, or other Perfon, being a Papift, or reputed Papift, or Per-fon profeffing the Popifh Religion, who fhall not fo refort, or repair to his or her Parifh-Church or Chapel, or fome fuch other ufual Place of Common Prayer as aforefaid;—or againft or concerning Perfons not taking and fubfcribing the Oath com-monly called the Oath of Supremacy, or the Declaration com-monly called the Declaration againft Tranfubftantiation;—

or the Declaration commonly called the Declaration against Tranfubftantiation and Invocation of Saints;—nor any Law requiring the Regiftry of the Names and real Eftates, or Inrollment of the Deeds and Wills of Popifh Recufants, or Papifts, or Perfons educated in the Popifh Religion, or whofe Parent or Parents fhall be a Papift or Papifts, or who fhall ufe or profefs the Popifh Religion; fhall extend, or be conftrued to extend, to any fuch Protefting Catholic Diffenter, who fhall have taken and fubfcribed fuch Oath of Allegiance and Abjuration and of Proteftation and Declaration as aforefaid: and in all Cafes where Perfons are required to take and fubfcribe the Oaths commonly called the Oath of Allegiance, the Oath of Abjuration, and the Oath of Supremacy, or the Declaration commonly called the Declaration againft Tranfubftantiation, or the Declaration commonly called the Declaration againft Tranfubftantiation and Invocation of Saints,—any fuch Protefting Catholic Diffenter as aforefaid fhall and may, at his or her Election, take and fubfcribe, in place of the fame, the Oath of Allegiance and Abjuration and of Proteftation and Declaration herein before mentioned and appointed to be taken as aforefaid;—and fuch laft mentioned Oath of Allegiance and Abjuration and of Proteftation and Declaration may and fhall alfo be adminiftered and taken, before the fame Perfons, and in the fame Manner, and fhall give the fame Benefits and Advantages, and fhall operate to and for all the fame Intents and Purpofes whatfoever (fave as hereinafter is excepted and provided), as the aforefaid Oaths commonly called the Oaths of Allegiance, Abjuration, and Supremacy, or the aforefaid Declaration againft Tranfubftantiation, or the aforefaid Declaration againft Tranfubftantiation and Invocation of Saints, in the room of which it is intended to be hereby fubftituted.

Provifo, For certifying and regiftering the Places of Worfhip, and Minifters of Protefting Catholic Diffenters.

Provifo, That no Affembly for Religious Worfhip of Protefting Catholic Diffenters fhall be had with the Doors locked barred, or bolted.

Provifo, For enabling Protefting Catholic Diffenters to exercife Parochial or Ward Offices by Deputy.

Provifo, To exempt Protefting Catholic Priefts from ferving upon Juries or Parochial or Ward Offices.

Provifo, To enable Juftices of Peace to tender the Oath prefcribed by the Act to any Perfon going to any Place of Affembly licenfed by the Act.

Provifo.

(6)

Proviso, That the Laws in force for Frequenting of Divine Service on the Lord's Day, shall continue in force against Offenders, unless they come to some Congregation or Assembly permitted by this Act, or by the Act of Toleration.

Proviso, That the Act shall not extend to Persons writing against the Trinity.

Proviso, That no Benefit in the Act shall extend to any Dissenting Catholic Ecclesiastic officiating in any Place of Congregation with a Steeple or Bell, or who shall exercise any of the Ceremonies of his Religion, or wear the Habit of his Order, except within some Place of Congregation licensed by the Act, or in a private House.

Proviso, That nothing therein contained shall be construed to exempt any such Protesting Catholic Dissenter, as aforesaid, from paying Tythes, or other parochial Duties, or any other Duties, to the Church or Minister, or from any Prosecution in any Ecclesiastical Court or elsewhere for the same; or to repeal any Part of the Statute made in the 26th Year of the Reign of his late Majesty King *George* the Second, intituled, " An Act " for the better preventing of Clandestine Marriages," or any Parts of any other Statute concerning Marriages; or to give any Ease, Benefit, or Advantage to any Person, who shall, by preaching, teaching, or writing, deny or gainsay the Oath of Allegiance and Abjuration and of Protestation and Declaration thereinbefore-mentioned, and appointed to be taken as aforesaid, or the Declarations or Doctrines therein contained, or any of them; or to repeal or affect any Law now in force concerning the Right of Succession to, or the Limitation of the Crown; or concerning the Election of any Member or Members to serve in Parliament; or to enable any Person to sit in either House of Parliament; or to be of his Majesty's Most Honourable Privy Council; or to hold, enjoy, or exercise any Office, civil or military, unless duly qualified in the Manner now required by Law; or to educate any Child a Papist; or to educate any Child, of Protestant Parents, a Protesting Catholic Dissenter.

Proviso, That nothing in the Act contained shall make it lawful to found, endow, or establish any Religious Order, or Society of Persons bound by Monastic or Religious Vows, within this Realm, or the Dominions thereunto belonging; and that all Uses, Trusts, and Dispositions, whether of real or personal Property, which immediately before the passing of the Act shall have been deemed to be superstitious or unlawful, shall continue to be so deemed and taken.

Proviso, That nothing in this Act contained shall extend, or be construed to extend, to that Part of *Great Britain* called *Scotland*.

HEADS OF A BILL FOR THE RELIEF OF PROTESTING CATHOLIC DISSENTERS.

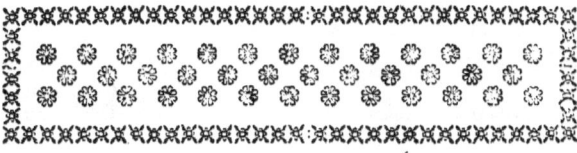

A.

B I L L

TO

Prevent unneceſſary Removals of the Poor; and to promote the granting of Certificates.

Note.—*The Figures in the Margin denote the Number of the Folios in the written Copy.*

WHEREAS ſome of the Laws now in being, relative to the Settlement of the Poor, have been found rather to have promoted than prevented unneceſſary Removals, and to have, in a great Meaſure, diſcouraged Pariſhes from granting Certificates: For Remedy thereof,

May it pleaſe your MAJESTY,

That it may be Enacted; **And be it Enacted** by the KING's Moſt Excellent Majeſty, by and with the Advice and Conſent of the Lords Spiritual and Temporal, and Commons, in this preſent Parliament aſſembled, and by the Authority of

A the

the same, That so much of the Statute, passed in the Third and Fourth Years of the Reign of King *William* and Queen *Mary*, intituled, "An Act for the better Explanation "and supplying the Defects of the former Laws for the "Settlement of the Poor," as Enacts, That if any Person, who shall come to inhabit in any Town or Parish, shall be charged with, and pay his Share towards the Public Taxes or Levies of the said Town or Parish, then he shall be adjudged and deemed to have a legal Settlement in the same, though no such Notice in Writing of the House of his or her Abode be delivered and published, as in the said Act is required, shall, from and after the   be   and the same is hereby   accordingly.

And be it further Enacted, That the Statute, passed in the Ninth and Tenth Years of the Reign of King *William* the Third, intituled, "An Act for explaining an Act, made the "last Session of Parliament, intituled, An Act for supplying "some Defects in the Laws for the Relief of the Poor of this "Kingdom," which Enacts, That no Person or Persons whatsoever, who shall come into any Parish by any Certificate given under and by virtue of the Statute of the Eighth and Ninth Years of the Reign of King *William* the Third, shall be adjudged, by any Act whatsoever, to have procured a legal Settlement in such Parish, unless he and they shall really and *bona fide* take a Lease of a Tenement of the yearly Value of Ten Pounds, or shall execute some annual Office in such Parish, being legally placed in such Office, shall from and after the   be and the same is hereby

Provided always, and be it hereby Declared and Enacted, That no such Certificate as aforesaid shall be construed to amount to a Notice in Writing, in order to gain a Settlement; nor shall any Person residing in any Parish, Township, or Place, under any such Certificate, gain any Settlement by virtue of any Notice in Writing of the House of his or her Abode, delivered to One of the Churchwardens or Overseers of the Poor, according to the Statutes made in the First Year of the Reign of King *James* the Second, and in the Third and Fourth Years of the Reign of King *William* and Queen *Mary*.

And

And be it further Enacted, That so much of the Statute, passed in the Twelfth Year of the Reign of her late Majesty Queen *Anne*, as Enacts, That if any Person shall be an Apprentice bound by Indenture to, or shall be a hired Servant to or with any Person whatsoever, who did come into or shall reside in any Parish, Township, or Place, by Means or Licence of a Certificate given under, and by virtue of the Statute passed in the Eighth and Ninth Years of the Reign of King *William* the Third, and not afterwards having gained a legal Settlement in such Parish, Township, or Place, such Apprentice, by virtue of such Apprenticeship, Indenture, or Binding, and such Servant by any such Hiring, or Service, shall not gain or be adjudged to have any Settlement in such Parish, Township, or Place, shall from and after the
be   and the same is hereby accordingly.

A

BILL

TO

Prevent unnecessary Removals of the Poor; and to promote the granting of Certificates.

1775.

A

BILL

FOR

Altering, explaining, and amending, several Acts of the Parliament of *Scotland*, respecting Colliers, Coalbearers, and Salters.

Note.—*The Figures in the Margin denote the Number of the Folios in the written Copy.*

WHEREAS, by the Statute Law of *Scotland*, as explained by the Judges of the Courts of Law there, many Colliers, and Coalbearers, and Salters, are in a State of Slavery or Bondage, bound to the Collieries and Salt Works where they work for Life, transferrable with the Collieries and Salt Works, when their original Masters have no further Use for them:

And whereas Persons are discouraged and prevented from learning the Art or Business of Colliers, or Coalbearers, and Salters, by their becoming bound to the Collieries and Salt Works for Life, where they shall work for the Space of One

A Year,

Year, by Means whereof there are not a sufficient Number of Colliers, Coalbearers, and Salters, in *Scotland*, for working the Quantities of Coal and Salt necessarily wanted, and many new-discovered Coals remain unwrought, and many are not sufficiently wrought; nor are there a sufficient Number of Salters for the Salt Works, to the great Loss of the Owners, and Disadvantage to the Public:

And whereas the emancipating or setting free the Colliers, Coalbearers, and Salters, in *Scotland*, who are now in a State of Servitude, gradually, and upon reasonable Conditions, and the preventing others from coming into such a State of Servitude, would be the Means of increasing the Number of Colliers, Coalbearers, and Salters, to the great Benefit of the Public, without doing any Injury to the present Masters, and would remove the Reproach of allowing such a State of Servitude to exist in a free Country:

May it therefore please Your MAJESTY,

That it may be Enacted; And be it Enacted by the KING's Most Excellent MAJESTY, by and with the Advice and Consent of the Lords Spiritual and Temporal, and Commons, in this present Parliament assembled, and by the Authority of the same, That from and after no Person, who shall begin to work as a Collier, Coalbearer, or Salter, or in any other Way, in a Colliery or Salt Work in *Scotland*, shall be bound to such Colliery or Salt Work, or to the Owner thereof, in any Way or Manner different from what is permitted by the Law of *Scotland* with regard to Servants and Labourers; and that they shall be deemed free, and shall enjoy the same Privileges, Rights, and Immunities with the rest of His Majesty's Subjects, any Law or Usage in *Scotland* to the contrary notwithstanding.

Provided always, That it shall be lawful for all Owners and Lessees of Collieries and Salt Works, and for Colliers, Coalbearers, and Salters, to take Persons bound by Contract or Indenture as Apprentices, to learn the Art or Business of Coalhewing, Coalbearing, or making Salt, for any Term of Years permitted by the Law of *Scotland* with regard to Apprentices in other Arts and Mysteries.

And

And be it further Enacted by the Authority aforesaid, That all Persons under the Age of   at the Commencement of this Act, employed as Colliers, Coalbearers, or Salters, in *Scotland*, shall, after   Service from and after the Commencement of this Act, be free from their Service and Servitude, and at Liberty to engage themselves as Servants or Labourers in any other Colliery or Salt Work, or in any other Kind of Labour whatever.

And be it further Enacted by the Authority aforesaid, That all Colliers and Salters in *Scotland*, above the Age of   and under the Age of   at the Commencement of this Act, after a Service of   and all Colliers and Salters above the Age of   but under the Age of   at the Commencement of this Act, after a Service of   and all Colliers and Salters above the Age of   at the Commencement of this Act, after a Service of   after their having respectively sufficiently instructed a Person as an Apprentice in the Art or Mystery of Coalhewing, or making of Salt, of the Age of   at least when such Instruction shall be perfected, shall be free from any other Servitude or Bondage to the Colliery or Salt Work to which they were bound.

Provided always, That every Collier or Salter claiming Liberty under the Authority of this Act shall, prior to his being freed from his Servitude or Bondage, obtain a Decree of the Sheriff Court of the County in which he resides, finding and declaring that he is entitled unto his Freedom under the Authority of this Act.

And be it Enacted by the Authority aforesaid, That for the Purpose of obtaining such Decree, it shall and may be lawful for the Collier or Salter claiming his Freedom, to present a Petition to the Sheriff Depute or Substitute of the County where he resides, stating his Claim of Freedom, and offering to prove the Facts which entitle him to it; and the Sheriff Depute or Substitute is hereby authorized and required to order the Petition to be served upon the Owner, Lessee, or Overseer of the Colliery or Salt Works to which the Petitioner is bound, and to order an Answer to be put in to the Petition in   Days after Service, stating the Objection or Objections to the Freedom claimed, if any such are

are intended to be made; and the Sheriff shall thereafter proceed in a summary Way, in taking the Proofs, and all other Procedure necessary, until a Decree shall be pronounced; and if the Decree of the Sheriff shall be against the Petitioner, finding him not entitled to Freedom, it shall nevertheless be competent to such Petitioner, at any Period after the Expiration of   to present a Second Petition, stating his Claim of Liberty of new, and which shall be proceeded upon in the same Manner as the former; and if the Petitioner fails in obtaining a Decree for him on the Second Petition, he may, after the Expiration of   from the Date of the Second Decree, present a Third Petition, which shall likewise be proceeded upon in the same Manner; and if he fails in obtaining Decree upon his Third Petition, he may present a Fourth; and so on, till he obtains a Decree declaring his Freedom;   at least being expired after a Decree upon One Petition, before it shall be competent to present another.

6 Provided always, and be it Enacted, That a Collier or Salter claiming his Liberty under the Authority of this Act, his not having instructed an Apprentice in Manner before directed, shall afford no Objection to such Collier or Salter obtaining a Decree of his Freedom, if he shall produce to the Sheriff a Writing, under the Hand of the Owner or Lessee of the Colliery or Salt Work to which he is bound, or of the Steward or Factor of the Owner, discharging the Obligation upon such Collier or Salter to have instructed an Apprentice in Manner before directed.

And be it further Enacted by the Authority aforesaid, That it shall not be competent for either of the Parties to remove the Proceedings upon any such Petition into the Court of Session in *Scotland* by Advocation, or to complain of any Decree by Appeal or Suspension, or to sue for Reduction of any such Decree; and that every Decree upon such Petition, finding and declaring the Freedom of the Petitioner, shall be final and conclusive against the Person to whom the Petitioner was bound.

And be it further Enacted by the Authority aforesaid, That when Colliers or Salters obtain their Freedom under the Authority of this Act, their Wives and Children, and

all

all others who make Part of their Family, and are Coalbearers, or otherwife affiftant to them, fhall likewife be free.

And be it further Enacted by the Authority aforefaid, That all Coalbearers, Salters, and other Labourers in Collieries or Salt Works, who are bound to any Colliery or Salt Work in *Scotland*, and do not belong to the Family of any particular Collier or Salter, fhall, after Service from the Commencement of this Act, be free from their Service and Servitude, and at Liberty to engage themfelves as Servants or Labourers in any other Colliery or Salt Work, or in any other Kind of Work whatfoever.

And be it further Enacted by the Authority aforefaid, That from and after all Colliers and Salters then free, and all Perfons that may thereafter become Colliers and Salters, and all Colliers and Salters bound to any Colliery or Salt Work upon the faid from the Time of obtaining their Freedom under the Authority of this Act, fhall be entitled to the Benefit of an Act, made in the Parliament of *Scotland* in the Year One thoufand Seven hundred and One, intituled, " Act for preventing wrongous Imprifonment, and againft " undue Delays in Trials," any Thing in the faid Act to the contrary notwithftanding.

A BILL

FOR

Altering, explaining, and amending, several Acts of the Parliament of *Scotland*, respecting Colliers, Coalbearers, and Salters.

1775.

A

B I L L

FOR

Dividing and Inclosing several Open and Common Fields, and other Commonable Lands and Grounds, within the Parish of *Woodstone*, in the County of *Huntingdon*.

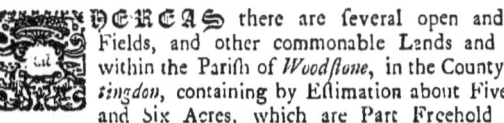**WHEREAS** there are several open and common Fields, and other commonable Lands and Grounds, within the Parish of *Woodstone*, in the County of *Huntingdon*, containing by Estimation about Five hundred and Six Acres, which are Part Freehold and Part Copyhold: *Preamble.*

And whereas *Carrier Thompson* is Lord of the Manor and of the Soil of *Woodstone* aforesaid, and the Reverend *Middlemore Ward*, Clerk, is Rector thereof, and in Right of the said Rectory intitled to certain Glebe Lands, and to both Great and Small Tithes of every Sort and Kind, arising, increasing, or happening within the

A said

said Fields; and the said *Carrier Thompson*, *Thomas Vaughan*, Esquire, *James Delarue*, Esquire, *William Edwards*, Gentleman, and Others, are the Owners and Proprietors of the said open Fields:

And whereas the Lands and Grounds of the several Proprietors in the said open Fields lie intermixed and dispersed, and are inconveniently situated, so that in their present Situation they are incapable of any considerable Improvement, and it would be advantageous to the several Proprietors thereof, and Persons intitled to and interested therein, to have the same divided and inclosed; **Yet** the same cannot be rendered effectual to answer the Intention of the Parties without the Aid and Authority of Parliament;

May it therefore please Your MAJESTY,

That it may be **Enacted; And be it Enacted**, by the KING's most Excellent MAJESTY, by and with the Advice and Consent of the Lords Spiritual and Temporal, and Commons, in this present Parliament assembled, and by the Authority of the same, That *William Pywell* of *Barnwell Castle*, in the County of *Northampton*, *John Newton* of *Laighton Bormswold*, in the County of *Huntingdon*, and *George Maxwell* of *Folksworth*, in the said County of *Huntingdon*, Gentlemen, and their Successors, to be elected in Manner herein aftermentioned, shall be and they are hereby appointed Commissioners for setting out, dividing, and allotting all the said open and common Fields and other commonable Lands and Grounds within the Parish of *Woodstone* aforesaid, and for putting this Act in Execution; subject to the Rules and Directions herein after-appointed.

Commissioners.

Provided always, and be it Enacted, by the Authority aforesaid, That no Person shall be capable of acting as a Commissioner in the Execution of any of the Powers given by this Act (except the Powers of giving and signing Notice of the First Meeting of the said Commissioners, and of administering the Oath herein after-directed) until he shall have taken and subscribed an Oath to the Effect following:

Commissioner's Oath.

I A. B. do swear, That I will faithfully, impartially, and honestly, according to the best of my Skill and Judgment, execute the Trust reposed in me as a Commissioner by virtue of an Act of Parliament "for Dividing and Inclosing the Open Fields within the Parish of "Wood-

" Woodſtone, *in the County of* Huntingdon," *without Favour or Affection to any Perſon whomſoever.*
                              So help me GOD.

Which Oath it ſhall and may be lawful for any One of the ſaid Commiſſioners to adminiſter, and he is hereby required to adminiſter the ſame to any other of the ſaid Commiſſioners.

And for the more certain Diviſion of the ſaid Lands, **Be it further Enacted,** by the Authority aforeſaid, That a true and diſtinct Survey ſhall be made of all the ſaid open Fields and of the preſent incloſed Lands within the ſaid Pariſh, before the   or as ſoon thereafter as conveniently may be, by ſuch Perſon or Perſons as the ſaid Commiſſioners, or any   of them, ſhall from time to time appoint; and ſuch Survey ſhall be reduced into Writing, and the Number of Acres, Roods, and Perches belonging to each Proprietor in the ſaid open Fields and preſent incloſed Lands ſhall be therein expreſſed and deſcribed, and ſuch Survey ſhall be laid before the ſaid Commiſſioners, or any   of them, at ſome or One of their Meetings to be held in purſuance of this Act.

Survey to be made.

Provided always, and be it Enacted, That no Perſon ſhall be capable of acting as Surveyor for the Purpoſes aforeſaid until he ſhall have taken and ſubſcribed an Oath to the Effect following:

Surveyor's Oath.

I A. B. *do ſwear, That I will faithfully, impartially, and honeſtly, according to the beſt of my Skill and Judgment, make a true and diſtinct Survey of all the open Fields and preſent incloſed Lands within the Pariſh of* Woodſtone, *in the County of* Huntingdon, *and reduce the ſame into Writing, and therein ſet forth the Number of Acres, Roods, and Perches belonging to each Proprietor in the ſaid open Fields and preſent incloſed Lands, and that I will lay ſuch Survey before the Commiſſioners appointed to put in Execution an Act of Parliament* " *for Dividing and Incloſing the Open Fields within the* " *Pariſh of* Woodſtone, *in the County of* Huntingdon," *purſuant to the Directions of the ſaid Act.*
                              So help me GOD.

Which Oath it ſhall and may be lawful to and for any One of the ſaid Commiſſioners to adminiſter, and he is hereby impowered and required to adminiſter the ſame accordingly.

                                                      And

Power to make a Survey.	**And be it further Enacted**, That the said Commissioners and the Surveyor or Surveyors appointed or to be appointed as herein before-mentioned, together with their and every of their Assistants, Servants, and Persons employed by them, shall have and they are hereby vested with full and free Power and Authority, at any Time or Times whatsoever, to enter into, view, examine, value, survey, and admeasure, for the Purposes of this Act, as well the open Fields and Grounds hereby directed to be divided and inclosed as also the ancient inclosed Lands within the said Parish of *Woodstone*.
Notice of Meetings to be given.	**And be it further Enacted**, That the said Commissioners, or any of them, shall and they are hereby required to give or cause to be given public Notice in the Parish Church of *Woodstone* aforesaid, upon some *Sunday* immediately after Divine Service, and also by a Writing affixed on One of the Doors of the said Church, of the Time and Place of their First and every subsequent Meeting for the Execution of this Act, at least Days before every such Meeting shall be held (Meetings by Adjournment only excepted);
Power to adjourn.	and shall then and from time to time afterwards adjourn themselves to meet at such Place or Places as they the said Commissioners, or any of them, shall from time to time think most convenient for putting this Act in Execution.

Provided always, That if no more than One Commissioner shall attend at any such Meeting, the Commissioner so attending shall have Power to adjourn such Meeting to such Time and Place as he shall think proper.

Election of Commissioners.	**And be it further Enacted**, That if any One or more of the Commissioners herein before-appointed or to be appointed by virtue of this Act shall, before the Execution of the Powers and Authorities hereby in them reposed, die or refuse to act, then and in such Case the surviving or other acting Commissioners or Commissioner (if any be) or otherwise the Persons interested in the said intended Inclosure, or the major Part of them in Number and Value, assembled at some Meeting to be held for that Purpose, shall from time to time, upon the Death or Refusal of such Commissioner or Commissioners to act, or as soon after as Occasion may require, and before any other Business is proceeded upon in the Execution of this Act, by Writing under his or their Hands or Seals or Hand and Seal, appoint One or more Commissioner or Commissioners, not interested in the said intended Inclosure, in the

Place

Place and Stead of such Commissioner or Commissioners so dying or refusing to act as aforesaid; and every such Commissioner or Commissioners so to be appointed shall have the like Powers and Authorities by virtue of this Act as the Commissioner or Commissioners in whose Place or Places he or they shall succeed was or were vested with; provided that Notice be given in the Parish Church of *Woodstone* aforesaid, on some *Sunday* immediately after Divine Service, of the Time and Place of Meeting to choose or appoint such new Commissioner or Commissioners, at least   Days before every such Meeting. *Notice of Elections.*

And be it further Enacted, That the said Commissioners, or any   of them, shall and may and they are hereby authorized and impowered, in the First Place, after setting out public and private Roads, Ways, and Drains, as herein-after is mentioned, to allot and appoint unto and for the said *Middlemore Ward* and his Successors, Rectors of the said Parish of *Woodstone* aforesaid, such Parcel or Parcels of the Lands and Grounds so intended to be inclosed as (Quantity, Quality, and Situation to be considered) shall in their Opinion and Judgment be equal in Value to and in full Satisfaction and Compensation for the Glebe Land in the said Fields now belonging to the said Rectory; and in the next Place to allot and appoint unto and for the said *Middlemore Ward* and his Successors, Rectors of the said Parish of *Woodstone*, so much of the said Lands and Grounds so intended to be inclosed as shall (Quantity, Quality, and Situation considered) be equal in Value to One Sixth Part of all the Residue of the Lands lying within and Part of the said open Fields subject to the Payment of Great and Small Tithes; which said Allotment so to be made as aforesaid shall be accepted, and be in Lieu of and as a full Satisfaction and Compensation for all Manner of Tithes whatsoever, as well Great as Small, belonging to the said *Middlemore Ward* and his Successors, Rectors of the said Parish of *Woodstone*, arising, growing, and renewing within the said open Fields, the usual and accustomed Mortuaries, *Easter* Offerings, and Surplice Fees only excepted. *Allotment to the Rector, for Glebe, and Tithes.*

Provided always, and be it Enacted, That the Outermost or Ring Fences of the several Parcels of Land so to be allotted to the said *Middlemore Ward* and his Successors, Rectors as aforesaid, in Lieu of and as a Compensation for Glebe Lands and Great and Small Tithes, shall be planted with young Quicks, which shall be guarded by and with Posts and Rails, at the Expence of the Proprietors of the several Tithable Lands and Grounds to be inclosed by virtue of this Act, in such Manner as the said Commissioners, *Rector's Allotment to be Ring fenced.*

B

or any of them, shall by their Award or Instrument in Writing hereafter mentioned ascertain, direct, and appoint; and that such Fences shall for ever after the making thereof be maintained and supported by the Rector of the said Parish for the Time being, or such other Persons and in such Manner as the said Commissioners, or any of them, shall by their said Award or Instrument direct and appoint.

Old Inclosures to remain tithable,

Provided also, and be it further Enacted, That all the old inclosed Lands within the said Parish of *Woodstone*, and every Part thereof, shall remain, continue, and be charged and chargeable with the Payment of Tithes to the said *Middlemore Ward* and his Successors, Rectors as aforesaid, in the same Manner the same now are, and as if this Act had not been made, unless the Proprietors thereof, or of any Part thereof, shall and do, before any Allotment shall be made of any Part of the Lands hereby intended to be inclosed, give Notice in Writing to the said Commissioners or their Successors, or any of them, of his, her, or their Desire and Intention of having his, her, or their ancient inclosed Lands, or any Part thereof, within the said Parish of *Woodstone* free and exonerated from the Payment of Tithes to the said *Middlemore Ward* and his Successors, Rectors as aforesaid; that then and in such

unless some Allotment shall be made in Lieu thereof.

Case it shall and may be lawful to and for the said Commissioners and their Successors, or any of them, and they are hereby authorized and required to assign, set out, allot, and appoint unto the said *Middlemore Ward* and his Successors, Rectors as aforesaid, such Parcel or Parcels of his, her, or their Part and Share of the said open Fields so intended to be inclosed as (Quantity, Quality, and Situation considered) shall in the Opinion and Judgment of the said Commissioners and their Successors, or any of them, be equal in Value to and in full Satisfaction and Compensation for all the Great and Small Tithes belonging to the said *Middlemore Ward* and his Successors, Rectors as aforesaid, arising, growing, or renewing within such ancient inclosed Lands within the said Parish of *Woodstone*, for which the said Allotment shall be given and assigned; which said Lands so to be allotted and assigned as aforesaid shall be accepted by the said *Middlemore Ward* and his Successors, Rectors as aforesaid, and shall be in Lieu of and as a full Satisfaction and Compensation for all the Great and Small Tithes arising, renewing, or increasing from, by, or out of the said ancient Inclosures for which such Lands shall be respectively given; and that from and immediately after the Execution of the Award or Instrument of the said Commissioners, as after mentioned, all Right and Claim to the Great and Small Tithes of such ancient inclosed

closed Lands, in respect of which such Allotments shall be made and assigned as aforesaid out of the said open Fields, shall cease and be for ever extinguished.

And be it further Enacted, That the said Commissioners, or any   of them (after making the several Allotments herein directed to be first made as aforesaid to the said *Middlemore Ward* and his Successors, as Rectors of the Parish of *Woodstone* aforesaid) shall and may and they are hereby required and directed to divide, allot, set out, and appoint such of the Lands and Grounds lying and being in the said open Fields so intended to be inclosed as aforesaid as shall not be set out for public Roads, Ways, and Drains, as after-mentioned, unto and amongst the said *Carrier Thompson, Thomas Vaughan, James Delaruc, William Edwards,* and the several other Proprietors and Persons interested therein, in Proportion to their several and respective Shares, Interest, and Right in, over, and upon the said open Fields, by such Ways and Means as to the said Commissioners, or any   of them, shall seem most just, reasonable, and expedient; in which Divisions and Allotments so to be had and made due Regard shall be had as well to the Quality as the Quantity, Situation, and Convenience of the Lands and Grounds so to be allotted and divided as aforesaid.

General Allotment.

Provided also, and be it Enacted, That all such Allotments of the said open Fields which shall by virtue of this Act be allotted or appointed unto or in Right of any Freehold Lands within the said open Fields, or any of them, shall for ever hereafter be deemed Freehold Land; and that all such Allotments of the said open Fields which shall by virtue of this Act be allotted or appointed unto or in Right of Copyhold Lands or Hereditaments within the said open Fields, or any of them, shall be deemed Copyhold Lands.

Allotments to be held by the same Tenure.

And be it further Enacted, That all and every Lease and Leases at Rack or extended Rent which shall at the Time of the Execution of the said Award be subsisting of all or any Part or Parts of the said open Fields and present inclosed Lands within the said Parish of *Woodstone,* or of the Tithes of the same, or any Part thereof, and all Agreements at Rack or extended Rent for any Time or Term therein, shall, immediately upon such Allotments and Division being made, and such Award or Instrument being executed as aforesaid, or within any less Time that the said Commissioners, or any   of them, shall by any Writing under their Hands and Seals appoint, cease, determine, and be void, the

Leases at Rack Rent vacated.

[8]

respective Owners or Proprietors of such Part or Parts of the said open Fields and present inclosed Lands, or of the Tithes of the same, or any Part thereof, who have made any such Lease or Leases, or Agreement or Agreements, making such Satisfaction to his, her, or their respective Lessee or Lessees, Tenant or Tenants, as the said Commissioners, or any   of them, shall ascertain as reasonable to be paid to such Lessee or Lessees, Tenant or Tenants on account thereof, or as an Equivalent for the same.

Satisfaction to be made for Leases vacated.

And be it further Enacted, That the said Commissioners, or any   of them, shall and may set out, appoint, and make such public Highways and all such Driftways, Horseways, and Footways in, over, and through and upon the several Lands and Grounds to be inclosed by virtue of this Act, as also divert, alter, or change all or any of the public Roads or private Ways now used in or over the said open Fields, so as the same do not alter, affect, or prejudice any Turnpike Roads in and through the said Parish; and also shall and may set out, appoint, and make such Ditches, Fences, Banks, Drains, Sluices, Shuttles, Bridges, Gates, Stiles, and other Works in, over, through, and upon the said several open Fields and Grounds intended to be inclosed by virtue of this Act as they the said Commissioners, or any   of them, shall think convenient, so that such of the said public Highways as shall be set out as Ways for Carriages shall be   Feet wide at least between the Ditches or Fences, and such of the said Ways as shall be set out for private Roads or Ways, or for Driftways, Horseways, or Footways respectively, shall be of such respective Widths within the Ditches or Fences as the said Commissioners, or any   of them, shall by their said Award direct or appoint.; which public Highways shall at all Times for ever after the Setting out and Appointment thereof as aforesaid be repaired and kept in Repair in such Manner as public Highways are by Law directed to be repaired, and that such Driftways, Horseways, and Footways, Ditches, Fences, Banks, Drains, Sluices, Shuttles, Bridges, Gates, Stiles, and other Works so to be set out, appointed, and made as aforesaid, shall be repaired and kept it Repair by such Person and Persons respectively, his, her, and their respective Heirs, Successors, and Assigns, and in such Manner as the said Commissioners, or any   of them, shall by their said Award or Instrument in Writing direct and appoint; and that after the making such public Highways, Driftways, Horseways, Footways, and such private Roads and Ways so to be set out, appointed, and made as aforesaid, it shall not be lawful for any Person or Persons to use any other Roads or Ways, either public or private, over or through the said Lands

Highways to be set out.

[9]

Lands hereby intended to be inclosed, either on Foot, or with Horses, Cattle, or Carriages; and that all the former Roads and Ways in, over, through, and upon the several open Fields hereby directed to be inclosed, which shall not be set out and appointed as Roads or Ways by the said Award so to be made as aforesaid, shall be deemed Part of the Lands to be inclosed by virtue of this Act, and shall be divided and allotted as Part of such Lands.

And be it further Enacted, That if any Difference or Dispute shall arise between the Parties interested in the said Division, or any of them, touching or concerning their respective Shares and Proportions which they or any of them ought to have upon such Division, or between any of the said Proprietors, or his, her, or their Lessees or Tenants respectively, touching the Loss which such Lessees or Tenants may hereafter sustain by reason of the said Inclosure, and the determining of such Leases as aforesaid, it shall and may be lawful for the said Commissioners, or any of them, and they are hereby impowered and required by Examination of Witnesses upon Oath (which Oath the said Commissioners, or any One or more of them, is or are hereby impowered to administer) and upon such other proper Enquiry, Evidence, and Proof as shall be laid before them, to hear and determine the same; and such Determination shall be binding and conclusive to all Parties.

Commissioners to determine Differences.

And be it further Enacted, That for the more convenient Situation and Disposition of the several Lands and Grounds of the several Proprietors in the said open Fields and of the said ancient Inclosures, it shall and may be lawful to and for the said *Middlemore Ward* and his Successors, Rectors as aforesaid, and to and for all or any of the said Proprietors, to exchange all or any of his, her, or their Messuages, Tenements, old Inclosures, or other Lands and Grounds within the said Parish of *Woodstone*, or within any adjoining Parish, Township, or Place for any other Messuages or Tenements, old Inclosures, or other Lands and Grounds within the said Parish of *Woodstone*, or within any adjoining Parish, Township, or Place, so as all and every such Exchange and Exchanges be made by and with the Consent and Approbation of the said Commissioners and their Successors, or any of them, to be ascertained, specified, and declared in the said Award or Instrument herein-after mentioned; and that all and every such Exchange and Exchanges so to be made as aforesaid shall be good, valid, and effectual in the Law to all Intents and Purposes whatsoever.

Power to exchange Lands.

C And

Commissioners to draw up an Award.

And be it further Enacted, That within the Space of   Calendar Months next after the Division and Allotments of the said open Fields shall be completed and finished, or so soon after as conveniently may be, the said Commissioners, or any   of them, shall form, draw up, and make an Award or Instrument in Writing under their Hands and Seals, which shall express the Quantity and Contents in Statute Measure of the Acres, Roods, and Perches contained in the said open Fields so intended to be inclosed as aforesaid, and the Quantity and Contents of each and every Part and Parcel thereof assigned and allotted to or taken in Exchange by each of the Parties intitled to Lands, Tithes, or other Property within the same, distinguishing the Copyhold Lands from the Freehold, and a Description of the Situation and Boundaries of such Allotments respectively, and contain proper Orders and Directions for and concerning the laying out and making the public Highways, and the Breadth thereof, and for and concerning the laying out, making, maintaining, cleansing, and keeping in Repair the Driftways, Horseways, and Footways, and all other private Roads and Ways, and all Ditches, Fences, Banks, Drains, Shuttles, Bridges, Gates, and Stiles in, upon, and over the said Lands intended to be inclosed, and also all such Orders, Regulations, and Determinations as are in and by this Act mentioned, directed, required, or authorized to be established and made concerning the same, and such other Orders and Regulations as shall be necessary and proper, conformable to the true Tenor of this Act, for the more easy, convenient, and effectual Execution thereof, and for preventing all Difficulties and Disputes in relation to the Matters herein contained; which said Award or Instrument shall be fairly ingrossed and written on Parchment, and signed by the said Commissioners, or any   of them, and shall, within the Space of   Calendar Months next after the Execution thereof, together with the Commissioners and Surveyors Oaths aforesaid (which shall be thereunto annexed) be inrolled in One of his Majesty's Courts of Record at *Westminster*, or by the Clerk of the Peace for the said County of *Huntingdon*, to the end Recourse may be had to the same by all Persons interested in the said intended Inclosure, for the Inspection whereof the Sum of   shall be paid, and no more; and a true Copy of the Whole or any Part or Parts thereof, whenever and so often as the same shall be required, shall be delivered to any Person or Persons interested in the said intended Division, purporting the same to be a true Copy (for which no more shall be paid than   *per* Sheet, each Sheet containing   Words, and so in Proportion for any Number of Words or Sheets) which said Copy, as well as the original Award, shall from time

Award to be inrolled.

time to time and at all Times thereafter be admitted and allowed in all Courts whatsoever as legal Evidence of the same.

And be it further Enacted, That the several Allotments and Divisions, and all Orders, Directions, Regulations, and Determinations so to be made as aforesaid, in and by such Award or Instrument, shall be binding and conclusive unto and upon all Persons intitled to or claiming any Lands, Tithes, Common Rights, or other Property in the said open Fields, and that the several Allotments to be made as aforesaid to the respective Proprietors and Persons interested as aforesaid, shall be in full Bar of and Compensation for all Manner of Tithes, Lands, Interest, Common Right, and Property whatsoever in the said open Fields; and that from and immediately after the Execution of the said Award or Instrument, all Right and Claim of, in, and unto all and any Manner of Great and Small Tithes in, upon, and over the said open Fields and Lands intended to be inclosed as aforesaid, and of such ancient inclosed Lands for which any Allotment shall be made in lieu of Tithes as aforesaid (except as herein-before mentioned) and all Right of Common upon the same, shall cease and be for ever extinguished.

Award to be binding to all the Parties.

And be it further Enacted, That within the Space of Calendar Months next after the Execution of the said Award or Instrument, the several Lands thereby allotted shall be inclosed, hedged, ditched, or fenced, and such Inclosures, Hedges, Ditches, and Fences shall at all Times thereafter be repaired and maintained by such Person or Persons, and in such Manner as the said Commissioners, or any of them, shall in such their Award or Instrument order and direct; and that convenient Gaps and Openings shall be left in the said Fences and Inclosures for the Space of Calendar Months next ensuing the Execution of the said Award or Instrument for the Passage of Cattle, Carts, and Carriages through the same, unless the said Commissioners, or any of them, shall order that the same shall be sooner made up.

Allotments to be fenced.

Provided always, and be it further Enacted, That if any Hedges or Fences now standing or growing upon any Part of the Lands hereby intended to be inclosed, shall be assigned, limited, and appointed by the said Commissioners, or any of them, as and for a Boundary Fence for any of the Inclosures to be made as aforesaid, all such Hedges shall be left for the Benefit of the Person or Persons to whom such new Inclosure shall belong by virtue of this Act, he, she, or they making such Allowance and Satisfaction

Satisfaction to be made for Hedges.

faction to the former Owners and Proprietors of such Hedges and Fences respectively, immediately before such Allotments are made, as the said Commissioners, or any of them, shall in that Behalf order and appoint; and in case there shall be any Tree or Trees growing in the said Hedges or Fences so assigned as aforesaid, and the former Owners thereof shall not chuse to fell the same, then it shall and may be lawful for any such former Owners, at any Time within   Calendar Months after such Allotments shall be made, to enter into and upon the Lands and Hedges upon which such Tree or Trees shall be standing and being, and to fell, cut down, and carry away the same, doing as little Damage as may be.

Trees to belong to former Proprietors.

And be it further Enacted, That where any Parcel of Land so to be allotted as aforesaid shall abut or adjoin upon any Freeboard belonging to the Proprietors of any Lands next adjoining to the Lands hereby intended to be inclosed, the Person or Persons to whom such Parcel of Land shall be allotted, shall and may and is and are hereby impowered to set up and erect Gates or any other Kind of Fence in, over, and upon such Freeboard, for preserving the Quicksets, Banks, Wood Plants, and other the Fences to be planted or set up on such Parcel of Land, until such Time as the Owner of such Freeboard shall sufficiently, and at his own Expence have ditched, fenced, and mounded the same Freeboard from the said Parcel of Land adjoining thereunto.

Not obliged to fence against Freeboards,

Provided always, That nothing in this Act contained shall extend or be construed to extend to compel or oblige any of the said Proprietors whose Allotments or Shares upon the said Division and Inclosure shall lie and be situate next and adjoining to any common Fields or inclosed Grounds, the Boundary of which is already fenced, to make or erect any Hedges, Ditches, or Fences next and adjoining to any Part of such Boundary Fence already made, for inclosing such their Allotments or Shares; but that the ancient Mound or Fence, Brook or Rivulet, or other sufficient Fences which adjoin to such Allotments, shall for ever be and remain a Boundary Fence for the Purpose of such Division, and shall from time to time be maintained, kept, cleansed, scoured, and repaired by the respective Owners thereof in the same Manner as before the Passing of this Act; any Thing herein contained to the contrary notwithstanding.

nor against the Boundary Fences of other Parishes.

And be it further Enacted and Declared, That it shall not be lawful for any Person or Persons to graze or keep any Sheep or Lambs

No Sheep to be kept in Lanes, &c.

Lambs upon any of the Lands to be divided and allotted by virtue of this Act, or in any Lanes, Ways, or Passages on either Side whereof any new Fences shall be made, for the Space of   Years after making the said Award or Instrument, unless the Party or Parties desirous of grazing or keeping such Sheep or Lambs shall first make a good and sufficient Guard against the Fence or Fences of the Allotment adjoining, so that no Damage may be done thereto.

unless properly guarded.

And be it further Enacted, That from and immediately after the Passing of this Act the said Commissioners, or any   of them, shall from time to time order, direct, and appoint the Course of the Husbandry that shall be used in the Tillage Part of all the said open Fields, until such Time as they shall have completed their said Award; and that all and every Persons Estate in the same Fields shall during that Space be liable and subject to such Directions as the said Commissioners, or any   of them, shall appoint, as well with regard to the stocking as to the ploughing, tilling, sowing, or laying down the same.

Commissioners to appoint the Course of Husbandry.

And be it further Enacted, That it shall and may be lawful to and for the said *Middlemore Ward* and his Successors, Rectors as aforesaid, by and with the Consent of the Lord Bishop of *Lincoln* for the Time being, to grant any Lease or Leases to any Person or Persons whomsoever of the Lands or Grounds to be allotted to the said *Middlemore Ward* and his Successors, in Right of the said Rectory, by virtue of this Act, or of any Part or Parts thereof, for any Number of Years, not exceeding   Years, to be computed from the   next after the Execution of the said Award or Instrument, so as the best and most improved yearly Rent or Rents be thereby reserved and made payable to the Rector of the said Parish of *Woodstone* for the Time being   and so as the usual Powers of Re-entry for Non-payment of such Rent or Rents, and such other necessary Covenants be inserted therein as is usual in Cases of the like Nature, and so as the Lessee or Lessees in such Leases to be named do execute a Counter-part of such Lease or Leases; any Law, Usage, or Custom to the contrary thereof in any-wise notwithstanding.

The Rector may grant Leases,

for Years.

And be it further Enacted and Declared, That he the said *Middlemore Ward* and his Successors, Rectors of the Parish of *Woodstone* aforesaid for the Time being, shall be immediately upon the Execution of the said Award or Instrument, and for ever thereafter, freed and exempt from finding, providing, and maintaining

Rector exempted from keeping a Bull and a Boar.

D   a Bull

a Bull and Boar, or either of them, for the Benefit of the Inhabitants and Persons occupying Lands and Grounds within the said Parish of *Woodstone*.

<small>Proprietors required to accept Allotments.</small>

And be it further Enacted, That all and every Person and Persons intitled to any Allotment or Allotments to be made as aforesaid, shall and is and are hereby required to accept such Allotment or Allotments within the Space of ⸺ Calendar Months after the Execution of the said Award or Instrument, and public Notice given in the Parish Church of *Woodstone* aforesaid, on a *Sunday* immediately after Divine Service, and also Notice in Writing affixed on One of the Doors of the said Church for that Purpose, signed by the said Commissioners, or any ⸺ of them, which Notice the said Commissioners, or any ⸺ of them, are hereby required to cause to be so published and given; and every Person or Persons who shall neglect or refuse to accept of his, her, or their respective Allotment or Allotments within the Time herein before limited, shall be totally excluded from any Estate or Right of Common in any of the Lands or Grounds to be allotted to any other Person or Persons as aforesaid.

<small>Guardians are impowered to accept;</small>

Provided always, and be it further Enacted, That the Guardians, Committees, Husbands, Trustees, or Attornies, or Persons acting as Guardians, Committees, Trustees, or Attornies for any Person being an Infant, Ideot, Lunatic, Feme-covert, or beyond the Seas, or otherwise incapable by Law to accept any such Allotment, shall be and they are hereby enabled and required to accept thereof for the Use of every Person so incapacitated, and such Acceptance shall be as valid and effectual as if every such Person respectively was capable of acting for himself or herself, and had in Person made such Acceptance; any Thing herein contained to the contrary in any-wise notwithstanding.

<small>but their Non-acceptance shall not prejudice Persons under any Incapacity.</small>

Provided nevertheless, That the Non-claim or Non-acceptance of any Guardian, Husband, Trustee, Committee, or Attorney shall not exclude or prejudice the Claim or Acceptance of any Infant, Feme-covert, or any other Person under such Disability or Incapacity as aforesaid, who shall claim or accept after such Disability or Incapacity shall be removed, or of any Person or Persons intitled as Heir, or in Remainder or Reversion after the Death of any Person dying under such Disability or Incapacity who shall claim or accept within ⸺ after his, her, or their Right, Title, or Interest shall have descended, vested, or accrued.

And

And be it further Enacted, That nothing in this Act contained shall revoke, make void, alter, annul, or any-ways affect any Settlement, Deed, or Will whatsoever, or prejudice any Person or Persons having any Right or Claim of Dower, Jointure, Portion, Debt, Rent, Incumbrance, or other Demand out of, upon, or affecting any Lands so intended to be inclosed as aforesaid, or any of the Messuages, Cottages, or present inclosed Lands to be exchanged pursuant to this Act, or any Part thereof (other than and except such Leases or Agreements at Rack-rent as aforesaid) but that the Lands to be allotted, and the Messuages, Cottages, and present inclosed Lands to be exchanged in pursuance of this Act, shall immediately after the making such Division and Allotments, and the Execution of the said Award, go, remain, and enure, and be held and enjoyed, and the several Proprietors to whom the same shall be allotted, and with whom the same shall be exchanged, shall, from and immediately after the Execution of the said Award, stand and be seised and possessed thereof respectively, to such and the same Uses, and upon such and the same Trusts, and subject to such and the same Wills, Settlements, Powers, Provisoes, Limitations, Remainders, Trusts, Charges, Rents, Incumbrances, and Demands whatsoever (except as aforesaid) as he, she, or they respectively should and would have stood seised or possessed of and in his, her, or their Lands, Interest, or Property in the said open Fields, or in the said Messuages, Cottages, or present inclosed Lands (in respect or in lieu of which such Allotments or Exchanges shall be respectively made) in case this Act had not been made; any Thing herein contained to the contrary notwithstanding.

This Act not to affect any Will or Settlement.

And be it further Enacted, That the Charges and Expences incident and attending the obtaining of this Act, and of making the said Survey, and of preparing and inrolling the said Award or Instrument, and all other the Charges and Expences of the said Commissioners, and other necessary Expences about and concerning the Premises, and the said Inclosures and Allotments thereof, shall be borne and defrayed by the Owners and Proprietors and Persons interested as aforesaid in the said Lands and Grounds so appointed and intended to be inclosed (except the said *Middlemore Ward* and his Successors, Rectors as aforesaid, in respect to the Lands and Grounds to be allotted and Provision made to him in lieu of his said Glebe and Tithes) by an equal Pound Rate, according to the Value of the Lands and Grounds each and every such Person and Persons shall have allotted, assigned, or exchanged to or with him, her, or them by virtue of this Act, to be settled, adjusted, and determined by the said Commissioners or their Successors.

Expences how to be paid.

[16]

ceffors, or any   of them; and that in cafe any of the Perfons aforefaid fhall refufe or neglect to pay his, her, or their Share or Proportion, Shares or Proportions of fuch Charges and Expences within the Time limited by the faid Commiffioners or their Succeffors, or any   of them, to fuch Perfon or Perfons as they, or any   of them, fhall appoint to receive the fame, then the faid Commiffioners or their Succeffors, or any   of them, fhall and may and they are hereby authorized and required, by Warrant under their Hands and Seals directed to any Perfon or Perfons whomfoever, to caufe the refpective Proportions of fuch Charges and Expences aforefaid, which fhall not be paid according to fuch Directions as aforefaid, to be levied by   of the Goods and Chattels of the Perfon or Perfons fo neglecting or refufing to pay the fame, rendering the Overplus (if any) on Demand to the Owner or Owners of fuch Goods and Chattels, after deducting the Cofts of taking fuch   or otherwife it fhall and may be lawful for the faid Commiffioners or their Succeffors, or any   of them, or any Perfon or Perfons authorized by them, to   of the Premifes fo to be allotted or exchanged to and with fuch Perfon or Perfons refufing or neglecting to pay as aforefaid, and to   the Rents and Profits thereof until thereby, therewith, or otherwife the Share or Shares, Proportion or Proportions of the faid Cofts and Charges fo ordered and directed by the faid Commiffioners or their Succeffors, or any   of them, to be paid by fuch Perfon or Perfons as aforefaid, and alfo all Cofts, Charges, and Expences occafioned by or attending fuch   of the Rents and Profits of the faid Premifes, fhall refpectively be fully paid and fatisfied.

Power to borrow Money. **And whereas** feveral Perfons who fhall or may be intitled to accept fuch Allotments as aforefaid may have Occafion to borrow Money to defray their refpective Shares and Proportions of the Charges and Expences incident to and attending the obtaining and executing this Act, and of inclofing their refpective Allotments, and cannot, by reafon of fome Settlement or other Difability, make an effectual Security thereof for the Money neceffary to be borrowed for thofe Purpofes; **Be it therefore Enacted,** by the Authority aforefaid, That it fhall and may be lawful for and for any of the Perfons to whom any Allotment or Allotments fhall be made by virtue of this Act, being Tenants for Life or in Tail, and alfo for the Truftees, Guardians, Committees, or Attornies, or any Perfon or Perfons acting as fuch, of any of the faid Owners and Proprietors, being under Coverture, Minors, Ideots, Lunatics, or beyond

beyond the Seas, and to and for any Person or Persons seised or possessed of any of the said Lands intended to be inclosed for any charitable Uses, or upon any Trust, by and with the Consent and Approbation of the said Commissioners and their Successors, or any of them, signified by Writing under their Hands and Seals, to charge the Lands and Grounds to be allotted to such Owners and Proprietors respectively by virtue of this Act with any Sum or Sums of Money for the Purposes herein-before mentioned, not exceeding for every Acre of the said Lands and Grounds; and for securing the Repayment of the said Sum or Sums of Money, with Interest, to grant, mortgage, lease, or demise the Lands and Grounds so to be charged unto any Person or Persons who shall advance such Money respectively, for any Term or Number of Years, so as such Grant or Demise be made with a Proviso or Condition to cease and be void, or with an express Trust to be surrendered, when such Sum or Sums of Money, with the Interest thereof, and the Charges occasioned by the preparing and executing such Security and of borrowing such Money respectively, which shall be ascertained therein, shall be satisfied and paid; and do also contain a Proviso that the Premises thereby mortgaged shall not be liable at any particular Interval of Time to the Payment of any further Sum for the Arrears of Interest than for in respect of the Monies so to be charged upon such Lands as aforesaid.

And it is hereby further Enacted, That all and every Person or Persons to whom any Grant, Mortgage, Lease, or Demise shall be made by virtue of this Act as a Security for any Sum or Sums of Money by him, her, or them lent and advanced on the Credit and for the Purposes in this Act mentioned, or who shall be intitled to the Money thereby secured, shall and may from time to time by any Deed or Deeds, Writing or Writings, under his, her, or their Hand and Seal or Hands and Seals, to be executed in the Presence of Two or more credible Witnesses, assign or transfer the same Security or Securities, or the principal Money and Interest thereby secured, and all Benefit thereof, and all his, her, or their Right, Title, and Interest in and to the same, unto any Person or Persons whomsoever, who may again in like Manner assign the same, and so *toties quoties*; and such Mortgagee or Mortgagees, Assignee or Assignees, his, her, and their Executors and Administrators, and all Persons claiming under them or any of them, shall and may use, take, and pursue all such lawful Methods, Courses, and Expedients in Law or Equity for recovering and obtaining Possession of the Premises so to be mortgaged, demised, or assigned

Securities may be transferred.

as

as aforesaid, in case of Nonpayment of the principal Money and Interest to be thereby secured, or any Part thereof, as is or are used, taken, and pursued in other Cases of the like Nature.

Commissioners to account. **And be it further Enacted,** That the said Commissioners and their Successors shall and they are hereby required, at or before the Time of signing the said Award, to deliver to the Proprietors, or to such Person or Persons as they or the major Part of them in Value shall by themselves, their respective Agents or Attornies, appoint to receive the same, a particular Account in Writing of all Monies by them the said Commissioners from time to time laid out and assessed in, about, or concerning the said Division and Inclosure; which Account the said Proprietors, or the major Part of them in Value, shall and may and they are hereby authorized and impowered, if they think proper so to do, finally to pass, settle, and allow.

Power of Appeal. **And be it further Enacted,** by the Authority aforesaid, That if any Person or Persons shall think him, her, or themselves aggrieved by any Thing done in pursuance of this Act, then and in every such Case (except the Cases where the Orders and Determination of the said Commissioners are directed to be final) he, she, or they may appeal to the next General Quarter-Sessions of the Peace which shall be held by Adjournment, or otherwise, in and for the said County of *Huntingdon,* within   Months next after the Cause of Complaint shall have arisen; and the Justices in their said General Quarter-Sessions, or any Adjournment thereof, are hereby required to hear and determine the Matter of every such Appeal, and to make such Order therein, and award such Costs as to them in their Discretion shall seem reasonable; which Determination of the said Justices shall be final and conclusive to all Parties concerned, and shall not be removed or removeable by *Certiorari* or any other Writ or Process whatsoever in any of his Majesty's Courts of Record at *Westminster* or elsewhere.

Saving to Lords of Manors. **Provided always, and be it Enacted and Declared,** That nothing in this Act contained shall prejudice, lessen, or defeat the Right, Title, or Interest of the said *Carrier Thompson,* his Heirs and Assigns, of, in, or to the Seigniories or Royalties, incident or belonging to the said Manor of *Woodstone,* or any other Manor or Lordship, or reputed Manor or Lordship, within the Jurisdiction or Limits whereof the said Lands, Grounds, and Premises hereby directed to be inclosed, or any Part or Parts thereof, are lying and being; but that he the said *Carrier Thompson,* his

Heirs

Heirs and Assigns, as Lord or Lords thereof, shall and may from time to time and at all Times hereafter hold and enjoy all Rents, Services, Courts, Perquisites and Profits of Courts, and all other Royalties and Privileges to the said Manors or Lordships, reputed Manors or Lordships, or to the said Lord or Lords thereof, or any claiming under him or them, incident or appendant, belonging or appertaining (other than and except such Right of Common as can or may be claimed by or belonging to him or them respectively as Lord or Lords, in, over, and upon the Lands and Grounds so to be divided and inclosed as aforesaid) in as full, ample, and beneficial a Manner to all Intents and Purposes as he or they ought or might have held and enjoyed the same before the Passing of this Act, or in case the same had never been made.

Saving always to the KING's most Excellent MAJESTY, his Heirs and Successors, and to all and every other Person and Persons, Bodies Politic and Corporate, his, her, or their Heirs, Successors, Executors, and Administrators (other than and except such Bodies Politic and Corporate, and such Person and Persons, his, her, and their Heirs, Successors, Executors, Administrators, and Assigns, to whom any Allotment shall be made by virtue of this Act, and all Persons claiming by, from, or under them, or any of them respectively) all such Estate, Right, Title, and Interest as they, every or any of them, had and enjoyed of, in, to, or out of the said Lands and Grounds before the Passing of this Act, or could or ought to have had and enjoyed in case the same had not been made; but no Person or Persons, Bodies Politic or Corporate, his, her, or their Heirs, Executors, Administrators, or Successors, shall have Power to disturb any of the Allotments to be made in pursuance of this Act, but shall accept the several Allotments which shall be made, in Lieu of the Tithes, Dues, Payments, Lands, Common Right, and other Interest in the said Lands and Grounds which he, she, or they would have been intitled to in case this Act had not been made.

General Saving.

[1776.]

A

BILL

FOR

Dividing and Inclosing several Open and Common Fields, and other Commonable Lands and Grounds, within the Parish of *Woodstone*, in the County of *Huntingdon*.

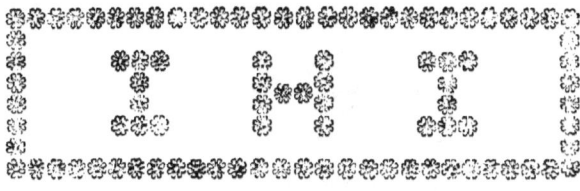

A

BILL

FOR

The Payment of Costs to Parties, and Charges to Constables, Witnesses, and others, on Complaints determined before Justices of the Peace out of Sessions; for making a Constables Rate; and for the Payment of Charges to Witnesses and Prosecutors of any Larceny or other Felony, in certain Cases.

Note.—*The Figures in the Margin denote the Number of the Folios in the written Copy.*

WHEREAS by the Laws now in being, His Majesty's Justices of the Peace are not sufficiently authorised, on Complaints that come before them out of Sessions, to award Costs against either the Person or Persons complaining, or the Person or Persons against whom any Complaint is made, as to Justice may appertain

A May

[2]

May it therefore please Your MAJESTY,

That it may be Enacted: **And be it Enacted** by the KING's Most Excellent MAJESTY, by and with the Advice and Consent of the Lords Spiritual and Temporal, and Commons, in this present Parliament assembled, and by the Authority of the same, That in all Cases whatsoever, where any Complaint shall be made before any of His Majesty's Justices of the Peace, for any County, City, Riding, Division, or Liberty, and any Warrant or Summons shall issue in consequence of such Complaint, that then it shall and may be lawful to and for any Justice or Justices of the Peace, who shall have heard and determined the Matter of the said Complaint, to award such Costs, and in Manner and Form, as to him or them shall seem fit, as well to the Party injured, as also a reasonable Satisfaction for the Trouble and Loss of Time of the Constable and Persons summoned to appear, and appearing, to give their Evidence before such Justice or Justices: And in case any Person, so ordered by the said Justice or Justices of the Peace to pay such Sum or Sums of Money as aforesaid, shall refuse or neglect, for the Space of   Days, to pay the said Sum or Sums of Money, it shall and may be lawful for the said Justice or Justices, by Warrant under his or their Hand and Seal, or Hands and Seals, to levy the said Sum or Sums by   of the Goods and Chattels of such Person so refusing or neglecting.

Provided nevertheless, That upon the Conviction of any Person or Persons upon any Penal Statute or Statutes, the said Costs, and Satisfaction for Charges, Trouble, and Loss of Time, shall be deducted by the said Justice or Justices, according to his or their Discretion, out of the said Penalty or Penalties, and the Remainder of the said Penalty or Penalties shall be paid to or divided among the Person or Persons, who would have been entitled to the Whole of the Penalty or Penalties, in case this Act had not been made.

And whereas Constables, Headboroughs, and Tythingmen, are or may be at great Charge and Loss of Time in doing the Business of their Parish or Township, and in many Cases are not sufficiently indemnified by the Laws now in being for the same: **Be it therefore Enacted,** That Constables, Headboroughs, or Tythingmen, may, at going out of Office, produce their Account of all such Charges and Recompence for the Loss of Time, in all such Cases not hitherto provided

provided for by the Laws heretofore made, or by this Act, to any of His Majesty's Justices of the Peace in and for the said County, Riding, Division, City, or Liberty; and they, together with the Churchwardens, and Overseers of the Poor, and other Inhabitants of the said Parish or Township, shall hereby have Power and Authority to make an indifferent Rate, and to tax all the Occupiers of Lands and Inhabitants, and all other Persons chargeable by the Statute made in the Forty-third Year of Queen *Elizabeth*, concerning the Office and Duty of Overseers of the Poor, within the said Parish or Township; which Account and Rate being approved of, and confirmed under the Hands and Seals of any Justices of the Peace as aforesaid, the said Constable, Headborough, or Tythingman, shall have Power, by Warrant under the Hand and Seal of One Justice of the Peace, to levy by of the Goods and Chattels of any Person or Persons refusing to pay the same.

And be it further Enacted, That in case any Person or Persons shall find him, her, or themselves, aggrieved by any such Account, Rate, or Assessment, or any Part thereof, or shall have any material Objection to any Person or Persons being put on or left out of such Rate, or to the Sum charged on any Person or Persons therein, or to such Account, or any Part thereof, or shall find him, her, or themselves aggrieved by any Neglect, Act, or Thing done or omitted by the said Constables, Headboroughs, or Tythingmen, or any of them, or by His Majesty's said Justices of the Peace, it shall and may be lawful for such Person or Persons, in any of the Cases aforesaid, giving reasonable Notice to the said Constables, Headboroughs, or Tythingmen, to appeal to the next General Quarter Sessions of the Peace for the County, City, Riding, Division, or Liberty, where such Parish, Township, or Place lies; and the Justices of the Peace there assembled, are hereby authorised and required to receive such Appeal, and hear and finally determine the same, and may award and order to the Party for whom the Appeal shall be determined such reasonable Costs as to the said Justices shall seem proper: Provided always, That in all Cities or Liberties which have not Justices of the Peace, it shall and may be lawful for any Person or Persons, in any of the Cases aforesaid, where an Appeal is given by this Act, to appeal, if he, she, or they shall
think

think fit, to the next General Quarter Sessions of the Peace for the County, Riding, or Division, wherein such City or Liberty is situate.

6 And whereas, by an Act passed in the Twenty-fifth Year of his late Majesty King *George* the Second, intituled, " An Act for the better preventing Thefts and Robberies, and for regulating Places of Public Entertainment, and punishing Persons keeping disorderly Houses," it was recited, that " Whereas many Persons are deterred from prosecuting Persons guilty of Felony, upon Account of the Expence attending such Prosecutions, which is a Cause of the Encouragement of Thefts ;" and it was therein, among other Things enacted, that it should and might be in the Power of the Court before whom any Person has been tried and convicted of any Grand or Petit Larceny, or other Felony, at the Prayer of the Prosecutor, and on Consideration of his Circumstances, to order the Treasurer of the County in which the Offence shall have been committed, to pay unto such Prosecutor such Sum of Money as to the said Court shall seem reasonable, not exceeding the Expences which it shall appear to the Court the Prosecutor was put unto in carrying on such Prosecution, making him a reasonable Allowance for his Time and Trouble therein; which Order the Clerk of Assize or Clerk of the Peace respectively was thereby directed and required forthwith to make out, and to deliver unto such Prosecutor, upon being paid for the same the Sum of One Shilling, and no more:

7 And whereas, by an Act passed in the Twenty-seventh Year of his late Majesty King *George* the Second, reciting that the Expence, as well as Loss of Time, in attending Courts of Justice, is a Discouragement to the poorer Sort to appear as Witnesses against Offenders, who thereby escape the public Justice, and the Punishment due to their Crimes, it was enacted, That when any poor Person shall appear on Recognizance in any Court to give Evidence against another accused of any Grand or Petit Larceny or other Felony, it should and might be in the Power of the Court, at the Prayer, and on the Oath of such Person, and on Consideration of his Circumstances, in open Court, to pay unto such Person such Sum of Money, as to the said Court shall seem reasonable, for his Time, Trouble, and Expence; which Order the proper Officer of such Court is required to make out and deliver to such Person, upon being paid for the same the Sum of Six Pence, and no more:

And

And whereas the said recited Acts of the Twenty-fifth and Twenty-seventh Years of his late Majesty King *George* the Second have been a great Encouragement towards bringing Offenders to Justice, in all such Cases as are within the Purview of the said Statutes; but, nevertheless, it has been found by Experience, that the said recited Statute of the Twenty-seventh Year of his said late Majesty, with regard to Persons appearing on Recognizance in any Court to give Evidence as aforesaid, extends only to such poor Persons as shall make Oath of their Poverty, such Court also considering their Circumstances:

And whereas the said Act of the Twenty-fifth Year of his said late Majesty, with regard to Prosecutors, directs the Court to consider the Circumstances of such Prosecutor, and also gives him Relief only where the Offender is convicted:

And whereas it is just and reasonable, and may tend in future to the due Prosecution of all Offenders against the Laws, that every Prosecutor to Conviction, and every Person so appearing on Recognizance, should be allowed his reasonable Expences, and also, in case he be poor, a reasonable Satisfaction for his Trouble and Loss of Time; and that such Allowance should be made to Prosecutors as aforesaid even though the Person so accused be acquitted: Provided it shall appear to such Court before whom the said Prisoner shall have been tried, that there was a reasonable Ground of Prosecution:

Be it further Enacted by the Authority aforesaid, That from and after the   Day of   it shall and may be in the Power of the Court before whom any Person has been convicted, or in case it shall appear unto the said Court, that there was a reasonable Ground of Prosecution, though such Person shall be acquitted, of any Grand or Petit Larceny, or other Felony, to grant to the said Prosecutor, upon the Prayer of such Prosecutor, a Certificate of such Prosecution, under the Hand of the Clerk of Assize or his lawful Deputy, or the Clerk of the Peace or his lawful Deputy, as the Case may be, he receiving for the same from the said Prosecutor the Sum of   and no more.

And be it Enacted by the Authority aforesaid, That from and after the   Day of   when any Person or Persons shall appear on Recognizance to give Evidence upon any Indictment for any Grand or Petit Larceny, or or other Felony, it shall and may be in the Power of the Court, at the Prayer of such Person or Persons, to grant to him, her, or them, a Certificate that such Person or Persons has or have appeared on Recognizance in such Court to give Evidence, under the Hand of the Clerk of Assize or his lawful Deputy, or the Clerk of the Peace or his lawful Deputy, as the Case may be, he receiving for the same, from the said Person or Persons, the Sum of   and no more.

And be it Enacted by the Authority aforesaid, That from and after the   Day of   His Majesty's Justices of the Peace shall, at every Quarter Sessions of the Peace wherein such Certificate or Certificates shall have been granted, or in case the same shall have been granted at the Assizes, then at the next Quarter Sessions of the Peace to be holden in and for the County, City, Riding, Division, or Liberty, either then examine into the said Certificate or Certificates, in Manner as hereinafter is mentioned, or appoint a Day or Days for the holding a special Sessions for the Purpose of examining the said Certificate or Certificates, within the Space of   after such General Quarter Sessions, at which Time or Times the Person or Persons having such Certificate as aforesaid, shall deliver in to the said Quarter Sessions, or Special Sessions, his, her, or their said Certificate, together with an Account in Writing of the reasonable Expences he, she, or they, shall have been put unto by Reason of the said Prosecution or the said Appearance on Recognizance, which said Account the said Justices of the Peace, or any   or more of them, shall examine into, upon Oath, or otherwise, and tax the same as to them shall seem meet, allowing to the said Person or Persons such Sum of Money as they shall think reasonable, not exceeding the Expences which it shall appear to them that the said Person or Persons was or were, *bona fide*, put unto by Reason of the said Prosecution or Appearance on Recognzance; and in case the said Person or Persons shall appear to them in poor Circumstances, then it shall and may be lawful for the said Justices of the Peace to allow to the said Person or Persons a reasonable Satisfaction for his, her, or their Trouble and Loss of Time, and the said Justices of the Peace may make out an Order, under the Hands and Seals of   or more of them, upon the Treasurer of the County, Riding, or Division, for the Payment

[7]

ment of the said Sum of Money to the said Person or Persons, upon being paid by him, her, or them, for the same, the Sum of   and no more; and such Treasurer is hereby authorized and required, upon Delivery of such Order, forthwith to pay unto such Person or Persons authorized to receive the same, such Sum of Money as aforesaid, and he shall be allowed the same in his Accounts.

And be it further Enacted by the Authority aforesaid, That if any Action or Suit shall be commenced against any Person or Persons, for any Thing done in Pursuance of this Act, the Defendant or Defendants in any such Action or Suit may plead the General Issue, and give this Act and the Special Matter in Evidence, at any Trial to be had thereupon, and that the same was done in Pursuance, and by the Authority of this Act; and if it shall appear so to have been done, the Jury shall find for the Defendant or Defendants; and if the Plaintiff shall be nonsuit, or discontinue his Action after the Defendant or Defendants shall have appeared, or if Judgment shall be given upon any Verdict or Demurrer against the Plaintiff, the Defendant and Defendants shall and may recover   Costs, and have the like Remedy for the same, as the Defendant or Defendants hath or have in other Cases by Law.

A

BILL

For the Payment of Costs to Parties, and Charges to Constables, Witnesses, and others, on Complaints determined before Justices of the Peace out of Sessions; for making a Constable's Rate; and for the Payment of Charges to Witnesses and Prosecutors of any Larceny or other Felony, in certain Cases,

1776.

A

BILL

[With the Amendments]

TO

Promote the Refidence of the Parochial Clergy, by making Provifion for the more fpeedy and effectual building, re-building, or repairing, Parfonage Houfes; and for erecting or repairing other neceffary Buildings upon the Glebes belonging thereto.

N. B. *The Words printed in* Italics, *and between Brackets, thus* [ ], *were inferted by the Committee.*

Note.—*The Figures in the Margin denote the Numbers of the Folios in the written Copy.*

WHEREAS many of the Parochial Clergy, for Want of proper Habitations, are induced to refide at a Diftance from their Benefices; by which Means the Parithioners lofe the Advantage of their Inftruction and Hofpitality, which were great Objects in the original Diftribution of Tythes and Glebes for the Endowment of Churches: **For** Remedy whereof,

1

May it please Your MAJESTY,

That it may be Enacted; And be it Enacted by the KING's most Excellent MAJESTY, by and with the Advice and Consent of the Lords Spiritual and Temporal, and Commons, in this present Parliament assembled, and by the Authority of the same, That from and after the [*Twenty-fourth*] Day of [*June One thousand Seven hundred and Seventy-seven,*] whenever the Parson, Vicar, or other Incumbent, of any Ecclesiastical Living, whereon there is no Parsonage House, or such House is become so ruinous and decayed that [*One Year*] neat Income and Produce of such Living will not be sufficient to re-build, or put the same, with the necessary Offices belonging thereto, in sufficient Repair, shall think fit to apply for the Aid and Assistance intended to be given by this Act, it shall and may be lawful for every such Parson, Vicar, or Incumbent (after having procured from some skilful and experienced Workman or Surveyor, a Certificate of the State and Condition of the Buildings on such Glebe, and of the Value of the Timber and other Materials thereupon, fit to be employed in such Buildings or Repairs, and also a Plan and Estimate of the Work proposed to be done, and laid the same, together with a just and particular Account in Writing, signed by him, of the annual Profits of such Living, before the Ordinary of the Diocese, and Patron of the Living, and obtained their Consent to such proposed new Buildings or Repairs, by Writing under their respective Hands, in the Form for that Purpose contained in the Schedule hereunto annexed) to borrow and take up at Interest, in the Manner hereafter mentioned, such Sum or Sums of Money as the said Estimate shall amount unto, not exceeding [*Two Years*] neat Income and Produce of such Living, after deducting all Rents, Stipends, Taxes, and other Outgoings; and, as a Security for the Money so to be borrowed, to mortgage the Glebe, Tythes, Rents, and other Profits and Emoluments, arising or to arise from such Living, to such Person or Persons who shall advance the same, by One or more Deed or Deeds, for the Term of [*Twenty-one Years,*] or until the Money so to be borrowed, with Interest for the same, and such Costs and Charges as may attend the Recovery thereof, shall be fully paid and satisfied, according to the Terms, Conditions, true Intent and Meaning of this Act; which Mortgage Deed or Deeds shall

be

be made in the Form or to the Effect for that Purpose contained in the said Schedule, and shall bind every succeeding Parson, Vicar, or Incumbent, of such Living, until the Principal and Interest, Costs and Charges, shall be paid off and discharged, as fully and effectually as if such Successor had executed the same.

And be it further Enacted, That every such Mortgagee shall execute a Counterpart of every such respective Mortgage Deed, to be kept by the Incumbent for the Time being; and a Copy of every such Mortgage Deed shall be registered with the Clerk of the Consistory Court of the Bishop of the Diocese for the Time being, after having been first examined by him with the Original, and shall be referred to upon all necessary Occasions (the Person inspecting the same paying [*Two Shillings and Six Pence*] for every Search) and shall be allowed as legal Evidence in case such Mortgage Deed shall happen to be lost or destroyed.

And be it further Enacted, That the Money so to be borrowed, shall be paid into the Hands of such Person or Persons as shall be nominated and appointed to receive and apply the same, for the Purposes aforesaid, by the Ordinary, Patron, and Incumbent, by Writing under their respective Hands, in the Form for that Purpose contained in the said Schedule; and the Receipt of the Person or Persons so to be nominated, shall be a sufficient Discharge to the Person or Persons who shall advance and lend the Money upon such Mortgage or Mortgages; and the Person or Persons so to be nominated shall enter into Contracts with proper Persons for such Buildings or Repairs as shall be approved by the Patron, Ordinary, and Incumbent, and shall be specified in an Instrument wrote upon Parchment, and signed by them, in the Form for that Purpose contained in the said Schedule; and shall inspect and have the Care of the Execution of such Contracts; and shall pay the Money for such Buildings and Repairs, according to the Terms of such Agreement, and shall take proper Receipts and Vouchers for the same; and, as soon as such Buildings or Repairs shall be completed, and the Money paid, shall make out an Account of his Receipts and Payments, and enter them in a Book, fairly wrote, which shall be signed by him, and laid before the Patron, Ordinary, and Incumbent, and examined by them; and when allowed, by Writing under their respective Hands, in the Form for that Purpose contained in the said Schedule, such

Allowance

Allowance shall be a full Discharge to the Person so nominated, in respect to the said Account; and if any Balance shall remain in the Hands of such Nominee or Nominees, the same shall be either laid out in some further lasting Improvements in Buildings upon such Glebe, or shall be paid and applied in the Discharge of so much of the said Principal Debt as such Balance will extend to pay, at the Discretion of the said Ordinary, Patron, and Incumbent, by Order signed by them, in the Form for that Purpose contained in the said Schedule; and an Account shall also be kept, made out, and allowed, of such further Disbursements, in Manner aforesaid; all which Accounts, when made out, completed, and allowed, shall be deposited, with the Vouchers, in the Hands of the said Clerk of the Consistory Court, and kept by him for the Use and Benefit of the Incumbents of such Living for the Time being; who shall have a Right to inspect the same whenever Occasion shall require, paying to such Clerk the Sum of [*Two Shillings and Six Pence*] for every such Inspection.

Provided always, and be it further Enacted, That every such Ordinary, before he shall signify his Consent in Manner aforesaid, shall cause an Enquiry to be made, and certified to him, by [*Two*] Clergymen within his Diocese, living near the Parish where such Buildings are proposed to be made or repaired, in the Forms for that Purpose specified in the said Schedule, of the State and Condition of such Buildings at the Time the Incumbent entered upon such Living, how long such Incumbent had enjoyed such Living, what Money he had received for Dilapidations, and how and in what Manner he had laid out the same; and if it shall appear to them that such Incumbent had, by wilful Negligence, suffered such Buildings to go out of Repair, then to certify the same to the said Ordinary, and also the Amount of the Damage which such Buildings had sustained by the wilful Neglect of such Incumbent; and such Incumbent shall pay the same into the Hands of the Nominee or Nominees to be appointed under the Authority of this Act, towards defraying the Expences of such Building or Repairs, before the Ordinary shall give his Consent as aforesaid.

And be it further Enacted, That the Incumbent of every such Living, and his Successors for the Time being, shall, and he and they is and are hereby required to pay the Interest arising upon every such Mortgage [*Half-yearly*,]

[5]

as the same shall become due, or within [*One Month*] after, and also [*Six Pounds*] per Centum of the Principal remaining due, by [*Half-yearly*] Payments; and that every such Incumbent who shall not reside [*Six Calendar Months*] in the Year upon such Living (computing such Year from the [*First Day of January*]) shall, instead of the said Sum of [*Six Pounds*] per Centum per Annum, pay the Sum of [*Eight Pounds*] per Centum per Annum of the Principal remaining due, by [*Half-yearly*] Payments (such Payments to be respectively made at the same Time such Interest shall be paid) until the whole Principal Money and Interest shall be fully paid and discharged; and that every such Incumbent shall annually, at his Expence, from the Time such Buildings authorized to be made by this Act shall be completed, insure, at One of the Public Offices established in London or Westminster for Insurance of Houses and Buildings, the House and other Buildings upon such Glebe, against Accidents by Fire, at such Sum of Money as shall be agreed upon by the Patron, Ordinary, and Incumbent.

8

And be it further Enacted, That at or before the Day on which the Money so to be borrowed and secured as aforesaid shall be paid, the Incumbent shall, with One sufficient Surety, become bound to the Ordinary of the Diocese and his Successors in a penal Sum to the Amount of the Sum so to be borrowed, with Condition that such Incumbent shall, as soon as such Building and Repairs shall be completed, and afterwards annually, so long as he holds the said Living, insure the House and Buildings upon such Glebe, in Manner and at the Sum aforesaid, against Accidents by Fire; and that every succeeding Incumbent of such Living shall give a Bond of the like Sort, with sufficient Surety, to the Ordinary of the Diocese, before he shall be instituted and inducted thereto, in such Penalty, not exceeding the Penalty aforesaid, as the Ordinary shall think proper; which Ordinaries are hereby required to take such respective Bonds, and keep them with Safety, that they may be transmitted to their respective Successors.

9

And be it further Enacted, That every such Parson, Vicar, or Incumbent, shall, at the Time he executes such Mortgage Deed or Deeds, also execute a Bond or Bonds to the Mortgagee or Mortgagees, in the Penalty of the Sum to be secured by each respective Mortgage Deed, conditioned

B

tioned for the due Payment and Discharge of the Interest and Principal [*Half-yearly*,] during the Time he shall enjoy such Living, according to the Direction and the true Meaning of this Act; and shall also, at the same Time, execute another Bond, with One sufficient Surety, to such Mortgagee, in a penal Sum equal to the Double of the Sum to be paid within the First Year for such Interest and Principal, conditioned for the Payment of such Sum or Sums of Money as such Parson, Vicar, or Incumbent, or his Representatives, in case of Avoidance of such Living by Death or otherwise, shall be liable to pay for the growing [*Half Year*] in which such Death or Avoidance shall happen, according to the Direction of this Act.

And, in order that the Payment for such [*Half Year*] may be justly and equitably ascertained and adjusted between the Successor and such Parson, Vicar, or Incumbent, so avoiding such Living, or his Representatives in case of Death or other Avoidance, in such Proportions as the Profits of such Living shall have been received by them respectively for the Year in which such Death or Avoidance shall happen; **Be it further Enacted**, That in case any Difference shall arise in adjusting or settling the Proportions aforesaid, the same shall be determined by Two indifferent Persons, the one to be named by the said Successor, and the other by the Person making such Avoidance, or his Representatives in case of his Death; and in case such Nominees shall not be appointed within the Space of [*Two Calendar Months next after such Death or Avoidance*,] or if they cannot agree in adjusting such Proportions within the Space of [*One Calendar Month*] after they shall have been appointed, the same shall be determined by some neighbouring Clergyman, to be nominated by the Ordinary of the Diocese, whose Determination shall be final and conclusive between the Parties; which Nominations and Determinations shall be made according to the Forms for that Purpose contained in the said Schedule, as near as conveniently may be.

And be it further Enacted, That where there shall be no Parsonage House upon any Ecclesiastical Living so described as aforesaid, or being one, the same shall be in such a State of Decay as aforesaid, and the Incumbent shall not reside in the same for such Time within the Year as aforesaid, it shall be lawful for the Patron of such Living, with the Consent of the
Ordinary,

Ordinary (in case the Incumbent shall not think fit to make such Application as aforesaid for building, repairing, or rebuilding such Parsonage House) to procure such Plan, Estimate, and Certificate, as herein directed, and to proceed in the Execution of the several Purposes of this Act in such Manner as the Parson, Vicar, or Incumbent is hereby authorized and directed to proceed, and to make and execute such Mortgage as aforesaid, which shall be binding upon the Incumbent and his Successors; and he and they shall be, and are hereby, made liable to the Payment of the Interest, Principal, and Costs, and also to the Expences of Insuring according to the Directions aforesaid, as fully and effectually as if he and they had respectively executed such Mortgage and Bond; and every such Incumbent and his Representatives shall be, and are hereby, also made respectively liable to the Proportion of the Payments for the [*Half Year*] which shall be growing at the Time of the Death of such Incumbent, or Avoidance of such Living, according to the Direction aforesaid.

12

𝔄𝔫𝔡 𝔟𝔢 𝔦𝔱 𝔣𝔲𝔯𝔱𝔥𝔢𝔯 𝔈𝔫𝔞𝔠𝔱𝔢𝔡, That all Sum and Sums of Money recovered or received by Suit or Compositions from the Representatives of any former Incumbent of such Living, and not laid out in the Repairs of such Buildings, shall go and be applied in Part of the Payments under such Estimate as aforesaid; and that all Money thereafter to be so recovered or received (in case the same cannot be had before such Buildings are completed, and the Money paid for the same) shall be applied, as soon as received, in Payment of the Principal then due on such Mortgage or Mortgages, as far as the same will extend.

13

𝔓𝔯𝔬𝔳𝔦𝔡𝔢𝔡 𝔞𝔩𝔴𝔞𝔶𝔰, 𝔞𝔫𝔡 𝔟𝔢 𝔦𝔱 𝔣𝔲𝔯𝔱𝔥𝔢𝔯 𝔈𝔫𝔞𝔠𝔱𝔢𝔡, That whenever the Patron of any Living, to which the Provisions of this Act are proposed to be extended, shall happen to be a Minor, it shall and may be lawful for the Guardian of every such Patron to transact the several Matters aforesaid for such Patron, who shall be bound thereby in such Manner as if he had been of full Age, and had done such Act, or given his Consent thereto.

𝔓𝔯𝔬𝔳𝔦𝔡𝔢𝔡 𝔞𝔩𝔰𝔬, 𝔞𝔫𝔡 𝔟𝔢 𝔦𝔱 𝔣𝔲𝔯𝔱𝔥𝔢𝔯 𝔈𝔫𝔞𝔠𝔱𝔢𝔡, That all Acts hereinbefore required to be done, or contented to, by the Ordinary and Patron, shall be done by the Ordinary alone, when such Ordinary shall happen to be the Patron of the Living;

[8]

ing; and that no Deed, Bond, Transfer, or other Writing, Inſtrument, or Proceeding, made, had, or done under the Powers or Authority of this Act, ſhall be charged or chargeable with any Stamp or Duty whatſoever, any Law or Statute to the contrary notwithſtanding.

14 **Provided likewiſe, and be it further Enacted,** That whenever any Controverſy or Diſpute ſhall ariſe touching the Reſidence of the Incumbent, with reſpect to any of the Matters contained in this Act, the ſame ſhall be adjuſted and determined by the Ordinary of the Dioceſe.

SCHEDULE

SCHEDULE,

To which the BILL refers.

FORM of the CONSENT of the Ordinary and Patron.

To be wrote on Parchment.

A. B. Rector, Vicar, &c. (as the Case shall be) of the Parish and Parish Church of   in the County of   within the Diocese of the Bishop of   having produced to us the Right Reverend   Ordinary of the said Diocese, and   Patron of the said Church and Living, a Certificate under the Hand of   a skilful and experienced Workman or Surveyor, of the State and Condition of the Buildings upon the Glebe belonging to the said Church, and of the Value of the Timber and other Materials thereupon fit to be employed about such Buildings, and also a Plan made by the said   of the Work proposed to be done by new Buildings and Repairs upon the said Glebe, and an Estimate of the Expence attending the same, after applying the said Materials, or the Money to arise from the Sale thereof, in such Buildings and Repairs; and also a particular Account in Writing, signed by the said *A. B.* of the annual Profits of such Living, and of the Rents, Stipends, Taxes, and other Outgoing, annually issuing thereout, pursuant to the Directions of an Act, passed in the Sixteenth Year of the Reign of His Majesty King *George* the Third, for promoting the Residence of the Parochial Clergy, by making Provision for the more speedy and effectual building, re-building, or repairing, Parsonage Houses, and for erecting or repairing other necessary Buildings upon the Glebes belonging thereto; and having considered such Certificate, Plan, and Account, we do approve thereof, and do consent that such Buildings and Re-

C   pairs

[10]

pairs shall be made as therein specified, and that the said *A. B.* do borrow and take up at Interest the Sum of   being, as appears to us from the said Account, a Sum not exceeding Two Years neat Income and Produce of the said Living; which Money is to be paid to   (a Person nominated by us and the said *A. B.*) and applied according to the Direction of the said Act.

---

17   FORM of the MORTGAGE.

THIS Indenture, made the   Day of   in the   Year of the Reign of His Majesty   and in the Year of our Lord   between the Reverend   Rector or Vicar, &c. of the Parish Church of   in the County of   and Diocese of the Bishop of   of the One Part, and   of   of the other Part. Whereas the said   pursuant to the Directions of an Act, passed in the Sixteenth Year of the Reign of His Majesty King *George* the Third, intituled " An Act to " promote the Residence of the Parochial Clergy, by making " Provision for the more speedy and effectual building, re-" building, or repairing, Parsonage Houses; and for erecting " or repairing other necessary Buildings upon the Glebes " belonging thereto," hath obtained the Consent of the Ordinary of the said Diocese, and the Patron of the said Church and Living, to borrow and take up at Interest the Sum of   to be laid out and expended in

18 building, re-building, or repairing (as the Case shall be) the Parsonage House, and other necessary Offices upon the Glebe belonging to the said Church, as appears by an Instrument signed by the said Ordinary and Patron, hereunto annexed: And whereas the said   hath agreed to lend and advance the said Sum of   upon a Mortgage of the Glebe, Tythes, Rents, and other Profits and Emoluments of the said Living, pursuant to the Direction and the true Intent and Meaning of the said Act: Now this Indenture witnesseth, That the said   in Consideration of the Sum of Five Shillings to him in Hand paid, and of the said Sum of   paid,

at

at or before the Sealing and Delivery hereof, into the Hands of   a Person or Persons (as the Case shall be) nominated by the said Ordinary, Patron, and Incumbent, to receive the same, pursuant to the Direction of the said Act (which Nomination is also hereunto annexed, and which Receipt of the said Sum of
the said   have or hath acknowledged by an Indorsement on the Back of this Deed) hath granted, bargained, sold, and demised, and by these Presents doth grant, bargain, sell, and demise, unto the said
his Executors, Administrators, and Assigns, all the Glebe Lands, Tythes, Rents, Modus's, Compositions for Tythe, Salaries, Stipends, Fees, Gratuities, and other Emoluments and Profits whatsoever, arising, coming, growing, renewing, or payable, to the Rector, Vicar, or Incumbent (as the Case shall be) of the said Living, in respect thereof, with all and every their Rights, Privileges, and Appurtenances thereunto belonging, to have, hold, receive, take, and enjoy the said Premisses, with their and every of their Appurtenances, unto the said   his Executors, Administrators, and Assigns, from henceforth, for and during the Term of   Years, fully to be complete and ended, in as full, ample, and beneficial Manner, and with such Remedies and Powers for obtaining and recovering the same and every Part thereof, to all Intents and Purposes, as the said   or his Successors, Rectors, Vicars, &c. (as the Case shall be) of the said Church, could or might, or ought to have held, enjoyed, received, taken, or recovered the same, if these Presents had not been made: And the said *A. B.* for himself, his Heirs, Executors, and Administrators, doth hereby covenant, promise, and agree, to and with the said
his Executors, Administrators, and Assigns, That he the said *A. B.* during the Time he shall continue Rector, Vicar, &c. of the said Parish and Parish Church, shall and will well and truly pay, or cause to be paid, unto the said
his Executors, Administrators, or Assigns, Interest for the said Sum of   or so much thereof as shall remain due at the End of every Year, to be computed from the Day of the Date of these Presents, after the Rate of   *per Centum per Annum*, by Two equal Half-yearly Payments, the First of the said Payments to begin and be made on the   Day of   next; and also, at the several Times before mentioned for Payment of the Interest as aforesaid, shall and

will

[right margin: 19, 20, 21]

will well and truly pay, or caufe to be paid, the Sum of   *per Centum per Annum* of the Principal which remained due at the Beginning of the Year in which every fuch Payment is to be paid, in cafe the faid *A. B.* fhall be refident upon the faid Living for the Time, and according to the true Intent and Meaning of the faid Act; and in cafe the faid *A. B.* fhall not refide upon the faid Living during the Time, and according to the true Intent and Meaning of the faid Act, he fhall pay, or caufe to be paid, the Sum of   *per Centum per Annum* of the faid Principal Money, by fuch Half-yearly Payments as aforefaid, inftead of the faid Sum of   *per Centum per Annum*, and fhall and will continue fuch refpective Payments of the faid Intereft, and on Account of the faid Principal Money, fo long as he fhall continue Rector, Vicar, &c. (as the Cafe fhall be) of the faid Parifh and Parifh Church, unlefs all the faid Principal Money, and Intereft for the fame, fhall be fooner paid and difcharged. Provided always, and thefe Prefents are upon this Condition, That if the faid *A. B.* and his Succeffors fhall well and truly pay, or caufe to be paid, the faid Principal Money, and Intereft for the fame, in Manner and at the Times aforefaid, according to the true Intent and Meaning of the faid Act and of thefe Prefents, and alfo all Cofts and Charges which fhall have been occafioned by the Non-payment thereof, thefe Prefents and every Thing herein contained fhall ceafe and be void. Provided alfo, That it fhall and may be lawful for the faid *A. B.* and his Succeffors peaceably and quietly to hold, occupy, poffefs, and enjoy, all and fingular the faid Glebe Lands, Tythes, Rents, Modufes, Compofition for Tythes, Stipends, Fees, Gratuities, and other Emoluments and Profits whatfoever, arifing or to arife from or in refpect of the faid Living, until Default fhall be made by him or them refpectively in the Payment of the Intereft and Principal, or fome Part thereof, at the Times and in the Manner aforefaid.

APPOINT-

APPOINTMENT of the NOMINEE.

To be wrote on Parchment.

WE whose Names are subscribed, being the Ordinary, Patron, and Incumbent, of the Rectory, Vicarage, &c. of   within the County of   and Diocese of the Bishop of   do hereby nominate and appoint   of   to receive the Money authorized to be raised, by an Act passed in Sixteenth Year of the Reign of His Majesty King *George* the Third, intituled, " An Act to promote the Re-
" sidence of the Parochial Clergy, by making Provision for
" the more speedy and effectual building, re-building, or
" repairing, Parsonage Houses; and for erecting or repairing
" other necessary Buildings upon the Glebes belonging there-
" to," for the Purpose of building, repairing, &c. the Parsonage House, &c. (as the Case shall be) to the said Rectory, Vicarage, &c. belonging, and to pay and apply the same, and to enter into Contracts with proper Persons for such Buildings or Repairs, and to inspect and take Care of the Execution of such Contracts, and to take such Receipts and Vouchers, keep such Accounts, and do and perform all such other Matters and Things which Nominees are authorized and required to do and perform in and by the said Act.

FORM of ORDER of the Ordinary, Patron, and Incumbent, for laying out or applying the Surplus Money.

WE whose Names are subscribed, being the Ordinary, Patron, and Incumbent, of the Rectory, Vicarage, &c. of   in the County of   and Diocese of the Bishop of   do hereby order, That the Sum of   now remaining in the Hands of   the Person nominated and appointed to receive and apply the Money raised for building, repairing, &c. the Parsonage House, &c. belonging to the said Rectory, Vicarage, &c. under the Act of Parliament passed

passed in the Sixteenth Year of the Reign of His Majesty King *George* the Third, intituled, " An Act to promote the " Residence of the Parochial Clergy, by making Provision " for the more speedy and effectual building, re-building, or " repairing, Parsonage Houses; and for erecting or repairing " other necessary Buildings upon the Glebes belonging there- " to," shall be [paid to   being the Person entitled to receive the Money now remaining due on the Mortgage made of the Glebe Lands, Tythes, and other Profits and Emoluments of the said Living, and applied in Part of Payment thereof, pursuant to the Direction of the said Act,] [or—applied in building or repairing, &c. (describing the same)— upon the Glebe belonging to the said Living.

FORM of CERTIFICATE from the Two Clergymen.

WE the Reverend *A. B.* of   in the County of   Clerk, and *C. D.* of   Clerk, being Two Clergymen within the Diocese of the Bishop of   do hereby certify to the said Bishop, pursuant to the Directions and Instructions sent by him to us, That we have made Enquiry into the State and Condition of the Buildings upon the Glebe belonging to the Rectory, Vicarage, &c. of   within the said Diocese, at the Time the Reverend   Clerk, the present Incumbent thereof, entered upon the said Living, which was in or about the Year of our Lord   and do find, [that the same have been kept in due and common Repair, without any wilful Neglect] [if the Case is so] or [that the same have, by wilful Negligence, been suffered to go to Decay, and that they have sustained Damage from a want of common and ordinary Repair, to the Amount of   Pounds; and we have also enquired into the Money received by the said   for Dilapidations, from the Representatives of the former Incumbent, and do find, that he hath received the Sum of   for such Dilapidations, and [that he hath expended the Whole, or   thereof, (as the Case may be) in the necessary Repairs of the Buildings] or [that the same hath not been laid out or expended in repairing the Buildings] upon the Glebe belonging to the said Living.

NOMINATION

NOMINATION of a Clergyman by the Bishop, to settle any Dispute about the Proportion of the Payments within the Year in which any Avoidance shall happen.

I The Right Reverend   Bishop of
pursuant to the Authority of an Act, passed in the Sixteenth 27 Year of the Reign of His Majesty King *George* the Third, intituled, " An Act to promote the Residence of the Parochial
" Clergy, by making Provision for the more speedy and effec-
" tual building, re-building, or repairing, Parsonage Houses;
" and for erecting or repairing other necessary Buildings upon
" the Glebes belonging thereto," do hereby nominate the Reverend   Clerk, being a Clergyman within my said Diocese, to adjust and determine the Matter in Dispute between the Reverend   Clerk, the present Incumbent of the Rectory, Vicarage, &c. of   within my Diocese, and   the Representatives of the   the last Incumbent, (in case of his Death) or the said   (in case of his Resignation or Promotion) concerning the due Proportion to be paid by each of the said Parties, of the Principal and Interest which accrued due within the Year in which such Death or other Avoidance happened, according to the Direction, true Intent and Meaning of the said Act.

AWARD and DETERMINATION of the Clergy- 28
man nominated by the Bishop.

I The Reverend *A. B.* of   in the County of   and Diocese of the Bishop of   Clerk, having been nominated by the said Bishop, pursuant to the Power given by an Act, passed in the Sixteenth Year of the Reign of His Majesty King *George* the Third, intituled, " An Act to
" promote the Residence of the Parochial Clergy, by making
" Provision for the more speedy and effectual building, re-
" building, or repairing, Parsonage Houses; and for erecting or
" repairing other necessary Buildings upon the Glebes belonging
" thereto," to adjust and determine the Matter in Dispute between the Reverend   Clerk, the present Incumbent of the Rectory, Vicarage, &c. of   within the

the said Diocese, and   the Representatives of the last Incumbent, (in case of his Death) or the said   (in case of his Resignation or Promotion) concerning the due Proportion to be paid by each of the said Parties, of the Principal and Interest which accrued due within the Year in which such [Death] [or Avoidance] happened, according to the Direction and true Intent and Meaning of the said Act; and having heard and duly considered the said Matter so referred to me as aforesaid, do award, adjudge, and determine, That the said   shall pay, in respect of the Interest and Principal which became due within the Year aforesaid, the Sum of   and that the said   shall pay, in respect of the same, the Sum of   being the Remainder thereof, according to the Provision and Direction of the said Act.

A

B I L L

[With the Amendments]

T O

Promote the Residence of the Parochial Clergy, by making Provision for the more speedy and effectual building, re-building, or repairing, Parsonage Houses; and for erecting or repairing other necessary Buildings upon the Glebes belonging thereto.

1776.

A

BILL

[With the Amendments]

FOR

The better ordering of the Militia Forces in that Part of Great Britain called Scotland.

N. B. *The Words printed in* 𝔅𝔩𝔞𝔠𝔨 𝔏𝔢𝔱𝔱𝔢𝔯, *and between Brackets, thus* [ ], *were left out by the Committee ; and the Words printed in* Italic, *between Brackets, and the Clauses at the End, marked* (A), (B), (C), (D), (E), (F), *were inserted by the Committee.*

Note.—*The Figures in the Margin denote the Number of the Folios in the written Copy.*

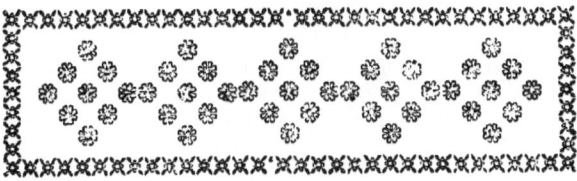WHEREAS it has been found, from Experience, that the well-ordering and disciplining the Militia in England and Wales has essentially contributed to the Safety, Peace, and Prosperity, of the United Kingdom:

And whereas it would further contribute to the same great and good Purposes, if a well-ordered and well-disciplined Militia was established in that Part of the United Kingdom called Scotland:

A   And

And whereas the Laws for the Regulation of the Militia in Scotland are defective and ineffectual; Be it therefore Enacted by the KING's Most Excellent MAJESTY, by and with the Advice and Consent of the Lords Spiritual and Temporal, and Commons, in this present Parliament assembled, and by the Authority of the same, That all Acts relating to the Militia, in that Part of Great Britain called Scotland, shall, from the passing of this Act, be, and are hereby [*repealed.*]

2 And be it Enacted, That in that Part of Great Britain aforesaid, there shall be [*Six thousand private*] Militia Men [**exclusive of Officers**] in the Whole, chosen by Lot, who shall be armed and arrayed in such Manner, and according to such Rules and Regulations as are hereinafter expressed.

And be it further Enacted, That for the Purpose of carrying this Act into Execution, His Majesty, His Heirs and Successors, may and shall issue forth Commissions [**to Commissioners of Militia, in each County, Stewartry, and Place**] [*of Lieutenancy for the several Counties and Stewartries*] within that Part of Great Britain aforesaid, and the respective [**Commissioners**] [*Lieutenants*] thereby appointed, [**or of them**] shall appoint [*Five or more*] Deputy [**Commissioners at the least**] [*Lieutenants*] if so many Persons, qualified as is hereinafter directed, can be found in each County [*or*] Stewartry [**or Place**] and if not, then shall appoint so many Persons, qualified as [**aforesaid**] [*hereinafter directed*] as can be therein found, and such Number of other Persons as shall be requisite to make up the Number [*of Five*] who shall be respectively qualified as hereinafter is expressed; and shall also, [*One Calendar Month*] at least before the General Quarter Sessions to be held on the [*First Tuesday in the Months of May and October*] in every Year, cause Advertisements to be pub-
3 lished in the Edinburgh Evening Courant [*and Caledonian Mercury*] and in some other News Paper for such County or [**Place**] [*Stewartry*] if any such there be, that all Gentlemen, willing to serve as Officers in the Militia of such County or [**Place**] [*Stewartry*] shall return their Names and Places of Abode, and Additions, to His Majesty's [**Commissioners of Militia**] [*Lieutenant of such County or Stewartry*] specifying the Rank in which they are willing to serve respectively; and His Majesty's [**Commissioner or Commissioners of Militia**] [*Lieutenant*] of each of such Counties [**and Places**]

or

or [*Stewartries*] [of them] out of the Gentlemen so offering to serve, shall appoint a proper Number of Lieutenant Colonels, Majors, and other Officers, qualified as hereinafter directed, to train and discipline the Persons so to be armed and arrayed, according to the Rules, Orders, and Directions, hereinafter provided; and shall certify to His Majesty the Names and Ranks of such Officers within [*One Calendar Month*] after they shall be so appointed; and in case His Majesty shall, within [*One Calendar Month*] after such Certificate, signify His Disapprobation of any such Person, His Majesty's [Commissioners of Militia] [*Lieutenant*] shall not grant a Commission to such Person, but shall grant Commissions to such Persons so appointed who shall not be disapproved of by His Majesty.

4.

And be it Enacted, That when [the Commissioner of] a [*Lieutenant of any*] County [*or*] Stewartry [or Place] shall be absent out of the Kingdom of Great Britain, or the Office of [Commissioner] [*Lieutenant*] shall be vacant, it shall be lawful for His Majesty to authorize and appoint under his Sign Manual [*Three*] Deputy [Commissioners] [*Lieutenants*] to grant Commissions to Officers to serve in the Militia for such County [*or*] Stewartry, [or Place] upon any Vacancy that shall happen during the Absence of the said [Commissioners] [*Lieutenant*] or the said Office shall be vacant, in such Manner and subject to such Approbation as aforesaid, and to proceed and do every other Act necessary or required to be done by His Majesty's [Commissioner] [*Lieutenant*] of any County [*or*] Stewartry, [or Place] for the carrying into Execution the several Powers of this Act.

Provided always, and be it Enacted, That no Deputation of any Deputy [Commissioner] [*Lieutenant*] nor any Commission of any Officer in the Militia, to be granted in pursuance of this Act, shall be vacated by reason of the Revocation, Expiration, or Discontinuance, of the Commission by which such respective [Commissioners] [*Lieutenant*] or Deputy [Commissioners] [*Lieutenant*] shall be appointed.

And be it further Enacted, That each Person so to be appointed a Deputy [Commissioner] [*Lieutenant*] shall be Proprietor and in Possession of Lands in Scotland [holden either of the Crown or of a Subject, and valued in the Cess Books of the County where they lie at] [*of the yearly Value*

5

Value of Three hundred Pounds Sterling] or shall be Superior of Lands yielding annually to the Superior not less than [*Three hundred Pounds Sterling*] or shall be Heir Apparent of some Person who shall be, in like Manner, Proprietor and in Possession of a like Estate as aforesaid [valued in the Cess Books of the County where they lie at] [*of the yearly Value of Five hundred Pounds Sterling*] or shall be Heir Apparent of a Superior of Lands yielding annually to the Superior not less than [*Five hundred Pounds Sterling*]: And each Person so to be appointed a Lieutenant Colonel shall be, in like Manner, Proprietor and in Possession of a like Estate as aforesaid, [valued, as aforesaid, at] [*of the yearly Value of Three hundred Pounds Sterling*] or shall be Superior of Lands, as aforesaid, yielding annually to the Superior not less than [*Three hundred Pounds Sterling*] or shall be Heir Apparent of some Person who shall be, in like Manner, Proprietor or in Possession of a like Estate, [valued, as aforesaid, at] [*of the yearly Value of Six hundred Pounds Sterling*] or shall be Heir Apparent of a Superior of Lands, as aforesaid, yielding annually to the Superior not less

6 than [*Six hundred Pounds Sterling*] And each Person so to be appointed a Major, or a Captain, shall be, in like Manner, Proprietor and in Possession of a like Estate as aforesaid, [valued, as aforesaid, at] [*of the yearly Value of Two hundred Pounds Sterling*] or shall be Superior of Lands, as aforesaid, yielding annually to the Superior not less than [*Two hundred Pounds Sterling*] or shall be Heir Apparent of some Person who shall be, in like Manner, Proprietor and in Possession of a like Estate, [valued, as aforesaid, at] [*of the yearly Value of Four hundred Pounds Sterling*] or shall be Heir Apparent of a Superior of Lands, as aforesaid, yielding annually to the Superior not less than [*Four hundred Pounds Sterling*] [or shall be a younger Son of some Person who shall be, or at the Time of his Death was, in like Manner, Proprietor and in Possession of a like Estate as aforesaid, valued, as aforesaid, at   or shall be a younger Son of some Person who shall be, or at the Time of his Death was, in like Manner, Superior of Lands as aforesaid, yielding annually to the Superior not less than   ] And that each Person so to be appointed a Lieutenant shall be, in like Manner, Proprietor and in Possession of a like Estate as aforesaid, [valued, as aforesaid, at]

7 [*of the yearly Value of One hundred Pounds Sterling*] or shall be Superior of Lands as aforesaid, yielding annually to the Superior not less than [*One hundred Pounds Sterling*] or shall be

Heir

[5]

Heir Apparent of some Person who shall be, in like Manner, Proprietor and in Possession of a like Estate [valued, as aforesaid, at] [*of the yearly Value of Two hundred Pounds Sterling*] or shall be Heir Apparent of a Superior of Lands, as aforesaid, yielding annually to the Superior not less than [*Two hundred Pounds Sterling*] or shall be a [younger] Son of some Person who shall be, or at the Time of his Death was, in like Manner, Proprietor and in Possession of a like Estate as aforesaid, [valued, as aforesaid, at] [*of the yearly Value of Two hundred Pounds Sterling*] or shall be a [younger] Son of some Person who shall be, or at the Time of his Death was, in like Manner, Superior of Lands as aforesaid, yielding annually to the Superior not less than [*Two hundred Pounds Sterling*] And that such Person so to be appointed an Ensign shall be, in like Manner, Proprietor and in Possession of a like Estate as aforesaid, [valued, as aforesaid, at] [*of the yearly Value of Sixty Pounds Sterling*] or shall be Superior of Lands, as aforesaid, yielding annually to the Superior not less than [*Sixty Pounds Sterling*] or shall be Heir Apparent of some Person who shall be, in like Manner, Proprietor and in Possession of a like Estate [valued, as aforesaid, at] [*of the yearly Value of One hundred Pounds Sterling*] or shall be Heir Apparent of a Superior of Lands, as aforesaid, yielding annually to the Superior not less than [*One hundred Pounds Sterling*] or shall be a [younger] Son of some Person who shall be, or at the Time of his Death was, in like Manner, Proprietor and in Possession of a like Estate as aforesaid, [valued, as aforesaid, at] [*of the yearly Value of One hundred Pounds Sterling*] or shall be a [younger] Son of some Person who shall be, or at the Time of his Death was, in like Manner, Superior of Lands, as aforesaid, yielding annually to the Superior not less than [*One hundred Pounds Sterling: One Moiety*] of which said Estates, required as Qualifications as aforesaid, shall be situated or arising within such respective County [or] Stewartry [or Place] in which he shall be appointed to serve.

Provided always, That in such Counties [or] Stewartries, [or Places] where [*Five*] Persons cannot be found, qualified as aforesaid, to act as Deputy [Commissioners] [*Lieutenants*] His Majesty's [Commissioner or Commissioners] [*Lieutenant*] of such County [or] Stewartry, [or Place] after having appointed so many Persons as can be found qualified as aforesaid, shall appoint such Number of Persons to be Deputy [Commissioners] [*Lieutenants*] as shall be requisite to

B make

make up the Number [*of Five*] who shall respectively be Proprietors and in Possession of a like Estate [valued at] [*of the yearly Value of One hundred Pounds Sterling*] or shall be Superior of Lands yielding annually to the Superior not less than [*One hundred Pounds Sterling*] [situated as] aforesaid [and every such Person shall be duly qualified to act and serve under such respective Commissions.]

[And be it Enacted, That when any Battalion of Militia shall be drawn out and embodied, His Majesty's Commissioner or Commissioners, or of them, may, upon Account of military Merit shewn in Time of actual Invasion or Rebellion, promote any Officer therein from a lower to a higher Commission, notwithstanding he shall not have the Qualification in point of Estate requisite for his Admittance unto such higher Rank; provided that no Person, not having the Qualification hereinbefore directed for a Captain, shall be promoted to a higher Rank than that of Captain.]

And be it Enacted, That His Majesty, from Time to Time, may signify His Pleasure to His [Commissioner or Commissioners] [*Lieutenant*] to displace any Deputy [Commissioners] [*Lieutenants*] and Commissioned Officers in the Militia; and thereupon the [Commissioner or Commissioners] [*Lieutenant*] shall displace such Deputy [Commissioners] [*Lieutenants*] or Officers, and shall appoint others in their Stead, with the like Qualifications in point of Estate, and according to the Rules and Directions herein prescribed for the Appointment of Deputy [Commissioners] [*Lieutenants*] and Commission Officers respectively.

And be it Enacted, That no Deputy [Commissioner] [*Lieutenant*] or Commission Officer in the Militia, shall act as such, until he shall have left with the Clerk of the Peace of the County [*or*] Stewartry [or Place] for which he shall be so appointed, his Qualification in Writing, signed by himself; and such Clerk of the Peace shall enter the same upon a Roll to be kept for that Purpose, and shall, in the Month of [*January*] in every Year, transmit to One of His Majesty's principal Secretaries of State, an Account of the Qualifications so left with him; and the said Secretaries of State shall cause Copies thereof to be annually laid before both Houses of Parliament.

And

And be it further Enacted, That every [Commissioner, [*Lieutenant*] for [a] [*each*] County or [Place] [*Stewartry*] and every Deputy [Commissioner] [*Lieutenant*] and Commission Officer in the said Militia, shall, at some General Quarter Sessions, or before the Sheriff Depute of the County for which they are appointed to serve, or his Substitute, within [*Six Calendar Months*] after he shall have accepted his Commission, take the Oaths in and by an Act, passed in the First Year of the Reign of His Majesty King George the First, intituled, " An Act for the further " Security of His Majesty's Person and Government, and " the Succession of the Crown in the Heirs of the late " Princess Sophia, being Protestants, and for extinguishing " the Hopes of the pretended Prince of Wales, and his " open and secret Abettors;" and also the Oath in and by an Act, passed in the Sixth Year of the Reign of His present Majesty, intituled, " An Act for altering the Oath " of Abjuration, and the Assurance, and for amending so " much of an Act, made in the Seventh Year of the Reign " of her late Majesty Queen Anne, intituled, An Act for the " Improvement and Union of the Two Kingdoms, as, after " the Time therein limited, requires the Delivery of certain " Lists or Copies, therein mentioned, to Persons indicted of " High Treason or Misprision of Treason," appointed to be taken; and shall also make, repeat, and subscribe, the Declaration in the said Act of the First of King George the First, directed to be made, repeated, and subscribed, by all Officers Civil and Military; and if any Person shall execute any of the Powers hereby conferred on Deputy [Commissioners] [*Lieutenants*] Lieutenant Colonels, or Majors (not being qualified as aforesaid) or shall not deliver in such Qualification, and take the Oaths, and make, repeat, and subscribe, the Declaration aforesaid, every such Person shall forfeit and pay the Sum of [*Two hundred Pounds Sterling*] and if any Person shall execute any of the Powers hereby conferred on Captains, Lieutenants, or Ensigns (not being qualified as aforesaid) and shall not deliver in such Qualification, and take the Oaths, and make, repeat, and subscribe, the Declaration, as is hereinbefore required, every such Person shall forfeit and pay the Sum of [*One hundred Pounds Sterling*] to be recovered by summary Action before the Court of Session at Edinburgh, [*One Moiety*] whereof shall go to the Use of such Person or Persons who shall sue for the same, and [*the other Moiety*] to the Uses hereinafter directed; and in every Action, Suit, or Information, brought against any Person for acting

as

as a Deputy [Commissioner] [*Lieutenant*] or as a Commissioned Officer, in the said Militia, not being qualified as
13 hereinbefore is directed, the Proof of his Qualification shall lie upon the Person against whom the same shall be brought.

Provided always, and be it Enacted, That nothing in this Act contained shall extend to restrain His Majesty's [Commissioner or Commissioners] [*Lieutenant*] of any County [*or*] Stewartry [or Place] from appointing any Peer or Heir Apparent of such Peer to be a Deputy [Commissioner] [*Lieutenant*] or Commission Officer in the Militia, within the County [*or*] Stewartry [or Place] wherein such Peer or Heir Apparent of such Peer shall respectively have some Place of Residence, or to oblige any Peer or Heir Apparent of such Peer (so appointed) to leave with the Clerk of the Peace for the County [*or*] Stewartry [or Place] for which he shall be appointed, any Qualification in Writing as aforesaid; but it shall be lawful for such Peer or Heir Apparent, so appointed, and taking the Oaths, and making, repeating, and subscribing, the Declaration aforesaid, to act as a Deputy [Commissioner] [*Lieutenant*] or Commission Officer respectively, although he shall not be seised or possessed of any such Estate as is required by this Act.

Provided also, and be it Enacted, That the Acceptance of an Appointment to be a Deputy [Commissioner] [*Lieutenant*] or of a Commission in the said Militia, shall not vacate the Seat of any Member returned to serve in Parliament.

And be it Enacted, That His Majesty's [Commissioners,
14 in such Counties, Stewartries, or Places, where there are more than One, or His Majesty's Commissioner, in such Counties, Stewartries, and Places, where there is only One] [*Lieutenant of each County or Stewartry*] with any [*Two*] Deputy [Commissioners] [*Lieutenants*] and on the Death or Removal, or in the Absence, of His Majesty's [Commissioner] [*Lieutenant*] any [*Three*] Deputy [Commissioners] [*Lieutenants*] at the End of every [*Four Years*] at their Annual Meeting, in case the Militia of such County [*or*] Stewartry [or Place] shall not be then embodied, and if they are then embodied, as soon after they are disembodied as conveniently may be, [*shall*] discharge some One Field Officer of each Battalion [*or Corps*] and such Number of Officers of each inferior Rank as shall be equal to the Number of Persons who shall have given
Notice

Notice in Writing to His Majesty's [Commissioner or Commissioners] [*Lieutenant One Calendar Month*] at least before such Meeting, that they are willing to serve as Field Officers, Captains, Lieutenants, or Ensigns, as the Case may require; provided that the Number of Vacancies to be made shall not exceed [*One Third*] of such Officers who shall have served for the Space of [*Three Years*] in each Rank respectively: Provided that nothing herein contained shall prevent any Officer, who has served [*Four Years*] from offering to serve in a higher Rank, if he be qualified as this Act requires to serve in such higher Rank.

And be it Enacted, That it shall be lawful for the [Commissioner] [*Lieutenant*] of any County [*or*] Stewartry [or Place, in which there is only One Commissioner, or for the Commissioner first named in His Majesty's Commission, where there are more, and for any such Commissioner first named for the Commissioner named in the Second Place, and so on] to act as [a Lieutenant Colonel of any Battalion of] [*Commanding Officer of the*] Militia, for such County [*or*] Stewartry [or Place, during such Time as there shall not be any Field Officer appointed for the Command of the same] according to the Establishment hereinafter mentioned; but no [Commissioner] [*Lieutenant*] shall, at any One Time, act as a Lieutenant Colonel to more than One Battalion.

And be it Enacted, That His Majesty, His Heirs and Successors, may and shall appoint One proper Person, who shall have served for the Space of [*Five Years*] in some of His Majesty's other Forces [or in any Corps of Militia that has been drawn out and embodied for the Space of   ] to be an Adjutant to each Battalion [or Independant Company] of Militia; and such Adjutant [if appointed out of His Majesty's other Forces] shall, during his Service in the said Militia, preserve his Rank in the Army in the same Manner as if he had continued in that Service; and it shall be lawful for His Majesty's [Commissioner or Commissioners] [*Lieutenant*] of any County [*or*] Stewartry [or Place] to grant unto the Adjutant to each Battalion [or Independant Company] a Commission of Lieutenant, or any inferior Commission therein, although such Adjutant shall not have an Estate to qualify him for such Commission, as is required by this Act: [*Provided always, That no Commission Officer upon Full Pay in His Majesty's Sea or Land Service, shall be capable of holding a Commission*

Commiſſion in the ſaid Militia, as long as he ſhall hold his Full Pay.]

And be it Enacted, That any Perſon who ſhall quit his Half Pay to ſerve as a Commiſſioned Officer in any Battalion or Independant Company of the ſaid Militia ſhall, upon his quitting the [**ſame**] [*ſaid Battalion or Independant Company*] or upon the unembodying thereof, be reſtored to his Half Pay, to re-commence from the laſt Quarter Day or Day of Payment next preceding.

And be it Enacted, That the [*Lieutenant*] Colonel, or, where there is no [*Lieutenant*] Colonel, the Commanding Officer, of each Battalion of Militia, ſhall appoint a Serjeant Major out of the Serjeants, and a Drum Major out of the Drummers, of ſuch Battalion.

17 And be it Enacted, That His Majeſty, His Heirs and Succeſſors, may and ſhall appoint, according to the Proportion of One Serjeant to [*Twenty*] Private Men, [*Two*] or more proper Perſons to be Serjeants to every Company in the ſaid Militia, [*who ſhall have ſerved for the Space of Three Years in His Majeſty's other Forces*] and from Time to Time, till ſuch Company ſhall have been inrolled, and formed for the Space of [*Three Years, or ſhall have been in actual Service for the Space of One Year*] when any Vacancies ſhall happen of ſuch Serjeants, ſhall fill up ſuch Vacancies, out of His Majeſty's other Forces, with ſuch proper Perſons, who ſhall have ſerved in ſuch other Forces for the Space of [*Three Years*] next preceding ſuch Appointment, or may appoint ſuch other Perſons to be Serjeants as have formerly ſerved in that Capacity for the Space of [*Six Years*] in His Majeſty's other Forces [**or out of any Corps of Militia that has been drawn out and embodied for the Space of**   ] which Serjeants ſo appointed ſhall take the following Oath; (that is to ſay)

" I A. B. do ſincerely promiſe and ſwear, That I will
" be faithful, and bear true Allegiance, to His Majeſty
" King George, His Heirs and Succeſſors; and I do
" ſwear that I am a Proteſtant, and that I will faith-
" fully ſerve as a Serjeant in the Militia, within the
" Kingdom of Great Britain, for the Defence of the
" ſame, until I ſhall be legally diſcharged."

And

And the Service in the Militia of such Persons so appointed out of His Majesty's other Forces, shall entitle them to the Benefit of Chelsea Hospital, in the same Manner as if they had continued to serve in the said Forces; and every Person appointed to be a Serjeant out of the Pensioners on the Establishment of Chelsea Hospital, shall be put again upon the said Establishment after he shall be discharged from the Militia, provided he brings a Certificate of his good Behaviour, under the Hand of the [*Lieutenant*] Colonel or Commanding Officer of the Corps in which he shall have served.

And be it Enacted, That after any Corps of Militia shall have been inrolled, and formed for the Space of [*Three Years*] or shall have been embodied, and called out into actual Service, for the Space of [*One Year*] the Captain or Commanding Officer of every Company of Militia, with the Approbation of the [*Lieutenant*] Colonel or Commanding Officer of each Corps of Militia, shall appoint Serjeants out of the Private Men of such Regiment or Corps, to fill up such Vacancies of Serjeants as may happen therein, which Serjeants so appointed shall take the like Oath as is hereinbefore required to be taken by Serjeants appointed by His Majesty (which Oath every Deputy Lieutenant, or Justice of the Peace, is hereby authorized to administer): Provided that no Person who shall keep any House of public Entertainment, or who shall sell any Ale, Wine, Brandy, or other Spirituous Liquors, by Retail, shall be capable of being appointed or continuing a Serjeant in the Militia. And it shall be lawful for the Commanding Officer of any Corps of Militia, on the Application of the Captain of a Company in such Corps, to displace any Serjeant belonging to such Company: Provided that any Person who shall be appointed from His Majesty's other Forces to be a Serjeant in the Militia, and shall be displaced as aforesaid, or shall for any Misbehaviour be reduced into the Ranks, and shall not, in One Month's Time after such Displacing or Reduction, be restored, shall be returned to the Company from which he was taken in His Majesty's other Forces, and shall there serve as a Private Soldier; and any Person who shall be appointed a Serjeant in the Militia, out of or from any Company of Militia, who shall be displaced as aforesaid, or shall be reduced into the Ranks, for Misbehaviour, shall serve, in the Ranks of such Company wherein he served before such Appointment, for such further Time as shall complete his [*Three Years*] Service as a Private Militia Man; and in case there be no Vacancy in such

[12]

such Company, he shall serve in any other Company in the same Corps.

And be it Enacted, That the Captain of every Company shall appoint Corporals out of the Private Men of his Company, in the Proportion of One Corporal to [*Twenty*] Private Men, and may displace such Corporals for Misbehaviour, and appoint others, as he shall see Occasion; and shall appoint [*Two*] Persons to be Drummers [*or Fifers*] to his Company, which Drummers or Fifers, when so appointed, and having received Pay as such, shall be deemed to be engaged, and compellable to serve in the same Corps until legally discharged; and such Captain may displace such Drummers or Fifers for Misbehaviour, and appoint others in their room.

And be it Enacted, That His Majesty's [𝕮𝖔𝖒𝖒𝖎𝖘𝖘𝖎𝖔𝖓𝖊𝖗 𝖔𝖗 𝕮𝖔𝖒𝖒𝖎𝖘𝖘𝖎𝖔𝖓𝖊𝖗𝖘] [*Lieutenant*] for any County [*or*] Stewartry [𝖔𝖗 𝕻𝖑𝖆𝖈𝖊] may and shall appoint a Clerk for the General Meeting within such County [*or*] Stewartry [𝖔𝖗 𝕻𝖑𝖆𝖈𝖊] and may displace such Clerk, if he shall think fit, and appoint another in his room; and the Deputy [𝕮𝖔𝖒𝖒𝖎𝖘𝖘𖎔𝖔𝖓𝖊𝖗𝖘] [*Lieutenants*] within their respective Subdivisions, or [*the major Part*] of them present, may and shall appoint a Clerk for their respective Subdivision, and may displace such Clerk, if they or [*the major Part*] of them present shall think fit, and appoint another in his room.

And be it Enacted by the Authority aforesaid, That when any Battalion of Militia shall be unembodied, the [*Lieutenant*] Colonel, or, where there is no [*Lieutenant*] Colonel, the Commanding Officer, of each Battalion or Corps of Militia, shall appoint a Clerk to such Battalion or Corps, and may displace such Clerk, if he shall think fit, and appoint another in his room.

And be it Enacted, That when any Corps of Militia shall be drawn out into actual Service, and during the Time they shall continue in such Service, the Commanding Officer of such Corps shall appoint an Agent to such Corps, and shall be accountable for, and make good, all Deficiencies that may happen in respect of the Pay, Cloathing, or public Stock, which shall be received by such Agent.

And

And be it further Enacted, That the Number of Private Men to be raised, by virtue of this Act, in that Part of Great Britain called Scotland, shall be,

For the County of Aberdeen [*Five hundred and Fifty-one.*]
For the County of Air [*Two hundred and Eighty.*]
For the County of Argyll [*Three hundred and Fourteen.*]
For the County of Bute [*Thirty-four.*]
For the County of Banff [*One hundred and Eighty-two.*]
For the County of Berwick [*One hundred and Twenty.*]
For the County of Caithness [*One hundred and Five.*]
For the County of Sutherland [*One hundred.*]
For the County of Dumfries [*One hundred and Eighty-eight.*]
For the County of Dumbarton [*Sixty-six.*]
For the County of Edinburgh [*Two hundred and Eighty-six.*]
[For the City and County of the City of Edinburgh, *One hundred and Forty-three.*]
For the County of Elgin [*One hundred and Forty-five.*]
For the County of Nairn [*Twenty-seven.*]
For the County of Fife [*Three hundred and Eighty-seven.*]
For the County of Kinross [*Twenty-three.*]
For the County of Forfar [*Three hundred and Twenty-six.*]
For the County of Haddington [*One hundred and Forty-one.*]
For the County of Inverness [*Two hundred and Eighty-two.*]
For the County of Kincardine [*One hundred and Nine.*]
For the Stewartry of Kirkcudbright [*One hundred.*]
For the County of Lanark [*Three hundred and Eighty-eight.*]
For the County of Linlithgow [*Eighty.*]
For the County of Orkney and Zetland [*One hundred and Eighty-three.*]
For the County of Peebles [*Forty-two.*]
For the County of Perth [*Five hundred and Sixty-four.*]
For the County of Renfrew [*One hundred and Twenty-six.*]
For the County of Ross [*Two hundred and Three.*]
For the County of Cromarty [*Twenty-four.*]
For the County of Roxburgh [*One hundred and Sixty-five.*]
For the County of Selkirk [*Nineteen.*]
For the County of Stirling [*One hundred and Seventy-six.*]
For the County of Clackmannan [*Forty-three.*]
For the County of Wigton or Galloway [*Seventy-eight.*]

And be it Enacted by the Authority aforesaid, That the Deputy [**Commissioners**] [*Lieutenants*] of each County [*or*] Stewartry [**or Place**] or [*any Three or more*] of them, at the least,

leaſt, ſhall hold [*as many*] General Meetings in [the firſt] [*this and every other*] Year after [*the paſſing of this Act*] for each County [*or*] Stewartry [or Place] aforeſaid [and One ſuch General Meeting every Year afterwards, for the Purpoſes hereinafter mentioned, and as many more ſuch General Meetings in each Year] as ſhall be neceſſary for carrying this Act into Execution; and of the Time and Place for holding each of ſuch General Meetings [*Twenty-one*] Days Notice, at the leaſt, ſhall be given in the Edinburgh Evening Courant, Caledonian Mercury, and Edinburgh Advertiſer, and alſo in ſome other weekly News Paper circulated in ſuch County [*or*] Stewartry [or Place] if any ſuch there be; and that if it ſhall appear to the Deputy [Commiſſioners] [*Lieutenants at ſuch General Meeting, or the major Part of them*] that it will tend to the eaſier Execution of this Act that there ſhould be Subdiviſion Meetings, it ſhall be lawful for them to divide the County [*or*] Stewartry [or Place] into as many Diſtricts as they ſhall think proper, for the Purpoſe of ſuch ſubdiviſion Meetings; and in caſe of the County [*or*] Stewartry [or Place] being ſo ſubdivided, there ſhall be [at leaſt] [*as many*] Meetings in [each of] ſuch Subdiviſions Yearly [and as many more ſuch Subdiviſion Meetings] as ſhall be neceſſary for carrying this Act into Execution; and in order to conſtitute a [Subdiviſion Meeting as aforeſaid, there ſhall be   Deputy Commiſſioners, or   Deputy Commiſſioners and One Juſtice of the Peace, or One Deputy Commiſſioner and   Juſtices of the Peace for ſuch County or Place, at the leaſt, preſent at ſuch Subdiviſion Meeting; and any Deputy Commiſſioner, or Juſtice of the Peace, for ſuch County, Stewartry, or Place, may act in the Execution of this Act in every Subdiviſion therein, with the ſame Power and Authority as in the Subdiviſion to which he may be particularly appointed] [*General or a Subdiviſion Meeting as aforeſaid, Two Deputy Lieutenants and One Juſtice of the Peace, or One Deputy Lieutenant and Two Juſtices of the Peace, for ſuch County or Stewartry, at the leaſt, ſhall be preſent at ſuch Meeting; and the Juſtices of the Peace in each County or Stewartry ſhall have the ſame Power, with reſpect to carrying this Act into Execution, as is hereby given to Deputy Lieutenants in all Caſes whatſoever, except to conſtitute a Meeting, there ſhall be One Deputy Lieutenant at the leaſt*]

And be it Enacted, That the Firſt General Meeting in purſuance of this Act ſhall be held on the [*Firſt Tueſday in the*

[15]

the Month of August One thousand Seven hundred and Seventy-six, and on the Thirtieth of April] in every [subsequent] Year, or so soon after as conveniently may be; and that the Deputy [Commissioners] [Lieutenants] or [any Three or more] of them, at the least, present at such Annual Meeting, shall, if it shall appear necessary, appoint the Subdivisions, and the Times and Places of holding the First Subdivision Meeting, in each District or Division in such County or [Place] [Stewartry] for that Year, and shall require the [Session Clerk] [Constable] in each Parish within the County [or] Stewartry [or Place, or such other Persons as they shall please to appoint] to return to the next General Meeting (in case there be no Subdivision made of the County [or] Stewartry [or Place] or, in case of such Subdivision, to the Deputy [Commissioners] [Lieutenants] at their respective First Subdivision Meetings) fair and true Lists, in Writing, of the Names of all the Men usually, and at that Time, dwelling within their respective Parishes and Places, between the Ages of [Eighteen] and [Thirty] Years complete, distinguishing their respective Ranks and Occupations (and, where the true Names of such Persons cannot be procured, the common Appellation of such Persons shall be sufficient) and which of the Persons so returned labour under any Infirmities incapacitating them from serving as Militia Men, having first affixed a true Copy of such List on the Door of [the] [every] Church [or] Chapel [and Place of public Worship] belonging to such Parish [or Place] on some Sunday Morning before they shall make such Return, (which Sunday shall be [Ten] Days at the least before the said Meeting) and also Notice in Writing, at the Bottom of such List, of the Day and Place of such General or Subdivision Meeting respectively, and shall then [and there] attend, and verify the Truth of such Lists by them respectively returned, upon Oath; and that all Persons who shall think themselves aggrieved may then [and there] appeal, and that no Appeal will be afterwards received.

And be it Enacted, That no Peer of this Realm, nor any Person who shall serve as a Commission Officer in His Majesty's other Forces, or in any one of His Castles or Forts, nor any Non-commission Officer or Private Man serving in any of His Majesty's other Forces, nor any Commission Officer serving, or who has served [Three Years] [as a Principal] in the Militia, nor any Person being a Member of any of the Universities, nor any Clergyman, nor any licensed Teacher of

any

any separate Congregation, nor any articled Clerk, Apprentice, Seaman, or Seafaring Man, nor any Person mustered and doing Duty in any of His Majesty's Docks, nor any Man [*not possessed of the Qualification necessary to enable him to be a Deputy Lieutenant or Commission Officer in the Militia*] who has a living Child [or 𝕮𝖍𝖎𝖑𝖉𝖗𝖊𝖓] born in lawful Wedlock, shall be compelled to serve personally, or provide a Substitute to serve, in the Militia.

27 And be it Enacted, That if such Deputy [𝕮𝖔𝖒𝖒𝖎𝖘𝖘𝖎𝖔𝖓𝖊𝖗𝖘] [*Lieutenants*] or Justices of the Peace shall, at any General or Sub-division Meeting respectively, receive Information, or shall suspect, that any Person inserted in any List, described as an Apprentice, has been fraudulently bound an Apprentice, in order to avoid serving in the Militia, they, or any [*Two*] of them, shall inquire into such Binding, and summon Witnesses, and examine them upon Oath, touching the Matter in Question; and if such Fraud shall appear, they, or any [*Two*] of them, shall appoint such Person so bound Apprentice to serve immediately in the Militia for the Parish or Place for which such List shall be returned, if there shall be a Vacancy, and if not, then upon the first Vacancy that shall happen therein; and the Person to whom such Apprentice shall be so bound shall forfeit and immediately pay the Sum of [*Ten Pounds Sterling*] to be recovered in such Manner, and to be applied to such Uses, as are hereinafter directed.

28 And be it Enacted, That if any [𝕾𝖊𝖘𝖘𝖎𝖔𝖓 𝕮𝖑𝖊𝖗𝖐, 𝖔𝖗 𝖔𝖙𝖍𝖊𝖗 𝕻𝖊𝖗𝖘𝖔𝖓] [*Constable*] to be appointed as above to return the Lists for any Parish or Place, shall refuse or neglect to return such Lists, or to comply with such Orders and Directions as aforesaid, or shall, in making such Return, be guilty of any Fraud or wilful Partiality, he shall forfeit and pay any Sum not exceeding [*Twenty Pounds Sterling*] to be recovered as hereinafter mentioned.

And be it further Enacted by the Authority aforesaid, That any Person who shall, by Gratuity, Gift, or Reward, or by Promise thereof, or [of] [*by*] any undue Means, or by Menaces, endeavour to prevail on any [𝕾𝖊𝖘𝖘𝖎𝖔𝖓 𝕮𝖑𝖊𝖗𝖐, 𝖔𝖗 𝖔𝖙𝖍𝖊𝖗 𝕻𝖊𝖗𝖘𝖔𝖓 𝖆𝖕𝖕𝖔𝖎𝖓𝖙𝖊𝖉 𝖆𝖘 𝖆𝖇𝖔𝖛𝖊] [*Constable*] to make a false Return of any List for any Parish [or 𝕻𝖑𝖆𝖈𝖊] or to erase or leave out of any such List the Name of any Person who ought to be returned; or who shall refuse to tell his Christian and Sirname,

or

or the Christian and Sirname of any Man lodging or residing within his or her House, to any Constable [**or other Officer authorized by this Act to demand the same**] every such Person shall forfeit and pay the Sum of [*Ten Pounds Sterling*] to be recovered as hereinafter is expressed.

And be it Enacted, That if the List of any Parish or Place shall be lost or destroyed, the Deputy [**Commissioners**] [*Lieutenants*] and Justices of the Peace in [the] [*each*] County [*or*] Stewartry [**or Place**] or in the Subdivision thereof respectively where such Neglect or Accident shall happen, shall cause a new List for such Parish [**or Place**] to be made, and returned to them, in such Manner as the List lost or destroyed was caused to be made, and returned to them, by the Deputy [**Commissioners**] [*Lieutenants*] at the General Meeting, or as near thereto as may be.

And be it Enacted by the Authority aforesaid, That every Person liable to serve in the Militia, having more than One Place of Residence, shall be deemed to reside or inhabit only in such Parish [**or Place**] where his Name shall be first returned in any List as aforesaid; and the Clerk of the General or Subdivision Meetings respectively, where his Name shall be so returned, shall grant him a Certificate thereof, upon Request, without Fee, and specify the Time in which such List was returned, to enable the Deputy [**Commissioners**] [*Lieutenants*] and Justices to determine in which Parish [**or Place**] he shall be deemed an Inhabitant for the Purpose aforesaid.

And be it Enacted by the Authority aforesaid, That the Deputy [**Commissioners**] [*Lieutenants*] and Justices of the Peace in the respective Counties [*or*] Stewartries [**or Places**] or in the Subdivisions thereof, as the Case shall be, after hearing such Persons who shall think themselves aggrieved by their Names being inserted in any such List, or by any others being omitted, shall order such List to be amended, as the Case shall require, and the Names of all Persons by this Act exempted to be struck out of the said List; and after such Lists are so regulated, a fair Copy thereof shall be made by the Clerk of each General or Subdivision Meeting, and signed by the Deputy [**Commissioners**] [*Lieutenants*] and Justices, or [*any Three or more*] of them acting at such Meeting; which Lists, if made up at a Subdivision Meeting, shall in the First Year after [*the passing of this Act*] forthwith be transmitted to the Clerk of the General Meeting for such County [*or*] Stewartry [**or Place**] who shall give a Receipt for the same; and the Clerk of the General Meeting for each County [*or*] Stewartry [**or Place**] shall forthwith transmit such Lists, or, in case of there being no Subdivision, the Lists made up in the same Manner at the General Meeting of such County [*or*] Stewartry [**or Place**] to His Majesty's [**Commissioner or Commissioners**] [*Lieutenant*] of such County or [**Place**] [*Stewartry*] who shall thereupon forthwith appoint a General Meeting of the Deputy [**Commissioners**] [*Lieutenants*] in such respective County or [**Place**] [*Stewartry*] giving at least [*Ten*] Days Notice thereof in Manner

31 aforesaid; and [*any Three*] or more Deputy [**Commissioners**] [*Lieutenants*] shall, at such General Meeting so appointed, direct what Number of Private Militia Men shall serve for each respective Subdivision, if any be within such County [*or*] Stewartry [**or Place**] to which they belong, towards raising the whole Number directed to be raised by such County [*or*] Stewartry [**or Place**; **and shall also appoint proper Times and Places for holding a Second Subdivision Meeting in each District or Division in such County, Stewartry, or Place**] where any Subdivisions are made as aforesaid; and the Clerk of such General Meeting shall forthwith transmit an Account in Writing, signed by the Deputy [**Commissioners**] [*Lieutenants*] or [*any Three or more*] of them present at such General Meeting, to each Clerk of every Subdivision Meeting in such County [*or*] Stewartry [**or Place**] of the Numbers of Private Militia Men to be raised in such Subdivision.

32 [**And be it further Enacted by the Authority aforesaid, That at every First Subdivision Meeting, where any Subdivisions are in every Year to be held, after the First Year from   as soon as all Appeals against the Lists are heard and determined, and all other Business finished, at such Meeting, as is required by this Act, the Deputy Commissioners and Justices present at such Meeting shall appoint a Second Meeting in such Subdivisions.**]

And be it further Enacted, That the Deputy [**Commissioners**] [*Lieutenants*] and Justices of the Peace [*or the greater Part of them, as aforesaid, at a General Meeting, or*] at their

[respective

[19]

[*respective* **Second**] Subdivision Meetings [*where Subdivisions shall be made*] as aforesaid, shall appoint what Number of Men shall serve for each Parish or [**Place or**] Parishes [**or Places**] when they shall think proper to join Two or more together in such [*County, Stewartry, or*] Subdivision [*respectively*] in Proportion to the Number appointed to serve for the same as aforesaid, and shall transmit an Account thereof, under their Hands, to the Clerk of the Peace, to be inrolled among the Records of [**Session**] [*the Quarter Sessions*] and also to the Receiver General of the Land Tax; and shall fix a Time and Place for holding a [**Third**] Meeting [in such **Subdivision**] for allotting the Men, and shall [issue an **Order**] [*give Notice*] to the [**Constables, or other Officers**] [*Constable*] of each Parish [**or Place within their respective Divisions**] [*respectively*] of the Number of Men so appointed to serve for such Parish or [**Place or**] Parishes [**or Places**] and of the Time and Place for holding another [**Subdivision**] Meeting, for choosing the Men by Lot.   33

[**And be it further Enacted, That in such Counties, Stewartries, or Places, where there are no Subdivisions, the General Meeting appointed by His Majesty's Commissioner or Commissioners, as above mentioned, with the Justices of the Peace, shall proceed to appoint what Number of Men shall serve for each Parish or Place, or Parishes or Places, and to act in all Respects in the same Manner as the Deputy Commissioners and Justices of the Peace are directed to do in such Counties, Stewartries, and Places, where there are Subdivisions.**]

And be it further Enacted, That at such subsequent General or Subdivision Meeting respectively appointed as above, any [*Three or more*] Deputy [**Commissioners**] [*Lieutenants*] and Justices of the Peace as aforesaid, shall cause the Number of Men appointed to serve as aforesaid, except as hereinafter excepted, to be chosen by Lot out of the Lists returned for such Parish or [**Place or**] Parishes [**or Places**] and shall again appoint a General or Subdivision Meeting, within the Space of [*One Calendar Month*] for swearing and inrolling the Men, and shall issue an Order to the [**Constables, or other Officers**] [*Constable*] to be appointed for each Parish [**or Place**] to give at least [*Ten*] Days Notice to every Man so chosen, or   34

leave

leave the same at his Place of Abode, to appear at such Meeting, and be sworn in and inrolled.

Provided always, and it is hereby Enacted, That it shall not be lawful for any Person to contract or agree with any Person, for any Sum or other Consideration, to indemnify or insure any Person, liable to serve in the Militia, against serving therein, or in like Manner to contract or agree to provide a Substitute for any Person who may be chosen by Lot to serve in the Militia, or to pay the Penalty of [*Ten Pounds Sterling*] by this Act laid on any Person chosen by Lot to serve in the Militia, who shall refuse or neglect to appear, and take the Oath, and serve in the Militia, or provide a Substitute; and if any Person shall offend herein, such Person shall, for every such Contract, Undertaking, or Agreement, forfeit and pay the Sum of [*One hundred Pounds Sterling*] to be recovered and disposed of as hereinafter is directed. Provided that nothing herein contained shall extend to prevent any Person, who shall have been chosen by Lot to serve in the Militia, from procuring, by himself or others, a proper Person to serve as his Substitute: Provided also that nothing in this Act shall extend to prevent Persons of the same Parish [or 𝔓lace] or of [*Two*] or more added together, from entering into Subscriptions amongst themselves for paying jointly for Substitutes, who may be provided for such of the Subscribers on whom the Lot may fall.

And be it further Enacted, That at the said General or Subdivision Meeting respectively, appointed as above, for [𝔠𝔥𝔬𝔬𝔰𝔦𝔫𝔤] [*swearing and enrolling*] the Men [𝔟𝔶 𝔏𝔬𝔱] the Constable [or other such like 𝔒fficer] of each Parish [or 𝔓lace] shall attend, and make a Return upon Oath of the Days when such Notice was served or left as aforesaid; and every Person so chosen by Lot shall, upon such Notice, appear at such Meeting, and, in case of his choosing to serve in Person, there take the following Oath; (that is to say)

" I A. B. do sincerely promise, and swear, That I will
" be faithful, and bear true Allegiance, to His Ma-
" jesty King George, His Heirs and Successors; and I
" do swear that I am a Protestant, and that I will
" faithfully serve in the Militia, within the Kingdom
" of Great Britain, for the Defence of the same, during
" the

"the Time for which I am inrolled, unless I shall be sooner discharged:"

(which Oath any One Deputy [**Commissioner**] [*Lieutenant*] or Justice of the Peace is hereby authorized to administer) and shall be inrolled to serve in the Militia of such respective County [*or*] Stewartry, [**or Place**] as a Private Militia Man, for the Space of [*Three Years*] [(**with the Exception to be afterwards**] [*(except as hereinafter is*] mentioned) in a Roll to be then and there prepared for that Purpose, or shall provide a fit Person, to be approved by any [*Three or more*] Deputy [**Commissioners**] [*Lieutenants*] or Justices of the Peace as aforesaid, at such Meeting, to serve as his Substitute, which Substitute, so provided and approved, shall take the Oath, and sign on the said Roll his Consent to serve as his Substitute during the said Term; and if any Person, so chosen by Lot to serve in the Militia, shall refuse or neglect to take the said Oath, and serve in the Militia, or provide a Substitute to be approved as aforesaid, who shall take the said Oath, and sign his Consent to serve as his Substitute, every Person so refusing or neglecting shall forfeit and pay [*Ten Pounds Sterling*] and at the Expiration of [*Three Years*] be liable to serve again or provide a Substitute; and the Clerk of each Subdivision Meeting [(**if any be**)] [*(where Subdivisions are appointed)*] shall make and send a fair Copy of such Roll of the Names of the Men sworn to serve in such Militia, and for what Parishes [**or Places**] respectively, signed by the Deputy [**Commissioners**] [*Lieutenants*] or Justices of the Peace, or [*Three*] of them at the least, present at such Subdivision Meeting, to the Clerk of the General Meeting.

And be it Enacted, That all Sums of Money arising by Forfeitures paid by, or levied upon, Persons refusing to serve in the Militia personally or by Substitute, shall be applied in the First Place, by any [*Three or more*] Deputy [**Commissioners**] [*Lieutenants*] or Justices of the Peace as aforesaid, within the respective Counties [*or*] Stewartries [**or Places**] or Subdivisions thereof, as the Case shall be, in providing a Substitute for the Person who shall have paid such Penalty; and if any Part of such Penalty shall remain after such Substitute shall be provided, the same shall be paid to the Clerk of the Corps, and be applied as Part of the Stock of such Corps.

And be it further Enacted, That no Perſon ſhall be admitted to ſerve as a Subſtitute in the Militia for any County [or] Stewartry [or 𝔓lace] who ſhall not have had his ordinary Reſidence in the County [or] Stewartry [or 𝔓lace] for which he ſhall offer to ſerve, for [*Twelve*] Calendar Months immediately preceding; nor ſhall any Perſon be admitted to ſerve as a Subſtitute, who ſhall before have ſerved for [*Three Years*] either for the County [or] Stewartry [or 𝔓lace] for which he is propoſed as a Subſtitute, or for any other in Scotland [*until the Expiration of Six Years from the Time of his former Service.*]

And be it further Enacted, That within [*One Calendar Month*] after the ſaid Rolls ſhall be made up by the General Meeting, in ſuch Counties [or] Stewartries [or 𝔓laces] where there are no Subdiviſions, or ſhall be returned from the Clerks of the Subdiviſion Meetings (where any are) to the Clerk of the General Meeting for each County [or] Stewartry [or 𝔓lace] the Deputy [𝔇ommiſſioners] [*Lieutenants*] therein ſhall hold another General Meeting, and ſhall at ſuch Meet-

39 ing form and order the Militia of ſuch County [or] Stewartry [or 𝔓lace] into Battalions, each conſiſting, where the Number of Militia Men will admit of it, of [*Eight Companies*] but in no caſe of leſs than [*Five*] Companies, of [*Eighty*] Men at the moſt, and [*Sixty*] at the leaſt, and ſhall appoint One Lieutenant Colonel and One Major to ſuch Battalion; and where the Number of private Men ſhall amount to [*Three*] Companies, or to any higher Number, under [*Five*] Companies, ſuch Militia ſhall alſo be formed into a Battalion, with One Major, and no other Field Officer; and ſhall appoint Captains to each Company, in every Battalion of Militia to which ſuch Field Officer or Officers ſhall not act as Captain, and ſhall alſo appoint One Lieutenant and One Enſign to each Company in ſuch Battalion (Grenadier Companies excepted) wherein there ſhall be One Captain and Two Lieutenants; and where the Number of Private Militia Men ſhall not be ſufficient to form a Battalion of [*Three*] Companies, of the Number of Men above ſpecified, ſuch Militia ſhall be formed into Independant Companies, each Company to conſiſt of [*One hundred and Ten*] Private Men at the moſt, and [*Sixty*]

40 at the leaſt, with One Captain, One Lieutenant, and One Enſign to each Company; and His Majeſty, His Heirs and Succeſſors, may, in caſe of the Militia being called out to

actual

actual Service, join together any Number of such Independant Companies, and therewith form a Battalion, or incorporate them with any Battalion of Militia, but so as the Number of Companies in such Battalion do not exceed, or fall short of, the Number of Companies of which a Battalion is hereinbefore allowed to consist.

And whereas the Militia Men appointed to serve as above for the Counties of Selkirk, Peebles, Bute, Clackmannan, Kinross, Nairn, and Cromarty, will be too few to compose an Independant Company in each of the said Counties; Be it therefore Enacted, That, for the Purposes of this Act, the following Counties shall be joined together, so as to form One joint Body of Militia for the Counties so joined; (that is to say) The Counties of Selkirk and Peebles shall be joined together, the Counties of Bute and Argyll, the Counties of Clackmannan and [*Sterling, and the Counties of*] Kinross [*and Fife, and*] the Counties of Nairn and Elgin, and the Counties of Cromarty and Ross [𝖆𝖓𝖉 𝖙𝖍𝖊 𝕮𝖔𝖒𝖒𝖎𝖘𝖘𝖎𝖔𝖓𝖊𝖗 𝖔𝖗 𝕮𝖔𝖒𝖒𝖎𝖘𝖘𝖎𝖔𝖓𝖊𝖗𝖘 𝖙𝖔 𝖇𝖊 𝖓𝖆𝖒𝖊𝖉 𝖋𝖔𝖗 𝖙𝖍𝖊 𝖗𝖊𝖘𝖕𝖊𝖈𝖙𝖎𝖛𝖊 𝕮𝖔𝖚𝖓𝖙𝖎𝖊𝖘 𝖘𝖔 𝖚𝖓𝖎𝖙𝖊𝖉 𝖋𝖔𝖗 𝖙𝖍𝖊 𝕻𝖚𝖗𝖕𝖔𝖘𝖊𝖘 𝖔𝖋 𝖙𝖍𝖎𝖘 𝕬𝖈𝖙, 𝖘𝖍𝖆𝖑𝖑 𝖍𝖆𝖛𝖊 𝖙𝖍𝖊 𝖘𝖆𝖒𝖊 𝕻𝖔𝖜𝖊𝖗𝖘, 𝖆𝖓𝖉 𝖕𝖗𝖔𝖈𝖊𝖊𝖉 𝖎𝖓 𝖆𝖑𝖑 𝕽𝖊𝖘𝖕𝖊𝖈𝖙𝖘, 𝖜𝖎𝖙𝖍 𝖗𝖊𝖌𝖆𝖗𖉉 𝖙𝖔 𝖇𝖔𝖙𝖍 𝕮𝖔𝖚𝖓𝖙𝖎𝖊𝖘, 𝖆𝖘 𝖎𝖋 𝖙𝖍𝖊𝖞 𝖜𝖊𝖗𝖊 𝖙𝖔 𝖆𝖑𝖑 𝕴𝖓𝖙𝖊𝖓𝖙𝖘 𝖆𝖓𝖉 𝕻𝖚𝖗𝖕𝖔𝖘𝖊𝖘 𝕺𝖓𝖊.]

And be it Enacted, That the Deputy [𝕮𝖔𝖒𝖒𝖎𝖘𝖘𝖎𝖔𝖓𝖊𝖗𝖘] [*Lieutenants*] for each County, [*or*] Stewartry, [𝖔𝖗 𝕻𝖑𝖆𝖈𝖊] or [*any Three or more*] of them at the least, at a General Meeting, when the Militia of such County [*or*] Stewartry [𝖔𝖗 𝕻𝖑𝖆𝖈𝖊] is not embodied and in actual Service, shall appoint the Time, and Place or Places, in every Year, when [𝖙𝖍𝖊] [*and where such*] Militia shall be trained and exercised for [*Twenty-eight Days*] together, as shall be least inconvenient to the Public; during which Time all the Provisions in any Act for punishing Mutiny and Desertion, and for the better Payment of the Army and their Quarters, shall extend to the Officers and Private Militia Men of every Corps of Militia, but not to extend to Life or Limb; and the Clerk of such General Meeting shall forthwith send Notice of the Time and Place of Exercise to the [𝕾𝖊𝖘𝖘𝖎𝖔𝖓 𝕮𝖑𝖊𝖗𝖐, 𝖔𝖗 𝖔𝖙𝖍𝖊𝖗 𝕺𝖋𝖋𝖎𝖈𝖊𝖗] [*Constable*] of the several Parishes [𝖔𝖗 𝕻𝖑𝖆𝖈𝖊𝖘] within the County [*or*] Stewartry [𝖔𝖗 𝕻𝖑𝖆𝖈𝖊] requiring them respectively to cause such Notice to be fixed on the Doors of the Churches or [𝕮𝖍𝖆𝖕𝖊𝖑𝖘] [*other Places of public Worship*]

belonging

belonging to their respective Parishes [or 𝕻𝖑𝖆𝖈𝖊𝖘] and all such Militia Men shall duly attend at the Time and Place or Places of Exercise so to be appointed; and if any Militia Man (not labouring under any Infirmity incapacitating him, or not having some other lawful Cause or Excuse) shall not appear at such Time, and Place or Places of Exercise, so appointed, he shall forfeit and pay the [𝕻𝖊𝖓𝖆𝖑𝖙𝖞] [*Sum*] of [*Twenty Pounds Sterling*] for every such Neglect, to be recovered [*in such Manner*] and applied to such Uses as hereinafter are directed: Provided that no Officer of the Militia, or Private Militia Man, shall be liable to any Penalty or Punishment for or on Account of his Absence during the Time he shall be going to vote at any Election of a Member to serve in Parliament, or returning from such Election.

And be it Enacted, That if any Militia Man, after having joined his Corps, shall desert during the Time of Annual Exercise, and not be apprehended till after the Expiration of the Time of such Annual Exercise, he shall incur the like Penalty, and be subject to the same Punishment, hereinbefore directed to be inflicted upon Militia Men not joining their Corps; and One Justice of the Peace in any County [*or*] Stewartry [𝖔𝖗 𝕻𝖑𝖆𝖈𝖊] wherein such Deserter shall be found, may proceed against him in the same Manner, and execute the like Powers, as in the Case of Militia Men not appearing at the Time and Place appointed for Annual Exercise.

43

And be it Enacted, That when the Militia shall be called out to be trained and exercised, and also when they shall be called out to actual Service, the Officers and Private Men serving in the said Militia shall be quartered and billeted, and the Carriages necessary for them shall be furnished and performed, in the same Manner as His Majesty's other Forces are ordered to be billeted and quartered, and provided with Carriages, in that Part of Great Britain called Scotland [𝖇𝖞 𝖆𝖓 𝕬𝖈𝖙, 𝖕𝖆𝖘𝖘𝖊𝖉 𝖎𝖓 𝖙𝖍𝖎𝖘 𝖕𝖗𝖊𝖘𝖊𝖓𝖙 𝖄𝖊𝖆𝖗 𝖔𝖋 𝕳𝖎𝖘 𝕸𝖆𝖏𝖊𝖘𝖙𝖞'𝖘 𝕽𝖊𝖎𝖌𝖓, 𝖎𝖓𝖙𝖎𝖙𝖚𝖑𝖊𝖉, " 𝕬𝖓 𝕬𝖈𝖙 𝖋𝖔𝖗 𝖕𝖚𝖓𝖎𝖘𝖍𝖎𝖓𝖌 𝕸𝖚𝖙𝖎𝖓𝖞 𝖆𝖓𝖉 𝕯𝖊𝖘𝖊𝖗𝖙𝖎𝖔𝖓; " 𝖆𝖓𝖉 𝖋𝖔𝖗 𝖙𝖍𝖊 𝖇𝖊𝖙𝖙𝖊𝖗 𝕻𝖆𝖞𝖒𝖊𝖓𝖙 𝖔𝖋 𝖙𝖍𝖊 𝕬𝖗𝖒𝖞 𝖆𝖓𝖉 𝖙𝖍𝖊𝖎𝖗 " 𝕼𝖚𝖆𝖗𝖙𝖊𝖗𝖘."]

And be it Enacted, That it shall be lawful for every Captain or Commanding Officer of each Company of Militia, to put the Corporals and Private Men of his Company under Stoppages, not exceeding [*Six Pence*] a Day, for the Purpose

pose of supplying them and their Wives with Necessaries, when called out to Annual Exercise; provided that such Captain or Commanding Officer shall account with each Corporal and Private Militia Man for the said Stoppages before they shall be dismissed from the said Annual Exercise, having first deducted what shall have been laid out for them for Necessaries, and Repair of Arms damaged by their [*wilful*] Neglect.

And be it Enacted, That all Muskets, delivered for the Service of the Militia, shall be marked distinctly in some visible Place with the Letter M. and the Name of the County [*or*] Stewartry [*or Place*] to which they belong; and the Captain of each Company of Militia shall have the Care and Custody of the Arms, Clothes, and Accoutrements, provided for his Company, and shall keep the same in some dry and secure Place, under Lock and Key, and the Serjeants of each Company are hereby required to take Care, that after the Annual Exercise is completed, every Militia Man shall return his Arms, Clothes, and Accoutrements, to his Captain, or to such Person or Persons as he shall appoint to receive the same, well cleaned, and in good Repair, or in Default thereof shall forfeit and pay any Sum not exceeding [*Three Pounds Sterling*] and the Serjeants and Drummers belonging to each Company shall be ordered and required, by the Captain or Commanding Officer of such Company, to assist in taking Care of the Arms, Clothes, and Accoutrements, thereto belonging, and in keeping the same clean, free from Rust, and fit for Service.

And be it Enacted, That if any Serjeant, or other Person, intrusted by the Captain or Commanding Officer of any Company of Militia with the Custody of any Arms, Clothes, or Accoutrements, belonging to such Company, shall deliver out any such Arms, Clothes, or Accoutrements, unless by the Order of such Captain, or Commanding Officer, he shall forfeit and pay any Sum not exceeding [*Three Pounds Sterling*] and if any Serjeant, Drummer, Corporal, or Private Militia Man, shall sell, pawn, or lose, any of his Arms, Clothes, or Accoutrements, or shall refuse or neglect to return the same in good Order to the Captain or Commanding Officer of the Company to which he belongs, or to such Person as he shall appoint to receive the same, when demanded, such Serjeant, Drummer, Corporal, or Private Militia Man, shall for every such

such Offence forfeit and pay any Sum not exceeding [*Three Pounds Sterling.*]

And be it Enacted, That if any Person shall knowingly buy, take in Exchange, conceal, or otherwise receive, contrary to the true Intent and Meaning of this Act, any Arms, Clothes, or Accoutrements, belonging to the said Militia, upon any Pretence whatsoever, every such Person shall forfeit and pay for every such Offence any Sum not exceeding [*Five Pounds Sterling*]

And be it Enacted, That the [*Lieutenant*] Colonel or Commanding Officer of every Battalion or Corps of unembodied Militia, as often as the same shall be called out to Exercise, within [*Thirty*] Days after such Exercise shall be finished, shall transmit to One of His Majesty's principal Secretaries of State a complete Return, signed by him, of the several Officers, Non-commissioned Officers, and Private Men, who served therein at the Time the same was so exercised, in Manner and Form following; the said Form being subject to such Alterations in making the same as is consistent with the particular Establishment of Militia in the County [*or*] Stewartry [𝖔𝖗 𝖕𝖑𝖆𝖈𝖊] from whence the Return is made.

RETURN of a Battalion or Corps of Militia at Annual Exercise.

Commissioned Officers.								Staff Officers.	Non Commissioned Officers.			Private.
Lieutenant Colonel.	Major.	Captains.	Captain Lieutenants.	Lieutenants.	Ensigns.			Adjutant.	Serjeants.	Corporals.	Drummers.	Private.

Present —
Absent —
Wanting to complete —

And

[28]

And that Part of the Return which gives an Account of the Number of Officers present during the Time of Exercise, shall be in the Form following; (to wit)

N° of Days.

48 Lieutenant Colonel — — —
Major — — — —
First Captain — — —
Second Captain — — —
Third Captain — — —
Fourth Captain — — —
Fifth Captain — — —
Sixth Captain — — —
First Lieutenant — — —
Second Lieutenant — — —
Third Lieutenant — — —
Fourth Lieutenant — — —
Fifth Lieutenant — — —
Sixth Lieutenant — — —
Seventh Lieutenant — — —
Eighth Lieutenant — — —
First Ensign — — —
Second Ensign — — —
Third Ensign — — —
Fourth Ensign — — —
Fifth Ensign — — —
Sixth Ensign — — —
Seventh Ensign — — —
Eighth Ensign — — —

49 And such Secretary of State shall cause a true Copy of such Return to be Annually laid before both Houses of Parliament, and that a like Return shall also be made to His Majesty's [Com= missioner or Commissioners] [*Lieutenant*] of such County or [Place] [*Stewartry*] and to the Auditor of His Majesty's Court of Exchequer, and to the Receiver General of the Land Tax, and to the Clerk of the Peace of such County [*or*] Stewartry, [or Place] and such Clerk of the Peace shall produce the same to the Justices of the Peace, at their next General Quarter Sessions, and shall afterwards file the same amongst the Records of such Sessions, and in Default thereof shall forfeit his Office

Office of Clerk of the Peace, and shall for ever after be disqualified from holding the same.

And be it Enacted, That in case of actual Invasion, or upon imminent Danger thereof, or in case of Rebellion in the Kingdom of *Great Britain*, or in any of His Majesty's Dominions, it shall be lawful for His Majesty (the Occasion being first communicated to Parliament, if the Parliament shall be then sitting, or declared in Council, and notified by Proclamation, if no Parliament shall be then sitting) to order and direct his [**Commissioner or Commissioners**] [*Lieutenant*] or any [*Three or more*] Deputy [**Commissioners**] [*Lieutenants*] of each County [*or*] Stewartry, [**or Place**] aforesaid, with all convenient Speed to draw out and embody all or any of the Battalions or Corps of Militia of their respective Counties [*or*] Stewartries [**or Places**] and shall order and direct them to be put under the Command of such General Officers, and to be led to such Parts of the Kingdom of Great Britain, as His Majesty shall think proper; and that the Officers of the Militia, and Private Militia Men, of the Battalions and Independant Companies, during the Time they shall be embodied, and in actual Service, as aforesaid, shall remain under the Command of such General Officers, and shall be intitled to the same Pay, to commence from the Day of the Date of His Majesty's Order by virtue of which they were called out into actual Service, as the Officers and Private Men in His Majesty's other Regiments of Foot receive, and no other; and the Officers of the Militia shall, during such Time as aforesaid, rank with the Officers of His Majesty's other Forces of equal Degree with them, as the youngest of their Rank; and the Officers, Drummers, Corporals, and Private Men, of such Militia, during the Time they shall be in such actual Service, shall be subject and liable to all such Articles of War, Rules, and Regulations, as shall be then by Act of Parliament in Force, for the punishing Mutiny and Desertion, and for the better Payment of the Army and their Quarters (excepting only as to such Particulars as are or shall be otherwise particularly provided for by this or any Act or Acts of Parliament hereafter to be made, for regulating the Militia Forces, within that Part of Great Britain aforesaid) and when such Militia shall be disembodied, and returned again to their respective Parishes, or Places of Abode, they shall be under the same Orders and Directions only, as they were before they were drawn out and embodied as aforesaid.

Provided always, and be it Enacted, That if, at the Time of calling out such Militia into actual Service, the Parliament

ment shall be separated by Adjournment or Prorogation, and on that Account will not meet within [*Fourteen*] Days, His Majesty shall forthwith issue a Proclamation for the Meeting of the Parliament upon such Day as he shall appoint, giving [*Fourteen*] Days Notice thereof, and the Parliament shall accordingly meet upon such Day, and continue to sit and act in like Manner, to all Intents and Purposes, as if it had stood adjourned or prorogued to the same Day.

Provided always, and be it Enacted, That no Officer serving in the Militia shall sit in any Court Martial upon the Trial of any Officer or Soldier serving in any of His Majesty's other Forces, nor shall any Officer serving in any of His Majesty's other Forces sit in any Court Martial upon the Trial of any Officer or Private Man serving in the Militia.

And be it further Enacted, That His Majesty's [Commissioner or Commissioners] [*Lieutenant*] or any [*Three*] Deputy [Commissioners] [*Lieutenants*] of every County [*or*] Stewartry [or Place] shall issue his or their Orders to the Constables [or other Officers] of the several Parishes [and Places] within their respective Divisions, forthwith to give Notice to the several Officers, Serjeants, Corporals, Drummers, Fifers, and Private Militia Men, or leave Notice in Writing at the usual Places of their respective Abodes, to attend at the Time and Place mentioned in such Order for calling out such Militia into actual Service; and if any such Officer, Serjeant, Corporal, Drummer, Fifer, or Private Militia Man, not labouring under any Infirmity incapacitating him to serve, nor having some lawful Excuse, shall not appear in pursuance of such Notice, he shall be considered as absent from his Corps without Leave, and shall be proceeded against accordingly; and if any Person shall knowingly harbour or conceal any such Officer, Serjeant, Corporal, Drummer, Fifer, or Private Militia Man, not attending when ordered out into actual Service as aforesaid, such Person shall for every such Offence forfeit and pay the Sum of [*Twenty Pounds Sterling.*]

And be it Enacted, That when the Militia of any County [*or*] Stewartry [or Place] shall be ordered out into actual Service, the [Commissioner or Commissioners] [*Lieutenant*] of such County [*or*] Stewartry [or Place] shall draw upon the Receiver General of the Land Tax in Favour of the Captain or Com-

Commanding Officer of each Company of Militia so ordered out, for such Sum as will amount to [*One Pound One Shilling Sterling*] for each Private Militia Man belonging to his Company, to be paid over by such Captain, or other Officer, to every such private Militia Man who belonged to his Company at the Time such Militia was ordered out into actual Service, on or before the Day appointed for marching, and to such Militia Man who shall be afterwards ordered out, when he shall join his Company then being in actual Service; and the Receiver General of the Land Tax shall be allowed the same in his Accounts. 54

And be it further Enacted, That it shall and may be lawful for any One Deputy [𝕮𝖔𝖒𝖒𝖎𝖘𝖘𝖎𝖔𝖓𝖊𝖗] [*Lieutenant*] at any Place in the County, or Stewartry, or Subdivision thereof, in which he usually acts, to swear and inroll any Substitute to serve for any Place in such County or Stewartry, or Subdivision thereof, provided such Substitute shall produce to such Deputy [𝕮𝖔𝖒𝖒𝖎𝖘𝖘𝖎𝖔𝖓𝖊𝖗] [*Lieutenant*] a Certificate, under the Hands and Seals of any [*Two*] other Deputy [𝕮𝖔𝖒𝖒𝖎𝖘𝖘𝖎𝖔𝖓𝖊𝖗𝖘] [*Lieutenants*] or Justice of the Peace acting in such County or Stewartry, or Subdivision thereof, certifying they have seen, and do approve of such Substitute as a proper Person to serve in the Militia; and such Person shall and may be sworn and inrolled by such Deputy [𝕮𝖔𝖒𝖒𝖎𝖘𝖘𝖎𝖔𝖓𝖊𝖗] [*Lieutenant*] provided the Clerk belonging to such County, Stewartry, or Subdivision thereof, shall attend with the Roll for that Purpose.

And be it further Enacted, That all such Militia Men whose Time of Service in the Militia shall be near expiring, and who shall be then absent from the County [*or*] Stewartry [𝖔𝖗 𝕻𝖑𝖆𝖈𝖊] to which they belong [*on actual Service*] shall be returned or marched back into the same, in order that they 55 may be near their respective Homes or Places of Abode as possible, at the Expiration of their said Service.

And be it further Enacted, That in every such County [*or*] Stewartry [𝖆𝖓𝖉 𝕻𝖑𝖆𝖈𝖊] wherein the Militia shall not be raised, and such Return as aforesaid shall not be delivered to the Clerk of the Peace before the General Quarter Sessions of the Peace to be held for such County [*or*] Stewartry [𝖔𝖗 𝕻𝖑𝖆𝖈𝖊] next after the [*Twenty-fifth Day of December*] in every Year, such Clerk of the Peace shall certify, under his Hand, to the Justices of the Peace there assembled, on the Day such Sessions shall

shall be opened, that he hath not received such Return, and shall file such his Certificate amongst the Records of such Sessions; and the Justices of the Peace at their said Sessions shall transmit the said Certificate to the Convenor of the Commissioners of Supply for the said County, who shall forthwith call a Meeting of the said Commissioners; and the Commissioners being so assembled shall proceed to raise and levy within such County or [Place] [Stewartry] the Sum of 56 [*Five Pounds Sterling*] in lieu of every Private Militia Man required to serve for the same as aforesaid, in such Manner and in such Proportions as the Land Tax or Cess have been usually levied in such County or [Place] [*Stewartry*] Provided that every Person duly qualified, who shall have served as an Officer in the Militia within the Kingdom of Great Britain for [*Three Years*] or who shall be then actually serving as an Officer, or who shall have duly offered to serve as an Officer in such Militia in Manner hereinbefore directed, shall not be liable to pay any Part or Share of such Rate or Assessment, nor shall his Lands, Tenements, or Hereditaments, be assessed or charged thereto; and the Deficiency thereby occasioned, shall be allowed to such County [*or*] Stewartry [or Place] by deducting the Sum which otherwise would have been charged on such Person, from the gross Amount of the Sums of [*Five Pounds Sterling*] per Man, hereinbefore directed to be raised in such County [*or*] Stewartry [or Place] provided that every Person claiming such Exemption shall file a Certificate of such 57 Service, or of his having offered to serve, with the Clerk of the Peace for the County or [Place] [*Stewartry*] wherein such Person shall claim to have such Exemption, and shall also deliver to him a List, under his Hand, of his Tenants and Farmers, and the Places of their Abode, and such Clerk of the Peace shall forthwith file the same amongst the Records of [Session] [*the Quarter Sessions*] And when any such Assessment shall be ordered to be made, such Clerk of the Peace shall certify to the Convenor of the Commissioners of Supply, and to the Receiver General of the Land Tax, the Names of all Persons who shall have filed such Lists, and the Names of their Tenants and Farmers inserted therein, in order that such Person or Persons, and his or their Lands, Tenements, and Hereditaments, may not be charged with such Assessment; and His Majesty's [Commissioner or Commissioners] [*Lieutenant*] of every County or [Place] [*Stewartry*] where any such Person shall have served as an Officer in the Militia thereof for the Space

of

[33]

of [*Three Years*] or who shall actually serve as an Officer of such Militia, shall, on Request, grant to him a Certificate thereof; and every such [**Commissioner or Commissioners**] [*Lieutenant*] Deputy [**Commissioner**] [*Lieutenant*] or Justice of the Peace, before whom such Person shall offer to serve as an Officer in the Militia, shall, on Request, grant him a Certificate thereof, in order that he may be exempted as aforesaid; and the said Assessment shall be made, levied, collected, and kept, distinct and separate from the Cess or Land Tax; and that every Tenant or Occupier of any Messuages, Lands, Tenements, or Hereditaments, who shall pay any Assessment made in pursuance of this Act, for the Purposes aforesaid, shall and may deduct and retain the same out of his or her Rent, except where there is a Covenant or Agreement to the contrary.

58

And be it Enacted by the Authority aforesaid, That the said Sums of [*Five Pounds Sterling*] directed to be raised for every Militia Man required to serve for each County [*or*] Stewartry [**or Place**] where such Militia shall not be raised as aforesaid, shall be paid to the Receiver General of the Land Tax within [*Six Calendar Months*] after the General Quarter Sessions of the Peace, that shall be held for such County [*or*] Stewartry [**or Place**] next after the [*Twenty-fifth Day of December*] in every Year, who shall, within [*One Calendar Month*] after the Receipt thereof, account for and pay the same into the Receipt of His Majesty's Exchequer at Westminster to be accounted for Yearly to Parliament, and applied to such Uses as Parliament shall direct; and in case the said Sums of Money shall not be raised and paid to the Receiver General of the Land Tax as aforesaid, the Receiver General shall immediately proceed to enforce the Payment thereof in the same Manner as is appointed, with regard to the Cess or Land Tax in that Part of Great Britain called Scotland, by an Act, passed in this present Year of His Majesty's Reign, intituled, " An Act " for granting an Aid to His Majesty by a Land Tax, to " be raised in Great Britain for the Service of the Year " One thousand Seven hundred and Seventy-six:" And the Receiver General of the Land Tax, for his Trouble in receiving such Sums of Money, and for his Trouble in giving Receipts for the same, and accounting for and paying it into His Majesty's said Exchequer, and doing the Duty in all other Respects required of him by this Act, shall be allowed [*Two Pence Sterling*] in the Pound [*Sterling*] out of the Money so received and paid by him, and no more; and every Officer ne-

59

I cessarily

cessarily employed in collecting the said Sums of Money in the several Parishes [AND PLACES] aforesaid, and in accounting for and paying the same to such Receiver General, and for doing the Duty in all other Respects required of him by this Act, in regard to the levying and collecting such Sums of Money respectively, shall be allowed [*One Penny Sterling*] in the Pound [*Sterling*] and no more, out of the Money so received by him.

And be it Enacted, That no Serjeant, Corporal, Drummer, Fifer, or Private Man, serving in the Militia, shall, during the Time of such Service, be liable to do any Highway Duty, commonly called Statute Work, or be appointed to serve as a Peace Officer, or Parish Officer, or be liable to serve in [ANY OF] His Majesty's [LAND OR] Sea Forces, unless he shall consent thereto.

And be it Enacted, That if any Non-commission Officer of the Militia, or Private Militia Man, shall be maimed or wounded in actual Service, he shall be equally entitled to the Benefit of Chelsea Hospital with any Non-commission Officer or Private Soldier belonging to His Majesty's other Forces; and that every such Person, having served in the Militia when called out into actual Service, and being a married Man, may set up and exercise any Trade in any Town or Place within the Kingdoms of Great Britain or Ireland, without any Molestation for or by Reason of the using such Trade, in like Manner as any Person who has served in His Majesty's Navy, or as a Soldier in his regular Land Forces, may do.

And be it Enacted, That it shall be optional to any Battalion or Independant Company of Militia, within that Part of the United Kingdom called Scotland, to be cloathed in the Highland Dress, if the Commanding Officer thereof shall think fit.

And be it Enacted, That every Private Militia Man who shall have served [*Three Years*] without being called out into actual Service, or who shall have served [*One Year*] in actual Service, shall, at the End of such Times respectively, be entitled to his Military Clothes for his own Use, in such Manner as the Commanding Officer of the Corps in which he served shall judge most for his Benefit.

And

And be it Enacted, That if any Servant hired by the Year, or otherwise, shall serve in the Militia, it shall be lawful for One Justice of the Peace, upon Complaint made on Oath by such Servant, to order so much of his Wages as shall appear to such Justice to be due to him, to be immediately paid him by his Master or Employer, in Proportion to the Service he has performed; and in Default of Payment the same shall be levied by [*Distress and Sale*] by Warrant from such Justice.

62

And be it further Enacted, That no Person having served personally, or by Substitute, [*Three Years*] in the Militia, shall be obliged to serve again until by Rotation it comes to his Turn; and when any Substitute, after having been approved as aforesaid, before the Expiration of the Term for which he was to serve, shall die, or be appointed a Serjeant in the Militia, or be legally discharged, the Person for whom he served shall not be obliged to serve himself, or to find another Substitute, but such Vacancy shall be filled up as in the Case of Vacancies occasioned by the Death or Discharge of Persons serving for themselves.

Provided always, That no Militia Man, having served as a Substitute, shall be thereby excused from serving for himself when he shall be chosen by Lot.

And be it further Enacted, That if any Serjeant Major, Drum Major, Drummer, or Fifer, engaged to serve as aforesaid, within that Part of Great Britain called Scotland, who shall have received Pay therein, shall, during the Time such Corps of Militia to which he belongs is not in actual Service, or out at Annual Exercise, misbehave, be negligent in his Duty, or be disobedient to the Orders of the Adjutant or other his superior Officer, he shall forfeit and pay any Sum not exceeding [*Thirty Shillings Sterling*] for every such Offence.

63

And be it further Enacted, That at the End of the [*First*] Year's Service of any Battalion or Independant Company of Militia [*One Third*] Part of the Private Men of such Battalion or Independant Company shall be discharged by Ballot, and the Private Men so discharged, and also such Vacancies as may have happened, shall be supplied by Ballot; and after the [*Second*] Year's Service of any Battalion or Independant Company of Militia, [*One other of the Two remaining Third Parts*] [Part] of the

[36]

the Private Men ſhall be diſcharged, and others ſupplied, in like Manner; and at the End of the [*Third*] Year's Service of any Battalion or Independant Company of Militia, the re‐
64. maining [*Third Part*] of the Private Men ſhall be diſcharged, and ſupplied, in like Manner; and from thenceforth a Ballot ſhall be regularly made each Year, for ſupplying the Private Men ſo diſcharged in Rotation, and alſo for ſupplying ſuch Va‐
cancies as may have happened in any Battalion or Independant Company of Militia.

And be it Enacted, That if any Militia Man ſhall change the Place of his Abode from One Pariſh [or 𝔓lace] to another, without the Conſent in Writing of the Captain or Commanding Officer of the Company to which he belongs, [and alſo of the Conſtable of the 𝔓ariſh or 𝔓lace for which he ſhall be inrolled to ſerve] and without giving Notice thereof [*in Writing*] to the Clerk of the County or Stewartry, or of the Subdiviſion Meeting, if the County or Stewartry be ſubdivided [in which] [*and alſo to the Conſtable of*] the Pariſh [or 𝔓lace] for which he ſerves [ſhall be ſituated] [*ſpecifying the Name of the Pariſh from whence, and to which, he ſhall remove, and of the Officer of whom he obtained ſuch Leave*] (which Clerk is hereby required to keep an Account of the ſame) he ſhall [*then*] forfeit and pay any Sum not exceeding [*Ten Pounds Ster‐
ling*.]

And be it further Enacted, That if any Perſon, who is ſworn and inrolled to ſerve in the ſaid Militia, ſhall inliſt into His Majeſty's other Forces, the Colonel or Commanding Officer of ſuch Regiment or Corps in which he ſhall ſo inliſt, ſhall pay to the Clerk of the Corps of Militia to which ſuch
65 Militia Man belongs, the Sum of [*Three Pounds Three Shillings Sterling*] which ſhall be accounted for and paid by him to the Commanding Officer of the Corps for which ſuch Militia Man was inrolled to ſerve, and ſhall be applied to‐
wards finding another Man to ſerve in ſuch Militia, in the room of the Perſon ſo inliſting; and if ſuch Colonel or Com‐
manding Officer ſhall, on Demand, refuſe to pay ſuch Sum of Money to the Clerk of the Corps of Militia, ſuch inliſting ſhall be from thenceforth [*null and void*] And if any Militia Man ſhall deny to any Officer, Serjeant, or other Per‐
ſon, recruiting for Men to inliſt and ſerve in His Majeſty's other Forces, that he is, at the Time of his offering to inliſt, a Militia Man then actually inrolled and engaged to ſerve

(which

(which the said Officer, Serjeant, or other Person, is hereby required to ask any Man offering to inlist) and shall inlist in His Majesty's other Forces, such Person so offending, and who shall thereof be convicted before any Justice of the Peace for such County or [Place] [Stewartry] shall be [committed to the Common Gaol of such County or Stewartry, there to remain without Bail, for any Time not exceeding Six Calendar Months,] over and above any Penalty or Punishment to which such Person so offending shall be otherwise liable by Law, and from the Day on which his Engagement to serve in the Militia shall end, and not sooner, except on Payment of such Sum of Money as aforesaid, he shall belong as a Soldier to such Corps of His Majesty's other Forces into which he shall have been so inlisted.

And be it further Enacted, That no Officer, Serjeant, or Commander of a Recruiting Party, of His Majesty's other Forces, shall beat up for Recruits in any Place where any Corps of Militia shall be assembled for Exercise, nor shall inlist any Militia Man within [Ten Days] before, or [Ten Days] after, their being so assembled: And if any Officer, Serjeant, or Commander of a Recruiting Party, shall beat up for Recruits, or inlist any Militia Man, where any Corps of Militia is, or within the Time aforesaid, either before or after any Corps of Militia shall be so assembled, the Officer, Serjeant, or Commander of such Recruiting Party, so offending, shall forfeit [*Twenty Pounds Sterling*] for every such Offence, and the inlisting such Militia Man shall be [*null and void*].

And it is hereby further Provided and Declared, That in case of the Militia being embodied, no Officer, Serjeant, or Commander of a Recruiting Party, of His Majesty's other Forces, shall inlist any Militia Man, under the Penalty aforesaid, and the inlisting such Militia Man shall be likewise [*null and void*].

And be it Enacted, That if any Person serving in any of His Majesty's Regular Forces shall offer to serve, and be enrolled, as a Substitute, in the Militia, he shall for every such Offence forfeit and pay any Sum not exceeding [*Ten Pounds Sterling*].

And be it further Enacted by the Authority aforesaid, That if any Clerk of the Peace shall be guilty of any Neglect of Duty, or shall not do and perform the several Acts, Matters, and Things, herein required of or by him to be done or performed, for the better and more effectual carrying this Act into Execution, and for which no Penalty or Forfeiture is herein directed to be inflicted or paid, every such Clerk of the Peace shall [*forfeit his Office, and be rendered incapable of holding the same, or any other Office, Civil or Military, under the Government.*]

And be it Enacted, That if any Constable [or other 𝔒𝔣𝔣𝔦𝔠𝔢𝔯] shall neglect or refuse to do any such Act as is hereby required to be done by him or them, for the better and more effectual carrying this Act into Execution, or shall neglect or refuse to obey the lawful Commands of the Deputy [𝔠𝔬𝔪𝔪𝔦𝔰𝔰𝔦𝔬𝔫𝔢𝔯𝔰] [*Lieutenants*] or Justices of the Peace, or any of them, in the Execution of the Powers hereby placed in them, or any of them, every such Constable, and other [𝔰𝔲𝔠𝔥 𝔩𝔦𝔨𝔢] Officer, shall for every such Offence, in like Manner, forfeit and pay [𝔱𝔥𝔢] [*any*] Sum [𝔬𝔣] [*not exceeding Forty Shillings Sterling*].

68

And be it further Enacted by the Authority aforesaid, That all Fines, Penalties, and Forfeitures, by this Act imposed, the Manner of Recovery whereof is not hereby particularly provided for, shall, on Complaint made before the Sheriff or Stewart [*Depute, or their respective Substitutes*] of such County [*or*] Stewartry [𝔬𝔯 𝔓𝔩𝔞𝔠𝔢] where the Cause of such Complaint shall arise, and sufficient Proof produced before such Sheriff or Stewart [*Depute, or their respective Substitutes*] on examining into the Truth of such Complaint, to induce him to adjudge and determine the Offender to be guilty of such Offence or Neglect wherewith he is charged, be by the Sheriff or Stewart [*Depute, or their respective Substitutes*] forthwith ordered to be paid; and in Default of such Payment the Sheriff or Stewart [*Depute, or their respective Substitutes*] shall grant a Warrant to levy the same by [*Distress and Sale*] of the Goods and Chattels of such Offender, rendering the Overplus (if any) on Demand, after deducting the Charges of such [*Distress and Sale*] to such Offender; and where the Goods and Chattels of such Offender shall not be sufficient to answer such Penalty, and the Expences of making such [*Distress and Sale*] such Sheriff or Stewart [*Depute, or their respective Substitutes*] shall [*commit him to the Common Gaol of the County*] where the Offence shall have been committed, for any Time not exceeding [*Three Calendar Months*] and [*One Half*] of all Fines, Penalties, and Forfeitures, by this Act imposed, the Application whereof is not otherwise particularly provided for, shall be paid to and to the Use of the Person or Persons who shall inform or prosecute for the same and [*the other Half*]

69

Half] shall be paid to the Clerk of the Corps of Militia serving for the County or [𝔓𝔩𝔞𝔠𝔢] [*Stewartry*] where such Offence shall be committed, and shall be made a Common Stock; and the said Clerk shall every [*Three Months*] account for the same to the Commanding Officer of such Corps, who shall apply the Sums thence arising to the necessary Purposes of the Corps, and if there be any Overplus, shall, out of such Overplus, cause Butts to be erected in some convenient Places, and shall direct the Clerk of such Corps to buy and provide, with some Part of the Money so arising, a proper Quantity of Gunpowder and Ball, to be used at proper Times, by the Militia Men of such Corps, in shooting at Marks; and to apply and dispose of such other Part of the Money aforesaid, as he shall think reasonable, in Prizes to be given to such Militia Man or Men who shall, by the Commanding Officer then present, 70 be adjudged to be the best Markfman, or in such other Ways, tending to the Encouragement and Improvement of the Corps, as the Commanding Officer shall direct.

Provided always, and it is hereby further Enacted, That if any Person shall think himself aggrieved by the Judgment or Determination of such Sheriff or Stewart [*Depute, or their respective Substitutes*] such Person may bring the said Determination or Judgment under the Review of the Court of Session [*or the Circuit Court of Justiciary, in all Counties or Stewartries where Appeals to the Circuit are competent*] in common Form; and till such Appeal shall be finally heard and determined, all Proceedings upon such original Judgment or Determination shall be suspended.

And be it further Enacted, That if any Suit or Action shall be brought or commenced against any Person for any Thing done in pursuance of this Act, such Action or Suit shall be commenced within [*Six Calendar Months*] after the Fact committed, and not afterwards.

And be it hereby Enacted, That this Act shall continue in Force for [*Seven*] Years, and till the End of the then next Session of Parliament.

CLAUSE (A.)

And be it Enacted, That His Majesty's Lieutenants, who are or shall be commissioned for the Militia of the City of Edinburgh, may and shall continue to list and levy the Train Bands and Guard of the said City in Manner as heretofore.

CLAUSE (B.)

Provided always, and be it further Enacted, That where any Parish shall be in more Counties or Stewartries than One, the Inhabitants of such Parish shall serve in the Militia of that County or Stewartry wherein the Church belonging to such Parish is situated; and that such Parish shall be deemed as Part of that County, and shall be subject to the Jurisdiction and Authority of the Deputy Lieutenants, Justices, and other Officers, of that County or Stewartry, to all the Intents and Purposes of this Act.

CLAUSE (C.)

And be it Enacted, That His Majesty's Lieutenants, or any Three Deputy Lieutenants, of any County or Stewartry; is and are hereby authorized, by Warrant under his Hand and Seal, or their Hands and Seals, to employ such Person or Persons as he or they shall think fit, to seize and remove the Arms, Clothes, and Accoutrements, belonging to the Militia of such County or Stewartry, whenever His Majesty's said Lieutenants, or the Deputy Lieutenants, shall adjudge it necessary to the Kingdom, and to deliver the said Arms, Clothes, and Accoutrements, into the Custody of such Person or Persons as His Majesty's said Lieutenants, or Deputy Lieutenants, shall appoint to receive the same, for the Purposes of this Act.

CLAUSE

Clause (D).

Provided always, and it is hereby Enacted, That when any Volunteer or Volunteers shall, on the Day appointed for the Ballot, offer to serve for any Parish or Parishes, and shall be approved of by the Deputy Lieutenant and Justices aforesaid, then, and in that Case only, so many Men shall be ballotted for as are sufficient to make up the Number allotted to that Parish or Parishes, and the Volunteer or Volunteers so offering themselves shall be inrolled, and deemed Militia Men to all Intents and Purposes.

Clause (E.)

And be it Enacted by the Authority aforesaid, That the Justices of the Peace of every County or Stewartry, at their Quarter Sessions respectively, in that Part of Great Britain called Scotland, shall appoint yearly One or more Constables, in every Parish within their respective County or Stewartry, for the Purpose of carrying this Act into Execution; which Constable or Constables shall be vested with all other Powers given to any Constable or Constables by any former Law.

Clause (F).

And be it Enacted, That if any Person being of the People called Quakers shall be chosen by Lot to serve in the Militia, and shall refuse or neglect to appear, or to take the Oath and serve in the Militia, or to provide a Substitute, to be approved as aforesaid, who shall take the said Oath, and subscribe his Consent to serve as the Substitute of such Quaker, then, and in every such Case, any Three Deputy Lieutenants shall, if they think proper, upon as reasonable Terms as may be, provide and hire a fit Person, who shall take the Oath, and subscribe his Consent to serve in the said Militia for the Space of Three Years, as the Substitute of such Quaker; and are hereby impowered and required to levy, by Distress and Sale of the Goods and Chattels of such Quaker, by Warrant under their Hands

Hands and Seals, such Sum or Sums of Money as shall be necessary, to defray the Expence of providing and hiring such Person to serve in the Militia for the Space of Three Years, as the Substitute of such Quaker so refusing or neglecting, rendering the Overplus, if any, on Demand, after deducting the Charges of such Distress and Sale, to such Quaker upon whom such Distress shall have been made as aforesaid; and in case any Measures shall be used, in taking such Distress, which may be by any such Quaker thought oppressive, it shall be lawful for such Quaker to complain thereof to the Deputy Lieutenants and Justices of the Peace, at their next Meeting, for such County, Stewartry, or Subdivision, who are hereby impowered and required to hear and finally determine the same, and to order the Parties to make such Satisfaction to each other as to them shall appear just and reasonable.

A
BILL
[With the Amendments]

FOR

The better ordering of the Militia Forces in that Part of Great Britain called Scotland.

1776.

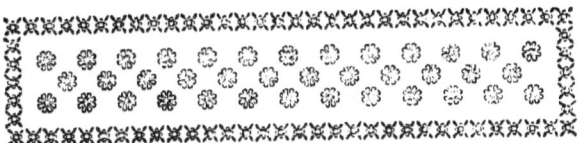

A

B I L L

TO

Reſtrain Apprentices, Tradeſmen, and other unqualified Perſons, from deſtroying the Game, in that Part of *Great Britain* called *Scotland*; and for granting to Proprietors of Lands in *Scotland* further Powers with regard to killing of Game.

Note.—*The Figures in the Margin denote the Number of the Folios in the written Copy.*

WHEREAS many Proprietors of Land in that Part of *Great Britain* called *Scotland*, are improperly reſtrained in the Uſe and Enjoyment of the Game upon their own Property:

And whereas many Tradeſmen, Apprentices, and other Perſons, neglect their Trades and Employments, and ſpend great Part of their Time in hunting, ſhooting, and otherwiſe deſtroying, Game, within that Part of *Great Britain*

A called

called *Scotland*, although not qualified by Law so to do, to the Ruin of themselves and Families, and to the Prejudice of the Public:

For Remedy whereof, **Be it Enacted** by the KING's Most Excellent MAJESTY, by and with the Advice and Consent of the Lords Spiritual and Temporal, and Commons, in this present Parliament assembled, and by the Authority of the same, That, from and after the   Day of   if any Person or Persons within that Part of *Great Britain* called *Scotland*, not being qualified by Law so to do, shall presume to shoot or fowl, hawk, hunt, keep or set Snares for, or shall keep or use any Dogs, Nets, Snares, or other Engines, to kill or destroy, the Game, or shall keep and use any Gun or Guns in destroying the Game, and shall be convicted of any of the said Offences, upon the Oath of One or more credible Witness or Witnesses, before the Sheriff of the County or Stewart of the Stewartry where the Offence shall be committed, or where the Offender shall be found, every such Offender shall, for the First Offence, forfeit and pay the Sum of   One Half to the Person or Persons upon whose Information such Offender shall be convicted, and the other Half to the Poor of the Parish where the Offence shall be committed, to be levied by   of the Offender's Goods and Chattels, by Warrant under the Hand of the Sheriff or Stewart before whom such Offender shall be convicted; and in case sufficient   cannot be found, such Sheriff or Stewart shall commit such Offender to the Common Gaol of the County or Stewartry where the Offence shall be committed, or where the Offender shall be found, there to remain for the Space of   unless such Penalty shall be sooner paid: And if any Person, being convicted as aforesaid, shall again offend in any of the said Cases, he shall forfeit and pay the Sum of   to be divided and levied in Manner above mentioned; and in case sufficient   cannot be found, the Sheriff or Stewart, before whom such Person shall be convicted of such Second or subsequent Offence, shall commit such Person in Manner aforesaid for the Space of   unless such Penalty shall be paid before the Expiration of that Period.

And be it further Enacted by the Authority aforesaid, That every

every Sheriff of a County, or Stewart of a Stewartry, in Confequence of Information upon Oath, fhall and may, by Warrant under their Hands refpectively, caufe Search to be made in the Day-time for any Dogs, Nets, or Engines, for deftroying of Game, which fhall be in the Cuftody of any Perfon or Perfons not qualified by Law to kill Game, and likewife to caufe Search to be made for any Gun or Guns kept and ufed by any unqualified or unlicenfed Perfon for killing and deftroying Game; and, in cafe fuch Dogs, Nets, or Engines, fhall be found in the Cuftody of any Perfon or Perfons not fo qualified, fuch Sheriff or Stewart refpectively fhall and may either caufe fuch Dogs, Nets, or Engines, to be deftroyed, or to be fold to the beft Bidder, and the Money arifing by fuch Sale to be given to the Poor of the Parifh where fuch Dogs, Nets, or Engines, fhall be found; and in cafe any Gun or Guns, kept and ufed for killing and deftroying Game, fhall be found in the Cuftody of any Perfon not fo qualified or licenfed, fuch Sheriff or Stewart refpectively fhall and may either caufe fuch Gun or Guns to be deftroyed, or to be fold to the beft Bidder, and the Money arifing by fuch Sale to be given to the Poor of the Parifh where fuch Gun or Guns fhall be found.

And be it further Enacted by the Authority aforefaid, That, notwithftanding any Law to the contrary now in Force in that Part of *Great Britain* called *Scotland*, every Proprietor of Land in that Part of the united Kingdom fhall be entitled to kill Game upon his own Property, and alfo to grant Licence under his Hand to any Perfon whatfoever to kill Game on the Property of the Perfon fo granting the Licence: But it is hereby Declared, That no Perfon whatever fhall have Power to grant Licence to any unqualified Perfon to hunt or kill Game upon the Eftate or Property of another; and, notwithftanding fuch Licence, fuch unqualified Perfon hunting or killing Game upon the Property of another, fhall be liable in the Penalties to which unqualified Perfons are liable by this or any other Law for Prefervation of the Game in that Part of *Great Britain* called *Scotland*.

And be it further Enacted by the Authority aforefaid, That the Conviction and Convictions of all and every Offender or Offenders againft this Act fhall be certified, by the Sheriff or Stewart refpectively by or before whom the Offender fhall be convicted, to the Seffion Clerk of the Parifh

where

where the Offence was committed, within   of such Conviction; and if, within   of such Conviction being so certified, the Penalty awarded by the Sheriff or Stewart is not paid, it shall be competent either for the Original Informer, or the said Session Clerk, to make Application to the Sheriff or Stewart, who, upon such Application, is hereby required to grant Warrant for   in Manner before directed.

6   And be it further Enacted, That this Act shall be deemed, adjudged, and taken to be, a Public Act; and shall be judicially taken Notice of as such by all Judges, Justices, and other Persons whomsoever, without specially pleading the same.

A

BILL

TO

Restrain Apprentices, Tradesmen, and other unqualified Persons, from destroying the Game, in that Part of *Great Britain* called *Scotland*; and for granting to Proprietors of Lands in *Scotland* further Powers with regard to killing of Game.

1775.

A

B I L L

FOR

Remedying some Defects in the several Acts passed for Paving, Cleansing, Lighting, and Regulating, the Squares, Streets, Lanes, and other Places, within the City and Liberty of *Westminster*, and Parts adjacent.

WHEREAS several Acts have been passed Preamble. in the Second, Third, Fourth, Fifth, and Eleventh Years of His present Majesty's Reign, for the Paving, Cleansing, Lighting, and Regulating, the Squares, Streets, Lanes, and other Places, within the City and Liberty of *Westminster*, and Parts adjacent:

And whereas there are some Defects in the said Acts, the remedying whereof would be of great Utility:

A May

[2]

May it therefore pleafe Your MAJESTY,

That it may be Enacted; And be it Enacted by the KING's moſt Excellent MAJESTY, by and with the Advice and Conſent of the Lords Spiritual and Temporal, and Commons, in this preſent Parliament aſſembled, and by the Authority of the ſame, That from and after

Powers relating to the Water Companies to be in Commiſſioners and Committees.

the ſeveral Powers, Rules, Regulations, Authorities, Matters, and Things, which, by the ſaid former Acts, any or either of them, are to be executed, obſerved, made, enforced, had, or done, by or with the Commiſſioners, their Agents or Officers, within the ſeveral Squares, Streets, Lanes, Alleys, or Places, now paved under their Direction, which may any Ways reſpect or relate to the ſeveral and reſpective Companies who furniſh Water to the Inhabitants of the City and Liberty of *Weſtminſter*, and the other Pariſhes and Places included in the Proviſions of the ſaid ſeveral Acts, any or either of them (except as hereinafter is excepted) ſhall be, and are hereby veſted in the ſeveral and reſpective Committees, and ſhall be executed, obſerved, made, enforced, had, and done, by or with them, their Agents and Officers, (within the ſeveral Squares, Streets, Lanes, Alleys, and Places, which ſhall be rated by the reſpective Committees, by virtue of the ſaid Act of the Eleventh Year of His preſent Majeſty) in as full and ample a Manner, to all Intents and Purpoſes, as hath been or may be done by or with the ſaid Commiſſioners, within the ſeveral Squares, Streets, Lanes, Alleys, or Places paved by virtue of the ſaid former Acts, any or either of them.

Liſt of Squares, Streets, &c. liable to be rated by Commiſſioners, to be tranſmitted to the Water Companies.

And be it further Enacted, That the Clerk to the ſaid Commiſſioners for putting the ſaid former Acts and this Act in Execution ſhall, within   tranſmit a true and perfect Liſt of the Names of all ſuch Squares, Streets, and Places, where the Owners and Occupiers of the Lands, Grounds, Houſes, Shops, Wharfs, Warehouſes, Coach Houſes, Stables, Cellars, Vaults, Buildings, Tenements, or Hereditaments therein, are now, or hereafter may be, liable by Law to be rated and aſſeſſed by the ſaid Commiſſioners, to the Secretary or Clerk to the reſpective Water Companies; and the reſpective Clerks to the ſeveral Committees ſhall alſo, within

The like by the Committees.

tranſmit to the ſaid Secretaries or Clerks to the ſaid Water Companies, a true and perfect

perfect List of all such Squares, Streets, Lanes, and Places, in their respective Parishes, Precincts, and Liberties, where the Owners and Occupiers as aforesaid are liable by Law to be rated and assessed by the said Committees respectively; and every such respective Committee is hereby required to appoint a public Place, within their respective Parish, Precinct, or Liberty, where Notices required by this Act to be given to the Committees by the Water Companies shall be brought and left; and every such Committee shall also, from Time to Time, transmit an Account of such public Place to the said Water Companies, immediately after the Appointment thereof, or as soon after as conveniently may be; and the respective Paviors to the Water Companies shall, from Time to Time, give or leave Notice for the Commissioners for Paving, at the Bridge Office at *Westminster*, or to such Person or Persons as the said Commissioners shall appoint to receive the same, when and where any of the Pavements have been broken or taken up, in any of the said Squares, Streets, Lanes, and Places mentioned in the List to be made by the said Commissioners, and the like when they, or either of them, shall have filled in and rammed down the Ground; and the Paviors to the respective Water Companies shall, from Time to Time, give or leave Notice to and for the several and respective Committees, at the public Places to be by them appointed as aforesaid, when and where any of the Pavements have been broken or taken up, in any of the Squares, Streets, Lanes, and Places included in the said List to be made by the respective Committees, and the like Notice when they, or either of them, have filled in and rammed down the Ground.
Commissioners and Committees to appoint a public Place to receive Notices from Water Companies.

Paviors to Water Companies to leave Notice, when Pipes are repaired and Ground filled in, at such public Places.

And be it further Enacted, That the said Commissioners, or the several and respective Committees, shall, and they are hereby authorized and required, from Time to Time, at any of their respective Meetings, as Occasion shall require, to contract with any Person or Persons for paving and keeping in Repair, by a separate Agreement, the Pavement over the Water Trenches belonging to any of the said Water Companies, within their respective Jurisdictions; but that no such Contract shall be made, unless, previous to the making thereof, Notice at the least shall be given in some of the public News-papers, expressing the Intention of such Contract, in order that any Person or Persons willing to undertake the same (not being Commissioners, or Members of the said Committees) may make Proposals for that Purpose, at the Time and Place in such Notice mentioned.

Obliging Commissioners to advertise their Contracts for Paving over Water Trenches.

And

Scavengers not to sweep Street Dirt into Common Sewers, or within Feet of the Grates, or within Feet of the Channel,	**And be it further Enacted,** That the Servants, Labourers, or Persons employed by the Savenger or Raker contracting with the Commissioners, or respective Committees, and all other Persons, shall take Care not to sweep or rake any of the Slop, Slush, Mud, Dirt, Dust, Rubbish, Ashes, Filth, or Soil, found in any of the Squares, Streets, Lanes, Courts, Yards, Mewses, Alleys, Passages, or Places, within the Limits aforesaid, into any of the Common Sewers, Drains, or Funnels, thereunto belonging; but shall sweep or rake the same together, so as to lie at the Distance of Feet at the least from each of the respective Grates belonging to or placed over every Common Sewer, Drain, or Funnel, and at the Distance of
where the Width of the Street will admit thereof.	Feet at the least from every Channel, in every Square, Street, Lane, Court, Yard, Alley, Mews, Passage, or Place, within the Limits aforesaid, where the Width of the Street, Lane,
Offender may be apprehended;	or Place, will admit thereof; and if any such Servant, Labourer, or other Person or Persons, shall offend in the Premises, it shall be lawful for any Person or Persons whatever, who shall see any such Offence committed, by virtue of this Act, and without any other Warrant, to apprehend the Offender or Offenders, and also for any Person or Persons to assist in apprehending such Offender or Offenders, and they are hereby authorized and required
and conveyed before a Magistrate;	so to do, and to convey him, her, or them so offending before One of His Majesty's Justices of the Peace for the County of *Middlesex,* or *Surrey,* or City and Liberty of *Westminster,* as the Case shall be; and such Justice shall proceed to examine upon Oath the Person or Persons who shall have apprehended, or assisted in apprehending, the Offender or Offenders, (who is and are hereby declared a competent Witness or Witnesses) or upon the Oath of any other Person or Persons who shall appear to give Information touching any such Offence or Offences, (which Oath or Oaths the said Justice is hereby authorized and required
and if convicted upon Oath	to administer;) and if the Party or Parties accused shall be convicted of any of the aforesaid Offences, either by his, her, or their own Confession, or by such Oath as aforesaid, he, she, or they so convicted shall forfeit and pay the Sum
to pay	of for every such Offence whereof shall be paid to the Person or Persons who shall apprehend the Offender, and to the Treasurer to the Commissioners, to be applied for the Purposes of the said former Acts and this Act, in the Parish, Precinct, or Liberty where the Offence was committed; and in case such Offen-
or be committed for any Time not	der or Offenders shall not immediately on such Conviction pay such

such Forfeiture, such Justice is hereby required to him or them to the   of the said Counties, or City and Liberty, respectively, there to be kept to hard Labour for any Space of Time not exceeding   nor less than   Days, to be computed from the Day of Commitment; and any such Offender or Offenders shall not be discharged before the Expiration of the Time for which he, she, or they shall be so committed, unless such Forfeiture shall be sooner paid: And in case the Person or Persons so offending shall be a Servant to or employed by any Scavenger or Raker, and cannot be apprehended, then and in every such Case the Scavenger or Raker employing such Offender or Offenders shall forfeit and pay the Sum of   to be applied as aforesaid.

exceeding

nor less than

Days.

And be it further Enacted, That if any Person or Persons, other than the Scavenger or Raker contracting with the said Commissioners or respective Committees, or those employed under him, shall presume to collect or gather, or put in any Cart or other Carriage, or shall carry away, any Coal Dust or Ashes, from any House or other Premisses, in any Square, Street, or Place within the Limits aforesaid, it shall be lawful for any of the Inspectors appointed either by the said Commissioners or respective Committees, and for the Scavenger or Raker contracting with the said Commissioners or respective Commitees, and for the Persons employed under him, by virtue of this Act, and without any other Warrant, to apprehend, or assist in apprehending, all and every the Person or Persons so offending, and convey him, her, or them before One of His Majesty's Justices of the Peace for the said County of *Middlesex*, or *Surrey*, or City and Liberty of *Westminster*, as the Case shall be; and such Justice shall proceed, with respect to the said Offence, in the same Manner as is hereinbefore directed, with regard to Persons sweeping or raking Slop, Mud, or other Things, into Sewers or Channels, and the Penalty, on Conviction, shall be disposed of, or the Offender   in like Manner, and for the like Time; and in case the Person or Persons who shall collect or gather, or put into any Cart or other Carriage, or shall carry away, any Coal Dust or Ashes, without being authorized by the Scavenger or Raker contracting with the Commissioners for putting the said former Acts and this Act in Execution, or with the said respective Committees, cannot be apprehended, then and in every

For punishing Persons stealing Ashes.

If Offender cannot be apprehended, Penalty to be laid on the Owner of the Cart, &c.

[6]

every such Case the Owner or Owners of the Cart or Carriage in which such Coal Dust or Ashes shall be placed, shall forfeit and pay the Sum of   Shillings for the First Offence, and for the Second and every other Offence the Sum of

Any Person may seize and remove Cart and Horses either to the Green Yard or to some secure public Place in the Parish;

Shillings; and it shall be lawful for any Person or Persons whatever, by the Authority of this Act, and without any other Warrant, to seize, or cause to be seized, any such Cart or Carriage, with the Horse or Horses, Beast or Beasts, drawing the same, and the Harness, Gears, and Accoutrements thereunto belonging, and drive, remove, or take, or cause the same to be driven, removed, or taken to the *Green Yard* at *Westminster*, or to some other convenient public Place to

there to be detained till demanded, and the Penalty paid.

be appointed for that Purpose by the Commissioners, there to be kept and detained until the Owner or Owners thereof, or his, her, or their known Servant or Servants, shall and do pay to the Person or Persons in whose Custody the same shall be, the said Penalty, together with the Charges of driving, removing, and taking the same, and of keeping any

If not demanded, and Penalty paid, in   Days, may be by Order of the Commissioners.

such Horse, or other Beast; and in case the same shall not be demanded, and the said Penalty and Charges paid, within   Days, then it shall be lawful for the said Commissioners, or respective Committees, where the Offence shall be committed, to order the same, or a competent Part thereof, to be   and the Money arising by such Sale shall be applied   to the Person who

Application of Penalty.

shall seize, drive, and remove, such Cart, Carriage, or Beast, Harness, Gear, or Accoutrements, and for the Purposes of the said former Acts or this Act, in the respective Parish, Precinct, Liberty, or Place where the Offence was committed, returning the Overplus of the Money (if any) after deducting the Penalty and Charges attending such Seizure, Driving, and Removal, and of maintaining such Horse or Horses, or other Beast, and of such Cart, Carriage, Horse, Beast, Harness, Gear, and Accoutrements, and what shall remain unsold, to the Owner or

Not to prevent Inhabitants using their own Ashes.

Owners thereof, upon personal Demand: Provided always, That nothing herein contained shall extend, or be construed to extend, to prevent the Inhabitants of any such Houses or Premisses from using their own Coal Dust or Ashes, within their respective Houses, Yards, or Gardens, or elsewhere.

Signs to be placed close to Houses.

And whereas Doubts have arisen as to the Manner how Signs and Sign Boards ought to be placed, within the Limits of the said Acts; Be it therefore further Enacted, That from and after   all Signs and

[7]

and Sign Boards, made, provided, or used, within the Limits of the said Acts, shall be placed and fixed close and flat to and against the Front Walls of the Houses, Warehouses, or Buildings of the Person or Persons to whom they respectively belong, and not otherwise, on Pain of being subject to the like Penalties and Forfeitures, for not complying therewith, as are, by the said Act of the Third Year of His present Majesty, to be recovered of Persons not complying with the said Act with respect to Signs.

And be it further Enacted, That if any Person or Persons whatever shall set or place, or wittingly cause, permit, or suffer to be set or placed, any Goods, Wares, or Merchandizes, upon either the Foot or Carriage Way, or on any Parts or Parts thereof, within the Limits of the said former Acts, every Person so offending shall for the First Offence forfeit and pay the Sum of
for the Second Offence the Sum of   and for
the Third and every other Offence the Sum of

Penalty on Persons setting Goods, &c. in the Streets.

And be it further Enacted, That if any Person or Persons shall keep open the Flat Entrance, on the Footway, into any Cellar, without having Side Doors to keep off Passengers, so as to prevent Accidents, or shall open any Hole or Funnel made in any Footway or Carriageway, within the Limits aforesaid, for the Purpose of conveying Coals, Wood, or other Things into any Vault or Cellar, for any longer Time than whilst Coals, or Wood, or other Things are actually delivering in or out of such Vault or Cellar; or shall set or place, or cause to be set or placed, on any of the Carriageways or Footways, any Casks, Package, Timber, Wood, or Wheels; or shall set or place, or cause to be set or placed, in, cross, or athwart any such Carriageways, any Coach, Cart, Common Stage Waggon, or other Waggon, Dray, or other Carriage, so as to occasion any Obstruction or Annoyance whatever, and shall not immediately remove the same, when required so to do by any Person or Persons whomsoever; or if any Brewer or other Persons shall draw Butts or Casks with Horses, out of any Cellar or Vault adjoining to any Foot Pavement, after the Hour of Eight in the Morning; or if any Person or Persons shall set or place any such Carriage, for the Purpose of loading or unloading thereof, or for any other Purposes, upon any Foot Crossing over the Carriageway, in any Square, Street, Way, Lane, or Place, within the Limits aforesaid; or if any Person or Persons shall set or place any

No Persons to leave open Funnels to Vaults;

or set Casks, &c. on Carriage or Foot Ways;

or set any Cart or Waggon across or athwart any Street,

or draw Butts or Casks out of Cellars;

or upon any Foot Crossing;

or set Carriages in the Street;

[8]

any Coach, Cart, or other Carriage, without any Horse or Horses fastened thereto, in any such Square, Street, Lane, or Place, on any Account or Pretence whatever, (except only in the Carriageway, for the Purpose of washing or cleaning the same, as hereinafter mentioned;) or if any Person or Persons shall set or place, or cause to be set or placed, any *or any Bricks or Materials for Building,* Stones, Bricks, Lime, Sand, Mortar, Wood, Timber, or any other Materials or Things whatever, for the Purpose of building any House, Shop, Warehouses, Coach Houses, Stables, or Tenements, or for any other Purpose, (unless the same shall *(unless inclosed in a Hoard)* be inclosed in a Hoard, erected and set up by and with the Consent of the Commissioners, as by the said former Acts *and shall not remove the same within* or some or One of them is particularly directed) and shall not remove such Stones, Bricks, Lime, Sand, Mortar, Wood, Timber, or other Materials or Things, within the Space of *Hours after Notice,* next after Notice in Writing to him or her given for that Purpose, or left at the Premisses where, or before which the same shall be, (or if empty, unoccupied, or in building, stuck or affixed against the Wall thereof, or against any Hoard or Pole belonging thereto or placed before the same) by any One of the said Commissioners or respective Committee Men, or by any Person or Persons appointed by the said Commissioners or Committees; every Person so offending shall for every or any of the said Offences forfeit and pay the Sum *forfeit* of   and any One of the said Commissioners *and any Person may seize the Goods, &c.* or Committee Men respectively, or any Person or Persons appointed for that Purpose either by the said Commissioners or respective Committees, may seize, or cause to be seized, any such Casks, Butts, Packages, Timber, Wood, or Wheels, or any such Coach, Cart, Common Stage Waggon, or other Waggon, Dray, or other Carriage, with the Horse or Horses, if any shall be thereunto belonging, together with their Harness, *and drive or remove them to the Green Yard at Westminster, or to some convenient Place;* Gears, or Accoutrements, and drive or remove, or cause the same to be driven or removed, to the *Green Yard* at *Westminster*, or to some other convenient public Place or Places to be appointed by the Commissioners, there to be kept and detained until the Owner or Owners thereof, or his, or her, or their known Servant or Servants, shall and do pay to the Person or Persons in whose Custody the same shall be, the said *and if not redeemed within   Days, Commissioners or Committees may cause the same to be sold.* Penalty, together with the Charges of removing the same, and of keeping such Horse or Horses (if any); and in case the same shall not be claimed, and the said Sum of   and Charges paid, within the Space of   Days next after such Seizure thereof, then it shall be lawful for the said Commissioners, or respective Committees, to cause

the

[9]

the fame, or a competent Part thereof, to be   for the Payment of the faid Penalty and Charges, returning to fuch Owner or Owners, upon perfonal Demand, the Goods or Things not fold, together with the Overplus (if any) of the Monies arifing by fuch

Provided always, That nothing in this Act contained fhall extend, or be conftrued to extend, to prevent or hinder Coaches or Carriages being fet or placed, any Time not exceeding   in the Carriageway only, to be wafhed and cleaned, before the Coach Houfe, in any fuch Places where Coaches and Carriages have heretofore been ufually wafhed and cleaned, in the Street before the Coach Houfe.

Allowing the Wafhing of Coaches, &c.

And, in order to determine what fhall be deemed and taken to be a Foot Crofling over the Carriageway, within the Meaning of this Act, **Be it further Enacted,** That the faid Commiffioners fhall caufe to be painted on a Board the following Words, FOOT CROSSING, in large plain Letters, and fhall caufe fuch Board to be hung up or affixed againft the Houfe, Wall, or other Buildings, oppofite, or as nearly as may be, to the Places they fhall appoint to be Foot Croffings; and the Place oppofite to fuch painted Board fhall be deemed and taken to be a Foot Crofling, within the Meaning of the faid former Acts and this Act; and if any Hackney Coach fhall ftand within   Fee of any fuch Foot Crofling, for a longer Time than is fufficient to take up or fet down a Fare, the Owner or Driver thereof fhall forfeit and pay the Sum of

For appointing Foot Croffings.

And whereas Quantities of Earth are frequently dug up, and large Holes left, in fome of the Squares, Streets, and Places, within the Limits aforefaid, for the Purpofes of making Vaults to Houfes or Tenements built or in building, or repairing, longer than is neceffary, and the Areas before Houfes or Tenements built or in building, or repairing, are left open, and without any Fence or Rails placed or fixed fo as to prevent Inconvenience or Danger to Paffengers; **Be it therefore further Enacted,** That if any Perfon or Perfons whomfoever fhall dig out any Earth, or leave any Hole, in any Street or Place, before any Houfe or Tenement built or in building, or repairing, within the Limits aforefaid, and fhall not inclofe the fame in a good and fufficient Manner (to be approved of by the Commiffioners) and fhall not, when needful, caufe the fame

Perfons digging Earth, or leaving Holes for making Vaults, &c. to inclofe the fame.

C   to

to be duly lighted or watched, or shall keep up such Inclosure longer than the Time limited by the Commissioners for that Purpose, or shall not fence or rail before the Area or Areas fronting to any Street or Place, in such Manner that the same shall not be inconvenient or dangerous to Passengers, every Person or Persons shall for every such Neglect or Offence forfeit the Sum of   and the like Sum of
 for every Week that such Nusance or Inconvenience shall be continued.

Penalty on driving Carriages, &c. on the Foot Pavements.

And be it further Enacted, That if any Person or Persons shall run, drive, draw, or roll, or cause to be run, driven, drawn, or rolled, on any of the Foot Pavements within the Limits aforesaid, any Wheel or Wheels, Sledge, or Wheelbarrow, Carriage, or Cask, or shall wilfully lead, ride, or drive any Horse, Ass, Mule, or Cattle, Coach, or other Carriage whatever, along or upon any Part of the said Foot Pavements; or if any Farrier shall permit or suffer any Horse to stand from his Shop upon any Part of the Foot Pavement; or if any Person or Persons whatever shall cast or throw any Tiles, Bricks, Wood, Rubbish, Dirt, or any other Matter or Thing (Snow excepted) from the Top or Roof, or out of or from any Part of any House or other Building, or from any Gutter belonging thereto, in any Square, Street, Lane, or Place; or shall rake or sweep between the Joints of the Stones, either of the Carriage or Foot Ways, under Pretence or for the Purpose of finding Nails, old Iron, or other Things; every Person so offending shall forfeit and pay the Sum of   and it shall be lawful in any of the said Cases, and

Any Person may apprehend the Offender.

as often as they or any of them shall happen, for any Person or Persons whatever, who shall see such Offence committed, to apprehend, and also for any other Person or Persons to assist in apprehending, the Offender or Offenders, and they are hereby authorized and required so to do, by the Authority of this Act, and without any other Warrant, and to convey him, her, or them before some Justice of the Peace for the said Counties, or City and Liberty of *Westminster*, as the Case shall be; and the Party or Parties accused being brought before any such Justice, he shall proceed to examine, upon Oath the Person or Persons who shall have apprehended or assisted in apprehending (and who is and are hereby declared a competent Witness or Witnesses) such Offender or Offenders, or upon the Oath of any other Witness or Witnesses who shall appear to give Information touching such Offence (which Oath or Oaths the said Justice

is

is hereby authorized and required to adminifter;) and if the Party or Parties accused shall be convicted of such Offence, either by his, her, or their own Confession, or upon such Oath or Oaths as aforesaid, he, she, or they so convicted of any such Offence respectively, shall immediately pay the said Sum of   and in case such Offender or Offenders shall not, upon such Conviction, pay such Forfeiture by him, her, or them incurred as aforesaid, the Justice before whom such Offender or Offenders shall be convicted is hereby required to   him, her, or them to the   for the said Counties, or City and Liberty of *Westminster*, as the Case may be, there to be kept to hard Labour for any Space of Time not exceeding   nor less than   Provided always, That it shall be lawful for any Brewer to roll or slide Casks or Butts upon a Pulley, to their Cellars or Vaults, in Courts or Places where Carriages cannot come, before the Hour of

Penalty.

Offenders not paying Penalty on Conviction to be

And be it further Enacted, That the Commissioners appointed, or to be appointed, by virtue of the said former Acts, or any or either of them, shall have, and they are hereby vested with, all the Powers and Authorities for removing Nusances, Annoyances, and Obstructions, and otherwise regulating the several Squares, Streets, Lanes, and Places within the Limits of the said recited Acts, or this Act, which have not been already new paved, or completed, by virtue of the said Acts, or any or either of them, as by the said Acts, or either of them, they are vested with, in the Squares, Streets, Lanes, and Places which have been new paved, or begun to be new paved, under their Direction.

Power vested in Commissioners to remove Nusances, &c.

And be it further Enacted, That no Person or Persons shall erect any Bulks or Stalls, or make any Dung Holes or Saw Pits, in any of the Squares, Streets, Lanes, Courts, Alleys, or Passages, within the Jurisdiction of the Commissioners, upon Pain that every Person so offending shall for every such Offence forfeit and pay any Sum not exceeding   nor less than   over and above the Expences of taking down such Bulks or Stalls, or filling up such Dung Holes or Saw Pits, according to the Direction of such Commissioners.

Persons not to erect Bulks, &c. in any of the Squares, Streets, &c.

And be it further Enacted, That if any Person or Persons shall, after the passing of this Act, throw at Oranges,

Persons not to throw at Oranges, &c.

or

[12]

<small>in any of the Squares, &c. nor make any Bonfires, or let off any Fire Works.</small>

or any Cock, Pigeon, or Fowl, or set up Oranges, or any Cock, Pigeon, or such like Fowl, to be thrown at, or shall make, or assist in the making, any Fire or Fires commonly called Bonfires, or shall set fire to, or let off, or throw any Squib, Serpent, Rocket, or Fire Works whatsoever, or fire off any Cannon, Gun, or Pistol, in any of the Footways or Carriageways of any of the Squares, Streets, Lanes, Alleys, and Places within the Jurisdiction of the said Commissioners, every Person so offending, in any of the said Cases, shall for the First Offence forfeit and pay the Sum of   and for the Second and every other Offence the Sum of   over and above such Penalties as are inflicted for or upon any or either of the said Offences by any Law or Statute now in being.

<small>Clerk to Commissioners to give Notice to Commissioners of Sewers when Contracts for new Paving are confirmed.</small>

And be it further Enacted, That the Clerk to the Commissioners for putting the said former Acts and this Act in Execution shall, and he is hereby required, within   after the Confirmation of any Contract for new paving any of the Squares, Streets, Lanes, and Places within the Limits aforesaid, transmit, or cause to be transmitted, to the Clerk or Surveyor to the Commissioners of Sewers, a List of the Names of every such Square, Street, Lane, or Place, for which a Contract for new paving hath been made and confirmed, to the End the said Commissioners of Sewers may cause the Sewer or Drain, in all or any such Squares, Streets, Lanes, or other Places, to be cleansed, emptied, and repaired, if they shall see Occasion so to do, previous to the new paving thereof.

<small>Houses and Lamp Irons to be numbered;</small>

And be it further Enacted, That it shall be lawful for the Commissioners for putting this Act in Execution, and for the respective Committees, from Time to Time, to cause every House, Shop, Warehouse, and Building, or other Tenement, and also every Lamp Iron, or Lamp, fixed or placed up by Order of the said Commissioners, or respective Committees, to be marked or numbered, in such Manner and in such Part thereof as the said Commissioners or respective Committees shall judge most proper for distinguishing the same;

<small>and Orders of Commissioners or Committees may be stuck up. Penalty on destroying the same.</small>

and also may order and cause to be affixed to or against any such House, Shop, Warehouse, Building, or other Tenement, any written, printed, or painted Order or Orders; and if any Person or Persons shall wilfully tear, destroy, pull down, cover, obliterate, or otherwise render illegible, or injure any such Marks, Numbers, Descriptions,

or

or any Part of them, or cause or procure the same to be done, any Person so offending shall for every such Offence forfeit and pay any Sum not exceeding   Shillings, nor less than

Provided always, That when any House, Shop, Warehouse, Building, or other Tenement shall be new painted, to or against which any such Marks or Numbers shall be painted, affixed, or described, the Person or Persons owning such House, Shop, Warehouse, Building, or Tenement, shall not be liable to pay the Penalty aforesaid, if, within   after finishing such Painting on the Outside of such House, Shop, Warehouse, Building, or Tenement, he, she, or they shall cause every such Mark or Number to be restored or re-painted, where such former Mark or Number was originally painted, affixed, or described. *Inhabitant to cause Number to be restored, when his House is new painted.*

And be it further Enacted, That it shall be lawful for the said respective Commissioners, and they are hereby authorized and empowered, yearly and every Year, after their Accounts are settled and adjusted for the preceding Year, to apply and appropriate the Whole or any Part of the Balance (if any) of the Rate levied and collected by virtue of the said Act of the Eleventh Year of His present Majesty, for repairing, cleansing, and lighting the Squares, Streets, and Places in the City and Liberties of *Westminster*, and Parts adjacent, towards discharging the Principal Sum borrowed on the Credit of the Rate of Six Pence in the Pound, for the Purpose of new paving the Squares, Streets, and Places within the Limits aforesaid, any thing in the said Act of the Eleventh Year of His present Majesty to the contrary thereof in anywise notwithstanding.

And whereas by the said recited Acts, or some of them, it is declared, that no Preference shall be given to any Person or Persons in the Re-payment of any Principal Sum or Sums of Money lent or advanced on the Credit, or by Way of Mortgage of the Tolls, Rates, or Annual Payment, by the said Acts, some or One of them, granted or made payable, but that all such Persons shall be deemed Creditors in equal Degree one with another, on the respective Tolls, Rates, or Annual Payment, whereon such Monies shall have been respectively lent or advanced: **And whereas** such Regulations may be attended with Inconveniencies, in paying off such Mortgages: **Be it therefore further Enacted,** That *Manner of repaying Money recited.*

[14]

<small>Manner of paying Money borrowed.</small> That it shall be lawful for the said Commissioners or respective Committees, as the Case may be, when and as often as the Surplus of any Tolls, Rates, or Annual Payment granted by the said former Acts, any or either of them, (after Payment of all Sums of Money charged thereon, and after all Purposes for which the same were respectively granted shall be satisfied and performed) shall amount to   of the Principal Sum borrowed, to cause the Number of all the Assignments or Securities for Money due and owing to the Creditors on the said respective Tolls, Rates, or Annual Payment, to be put separately into a Box or Glass, and that so many Numbers of the said Assignments or Securities shall be drawn out of the said Box or Glass, by the Clerk to the said Commissioners or respective Committees, in the Presence of   or more Commissioners or Committee Men, as the Case may be, at some or One of their Meetings, as shall make up the Sum then intended to be paid off; and that   Calendar Months Notice in Writing, or printed, and signed by the Clerk to the said Commissioners or respective Committees, shall be given to the Person or Persons who shall be entitled to such Assignment or Assignments, Security or Securities, so drawn out, or shall be left at his, her, or their last or usual Place of Abode, that his, her, or their Assignment or Assignments, Security or Securities, Principal and Interest, will be paid off, or so much thereof as shall be so drawn out as aforesaid; and that at the Expiration of the said   Calendar Months, to be computed from the Day of such Notice being given, or left as aforesaid, all Interest on such Assignment or Assignments, Security or Securities, shall cease and determine.

<small>Clause to make it Felony to counterfeit Assignments or Certificates.</small> **And be it further Enacted,** That if any Person or Persons whomsoever shall forge, counterfeit, or alter any Assignment or Certificate authorized or directed to be made, given, or granted by the said former Acts, any or either of them, relative to the borrowing, collecting, receiving, or paying of any Money, every such Person so offending in any of the Cases aforesaid, and being thereof lawfully convicted, shall be adjudged guilty of Felony without Benefit of Clergy.

<small>Rates may be collected before Quarter Day, where Persons are removing.</small> **And be it further Enacted,** That in order to avoid the Loss that frequently happens from Tenants or Occupiers of Houses and Tenements, who frequently quit and remove from such Houses and Tenements before the Quarter Day on which the Rates and Assessments charged by virtue of the said former Acts,

[15]

Acts, or some or One of them, on the said Houses or Tenements, become due and payable, it shall be lawful for the Receiver appointed by the Commissioners, and the Collectors appointed by any of the respective Committees before any such Quarter Day, or at any other subsequent Time (Oath being first made before One of His Majesty's Justices of the Peace for the Counties of *Middlesex* or *Surrey*, or City and Liberty of *Westminster*, as the Case may be, (which Oath such Justice is hereby required to administer) that there is good Cause to suspect that such Tenant or Occupier intends to remove before the next Quarter Day) to ask, demand, and receive the respective Rates and Assessments that would be due and payable on the then next Quarter Day; and in case of Non-payment thereof, to enforce the Payment of such Rates and Assessments in the same Manner, and with the same Powers, as they could or might, by virtue of any of the said former Acts, in case of Non-payment of such Rates and Assessments upon or after the Quarter Day on which the same became due and payable.

And whereas in some Cases Persons remove from their Houses, Shops, Wharfs, Warehouses, Coach Houses, Stables, Cellars, Vaults, Buildings, Tenements, or Hereditaments, without paying the Rates assessed on them, and other Persons do enter, and occupy the Premisses Part of the Year, whereby several Sums of Money may be annually lost; Be it therefore Enacted, That where any Person or Persons shall come into or occupy any Land, Ground, House, Shop, Wharf, Warehouse, Coach House, Stable, Cellar, Vault, Building, Tenement, or Hereditament, out of or from which any other Person rated or assessed by virtue of this Act shall be removed, or which, at the Time of making such Rate, was empty or unoccupied, that then every such Person so removing from, and every Person so coming into or occupying the same, shall be liable to pay such Rate or Assessment, in Proportion to the Time that such Person or Persons occupied the same respectively, in the same Manner, and under the like Penalty of Distress, or by Action, as if such Person so removing had not removed, or if such Person so coming in or occupying had been originally rated and assessed in such Rate; which said Proportion, in Case of Dispute, shall be ascertained by any of His Majesty's Justices of the Peace for the Counties of *Middlesex* or *Surrey*, or City and Liberty of *Westminster*, as the Case may be.

Justices to settle Proportion of Rate to be paid by Persons going out and coming into Houses, &c. between Quarter Days.

And,

On Refusal to pay Rates, how to be recovered.

And, for the better and more effectual recovering the Rates and Assessments directed to be made by any of the said Acts, **Be it further Enacted**, That in case any of the Inhabitants or Occupiers, or any Owner or Owners, Proprietor or Proprietors, Lessee or Lessees, of any Land, Ground, House, Shop, Wharf, Warehouse, Coach House, Stable, Cellar, Vault, Building, Tenement, or Hereditament, within the Limits aforesaid, or in case any Church Warden or Chapel Warden for the Time being of any Parish Church, Church Yard, or Chapel, or any Treasurer, Owner, or Proprietor, of any Meeting House, School, Market, void Space of Ground, Fence Walls or other Walls, Wharfs, Warehouses, or other public Building whatsoever, made liable to pay any Rate or Assessment, made, laid, and assessed by virtue of the said Acts, or any of them, shall refuse or neglect to pay the same, and all Arrears due thereon, it shall be lawful for such Receiver or Collectors, by Warrant under the Hand and Seal of any Justices of the Peace for the said Counties of *Middlesex* or *Surrey*, or City and Liberty of *Westminster*, as the Case shall be, (which Warrant any such Justices are hereby authorized and required to grant) in any Place within the Jurisdiction of such Justices, or out of the Limits thereof, such Warrant being first backed or countersigned by some Magistrate of the County, City, Liberty, or Place, where the Distress is to be made (which Warrants such Magistrate is hereby required to back or countersign without Fee or Reward) to collect or   such Rate, and all Arrears due thereon, by   of the Goods and Chattels of the Party so neglecting or refusing to pay, wheresoever such Goods and Chattels shall or may be found; and if, within   Days next after such   shall be made, the said Rate or Rates, Assessment or Assessments, together with all Arrears due thereon, shall not be paid, together with the reasonable Charges of taking and keeping such   the said Receiver or Collectors shall cause the said Goods and Chattels to be   or such Part thereof as shall be sufficient to pay the said Rate or Rates, Assessment or Assessments, together with all Arrears due thereon, and the reasonable Charges of making such   returning the Overplus (if any be) to the Owner or Owners of such Goods and Chattels respectively, upon Demand thereof made; and in case any Person or Persons liable by the said Acts, or any of them, to pay any Rate or Assessment, shall be under Commission of Bankruptcy, or if his, her, or their Goods and

and Chattels, or any of them, shall at the Time any Rate or Assessment shall be due and be demanded, be taken in Execution, or assigned by any Bill of Sale, or otherwise, in every such Case, the Rate or Assessment, and all Arrears thereon, (not exceeding One Year) due from any such Person or Persons, shall and may be on the Goods and Chattels of the Assignee or Assignees of any such Bankrupt, and on the Goods and Chattels of the several and respective Persons having such Execution or Bill of Sale, in the same Manner as is herein directed for the Recovery of Rates or Assessments from any other Persons; and the Receipt of the Receiver or Collector appointed to recover any such Rate or Assessement shall be a legal Discharge to the Assignee, or other Person or Persons, paying any such Rate or Assessment, or on whose Goods and Chattels the same, or any Part thereof, may have been

Provided always, and it is hereby Enacted and Declared, That the said Commissioners or respective Committees may nevertheless, if they think proper so to do, sue, in the Name of the Clerk, Treasurer, or other proper Officer; all and every Person and Persons made liable to the Payment of all and every such Rate and Rates, for all or any of the Rates or Assessments which shall be made by virtue of the said Acts, or any of them, and all Arrears due thereon and unpaid, either in any of His Majesty's Courts of Law at *Westminster*, or in any Court for the Recovery of small Debts, as the Case may be, within the respective Parishes, Precincts, or Liberties, subject to the Powers of the said former Acts and of this Act.

Commissioners or Committees may sue for Rates.

And be it further Enacted by the Authority aforesaid, That all Penalties and Forfeitures by this Act imposed, (the Manner of recovering whereof is not hereby otherwise particularly directed) shall be
of the Offender's Goods and Chattels, by Warrant under the Hands and Seals of any of His Majesty's Justices of the Peace for the said County of *Middlesex*, or County of *Surrey*, or City and Liberty of *Westminster*, as the Case may be; which Warrant such Justices are hereby empowered and required to grant, upon the Confession of the Party or Parties, or upon the Information of One or more credible Witness or Witnesses upon Oath (which Oath such Justices are hereby empowered and required to administer) and the Informer, and also any Inhabitant or Inhabitants, is and are hereby declared to be a competent Witness and Witnesses; and
of the Penalties and Forfeitures, when recovered,

Penalties may be levied.

Informer deemed a credible Witness.

E (after

(after rendering the Overplus (if any be) upon Demand, to the Party or Parties whose Goods and Chattels shall be so   and the Charges of making such and the keeping and Sale thereof, being first deducted, or such Part or Parts thereof as is or are not hereinbefore otherwise disposed of) shall, if not otherwise disposed of, be paid to the Informer or Informers; and   to the Treasurer or Treasurers to the said Commissioners for the

Application of Penalties. Time being, and shall be applied to and for the Purposes of the said former Acts and this Act, in the respective Parish, Precinct, Liberty, or Place where the Offence was committed, and not elsewhere; and in every Case where   is directed to be taken by the said former Acts or this Act, and sufficient   shall not be found, and such Penalties and Forfeitures shall not be forthwith paid, it shall be lawful for such Justice or Justices of the Peace, and he and they is and are hereby authorized and required, by Warrant under his or their Hand and Seal, or Hands and Seals, to cause such Offender or Offenders to be   of the County or Place, there to remain without Bail or Mainprize, for any Time not exceeding   nor less than   unless such Penalties and Forfeitures, and all reasonable Charges, shall be sooner paid and satisfied.

Form of Conviction. **And** for the more easy and speedy Conviction of Offenders against the said former Acts, or this Act, **Be it Enacted** by the Authority aforesaid, That all and every Justice and Justices of the Peace before whom any Person or Persons shall be convicted of any Offence against the said former Acts, any or either of them, or this Act, shall and may cause the Conviction to be drawn up in the following Form of Words, or any other Form of Words to the same Effect:

" Be it remembered, That on the
" Day of   in the   .
" Year of His Majesty's Reign, *A. B.* is convicted be-
" fore   of His Majesty's Justices of the
" Peace for the County of
" or City and Liberty of *Westminster*" (as the Case shall be, specifying the Offence, and Time and Place when and where the same was committed.)

And

And be it further Enacted, That if any Person or Persons shall think himself, herself, or themselves aggrieved by any Rate or Rates, Assessment or Assessments, made either by the Commissioners or respective Committees, by virtue of the said former Acts, or any of them, such Person or Persons may and shall first apply, in Writing under his, her, or their Hands, by Way of Appeal, for Relief, to the said Commissioners or respective Committee who made the same, at their First, Second, or Third Meeting next after Demand made of such Rate or Rates, Assessment or Assessments, respectively; and the said Commissioners or Committees are hereby authorized and impowered to administer an Oath to any Person or Persons who shall attend on such Appeal to give Evidence, if the said Commissioners or Committees shall think it necessary and proper, and to give such Relief, or to make such other Order in the Premises as to them respectively shall seem meet; and in case any Person or Persons so applying to any Committee shall not be satisfied with the Order and Determination of such Committee, such Person or Persons may appeal to the said Commissioners, at their First, Second, or Third Meeting next after such Determination of the said Committee, giving to such Committee, or their Clerk Notice in Writing of such Appeal; and the said Commissioners shall and may, and are hereby enabled and impowered thereupon to hear and determine, and make such Order therein, as to them shall seem meet; and if any Person or Persons appealing to the said Commissioners (with respect to any Rate made either by the Commissioners, or by any Committee) shall be dissatisfied with the Order and Determination of the said Commissioners, the Person or Persons rated shall nevertheless be obliged to pay the Rate or Assessment appealed against, according to the Order of the said Commissioners in the Premises, and then the Person or Persons may appeal to the Quarter Sessions of the Peace, to be holden in and for the County of *Middlesex* or *Surrey*, or City and Liberty of *Westminster*, as the Case may be, within   Calendar Months next after such Determination of the said Commissioners, such Appellant giving, or causing to be given,   Days Notice at least, in Writing, of his or her Intention to bring such Appeal, and of the Matter thereof, to the Clerk to the said Commissioners, and also to the Clerk of the Committee whose Rate is appealed against, and, within   Days next after such Notice, entering into Recognizance before some Justice of the Peace for such County, City, and Liberty respectively, with

Allowing an Appeal against any Rate.

sufficient

sufficient Sureties, conditioned to try such Appeal, and to abide the Order of, and to pay such Costs as shall be awarded by the Justices at such Quarter Session; and the Justices at such Session, upon due Proof of such Notice having been given as aforesaid, and the entering into such Recognizance, shall hear and determine the Causes and Matters of such Appeal in a summary Way, and award such Costs to the Parties appealing, or appealed against, as they the said Justices shall think proper, not only on Account of the said Appeal to the said Quarter Sessions, but also on Account of the Appeal to the said Commissioners; and the Determination of such Quarter Session shall be final, binding, and conclusive unto and upon all Parties.

Limitation of Actions. **And be it further Enacted,** That no Action or Suit shall be commenced against any Commissioner or Commissioners, or any Person or Persons acting under them, or against any Committee Man or Committee Men, or any Person or Persons acting under the respective Committees, for any Thing done in pursuance of this Act, or by the Direction of the said Commissioners or Committees, until after the Expiration of   Days next after Notice thereof shall be given in Writing to the Clerk to the said Commissioners, or Clerk to the said Committee, as the Case shall be, or after sufficient Satisfaction, or Tender thereof, hath been made to the Party or Parties aggrieved, or after   Calendar Months next after the Fact committed for which such Action or Actions, Suit or Suits, shall be brought; and every such Action shall be brought, laid, and tried in the County of *Middlesex* or *Surrey*, as the Case shall be, and not elsewhere; and that the Defendant or Defendants, and every of them, in every such Action or Suit, may plead the General Issue, and give the special Matter in Evidence at any Trial or Trials to be had thereupon, and that the Matter or Thing for which such Action or Suit shall be so brought, was done in pursuance and by the Authority of this Act; and if the said Matter or Thing shall appear to have been so done, or if it shall appear that such Action or Suit was brought without giving such Notice, or before the Expiration of Twenty-one Days after Notice thereof given as aforesaid, or that sufficient Satisfaction was made or tendered as aforesaid, or if such Action or Suit was not commenced within the Time before limited for that Purpose, or shall be laid in any County or Place other than the said County of *Middlesex* or *Surrey*, as the Case may be, then

the

the Jury shall find for the Defendant or Defendants therein; and if a Verdict or Verdicts shall be found for such Defendant or Defendants, or if the Plaintiff or Plaintiffs in such Action or Suit shall become nonsuited, or suffer a Discontinuance of such Action or Suit, or if, upon any Demurrer in such Action or Suit, Judgment shall be given for the Defendant or Defendants, then, and in either of the Cases aforesaid, such Defendant or Defendants shall have Costs, and shall have such Remedy for recovering the same as any Defendant or Defendants may have for his, her, or their Costs in any other Cases by Law. Costs.

And be it further Enacted, That this Act shall be deemed and taken to be a Public Act, and shall be judicially taken Notice of as such by all Judges, Justices, and other Persons whatsoever, without specially pleading the same, or giving the same in Evidence. Public Act.

A BILL

FOR

Remedying some Defects in the several Acts passed for Paving, Cleansing, Lighting, and Regulating, the Squares, Streets, Lanes, and other Places, within the City and Liberty of *Westminster*, and Parts adjacent.

1776.

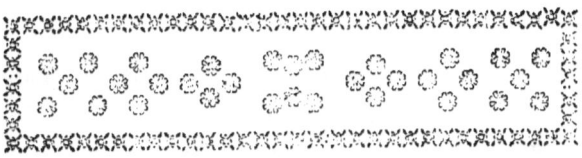

A

BILL

FOR

The further advancing the Cultivation, Improvement, and Regulation, of the Common Arable Fields, Common Meadows, and Commons of Pasture, in this Kingdom.

Note.—*The Figures in the Margin denote the Number of the Folios in the written Copy.*

WHEREAS, by an Act passed in the Thirteenth Year of the Reign of His present Majesty, intituled, " An Act for the better Cultivation, Improvement, and Regulation, of the Common Arable Fields, Wastes, and Commons of Pasture, in this Kingdom," it is, amongst other Things, Enacted, That Three Fourths in Number and Value of the Occupiers of such Common Fields, with such Consent and under such Restrictions as are therein mentioned,

A   may

may come to an Agreement for keeping the same in a particular Course of Husbandry, and under particular Regulations, for the Term of Six Years, or Two Rounds, according to the ancient and established Course of each Parish respectively:

𝔄𝔫𝔡 𝔴𝔥𝔢𝔯𝔢𝔞𝔰 the said Act has been carried into Execution with great Advantage in several Places; but it appears that the Ends of the same might be greatly advanced, and the Benefits arising therefrom increased, if Encouragement was given to the laying together of the Lands of the several Occupiers, which lie dispersed in different Places in such Fields, into more convenient Plots for the Occupation of the same:

May it therefore please Your MAJESTY,

That it may be Enacted; 𝔄𝔫𝔡 𝔟𝔢 𝔦𝔱 𝔈𝔫𝔞𝔠𝔱𝔢𝔡 by the KING's Most Excellent MAJESTY, by and with the Advice and Consent of the Lords Spiritual and Temporal, and Commons, in this present Parliament assembled, and by the Authority of the same, That wheresoever such general Agreement shall be entered into for the Cultivation of any Common Field, as is authorized and described by the said above-recited Act, it shall and may be lawful for any Occupiers of Lands in such Common Fields, or their Guardians or Trustees; with Consent in Writing first had and obtained from the Owner or Owners, his or their Guardians and Trustees; and also of each and every Mortgagee, Annuitant, or other Person having a Security affecting the same; and also of the Lord of the Manor, in respect to any Lands which shall be Copyhold; to make Exchanges between themselves of any Lands, as they shall find convenient; which Exchanges shall be good and binding upon all Persons who shall come to the Property or Occupation of such Lands during the Term of the said general Agreement, any Disability or Imperfection of the Estate of such Owner or Occupier notwithstanding.

𝔓𝔯𝔬𝔳𝔦𝔡𝔢𝔡 𝔞𝔩𝔴𝔞𝔶𝔰, 𝔞𝔫𝔡 𝔟𝔢 𝔦𝔱 𝔈𝔫𝔞𝔠𝔱𝔢𝔡, That the Compensation which may be necessary to be given for the Difference that may be of Quantity and Value in the said Lands so exchanged, shall be by Payment of a Yearly Sum of Money, and not by any Fine or Foregift; otherwise such Agreement shall be null and void to all Intents and Purposes whatsoever.

𝔓𝔯𝔬𝔳𝔦𝔡𝔢𝔡

Provided also, and be it Enacted, That such Lands so exchanged shall be surveyed and planned, and shall be distinguished by proper Bound Stones; and a Copy of such Agreement, together with a Copy of such Plan, shall be lodged in the Parish Chest, and also, if Copyhold, delivered to the Lord's Steward, to be inrolled in the Lord's Court, after the Execution of the same; otherwise the same shall be null and void to all Intents and Purposes whatsoever.

And be it further Enacted, That every Landlord, Mortgagee, or other Creditor, or any other Person whatsoever, having any Right or Demand affecting any of such exchanged Lands, shall, during the Continuance of such Agreement, have the same Right and Remedy in and against any such Land taken in Exchange, as he would have had against the Land given in Exchange for it.

And whereas it would greatly conduce to the better manuring of such Common Fields, especially those Parts which lie remote from the Dwellings and Homesteads of the Occupiers of the same, if they were enabled to inclose, and hold inclosed, a small Portion of the same, for the Purpose of a Foddering Yard, Sheepcote, or such like Convenience; **Be it Enacted** by the Authority aforesaid, That it shall and may be lawful for every such Occupier, with Consent of the Owner, to inclose, and hold inclosed, any Parcel or Parcels of their Lands in such Common Fields, not exceeding in the Whole the Quantity of
provided the same do not interrupt or obstruct any public or private Road.

And whereas many small Trespasses, and Breaches of the Regulations agreed to according to the Act above recited, may be committed, with regard to which the Remedy by Action in any of His Majesty's Courts of Record at *Westminster* may be thought too troublesome and expensive; **Be it Enacted** by the Authority aforesaid, That upon Information being made by the Field Master or Field Reeve for the Time being, before One Justice of the Peace for the County, Riding, or Division, wherein the Township shall lie, and Proof made thereof by the Oath of One or more credible Witnesses, such Justice may order the Party offending to pay a Sum not exceeding which Penalty,

[4]

Penalty, in case such Person shall not pay the same within   Days after Demand, shall, by virtue of a Warrant under the Hand and Seal of the said Justice of the Peace, be levied by   of the Goods and Chattels of the Party so offending, if not redeemed within   Days, rendering the Overplus of the Value of the Goods (if any) to the Owner, after deducting the Charges of taking and making such   and all the Sums so recovered, shall be employed and accounted for according to the Orders and Directions of such Majority of Owners and Occupiers, as is directed by the said above recited Act, for and towards the better Cultivation of the said Common Field Lands, or Improvement of the said Commons of Pasture, or Wastes.

A

B I L L

FOR

The further advancing the Cultivation, Improvement, and Regulation, of the Common Arable Fields, Common Meadows, and Commons of Pasture, in this Kingdom.

1777.

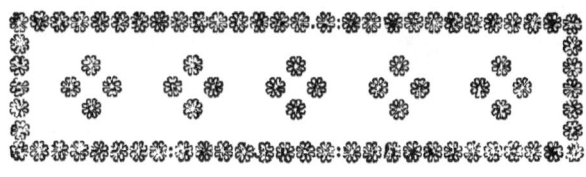

A

B I L L

[With the Amendments]

T O

Explain and amend the Laws now in being relating to Sewers.

Note.—*The Figures in the Margin denote the Number of the Folios in the written Copy.*

WHEREAS Commissions of Sewers have issued and been directed into divers Parts of the Realm, in a Manner suitable to the Circumstances of Time and Place then and there requisite:

And whereas, by an Act passed in the Twenty-third Year of the Reign of King *Henry* the Eighth, intituled " A Bill of Sewers, with a new Proviso, &c." it was Enacted, That Commissions of Sewers, according to One prescribed Manner, Form, Tenor, and Effect, therein recited, should be directed into all Parts of the Realm; which Act, at first temporary, was, by an Act passed in the Third and Fourth Years of the Reign of King *Edward* the Sixth, made perpetual:

And whereas many of the Provisions, by a Change of divers Circumstances, in the Course of a long Period of Years, cease to have the Effect proposed, and are no longer sufficient Remedy to the Reformation of the Premises, as therein and thereby intended:

And whereas, amongst other Things, it was by the said Bill of Sewers Enacted "That if any Manner of Person or Persons, of "what Estate or Degree soever he or they be of, that from "henceforth doth take upon him or them to sit, by vir- "tue of any of the said Commissions, not having Lands "and Tenements, or other Hereditaments, in Fee Simple, "Fee Tail, or for Term of Life, to the clear yearly Va- "lue of Forty Marks, above all Charges, to his own Use, "except he be resiant and free of any City, Borough, "or Town Corporate, and have moveable Substance of the "clear Value of One hundred Pounds, or else be learned "in the Laws of this Realm in and concerning the same, "that is to say, admitted in One of the Four principal "Inns of Court for an Utter Barrister, shall forfeit Forty "Pounds for every Time that he shall attempt so to "do:"

Now whereas, from the different Value of Money, Lands, and other Circumstances, the Qualification therein, by the Tenor of the said Act described, is no longer such as the true Meaning thereof requireth, or such as in like Cases is now required:

May it please Your MAJESTY,

That it may be Enacted; And be it Enacted by the KING's Most Excellent MAJESTY, by and with the Advice and Consent of the Lords Spiritual and Temporal, in this present Parliament assembled, and by the Authority of the same, That from and after the passing of this Act so much of the said Act of the Twenty-third Year of the Reign of *Henry* the Eighth, as relates to the Qualification aforesaid of Persons acting as Commissioners of Sewers, shall be, and the same is hereby declared to be repealed, respecting all Commissions of Sewers hereafter, after the passing of this Act, issued, and respecting all Commissioners of Sewers hereafter, after the passing of this Act, named and appointed as Commissioners of Sewers.

And

[3]

And be it further Enacted by the Authority aforesaid, That no Person (except as hereinafter is excepted) shall be capable of acting as a Commissioner of Sewers, under any Commission hereafter, after the passing of this Act, issued, unless he shall have, [either in Law or Equity, to and for his own Use and Benefit, in Possession, a Freehold, Copyhold, or Customary Estate for Life, or for some greater Estate, or an Estate for some long Term of Years determinable upon One or more Life or Lives, or for a certain Term originally created for Twenty-one Years or more, in] Lands, Tenements, or Hereditaments, [lying or being in that Part of Great Britain called *England*, or the Principality of *Wales*] of the clear yearly Value of [One hundred Pounds] over and above what will satisfy and discharge all Incumbrances that affect the same, and over and above all Rents and Charges payable out of or in respect of the same; or who shall not be seised of or entitled unto, in Law or Equity, to and for his own Use and Benefit, the immediate Reversion or Remainder of and in Lands, Tenements, or Hereditaments, lying or being as aforesaid, which are leased for One, Two, or Three Lives, or for any Term of Years determinable upon the Death of One, Two, or Three Lives, upon reserved Rents, and which are of the clear yearly Value of Three Hundred Pounds, and unless One Third Part of such Qualification afore described and defined lieth and is within the Precincts of the Jurisdiction of the Commission of Sewers for which the Person qualifies and acts as a Commissioner; and who shall not at the Time, or before he takes upon himself to act as a Commissioner of Sewers, at some General or Quarter Sessions, or Court of Sewers, in the District for which he is commissioned, and does or shall intend to act, first take and subscribe the Oath following; *videlicet:*

" I *A. B.* do swear, That I truly and *bona fide* have
" such an Estate, in Law or Equity, to and for my
" own Use and Benefit, consisting of
"   " [specifying the Nature of
such Estate, whether Messuage, Land, Rent, Tythe,
Office, Benefice, or what else] " as doth qualify me
" to act as a Commissioner of Sewers under the
" Commission issued for" [here describing the Place
or District to which the Jurisdiction of the Commission
                                                    extends,

extends, as described in the Commission; except where it consists of an Office, Benefice, or Ecclesiastical Preferment, which it shall be sufficient to ascertain by their known and usual Names] "is lying, or being, or issuing
" out of Lands, Tenements, or Hereditaments, being
" within the Parish, Township, or Precinct, of
"   or in the several Parishes,
" Townships, or Precinct of
" in the County of   or in the several
" Counties of
"   " [as the Case may be]
" and that One Third Part thereof doth lie within
" the Precincts of the Jurisdiction of the said Com-
" mission."

Which Oath, so taken and subscribed as aforesaid, shall be kept by the Clerk of the Sewers of the said District for the Time being, among the Records of the Sewers for the said Parts.

And be it further Enacted by the Authority aforesaid, That every such Clerk of the Sewers shall, upon Demand for that Purpose made, forthwith deliver a true and attested Copy of the said Oath, in Writing, to any Person paying for the same the Sum of Two Shillings and no more; which being proved to be a true Copy of such Oath to be kept amongst the Records as aforesaid, shall be admitted to be given in Evidence upon any Issue, in any Action, Suit, or Information, to be brought upon this Act.

And be it further Enacted by the Authority aforesaid, That from and after the Time at which this Act shall take Effect and be in Force, respecting any Commission of Sewers hereafter, after the passing of this Act, issued, any Person who shall act as a Commissioner of Sewers under such Commission, within that Part of *Great Britain* called *England*, or the Principality of *Wales*, without having taken and subscribed the said Oath as aforesaid, or without being qualified according to the true Intent and Meaning of this Act, shall for every such Offence forfeit the Sum of One hundred Pounds, One Moiety to the Use of the Poor of the Parish in which he most usually resides, and the other Moiety to the Use of such Person or Persons who shall sue for the same, to be recovered, together with full Costs of Suit, by Action of Debt, Bill, Plaint, or Information, in any of His Majesty's Courts of Record at *Westminster*, in which no Essoign, Protection, Wager of Law, or more than One Imparlance, shall be allowed; and in every such Action, Suit, or Information, the Proof of his Qualification shall lie on such Person against whom the same is brought.

Provided always, and be it further Enacted by the Authority aforesaid, That if the Defendant in any such Action, Suit, or Information, shall intend to insist upon any Lands, Tenements, or Hereditaments, not contained in such Oath as aforesaid, as his Qualification to act as a Commissioner of Sewers, in Part or in the Whole (provided always, that One Third Part thereof be and lies within the Precincts of the Jurisdiction of the Commission under which he acted) at the Time of the supposed Offence wherewith he is charged, he shall at or before the Time of his Pleading deliver to the Plaintiff or Informer, or his Attorney, a Notice in Writing, specifying such Lands, Tenements, and Hereditaments, other than those contained in the said Oath, and the Parish, Township, Precinct, or Place, or Parishes, Townships, Precincts, or Places, and the County or Counties, wherein the same are respectively situate, lying, or being, (Offices and Benefices excepted, which it shall be sufficient to ascertain by their known and usual Names) and if the Plaintiff or Informer, in any such Action, Suit, or Information, shall think fit thereupon not to proceed any farther, he may, with the Leave of the Court, discontinue such Action, Suit, or Information, on Payment of such Costs to the Defendant as the Court shall award.

Provided also, and it is hereby further Enacted by the Authority aforesaid, That upon the Trial of the Issue in any Action, Suit, or Information, to be brought as aforesaid, no Lands, Tenements, or Hereditaments, which are not contained in such Oath and Notice as aforesaid, or one of them, shall be allowed to be insisted upon by the Defendant as any Part of his Qualification.

And be it further Enacted and Declared by the Authority aforesaid, where the Lands, Tenements, or Hereditaments, contained in the said Oath, or Notice, are, together with other Lands, Tenements, and Hereditaments, belonging to the Person taking such Oath, or delivering such Notice, liable to any Charges, Rents, or Incumbrances, That, within the true Intent and Meaning, and for the Purposes, of this Act, the Lands, Tenements, and Hereditaments, contained in the said Oath, or

Notice, shall be deemed and taken to be liable and chargeable only so far as the other Lands, Tenements, and Hereditaments so jointly charged, are not sufficient to pay, satisfy, or discharge the same.

𝕻𝖗𝖔𝖛𝖎𝖉𝖊𝖉 𝖆𝖑𝖜𝖆𝖞𝖘, That where the Qualification required by this Act, or any Part thereof, consists of Rent, it shall be sufficient to specify in such Oath, or Notice, as aforesaid, so much of the Lands, Tenements, or Hereditaments, out of which such Rent is issuing, as shall be of sufficient Value to answer such Rent.

𝕻𝖗𝖔𝖛𝖎𝖉𝖊𝖉 𝖆𝖑𝖜𝖆𝖞𝖘, 𝖆𝖓𝖉 𝖇𝖊 𝖎𝖙 𝕰𝖓𝖆𝖈𝖙𝖊𝖉 by the Authority aforesaid, That in case the Plaintiff or Informer in any such Action, Suit, or Information, shall discontinue the same otherwise than aforesaid, or be nonsuit, or Judgment be otherwise given against him, that then, and in any of the said Cases, the Person against whom such Action shall have been brought shall recover Treble Costs.

𝕻𝖗𝖔𝖛𝖎𝖉𝖊𝖉 𝖆𝖑𝖜𝖆𝖞𝖘, 𝖆𝖓𝖉 𝖇𝖊 𝖎𝖙 𝖋𝖚𝖗𝖙𝖍𝖊𝖗 𝕰𝖓𝖆𝖈𝖙𝖊𝖉 by the Authority aforesaid, That only One Penalty of One Hundred Pounds shall be recovered from the same Person, by virtue of this Act, for the same or any other Offence committed by the same Person, before the bringing of the Action, Suit, or Information, upon which One Penalty of One Hundred Pounds shall have been recovered, and due Notice given to the Defendant of the Commencement of such Action, Suit, or Information, any Thing in this Act to the contrary notwithstanding.

𝕻𝖗𝖔𝖛𝖎𝖉𝖊𝖉 𝖆𝖑𝖜𝖆𝖞𝖘, 𝖆𝖓𝖉 𝖇𝖊 𝖎𝖙 𝕰𝖓𝖆𝖈𝖙𝖊𝖉 by the Authority aforesaid, That where an Action, Suit, or Information, shall be brought, and due Notice given thereof as aforesaid, no Proceedings shall be had upon any subsequent Action, Suit, or Information, against the same Person, for any Offence committed before the Time of giving such Notice as aforesaid; but the Court where such subsequent Action, Suit, or Information, shall be brought, may, upon the Defendant's Motion, stay Proceedings upon every such subsequent Action, Suit, or Information; so as such first Action, Suit, or Information, be prosecuted without Fraud, and with Effect; it being hereby declared, that no Action, Suit, or Information, which shall not be so prosecuted, shall be deemed or construed to be an Action, Suit, or Information, within the Intent and Meaning of this Act.

𝕻𝖗𝖔𝖛𝖎𝖉𝖊𝖉

Provided always, That every Action, Bill, Plaint, or Information, given by this Act, shall be commenced within the Space of Six Calendar Months after the Fact upon which the same is granted shall have been committed.

Provided always, That when any Corporation hath any Estate in Lands, Tenements, or other Hereditaments, to the clear yearly Value of One Hundred Pounds, as hereinbefore described, lying and being within the Precincts of the Jurisdiction of any Commission of Sewers, the chief Magistrate of such Corporation, by whatever Name described or distinguished (in case such Office be named and appointed in and by such Commission) shall and may act as a Commissioner under such Commission, during his Continuance in such Office, any Thing herein contained to the contrary notwithstanding.

Provided also, That in case any Commission of Sewers extends, or shall extend, only to the Sewers within the Precincts of the Jurisdiction of any City, Borough, or Town Corporate, then and in every such Case any Person or Persons named in such Commission, and having Lands, Tenements, or other Hereditaments, in Fee Simple, Fee Tail, or for Term of Life, lying and being within such Precincts respectively, to the clear yearly Value of Forty Marks, above all Charges, to his own Use, or being a Magistrate having the Power to act as a Justice of the Peace, and being resiant and free of such City, Borough, or Town Corporate, and having therein moveable Substance to the Value of One Hundred Pounds, and being named and appointed in such Commission, may, being duly sworn, act as a Commissioner or Commissioners under such Commission.

And be it further Enacted by the Authority aforesaid, That if any Person shall presume to act in any Case whatsoever as a Commissioner of Sewers, without being duly sworn as by Law directed, every such Person shall for every such Offence forfeit and pay the like Sum of Forty Pounds, to be recovered and applied in Manner as hereinbefore directed.

Whereas by the Continuance of the Term for which the Commission of Sewers is now by Law to stand and endure, great Inequality and many Inconveniences may arise, contrary to the original Intent and Spirit thereof, in the Administration

ministration and Execution of the Powers therein contained, if Provision be not made for Remedy thereof; **Be it therefore Enacted** by the Authority aforesaid, That, at any Time during the Continuance of any Commission of Sewers, if any Person not named as a Commissioner in such Commission, comes by Devise, Inheritance, or Purchase, into the Possession of any Lands, Tenements, or other Hereditaments, in Fee Simple, Fee Tail, or for Term of Life, or for some greater Estate, or an Estate for some long Term of Years determinable upon One or more Life or Lives, or for a certain Term originally created for Twenty-one Years or more, in Lands, Tenements, or Hereditaments, lying and being within the Precincts of the Jurisdiction of the said Commission, to the clear Yearly Value of Two Hundred Pounds, above all Charges, to his own Use, should apply by Petition to the Chancellor, together with the other great Officers already by Law impowered to issue the Commission of Sewers, the said Chancellor, together with the other great Officers, if he or they shall see Cause, and if the Persons already named in the said Commission, or a Quorum thereof, do not make any just Cause of Objection thereto, may order the Name of such Person or Persons duly qualified, to be added to and inserted in the said Commission as aforesaid; and such Person or Persons so qualified and so named, and taking the Oath as by the Law of Sewers directed to be taken by a Commissioner of Sewers, shall be held and deemed a lawful Commissioner in the said Commission of Sewers, and may sit and act under and by virtue of the same, as though he or they was or were originally, at the first sealing thereof, named as Commissioner or Commissioners therein; any Law, Statute, or Custom, to the contrary notwithstanding.

And whereas Commissioners of Sewers are impowered by Law to act in certain Cases according to their Wisdom and Discretion; which Power may be attended with Inconveniencies, if exercised without such Commissioners having competent Knowledge or proper Information in the Premisses; **Be it therefore further Enacted** by the Authority aforesaid, That in Cases where the Law directs that the said Commissioners shall be governed by their Wisdom and Discretion, no Order shall be made as to any Matter or Thing to be done in the Premisses, without a View of such Premisses by the Commissioners themselves, or by Survey and Report of some Surveyor, or other Officer, duly

and

and according to Marſh Law appointed, and ſworn to make ſuch Survey and Report, ſhall precede or accompany ſuch Acts and Orders reſpectively of ſuch Commiſſioners.

𝔄𝔫𝔡 𝔴𝔥𝔢𝔯𝔢𝔞𝔰 Commiſſioners of Sewers are by Law authorized to depute and aſſign diligent, faithful, and true Keepers, Bailiffs, Surveyors, Clerks, Collectors, Expenditors, and other Miniſters and Officers, for the Safety, Conſervation, Reparation, Reformation, and Making, of the Premiſſes, and every of them, but frequently do neglect ſo to do; 𝔅𝔢 𝔦𝔱 𝔣𝔲𝔯𝔱𝔥𝔢𝔯 𝔈𝔫𝔞𝔠𝔱𝔢𝔡 by the Authority aforeſaid, That in all Caſes (where ſuch Officers and Miniſters are not, by the Cuſtom of the Marſh or otherwiſe, choſen and appointed) all ſuch Commiſſioners ſhall, and are hereby required to depute and aſſign diligent, faithful, and true Keepers, Bailiffs, Surveyors, Clerks, Collectors, Expenditors, or other Miniſters and Officers, and to appoint ſuch Officers and Miniſters, ſo aſſigned and deputed, ſuch reaſonable Wages, or ſuch Sums of Money or Fees, as by the Diſcretion of the ſaid Commiſſioners, or any Six of them, ſhall be thought reaſonable, as Matters and Things to be done may require, to the Purport, Effect, Words, and true Meaning, of their Commiſſion; and the ſaid Commiſſioners are hereby further required, at every General or Quarter Seſſions, or Court of the Sewers, to give their Charge to the ſame Officers and Miniſters, and from Time to Time to give Inſtructions and iſſue their Orders to the ſaid Miniſters and Officers, according to their Wiſdom and Diſcretions.

𝔄𝔫𝔡 𝔟𝔢 𝔦𝔱 𝔈𝔫𝔞𝔠𝔱𝔢𝔡 by the Authority aforeſaid, That every Clerk, Dykereeve, Keeper, Bailiff, Surveyor, Collector, Expenditor, or other Miniſter or Officer, whether choſen according to the Cuſtom of the Marſh or appointed by the Commiſſioners, and concerned in and for the Receipt and laying out of Monies, or charged with the Care, Uſe, and Keeping, of any Utenſils, Stores, or other Materials whatſoever, uſed or to be uſed in or belonging to the Premiſſes, ſhall account, and produce his or their Vouchers, for all and every Sum and Sums of Money that he or they ſhall receive or pay by virtue of his or their Office or Offices, or committed to his Charge and Cuſtody; and ſhall account for the Uſe and Expenditure of the ſame to the Commiſſioners of Sewers under whom he or they acts or act, when and as often as thereunto required by them ſo to do; and ſhall, whenever his or their Office or Offices cease and determine, pay over the Balance of such Accounts, and deliver over all such Utensils, Stores, and other Materials, as do remain in his or their Hands, to such Person or Persons as shall succeed him or them in the said Office or Offices, or as the said Commissioners of Sewers shall direct and appoint to receive the same; and all Officers and Ministers so accounting as aforesaid, shall verify their Accounts upon Oath, if thereunto required by the said Commissioners of Sewers (which Oath the said Commissioners, or any Six of them, are hereby empowered to administer) and if any such Clerk, Dykereeve, Keeper, Bailiff, Surveyor, Collector, Expenditor, or other Officer or Minister, shall neglect or refuse to account for any Sum or Sums of Money by him collected or received by virtue of his Office, or to account for such Utensils, Stores, or other Materials, as aforesaid, or to verify such Accounts upon Oath, or to produce his or their Vouchers for all and every Sum and Sums of Money which he or they shall have received or paid as aforesaid, and for the Charge and Expenditure of all such Utensils, Stores, and Materials, as aforesaid, as often as required so to do by the said Commissioners of Sewers; or to pay over the Balance remaining in his or their Hands, and to deliver over all such Utensils, Stores, and other Materials, as aforesaid, to such Person or Persons as shall succeed him or them in his or their said Offices, or to such Person or Persons as the said Commissioners shall appoint to receive the same; or shall not deliver up to the said Commissioners, or to their Order, within Fourteen Days after being required so to do, all the Books, Papers, and Writings, in his or their Custody or Power, relating to his or their Charge in the Execution of his or their Office or Offices; then, and in each or any or either of the Cases aforesaid, it shall and may be lawful to and for the said Commissioners of Sewers to commit such Clerk, Keeper, Bailiff, Surveyor, Collector, Expenditor, or other Officer or Minister, so offending, to the County or Common Gaol, there to remain until he or they shall have made a full, true, and perfect Account, Payment, and Delivery, as aforesaid, or until he or they shall have compounded with the said Commissioners of Sewers for the same, and have paid such Composition, or shall have given Security for the same, in such Manner as they shall appoint (which Composition the said Commissioners are hereby empowered to make) and until he or they shall have delivered up all such Books, Papers, and Writings, as aforesaid, or shall have given Satisfaction to the said Commissioners of Sewers in respect thereof.

And

And be it further Enacted by the Authority aforesaid, That if any Person holding and executing any of the Offices aforesaid shall die before the Expiration of his Office, or before he shall have accounted, and discharged himself, as afore required and directed, his Executor or Administrator, Executors or Administrators, shall, within a reasonable Time after his Decease, deliver over to his Successor, or to such Persons as the Commissioners of Sewers shall direct, all Books, Papers, and Writings, and Accounts, belonging to and concerning his said Office, except such as are necessary for the making up his Accounts, and then such are to be delivered over with his Accounts, as also all Utensils, Stores, and other Materials whatsoever, remaining in his Charge at the Time of his Decease, or which shall come into the Custody and Power of such his Executor or Administrator, Executors or Administrators; and such Executor or Administrator, Executors or Administrators, shall be liable to pay, and shall pay, out of the Assetts of such deceased, all Sums of Money remaining due, which the said Officer or Minister collected or received, or for which he was accountable by virtue of his said Office, before any of his other Debts are paid or satisfied; or in case any Person exercising any of the Offices aforesaid, shall, before he hath accounted and discharged himself, as hereinbefore required, become a Bankrupt, then and in such Case the Assignees of such Bankrupt shall be in like Manner liable to, and in like Manner required to do and perform all such Matters and Things as the Executors or Administrators hereinbefore mentioned are liable to, and are required to do and perform.

And, in order to prevent and remedy the many Inconveniences which do, and the Mischiefs which may, arise through Delay or Default of Payment of Rates and Assessments; and in order to ascertain what may be held and deemed to be an Arrearage; Be it further Enacted by the Authority aforesaid, That where the Custom of the Country is, or where any special Occasion requires, that the Commissioners of Sewers do, as by Law empowered, of their own Act lay any Rate, Tax, or Assessment, then and in such Case they shall forthwith, after the laying any such Rate, Tax, or Assessment, issue a Precept to the Dykereeve, Collector, Expenditor, or any other Minister or Officer, who is empowered and ordered to collect the same, directing him or them to affix upon the principal Door of the Church, or in some other public Place in the Town or District wherein the Lands and Tenements so rated, taxed, or assessed, do lie, Notice of such Rate, Tax, or Assessment, so

laid,

laid, and of the Times fixed for the Payment thereof; which Precept fo iffued, and fo directing, fhall be held and deemed to be fufficient Notice thereof; and that, where the Cuftom of the Country is, that the Dykereeves or Sewers Rates and Affeffments are laid at a Dykereeve's, Sewer, Leet, Town, or other Meeting, by the Commonalty, or Landowners and Landholders, of that Leet, Town, or Diftrict, then and there previous Notice fhall be, and is hereby required to be given, by the Dykereeve, Expenditor, or other Officer or Minifter, or by his or their Deputy, or Deputies, at the Time of Divine Service, or in fome other public Place in the Town or Diftrict, at leaft Seven Days before fuch Meeting, that a Leet, Dykereeve or Sewers, Town, or other Meeting, as by the Cuftom of the Country it fhall be named, is to be held for the Purpofe of confidering on the laying a Rate, Tax, or Affeffment, on the Lands and Tenements within the Precincts of the Jurifdiction of the fame; and that the faid Officer or Officers, or his or their Deputy or Deputies, fhall call upon the Landholders and Landowners, in the faid Notice, to attend him or them on fome One Day, as fuch Officer or Officers aforefaid fhall fix, previous to the Meeting, in order to their taking a View and Survey of the Premiffes, and in order to examine and advife what Rates, Taxes, or Affeffments, may be neceffary and proper to be laid; and that when fuch Rates, Taxes, or Affeffments, are laid, then and there the Times of Payment of the fame fhall be fixed; and the Dykereeve, Bailiff, Expenditor, or other Officer or Minifter, who is authorized and directed to collect the fame, is hereby required forthwith to fix upon the principal Door of the Church, or in fome other public Place of the Town or Diftrict, Notice of fuch Rate, Tax, or Affeffment, and of the Time or Times of Payment fo fixed as aforefaid; which fhall be held and deemed to be due and legal Notice thereof: And all fuch Rates, Taxes, or Affeffments, fo laid, and not paid at the Times fo fixed and notified, fhall be held and deemed to be Arrearages, and the Dykereeve, Bailiff, Expenditor, or other Officer or Minifter, or his or their Deputy or Deputies, are hereby authorized and required forthwith to diftrain for the fame, and the faid Diftrefs to prize and fell, or caufe to be prized and fold, in cafe the faid Arrears are not paid in Five Days after the making fuch Diftrefs, or to take and ufe fuch other Procefs thereupon, according to the Powers by the Laws and Commiffion of Sewers vefted in him or them by virtue of his or their Office or Offices.

Provided

Provided always, That if, when the Dykereeve, or other Officer or Minister, Officers or Ministers, or his or their Deputies, as aforesaid, shall, as above directed, have given Notice to the Landowners and Landholders to meet and attend him or them, in order to their taking a View and Survey of the Premisses, such Landowners and Landholders shall neglect so to do, such Rates, Tax, or Assessment, as afore named, may nevertheless be laid from the Report of such Officer or Minister, Officers or Ministers, or his or their Deputies, as shall appear to be requisite, any Thing herein contained to the contrary notwithstanding.

And be it further Enacted by the Authority aforesaid, That if the Landowners, being Inhabitants, or Landholders, or the most Part of them, inhabiting within any such Town or District for which Notice of such Meeting as aforesaid for the Purpose of laying such Rate, Tax, or Assessment, as aforesaid, was given, shall not be at the Place at the Hour and Time by such Dykereeve, or other Minister or Officer, his or their Deputy or Deputies, as aforesaid, so appointed, every of the said Landowners, being an Inhabitant, and every Landholder, that shall so make Default, shall forfeit and pay Five Shillings for every Time he or they shall not, upon such Notice as aforesaid, repair, at the Time, to the Place by such Dykereeve, or Officer or Minister, his or their Deputy or Deputies, as aforesaid, so appointed, the said Default to be presented by the said Officer or Minister, his or their Deputy or Deputies, at the next Sessions or Court of Sewers, upon his or their Oath or Oaths; and upon such Presentment the Commissioners, or any Six of them, sitting in such Sessions or Court, are hereby authorized and required to fine the said Landowners and Landholders in the said Sum accordingly; the said Fine to be levied and paid as all other Fines are by the Laws of Sewers, or by this Act, directed to be levied and paid.

And be it Enacted by the Authority aforesaid, That if, by Want of the Appearance of Six of such Landowners or Landholders as aforesaid, at such Meeting as aforesaid, for the Purpose aforesaid, or through their not agreeing upon any Rate, Tax, or Assessment, the Dykereeve, or other Minister or Officer, or his or their Deputy or Deputies, who hath or have Charge of the Preservation of the Defences and Sewers of the Town or District, shall think the Country may be endangered, such Dykereeve, or such other Officer, his or their Deputy or Deputies,

Deputies, which did give such Warning or Notice as aforesaid, shall resort unto some Two of the Commissioners of Sewers acting, as by Law directed, for the District wherein the Premisses do lie; and such Commissioners, if upon the Oath or Oaths of the Officer or Minister, his or their Deputy or Deputies, presenting the Matter, they shall see Cause, are hereby authorized to rate and assess such Acre Shott, as they in their Discretions shall see necessary, for the present imminent Case so presented; and they shall deliver the said Assessment, under their Hands, to the said Dykereeve, or other Officer or Minister, his or their Deputy or Deputies, as aforesaid, who shall forthwith publish or give Notice, in Manner as before by this Act directed, of every such Acre Shott so assessed; and such Officer or Minister, his or their Deputy or Deputies, are hereby empowered to collect and gather the same in the Manner as he or they are empowered to gather and collect all other Rates, Taxes, or Assessments, of the Sewers.

14. *And be it Enacted* by the Authority aforesaid, That if any Person be chosen a Dykereeve by Reason of his Lands, within any Town wherein he doth not inhabit, then it shall be lawful for any Two Commissioners of Sewers, with the Consent of Four of the Inhabitants of the said Town, to choose some sufficient Man in his Room, as shall seem good to the said Commissioners and Inhabitants, the said Commissioners making him such Allowance for his Pains in that Behalf, as shall seem good in their Discretion, so that the Sum of Money allowed unto any of them exceed not the Sum of Forty Shillings, and the said Deputy, so appointed, to undergo all such Pains and Forfeitures as are before specified in any Laws aforesaid; and the Dykereeve that payeth any such Sum to any Deputy so appointed and allowed as aforesaid, to be thereof discharged.

And be it further Enacted by the Authority aforesaid, That if any Person, duly qualified, shall duly, according to Marsh Law, be chosen a Keeper, Bailiff, Dykereeve, Surveyor, Collector, or any other Officer or Minister, for the Execution of the Laws of Sewers in the Town wherein he is an Inhabitant, and shall refuse to take upon him, and to execute, such Office, or shall not well and sufficiently, with his or their best Diligence and Endeavour, execute the same, then he or they to forfeit the Sum of Ten Pounds, to be levied by any Six or more Commissioners of the Sewers, whereof Three to be of the Quorum,

or

or by any other Person or Persons assigned by them, under their Hands and Seals, to levy the same.

And be it Enacted by the Authority aforesaid, That every Keeper, Bailiff, Dykereeve, Surveyor, or other Officer or Minister, of any Town, having Charge and Care of the Preservation and Reparation of the Banks and Sewers in and belonging to the said Town or District, shall, as soon as he is elected to the said Office as aforesaid, with all convenient Speed, and from Time to Time, make a Survey of all the Banks and Sewers within their several Towns and Parishes, and the Wood Shores and Counter Shores thereof, and, as he or they shall find any Default, from Time to Time, make a Remembrance thereof in Writing, and thereupon shall give present Warning to the Owner, Farmer, or Occupier, of such Lands whose Banks or Shores shall be found in Default, charging them to see the said Banks and Wood Shores, without Delay, to be made according to the Form as by Law directed, by a Time to be limited; and if, after such Warning given, the Persons that ought to repair the same shall not endeavour themselves for the speedy repairing, heightening, and amending, as the Case may require, of the said Banks, Wood Shores, and Counter Shores, that then it shall and may be lawful for the said Dykereeve or Dykereeves, or other Officers or Ministers, their Deputy or Deputies, within whose Charge any such Default shall be found, presently to make the said Banks and Shores, and to take, for every Penny disbursed by him or them, Two Pence.

And be it Enacted by the Authority aforesaid, That if any Person or Persons which shall make Default in repairing, in Heighth or Breadth, or making, any of the said Banks or Shores, after Warning given as aforesaid, shall also make Default in paying the Monies disbursed and forfeited, by the Space of Ten Days next after any of the Dykereeves, or other Officers or Ministers, his or their Deputy or Deputies, as aforesaid, of any of the said several Towns, shall have repaired the same Banks, Walls, and Shores, or any of them, immediately before or after Divine Service, in any the said Parish Churches or Chapels of the same Town wherein the Land so charged to the said Sea Banks do lie, shall have demanded the same, that then it shall and may be lawful for the said Dykereeve or Dykereeves, Officer or Officers, Minister or Ministers, as aforesaid,

his

his or their Deputy or Deputies, to enter into any of his or their Lands or Tenements lying within the Precincts of this Commission, and to distrain, as well for the Money so expended and disbursed, as also for the Sum or Sums so forfeited, in Manner and Form as by the Power and Authority of this Act is directed in such Cases; and if any of the Dykereeves, or other Officer or Minister, Officers or Ministers, his or their Deputy or Deputies, as aforesaid, of any of the said Towns, shall, for the avoiding of present Danger, and for the Preservation of any Place within the Precincts aforesaid, before or without Warning thereof given to the Owner or Owners of any such Lands as be charged with the repairing, in Breadth, Height, or other amending, of such Banks or Shores, repair, heighten, or make, or cause to be repaired, heightened, or made, the said Banks or Shores, or any Part thereof, and that the Owners, Farmers, or Occupier, or Township, chargeable to the making, heightening, and repairing, of the said Banks and Shores, shall not, within Ten Days next after Demand openly made, in the Church or Chapel as is aforesaid, by the Dykereeve or Dykereeves, Minister or Officer, Ministers or Officers, his or their Deputy or Deputies, as aforesaid, pay such Sum or Sums of Money as he or they shall have expended or disbursed for the Charge aforesaid, that then it shall be lawful for the said Dykereeve or Dykereeves, Minister or Officer, Ministers or Officers, his or their Deputy or Deputies, as aforesaid, to distrain, and take for every Penny so disbursed Two Pence, and the Distress so taken to cause to be prized and sold, in Manner and Form as by this Act is directed and provided; and if no Distress sufficient can be found in any of the Lands and Tenements of such Person and Persons which ought to pay the same, then it shall and may be lawful for Six Commissioners, whereof Three to be of the Quorum, to demise, sell, and set over, such Lands and Tenements, or any Part or Parcel of them, to such Person or Persons, and for such Term and Terms, as by the Discretion of the said Commissioners shall seem good.

And whereas great Losses have happened, and do daily happen, where Banks have, at the great Cost and Charges of the Owners thereof, been sufficiently made, by the not making and repairing of the Banks next or near adjoining in due and convenient Time; Be it further Enacted by the Authority aforesaid, That if any of the Banks or Shores of any Person

or

or Perſons, within the Precincts of the Juriſdiction of any Commiſſion of Sewers, ſhall be in Decay, and the Banks or Shores of any other next adjoining ſhall be ſufficient, and not in Decay, that then it ſhall be lawful for the Perſon or Perſons whoſe Banks ſhall be ſtanding, and not in Decay, but in Danger to take Hurt, upon Notice given to, and Default of, him or them, his or their Farmer or Farmers, whoſe Banks ſhall be ſo in Decay, to put forth the ſaid Banks next or near adjoining to him, and to cauſe the ſame to be ſufficiently made and repaired, ſo often as Need ſhall require, and to levy and take of the Perſon or Perſons who are bound to repair and keep up the ſame, by way of Diſtreſs or otherwiſe, for every Groat by him or them diſburſed for the making or repairing of the ſaid Banks ſo in Decay, Six Pence of lawful Money, in ſuch Manner and Form as the Dykereeves and Surveyors, or other Officers or Miniſters, his or their Deputy or Deputies, as aforeſaid, might take the ſame in any Caſe before expreſſed.

Provided, That no private Perſon that ſhall make, or cauſe to be made, any ſuch Banks ſo in Decay as aforeſaid, ſhall take any Diſtreſs before he hath delivered a true Account of the Monies ſo by him or them diſburſed, unto the Owner, or unto Six Commiſſioners of Sewers, and have obtained a Warrant under the Hands and Seals of the ſaid Commiſſioners, for the taking of ſuch Diſtreſs; and that every Diſtreſs ſo taken may be prized and ſold as aforeſaid; and every ſuch Sale ſhall be as good and available, to all Conſtructions, as if the ſame had been made or done by the Dykereeve or Dykereeves, their Deputy or Deputies, or by any other Officer whatſoever.

Provided always, That if the Cattle, Goods, or Things, which ſhall be at any Time ſo taken, diſtrained, and ſold, as aforeſaid, ſhall amount unto any more or greater Sum than ſhall be by him or them diſburſed and forfeited, by virtue and force of this Act, that then every ſuch Perſon who ſhall take any ſuch Diſtreſs, ſhall as well pay or cauſe to be paid, or ſatisfied, to the Owner or Owners of the ſaid Diſtreſs or Diſtreſſes, upon Requeſt by him or them made, the Surpluſage of all ſuch Sum and Sums of Money that ſhall remain in his or their Hands, as alſo to deliver to the Owner or Owners of the ſaid Diſtreſs or Diſtreſſes, upon like Requeſt, a true and perfect Bill of all the Money as well expended and diſburſed, as alſo received and taken, by virtue of this Act.

𝔄𝔫𝔡 𝔟𝔢 𝔦𝔱 𝔈𝔫𝔞𝔠𝔱𝔢𝔡 by the Authority aforesaid, That in all Cases wherein any Officer or Minister, or other Person, acting under and by Authority of any Commission of Sewers, is empowered to make Distress and Sale of the Goods and Chattels of any Person or Persons within the Precincts of the Jurisdiction of such Commission aforesaid, for Neglect or Refusal of Payment of the Arrears of any Rate, Tax, or Assessment, as by the Laws of Sewers are directed to be made, or for any Forfeit or Penalty incurred, or on Account of any Fine or Amerciament, such Officer or Minister, or such other Person, may in such Case make Distress and Sale in like Manner and Form, and under the like Protections, respecting the Powers of the Commission and Commissioners of Sewers, as by the Powers given and Provisions made in and by the several Laws in force, directing the Mode of Distress and Sale for Rent, but more especially by an Act passed in the Eleventh Year of the Reign of King *George* the Second, intituled, " An Act for the " more effectual securing the Payment of Rent, and prevent- " ing Frauds by Tenants," are enacted.

𝔓𝔯𝔬𝔳𝔦𝔡𝔢𝔡 𝔞𝔩𝔴𝔞𝔶𝔰, That in the Case wherein this last-mentioned Act directs that Recourse be had to Two Justices of the Peace, from whom there may be an Appeal to the Quarter Sessions of the Peace, there shall, in the like Case arising in any like Manner respecting the Laws of Sewers, Recourse be had to Two Commissioners of Sewers, and in Case of an Appeal from them, such Appeal shall lie to the next Sessions or General Court of Sewers; who are hereby empowered to receive, hear, and determine upon, such Appeal.

𝔄𝔫𝔡, in order to prevent all such Danger as the Drainage of the Country may be liable to, by Persons, without being duly authorized, taking upon themselves wilfully to obstruct any of the Sewers, or Works of Sewers, or in any Manner to pervert or alter the Operations thereof; 𝔅𝔢 𝔦𝔱 𝔈𝔫𝔞𝔠𝔱𝔢𝔡 by the Authority aforesaid, That if any Person or Persons shall wilfully, to the Annoyance or endangering of the Country, or to obstructing the Drainage thereof, or without being duly and legally authorized, open or shut, pull up or let down, any Door or Doors of any Tunnel, Sluice, Lock, Gole, or Gote, or in like Manner, and with like Intent, obstruct, streighten, or widen, or any ways alter, any Tunnel, Streight, Drain, Run, or Sewer, by whatever Name such may be called or described, or shall in like Manner, and with like Intent, put down or raise, or lower, enlarge, or lessen, any Wear, Head, or Dam, or any ways da-

mage

mage any inland Bank, not being the Bank of any River or main Drain, being within and under the Jurisdiction of the Sewers Law, and shall, on the Oath or Oaths of One or more credible Witness or Witnesses, be convicted thereof before any Two or more Justices of the Peace acting for the County, Division, or Place wherein the Offence shall have been committed, such Offender or Offenders shall for every such Offence forfeit and pay, according to the Nature of his or their Offence, any Sum not exceeding Fifty Pounds, nor less than Five Pounds, at the Discretion of the said Justices, and such Offender or Offenders shall moreover be liable to pay, and shall pay, all such Expences as the Reparation of the Damages done to any of the Works or Defences of the Sewers, by their Offence, shall have cost (the said Costs being first examined and allowed by the Commissioners of Sewers) to the Person or Persons, Officer or Officers, who by Law shall be charged with the Care, Preservation, and Reparation, of the Works of the Sewers in the said Parts, and who shall have actually repaired the same; and such Offender or Offenders neglecting or refusing to pay the same, shall be committed to the County Gaol, there to remain until the same shall be so paid as herein required.

Provided always, That nothing herein contained shall extend, or be construed to extend, to prevent any Person or Persons, who shall be injured in their private Property by any of the Offenders aforesaid, from suing for Trespass or Damage, or from recovering Damages, in His Majesty's Courts of Law.

And be it further hereby Enacted, That if any Person or Persons do wilfully and maliciously break, or any ways demolish, any Tunnel, Ditch, Gutter, Sewer, Clough, Lock, Sluice, Gole, or Gote; or cut or break down, burn, or demolish, any Sea Bank, or any Bank of any River or main Drain, or any other the Works of Defence made, erected, set up, or that shall be hereafter made, erected, or set up, by and under the Jurisdiction of any Commission of Sewers; or shall steal any Timber, Bricks, Deals, or any other Materials, actually employed in, and being Part or Parts of, such Works and Defences; such Offender or Offenders shall be judged guilty of Felony, and shall be subject and liable to the like Pains and Penalties as in the Case of Felony; and the Court by and before whom such Person or Persons shall be tried and convicted, shall have full Power and Authority to transport such Felon or Felons to some of His Majesty's Plantations, for any Term

of

of Years, not more than Seven Years nor less than Three Years, in like Manner as other Person or Persons convicted of Felony are directed to be transported by the Laws and Statutes of the Realm, or to assign such other Punishment as any Statute may or shall assign to such Persons convicted of Felony, in lieu of the Punishment of Transportation.

And be it Enacted by the Authority aforesaid, That any Person appointed or to be appointed a Commissioner, in or by virtue of any Commission of Sewers, who shall be a Justice of the Peace, may, and is hereby authorized, empowered, and required to act as a Justice of the Peace within the Precincts of the Jurisdiction of such said Commission, in the Execution of such Powers and Authorities as are by the Laws and Statutes of the Realm, and by this Statute, given to any Justice of the Peace, notwithstanding his or their being a Commissioner or Commissioners of Sewers, provided such Justice be otherwise qualified, and not interested in the Matter in Question, other than as a Commissioner of Sewers.

And whereas the Commissioners of Sewers are by the "Bill of Sewers with a new Proviso, &c." afore named, created a Court to hear and determine all and singular the Premises specified in the said Act, as well at the Suit of Our Lord the King, as at the Suit of any other whatsoever, complaining before them, or Six of them; Be it Enacted by the Authority aforesaid, That without a Jury of lawful Men, sworn and acting as the Law requires, the said Commissioners shall not hear, nor without a Verdict or Presentment of such Jury on the Matter of Fact, determine, give Judgment, or make any Decree whatsoever in their judicial Capacity.

And be it further Enacted by the Authority aforesaid, That no Person whatsoever shall sit and act as a Commissioner of Sewers, to hear and determine in any Case whatsoever in which he is (other than as a Commissioner) personally, or by Reason of his Property, or of any Property in Right of which he is qualified to be a Commissioner of Sewers; in any Manner whatsoever, directly or indirectly, interested or concerned in the Case, under the Penalty of forfeiting and paying the Sum of One hundred Pounds for every Time that he shall so sit and act, One Half thereof to Our Sovereign Lord the King, and the other Half to the Use of him or them who shall sue for the same, in any of the King's Courts at *Westminster*, by Action of Debt, or on the Case, Bill, Plaint, or Information, wherein no Essoign, Protection,

tection, or Wager of Law, nor more than One Imparlance, shall be allowed; and any Person or Persons having any Cause to be heard and determined before the said Court of Sewers may and shall have Challenge against any Commissioner so concerned and interested.

And be it further Enacted by the Authority aforesaid, That in all Cases relative to and concerning the Execution of the Laws of Sewers, any Person aggrieved by any Justice or Justices of the Peace shall have Appeal to, and be heard on the Matter of such Complaint at, any General or Quarter Sessions of the Peace to be held within Four Months, for the County or Precinct wherein such Justice or Justices of the Peace acted; and any Person aggrieved by any inferior Officer or Minister of the Sewers, whether deputed and assigned by the Commissioners of Sewers, or chosen and appointed according to the Custom of the Country, such Person so aggrieved shall have Appeal to, and be heard by, the next Sessions or Court of Sewers, on the Matter of such Complaint; and the Justices of the said General or Quarter Sessions, and the Commissioners of the said Sessions or Court of Sewers, as the Matter shall come respectively before them, are hereby respectively authorized and required, if the Appellant shall make good the Matter of his Complaint, to give such Relief, and to award such Damage and Costs, as the Nature of the Case shall appear to them to require; as also, where, on such Appeal, the Appellant shall not make good the Matter of his Complaint, or where such Appeal shall appear to them to be frivolous or vexatious, to give to the Justice or Justices, Officer, or Minister, against whom such Appeal was made, such Relief, and to award to him such Costs and Damages, as the Nature of the Case shall appear to them to require.

Provided always, That nothing herein contained shall extend, or be construed to extend, by such Right of Appeal, to suspend or obstruct any Order, Act, Matter, or Thing, which may be necessary to be executed or done for the immediate Safety and Defence of the Country, within the Premisses, or to absolve any Person from obeying such Order, or from doing such Act, Matter, or Thing, in such Case of immediate Necessity, however so much such Person or Persons may think himself or themselves aggrieved thereby, his and their Right of Appeal for Relief and Remedy remaining at the same Time notwithstanding.

And be it further Enacted by the Authority aforesaid, That no Law made or to be made by the said Commissioners of Sewers shall have any Force or Effect, unless such Law be made at a General Quarter Sessions or Court of Sewers; and unless Duplicates thereof, written on Parchment, and indented, be signed and sealed by Six or more of the said Commissioners then and there present, whereof Three shall be of the Quorum; and unless, being so made, signed, and sealed, One Part thereof shall be transmitted to His Majesty's Most Honourable Privy Council, and shall there receive His Majesty's Royal Assent in Council, certified by One of the Clerks of the said Council to the said Commissioners.

Provided always, That nothing herein contained shall extend, or be construed to extend, to the restraining the Commissioners of Sewers, in their Court of Sewers, from making Ordinances respecting any particular Case within the Premises, upon Authority of Law already in force, nor to abate the Force and Effect of such Ordinances so made and ordained accordingly.

And, to the Intent that any Person or Persons who may think himself or themselves in Danger of being aggrieved or damaged by any such Law as aforesaid, made at such Sessions or Court of Sewers, may have Time to petition to be heard at the Council Board against such Law receiving such Royal Assent; Be it further Enacted by the Authority aforesaid, That whenever the Commissioners of Sewers shall make any new Law, or repeal any old Law, they shall, by their Clerk, give public Notice of their having made or repealed such Law, in some public News-paper which is most generally circulated and most in use in those Parts or County wherein the Premisses lie and are situated, One Calendar Month at least before it is transmitted to the Privy Council.

And be it further enacted that where any work or works are ordered to be done by presentment of a Jury or by view of Commissioners if any Juryman shall have any part share or interest directly or indirectly in any Contract or Bargain for work or materials to be made done or provided upon for or on account of any of the works whatsoever under the Jurisdiction of the Commissioners of Sewers or shall upon his own account directly or indirectly sell or dispose of any Brick Timber Stone or other materials to be used or employed in making or repairing such works as aforesaid (unless a licence in writing for such contract or bargain or for the sale of such materials be first obtained under the hands and seals of two Commissioners) he shall forfeit for every such offence the sum of Ten Pounds to be levied by distress and sale of his Goods & Chattells by Warrant under the hands and seals of   Commissioners.

And be it further enacted that where any works are ordered to be done by presentment of a Jury or by view of Commissioners, ~~that~~ if any Juryman shall have any part share or interest directly or indirectly in any Contract or Bargain for work or materials to be made done or provided upon for or on Account of any of the Works whatsoever under the Jurisdiction of the Commissioners of Sewers or shall upon his own Account directly or indirectly sell or dispose of any Brick Timber Stone or other Materials to be used or employed in making or repairing such Works as aforesaid (unless a licence in writing for such contract or bargain or for the sale of such Materials be first obtained under the hands and seals of two Commissioners) he shall forfeit for every such Offence the sum of Ten Pounds to be levied by Distress and sale of his Goods & Chattels by Warrant under the hands & seals of two Commissioners

A BILL

[With the Amendments]

TO

Explain and amend the Laws now in being relating to Sewers.

1777.

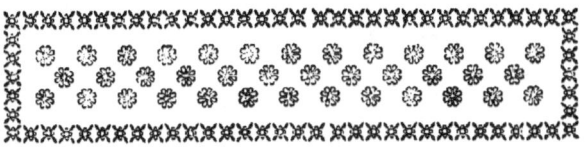

A
B I L L
T O

Oblige the Minister and Churchwardens, or other proper Officers, in every Parish and Place within that Part of *Great Britain* called *England*, to make Returns upon Oath of all Charitable Donations, for the Benefit of Poor Persons, within such respective Parishes or Places; distinguishing, as far as may be, by whom, when, and in what Manner, and for what Purposes, given, likewise whether such respective Donations were in Land or Money, and in whom now vested, and what is the Annual Produce thereof, respectively.

Note.—*The Figures in the Margin denote the Number of the Folios in the written Copy.*

WHEREAS it may be proper that the Legislature, who are extending their Enquiries into the State and Condition of the Poor, should be informed of the several Charitable Donations for the Use and Benefit of Poor Persons; which Information cannot be effectually obtained without the Aid and Assistance of Parliament:

A May

May it therefore please Your MAJESTY,

That it may be Enacted; **And be it Enacted** by the KING's Most Excellent MAJESTY, by and with the Advice and Consent of the Lords Spiritual and Temporal, and Commons, in this present Parliament assembled, and by the Authority of the same, That a sufficient Number of printed Copies of this Act shall, as soon as conveniently may be after the passing hereof, be transmitted by *George White*, Esquire, One of the Clerks of the House of Commons, to the Clerks of the Peace of every County in *England* and *Wales*; and that the said several Clerks of the Peace shall, and they are hereby required, with all convenient Speed, to cause the same to be distributed amongst the acting Justices of the Peace within their respective Counties, and also within all Cities, Boroughs, and other Places, having separate Jurisdictions, and Magistrates situate within their said respective Counties; and also to cause a sufficient Number of the Schedule, to this Act annexed, to be printed, and delivered to the High Constables, or other proper Officers, within every such County, and also to the Town Clerk, or other proper Officer, of every such City, Borough, or Place, on or before the

and also to receive the Answers and Returns made by the Minister and Churchwardens, pursuant to the Directions hereinafter given, and transmit the same to the Clerk of the Parliaments, with all convenient Speed, in order that the same may be inspected by the Members of both Houses of Parliament, upon Pain of forfeiting for every Neglect and Default a Sum not exceeding
nor less than

And be it further Enacted, That the several Justices of the Peace, within their respective Jurisdictions in *England* and *Wales*, shall, as soon as conveniently may be after the said   appoint a Time and Place, or Times and Places (which Time or Times shall be on or before the then next   for the Minister and Churchwardens of the several Parishes, Townships, and Places, within their respective Jurisdictions, to attend them at such Meeting or Meetings for the Purposes of this Act, with Returns and Answers to the Questions stated in the Schedule to this Act annexed, and cause Notice thereof to be given to such Minister and Churchwardens respectively,
and

and also to the High Constable, or, where there are no High Constables, to such other proper Officers who have the Execution of Precepts from Justices of the Peace to inferior Officers, within such respective Jurisdictions, and also to the Town Clerks, or other proper Officers, of such Cities, Towns, and Places, requiring their Attendance at such Meetings for the Purposes of this Act.

And be it further Enacted, That the said Justices of the Peace shall, and they are hereby also required, at such Meeting or Meetings so to be appointed by them as aforesaid, to receive and take the Answers and Returns to be made by the Minister and Churchwardens, pursuant to the Directions aforesaid, and then and there administer to them respectively the Oath contained in the said Schedule; and such Justices, if they see Cause, may examine such Minister and Churchwardens upon Oath, touching any of the Matters contained in such Questions and Answers; and the said Justices shall then deliver such Answers and Returns to the respective High Constables, Town Clerks, or other proper Officers, as aforesaid, in order that the same may be by them transmitted to the Clerks of the Peace, as herein is directed.

And be it further Enacted, That the several High Constables, Town Clerks, or other proper Officers, so described as aforesaid, within the respective Jurisdictions aforesaid, shall receive from the said Clerks of the Peace the said printed Schedules, and deliver, or cause to be delivered, One such Schedule to the Minister, and also to the Churchwarden or Churchwardens, in every Parish, Township, or Place within their respective Limits; and, when required by the respective Justices of the Peace as aforesaid, attend the said respective Meetings, and then and there receive the several Answers and Returns made by the Minister and Churchwardens, and indorse upon the Back of each of them the Name of the Hundred, Rape, Wapentake, Lathe, Precinct, Soke, Franchise, Liberty, City, Town, or County Corporate, wherein the Parish, Township, or Place, therein mentioned is situate, and transmit the same, together with a true and perfect List of the Names of the Minister and Churchwardens of every Parish, Township, or Place, to whom such Schedules had been delivered by them respectively as aforesaid, to the several

veral Clerks of the Peace at the then next   or the Adjournment thereof (which Adjournment the Juſtices at ſuch   are required to make, to ſome convenient Day within   after ſuch in Caſes where any ſuch Returns ſhall not be made at the ſaid   and every ſuch High Conſtable, Town Clerk, or other proper Officer, ſhall forfeit for every Default or Neglect, a Sum not exceeding   nor leſs than

       𝖆𝖓𝖉 𝖇𝖊 𝖎𝖙 𝖋𝖚𝖗𝖙𝖍𝖊𝖗 𝕰𝖓𝖆𝖈𝖙𝖊𝖉, That the Miniſter and Church-wardens of every ſuch Pariſh, Townſhip, and Place ſhall, and are hereby required to attend the Juſtices of the Peace at ſuch Meeting or Meetings, and then and there deliver to the ſaid Juſtices, in Writing ſigned by them, a juſt and true Anſwer and Return to the ſaid Queſtions, upon Oath, as before directed; and that every Miniſter and Churchwarden making Default in any of the Matters hereby required,
7 ſhall for every ſuch Neglect or Default forfeit a Sum not exceeding   nor leſs than   at the Diſcretion of the Juſtice or Juſtices before whom Complaint thereof ſhall be made: And in order to enable the Miniſter and Churchwardens to make Anſwers and Returns as aforeſaid, they are hereby authorized and impowered to inſpect any Deed, Inſtrument, or other Writing, relating to ſuch Charitable Donations, and to take Copies of ſuch Part or Parts thereof as ſhall be neceſſary for the Purpoſes of this Act; and every Perſon or Perſons in whoſe Cuſtody or Power any ſuch Deed, Inſtrument, or Writing ſhall be, ſhall, and he and they is and are hereby required to produce, or cauſe the ſame, or a true Copy thereof, in caſe the Original ſhall be in the Hands of a Perſon living above   from ſuch Pariſh or Place, to be produced to the ſaid Miniſter and Churchwardens for the Purpoſes aforeſaid, upon Pain of forfeiting for every Default or Neglect in the Premiſes a Sum not
8 exceeding   nor leſs than   at the Diſcretion of the Juſtice or Juſtices before whom Complaint thereof ſhall be made.

       𝖆𝖓𝖉 𝖇𝖊 𝖎𝖙 𝖋𝖚𝖗𝖙𝖍𝖊𝖗 𝕰𝖓𝖆𝖈𝖙𝖊𝖉, That there ſhall be paid and allowed for the Trouble and Expences of the ſeveral Perſons employed in the Tranſactions aforeſaid, for every Re-
.turn

[5]

turn which shall be so made and transmitted to the Clerks of the Peace, pursuant to the Directions aforesaid, the Sums following, and no more; *(viz.)* To the Clerk of the Peace, for the Return which shall be made from every Parish, Township, or Place, the Sum of
to the High Constable, Town Clerk, or other proper Officer, for the like, the Sum of
to the Churchwardens, for the like, the Sum of
to the Clerks of the Justices of the Peace, for the like, the Sum of
And that the Justices of the Peace, at their respective Quarter Sessions which shall be held next after
shall, and are hereby required to make an Order upon their respective Treasurers, to pay the same out of the Rates to be made and collected for the respective Counties, Ridings, Divisions, Precincts, Sokes, Franchises, Liberties, Cities, Towns, and Counties Corporate.

And be it further Enacted, That the several Forfeitures and Penalties inflicted by this Act shall, if not immediately paid, be   of the Offender's Goods and Chattels, by virtue of a Warrant under the Hand and Seal of any Justice of the Peace having Jurisdiction where such Offender shall dwell, rendering to the said Offender the Overplus (if any) after the Charge of such   shall be deducted; and in case sufficient   shall not be found, then it shall be lawful for such Justice to   such Offender to   there to remain without Bail or Mainprize for a Term not exceeding   unless the said Forfeiture and Charges shall be sooner paid; and the said Forfeitures, when   shall be paid and applied   to the Informer, and the other Half to the said respective Treasurers, in Aid of the Rates aforesaid; and any Person shall be deemed a competent Witness for the Execution of any of the Purposes of this Act, notwithstanding his paying, or being liable to pay, to such Rates.

B   SCHEDULE

SCHEDULE.

QUESTIONS, to which, by virtue of an Act passed in the Seventeenth Year of His Majesty King George the Third, intituled, "An Act to oblige the Minister and Churchwardens, or other proper Officers, in every Parish and Place within that Part of Great Britain called England, to make Returns upon Oath of all Charitable Donations, for the Benefit of Poor Persons, within such respective Parishes or Places; distinguishing, as far as may be, by whom, when, and in what Manner, and for what Purposes, given, likewise whether such respective Donations were in Land or Money, and in whom now vested, and what is the Annual Produce thereof, respectively," Answers are to be returned by the Ministers and Churchwardens *(or Churchwarden, where but One)* of every Parish, Township, and Place, in Writing, upon Oath, and signed by them; for which Purpose the said Minister and Churchwardens are to attend the Justices of the Peace within their respective Jurisdictions, at such Times and Places as they shall appoint, on Pain of forfeiting for every Default or Neglect a Sum not exceeding   nor less than

FIRST QUESTION.

WHAT Charitable Donations are there, for the Benefit of Poor Persons, within your Parish (or Place) by whom, when, in what Manner, and for what particular Purpose, were they given?

SECOND QUESTION.

Were the respective Donations in Land or Money; in whom are they now vested; and what is the Annual Produce thereof, respectively?

FORM

FORM of the OATH.

YOU shall swear, That the Answers and Return now made by you, to the Questions contained in the Schedule hereunto annexed, is a full and true Answer to the said Questions, to the best of your Knowledge, Information, and Belief.

To be indorsed by the High Constable, Town Clerk, or other proper Officer, receiving the Returns from the Justices.

ANSWERS returned to those Questions, of the Parish [or Place] of   [in the Hundred, Rape, Wapentake, Lath, Precinct, Soke, Franchise, Liberty, City, Town, or County Corporate, as the Case shall be] the   Day of

A

BILL

TO

Oblige the Minister and Churchwardens, or other proper Officers, in every Parish and Place within that Part of *Great Britain* called *England*, to make Returns upon Oath of all Charitable Donations, for the Benefit of Poor Persons, within such respective Parishes or Places; distinguishing, as far as may be, by whom, when, and in what Manner, and for what Purposes, given, likewise whether such respective Donations were in Land or Money, and in whom now vested, and what is the Annual Produce thereof, respectively.

1777.

A

BILL

TO

Promote the Refidence of the Parochial Clergy, by making Provifion for the more fpeedy and effectual building, re-building, repairing, or purchafing, Houfes, and other neceffary Buildings and Tenements, for the Ufe of their Beneficcs.

Note.—*The Figures in the Margin denote the Number of the Folios in the written Copy.*

𝕳𝕰𝕽𝕰𝕬𝕾 many of the Parochial Clergy, for Want of proper Habitations, are induced to refide at a Diftance from their Benefices, by which Means the Parifhioners lofe the Advantage of their Inftruction and Hofpitality, which were great Objects in the original Diftribution of Tythes and Glebes for the Endowment of Churches: 𝖋𝖔𝖗 Remedy whereof,

1

A May

[2]

May it please Your MAJESTY,

That it may be Enacted; And be it Enacted by the KING's Most Excellent MAJESTY, by and with the Advice and Consent of the Lords Spiritual and Temporal, and Commons, in this present Parliament assembled, and by the Authority of the same, That from and after the Twenty-fourth Day of *June*, One thousand Seven hundred and Seventy-seven, whenever the Parson, Vicar, or other Incumbent, of any Ecclesiastical Living, Parochial Benefice, Chapelry, or perpetual Curacy, whereon there is no House of Habitation, or such House is become so ruinous and decayed, or so mean, that One Year's neat Income and Produce of such Living will not be sufficient to build, re-build, or put the same, with the necessary Offices belonging thereto, in sufficient Repair, shall think fit to apply for the Aid and Assistance intended to be given by this Act, it shall and may be lawful for every such Parson, Vicar, or Incumbent (after having procured from some skilful and experienced Workman or Surveyor, a Certificate, containing a State of the Condition of the Buildings on their respective Glebes, and of the Value of the Timber and other Materials thereupon, fit to be employed in such Buildings or Repairs, or to be sold, and also a Plan and Estimate of the Work proposed to be done (such State and Estimate to be verified upon Oath, taken before some Justice of the Peace, or Master in Chancery, Ordinary or Extraordinary) and laid the same, together with a just and particular Account in Writing, signed by him, and verified upon Oath, taken as aforesaid, of the Annual Profits of such Living, before the Ordinary and Patron of the Living, and obtained their Consent to such proposed new Buildings or Repairs, by Writing under their respective Hands, in the Form for that Purpose contained in the Schedule hereunto annexed) to borrow and take up at Interest, in the Manner hereafter mentioned, such Sum or Sums of Money as the said Estimate shall amount unto, after deducting the Value of Timber or other Materials which may be thought proper to be sold, not exceeding Two Years neat Income and Produce of such Living, after deducting all Rents, Stipends, Taxes, and other Outgoings, excepting

only

only the Salaries to the Assistant Curate, where such a Curate is necessary; and as a Security for the Money so to be borrowed, to mortgage the Glebe, Tythes, Rents, and other Profits and Emoluments, arising or to arise from such Living, to such Person or Persons who shall advance the same, by One or more Deed or Deeds, for the Term of Twenty-one Years, or until the Money so to be borrowed, with Interest for the same, and such Costs and Charges as may attend the Recovery thereof, shall be fully paid and satisfied, according to the Terms, Conditions, true Intent and Meaning of this Act; which Mortgage Deed or Deeds shall be made in the Forms or to the Effect for that Purpose contained in the said Schedule, and shall bind every succeeding Parson, Vicar, or Incumbent, of such Living, until the Principal and Interest, Costs and Charges, shall be paid off and discharged, as fully and effectually as if such Successor had executed the same.

And be it further Enacted, That every such Mortgagee shall execute a Counterpart of every such Mortgage, to be kept by the Incumbent for the Time being; and a Copy of every such Deed of Mortgage shall be registered in the Office of the Registrar of the Bishop of the Diocese where the Parish lies, or the Ordinary having Episcopal Jurisdiction therein for the Time being, after having been first examined by him with the Original, which Officer shall be entitled to Demand and receive the Sum of Five Shillings, and no more, for registering the same; and such Deed shall be referred to upon all necessary Occasions, the Person inspecting the same paying One Shilling for every such Search; and the said Deed, or a Copy thereof, certified under the Hand of the Registrar, shall be allowed as legal Evidence, in case such Mortgage Deed shall happen to be lost or destroyed.

And be it further Enacted, That the Money so to be borrowed shall be paid into the Hands of such Person or Persons as shall be nominated and appointed to receive and apply the same, for the Purposes aforesaid, by the Ordinary, Patron, and Incumbent, by Writing under their respective Hands, in the Form for that Purpose contained in the said Schedule, after such Nominee shall have given a Bond to the Ordinary, with sufficient Surety, in double the Sum so to be borrowed or raised, with

Condition

Condition for his duly applying and accounting for the same according to the Directions of this Act; and the Receipt of the Person or Persons so to be nominated shall be a sufficient Discharge to the Person or Persons who shall advance and pay the Money: And the Person or Persons so to be nominated, shall enter into Contracts with proper Persons, for such Buildings or Repairs as shall be approved by the Ordinary, Patron, and Incumbent, and shall be specified in an Instrument written upon Parchment, and signed by them, in the Form for that Purpose contained in the said Schedule; and shall inspect and have the Care of the Execution of such Contracts, and shall pay the Money for such Buildings and Repairs, according to the Terms of such Agreements, and shall take proper Receipts and Vouchers for the same; and as soon as such Buildings or Repairs shall be compleated, and the Money paid, shall make out an Account of his Receipts and Payments, together with the Vouchers for the same, and enter them in a Book, fairly written, which shall be signed by him, and laid before the Ordinary, Patron, and Incumbent, and examined by them, and when allowed, by Writing under their respective Hands, in the Form for that Purpose contained in the said Schedule, such Allowance shall be a full Discharge to the Person so nominated, in respect to the said Accounts; and if any Balance shall remain in the Hands of such Nominee or Nominees, the same shall be laid out in some further lasting Improvements in building upon such Glebe, or shall be paid and applied in Discharge of so much of the said Principal Debt as such Balance will extend to pay, at the Discretion of the said Ordinary, Patron, and Incumbent, or Two of them, of which the said Ordinary to be One, by Order signed by them, in the Form for that Purpose contained in the said Schedule; and an Account shall also be kept, made out, and allowed, of such further Disbursements, in Manner aforesaid: All which Accounts, when made out, completed, and allowed, shall be deposited, with the Vouchers, in the Hands of the said Registrar, and kept by him, for the Use and Benefit of the Incumbents of such Living for the Time being, who shall have a Right to inspect the same, whenever Occasion shall require, paying to such Registrar, or Deputy Registrar, the Sum of One Shilling for every such Inspection.

Provided

Provided always, and be it further Enacted, That every such Ordinary, before he or they shall signify his or their Consent, in Manner aforesaid, shall cause an Enquiry to be made, and certified to him or them by the Archdeacon, Chancellor of the Diocese, or other proper Persons living in or near the Parish where such Buildings are proposed to be made or repaired, in the Forms for that Purpose specified in the said Schedule, of the State and Condition of such Buildings at the Time the Incumbent entered upon such Living or Benefice, how long such Incumbent had enjoyed such Living or Benefice, what Money he had received, or may be entitled to receive, for Dilapidations, and how and in what Manner he had laid out what he had so received; and if it shall appear to them that such Incumbent had, by wilful Negligence, suffered such Buildings to go out of Repair, then to certify the same to the said Ordinary, and also the Amount of the Damage which such Buildings had sustained by the wilful Neglect of such Incumbent; and such Incumbent, if the Ordinary require it, shall pay the same into the Hands of the Nominee or Nominees to be appointed under the Authority of this Act, towards defraying the Expences of Building or Repairs, before the Ordinary shall give his Consent as aforesaid.

And be it further Enacted, That the Incumbent of every such Living or Benefice, in Cases where such Mortgage or Mortgages shall be made, as aforesaid, and his Successors for the Time being, shall, and he and they, is and are hereby required to pay the Interest arising upon every such Mortgage, Half Yearly, as the same shall become due, or within One Month after, and also Five Pounds *per Centum per Annum* of the Principal remaining due, by Half Yearly Payments; and that every such Incumbent who shall not reside Six Calendar Months in the Year upon such Living, computing such Year from the First Day of *January*, shall, instead of the said Sum of Five Pounds *per Centum per Annum*, pay the Sum of Ten Pounds *per Centum per Annum*, of the Principal remaining due, by Half Yearly Payments, such Payments to be respectively made at the same Time such Interest shall be paid, until the whole Principal Money and Interest shall be fully paid and discharged; and that every such Incumbent shall, Annually, at his own Expence, from the Time such Buildings authorized

rized to be made by this Act shall be completed, insure, at One of the public Offices established in *London* or *Westminster* for Insurance of Houses and Buildings, the House and other Buildings upon such Glebe, against Accidents by Fire, at such Sum of Money as shall be agreed upon by the Ordinary, Patron, and Incumbent; and in Default of the Payment of either the Principal or Interest, in Manner aforesaid, or Neglect of the Incumbent to make such Insurance, the Ordinary shall have Power to sequester the Profits of the Living till such Payment or Insurance shall be made.

And, in order that the Payment of such Half Year may be justly and equitably ascertained and adjusted, between the Successor, and such Parson, Vicar, or Incumbent, so avoiding such Living or Benefice, or his Representatives, in case of Death or other Avoidance, in such Proportions as the Profits of such Living shall have been received by them respectively, for the Year in which Death or Avoidance shall happen; **Be it further Enacted,** That in case any Difference shall arise in adjusting or settling the Proportions aforesaid, the same shall be determined by Two indifferent Persons, the one to be named by the said Successor, and the other by the Person making such Avoidance, or his Representatives, in case of his Death; and in case such Nominees shall not be appointed within the Space of Two Calendar Months next after such Death or Avoidance, or if they cannot agree in adjusting such Proportions within the Space of One Calendar Month after they shall have been appointed, the same shall be determined by some neighbouring Clergyman, to be nominated by the Ordinary, whose Determination shall be final and conclusive between the Parties; which Nominations and Determinations shall be made according to the Forms for that Purpose contained in the said Schedule, as near as conveniently may be.

And be it further Enacted, That where there shall be no House of Habitation upon any Ecclesiastical Living or Benefice, so described as aforesaid, exceeding in clear Yearly Value One hundred Pounds *per Annum,* or being one, the same shall be so mean, or in such a State of Decay as aforesaid, and the Incumbent shall not reside in the Parish for such Time within the Year as aforesaid, it shall be lawful for the Ordinary of such Living or Benefice, with the Consent of the Patron (in case the Incumbent shall not

think

think fit to lay out One Year's Income, where the same may be sufficient, to put the House and Buildings in proper and sufficient Repair, or to make such Application as aforesaid for building, repairing, or re-building such Parsonage House) to procure such Plan, Estimate, and Certificate, as herein directed, and to proceed in the Execution of the several Purposes of this Act in such Manner as the Parson, Vicar, or Incumbent, is hereby authorized and directed to proceed, and to make and execute such Mortgage as aforesaid, which shall be binding upon the Incumbent and his Successors, and he and they shall be, and are hereby made liable to the Payment of the Interest, Principal, and Costs; and every such Incumbent, and his Representatives, shall be, and are hereby, also made respectively liable to the Proportion of the Payments for the Half Year which shall be growing at the Time of the Death of such Incumbent, or Avoidance of such Living, according to the Directions aforesaid; which said Interest, Principal, and Costs, and Proportion of Payments growing at the Time of the Death of such Incumbent or Avoidance, shall and may be recovered against such Incumbent, his Successors, or Representatives, respectively, by Action of Debt, in any Court of Record.

And be it further Enacted, That all Sum and Sums of Money recovered, or received by Suit or Compositions from the Representatives of any former Incumbent of such Living or Benefice, and not laid out in the Repairs of such Buildings, shall go and be applied in Part of the Payments under such Estimate as aforesaid; and that all Money thereafter to be recovered or received, in case the same cannot be had before such Buildings are completed, and the Money paid for the same, shall be applied, as soon as received, in Payment of the Principal then due, as far as the same will extend; or in case the said Mortgage Money shall have been discharged, all such Money arising from Dilapidations shall be paid into the Hands of the Nominee to be appointed as aforesaid, or of some other Person or Persons to be nominated by the Ordinary, Patron, and Incumbent, in case such Nominee shall be dead, or shall decline to act therein, to be laid out and expended in making some additional Buildings or Improvements upon the Glebe of such Living or Benefice, to be approved by the Ordinary, Patron, and Incumbent;

hem; and in the mean Time, or in case such Buildings shall not be necessary, then in Trust; to lay out the same in Government or other good Securities, and pay the Interest thereof to the Incumbent for the Time being.

Provided always, and be it further Enacted, That
15 where new Buildings are necessary to be provided or erected for the Habitation and Residence of the Rector, Vicar, or other Incumbent, pursuant to the Authority hereby given, it shall and may be lawful for the Ordinary, Patron, and Incumbent, of every such Living or Benefice to contract, or to authorize, if they shall think fit, the Person so to be nominated by them as aforesaid to contract, for the absolute Purchase of any House or Buildings, in a Situation convenient for the Habitation and Residence of the Rector or Vicar of such Living or Benefice, and not at a greater Distance than One Mile from the Church belonging to such Living, Benefice, or Chapelry, and also to contract for any Land adjoining or lying convenient to such House or Building, or to the House or Building belonging to any Parochial Living or Benefice, having no Glebe lying near or convenient to the same, not exceeding Two Acres, if the Annual Value of such Living shall be less than One Hundred Pounds *per Annum*, nor Two Acres for every One Hundred Pounds *per Annum*, if of greater Value, and to cause the
16 Purchase Money for such House or Buildings to be paid out of the Money to arise under the Powers and Authorities of this Act; in all which Cases the said Buildings and Lands shall be conveyed to the Patron of such Living or Benefice, and his Heirs, in Trust, for the sole Use and Benefit of the Rector, Vicar, or other Incumbent, of such Living or Benefice, for the Time being, and their Successors, and shall be annexed to such Church or Chapel, and be enjoyed and go in Succession with the same for ever; but no Contract so made by the Nominee shall be valid, until confirmed by the Ordinary, Patron, and Incumbent, by Writing under their Hands; and every such Purchase Deed shall be in the Form or to the Effect contained in the Schedule hereunto annexed, and shall be registered in such Manner, and in such Office, as the other Deeds are hereby directed to be registered.

Provided

Provided also, and be it further Enacted, That when any Land lying near to the Parsonage House and Buildings shall be thought fit to be taken and used as a Conveniency for the same, the Purchase Money or Equivalent for such Land shall be raised and had by Sale or Exchange of some Part of the Glebe or Tythes of such Living or Benefice, which shall appear to the said Ordinary, Patron, and Incumbent, most convenient for that Purpose; and every such Sale or Exchange shall be by Deed, in the Form or to the Effect contained in the Schedule hereunto annexed, and registered as hereinbefore directed.

And be it further Enacted, That it shall and may be lawful for the Governors authorized or appointed to regulate and superintend the Bounty given by her late Majesty Queen *Anne*, for the Augmentation of the Maintenance of the Poor Clergy, to advance and lend any Sum or Sums of Money, not exceeding the Sum of One Hundred Pounds, out of the Money which has arisen, or shall from Time to Time arise, from that Bounty, for promoting and assisting the several Purposes of this Act, with respect to any such Livings or Benefices as shall not exceed the clear annual improved Value of Fifty Pounds; and such Mortgage and Security shall be made for the Re-payment of the Principal Sums so to be advanced, as are hereinbefore mentioned, but no Interest shall be paid for the same.

And be it further Enacted, That it shall and may be lawful for the Master and Fellows of any College or Hall, within the Universities of *Oxford* and *Cambridge*, or for any other Corporate Bodies possessed of the Patronage of Ecclesiastical Livings or Benefices, to advance and lend any Sum or Sums of Money, of which they have the Power of disposing, in order to aid and assist the several Purposes of this Act, for the building, re-building, repairing, or purchasing, of any Houses or Buildings for the Habitation and Convenience of the Clergy, upon Livings or Benefices under the Patronage of such College or Hall, upon the Mortgage and Security directed by this Act for the Re-payment of the Principal, without taking any Interest for the same.

And be it further Enacted, That whenever the Patron of any Living or Benefice, to which the Provisions of this Act are proposed to be extended, shall happen to be a Minor, Idiot, or Lunatic, it shall and may be lawful for the Guardian or Committee of every such Patron, to transact the several Matters aforesaid for such Patron, who shall be bound thereby, in such Manner as if he had been of full Age, of sound Mind, and had done such Act, or given his Consent thereto.

Provided also, and be it further Enacted, That all Acts hereinbefore required to be done or consented to by the Ordinary and Patron, shall be done by the Ordinary alone, when such Ordinary shall happen to be the Patron of the Living; and that no Deed, Bond, Transfer, or other Writing, Instrument, or Proceeding, made, had, or done, under the Powers or Authority of this Act, shall be charged or chargeable with any Stamp Duty, or Fee of Office, except as herein mentioned, any Law or Statute to the contrary notwithstanding.

Provided always, and it is hereby further Enacted, That in all Cases where any Act is required to be done by the Ordinary, in the Execution of any of the Purposes of this Act, and such Ordinary shall be a Body Corporate Aggregate, every such Act shall be done and signified under the Seal of such Body Corporate.

Provided always, and be it further Enacted, That where the Incumbent of any Chapelry or perpetual Cure shall be nominated by the Rector or Vicar of the Parish wherein the same is situated, in every such Case the Consent of such Rector or Vicar, together with the Consent of the Patron of such Rectory, shall be necessary, in all such Matters wherein the Consent of the Patron is required by the former Provisions of this Act.

Provided likewise, and be it further Enacted, That whenever any Controversy or Dispute shall arise, touching the Residence of the Incumbent, with respect to any of the Matters contained in this Act, the same shall be adjusted and determined by the Ordinary of the Diocese.

𝔓𝔯𝔬𝔳𝔦𝔡𝔢𝔡 𝔞𝔩𝔰𝔬, 𝔞𝔫𝔡 𝔟𝔢 𝔦𝔱 𝔣𝔲𝔯𝔱𝔥𝔢𝔯 𝔈𝔫𝔞𝔠𝔱𝔢𝔡, That it shall and may be lawful for the Patron, Ordinary, and Incumbent, of any such Living or Benefice as aforesaid, by Writing under their Hands, to make such Allowance to the Person or Persons to be nominated by them, for the Purpose of paying and applying the Money so to be raised as aforesaid, as they shall think fit, not exceeding the Sum of Five Pounds for every One hundred Pounds so to be laid out and expended as aforesaid.

SCHEDULE

SCHEDULE

To which the Bill refers.

FORM *of the* CONSENT *of the Ordinary and Patron, to be written on Parchment.*

*A*B. Rector, Vicar, &c. (as the Case shall be) of the Parish, Chapelry, or perpetual Curacy (as the Case shall be) of   in the County of   under the Jurisdiction of the Ordinary, having produced to us the said Ordinary and   Patron of the said Church and Living, a Certificate under the Hand of   a skilful and experienced Workman, or Surveyor, of the State and Condition of the Buildings upon the Glebe belonging to the said Church, Chapelry, or perpetual Curacy (as the Case shall be) and of the Value of the Timber, and other Materials, thereupon, fit to be sold, or employed about such Buildings; and also a Plan, made by the said   of the Work proposed to be done by new Buildings and Repairs upon the said Glebe, and an Estimate of the Expence attending the same, after applying the said Materials, or the Money to arise from the Sale thereof, in such Buildings and Repairs; and also a particular Account in Writing, signed by the said *A. B.* of the Annual Profits of such Living, and of the Rents, Stipends, Taxes, and other Outgoing, Annually issuing thereout, verified upon Oath, pursuant to the Directions of an Act, passed in the Seventeenth Year of the Reign of His Majesty King *George* the Third, to promote the Residence of the Parochial Clergy, by making Provision for the

more

more speedy and effectual building, re-building, repairing, or purchasing, Houses, and other necessary Buildings and Tenements, for the Use of their Benefices; and having considered such Certificate, Plan, and Account: Now, we do approve thereof; and do consent, that such Buildings and Repairs shall be made as therein specified; and that the said *A. B.* do borrow and take up at Interest the Sum of   being the Estimate of the Expences, after deducting the Value of the Timber, and other Materials, thought proper to be sold, and which appears to us, from the said Account, a Sum not exceeding Two Years neat Income and Produce of the said Living; which Money is to be paid to
(a Person nominated by us and the said *A. B.*) and applied according to the Direction of the said Act.

FORM *of the* MORTGAGE.

THIS Indenture, made the   Day of   in the   Year of the Reign of His Majesty   and in the Year of our Lord   between the Reverend   Rector or Vicar, *&c.* of the Parish Church, Curacy, or Chapelry, of   in the County of   and the Diocese of the Bishop of   of the one Part, and   of   of the other Part. Whereas the said   pursuant to the Directions of an Act, passed in the Seventeenth Year of the Reign of His Majesty King *George* the Third, intituled, "An Act to promote the Residence of the Parochial Clergy, by making Provision for the more speedy "and effectual building, re-building, repairing, or purchasing, Houses, and other necessary Buildings and Tenements, for the Use of their Benefices," hath obtained the Consent of the Ordinary of the said Diocese, and the Patron of the said Church and Living, to borrow and take up at Interest the Sum of   to be laid out and expended in building, re-building, or repairing (as the Case shall be) the Parsonage House, and other necessary Offices, upon the Glebe belonging to the said Church, Chapel, or Curacy, as appears by an Instrument signed

signed by the said Ordinary and Patron, hereunto annexed:
And whereas the said   hath agreed to
lend and advance the Sum of   upon
a Mortgage of the Glebe, Tythes, Rents, and other Profits and Emoluments, of the said Living, pursuant to the Direction and the true Intent and Meaning of the said Act: Now this Indenture witnesseth, That the said
24   in Consideration of the Sum of Five
Shillings to him in Hand paid, and of the Sum of
                    paid at or before the Sealing and
Delivery hereof, into the Hands of
a Person, or Persons, (as the Case shall be) nominated by the said Ordinary, Patron, and Incumbent, to receive the same, pursuant to the Direction of the said Act (which Nomination is also hereunto annexed, and which Receipt of the said Sum of
the said   have, or hath, acknowledged, by an Indorsement on the Back of this Deed) hath granted, bargained, sold, and demised, and by these Presents doth grant, bargain, sell, and demise, unto the said   his Executors, Administrators, and Assigns, all the Glebe Lands, Tythes, Rents, Moduses, Compositions for Tythe, Salaries, Stipends, Fees, Gratuities, and other Emoluments and Profits whatsoever, arising, coming, growing, renewing, or payable, to the Rector, Vicar, or Incumbent (as the Case shall be) of the said Living in respect thereof, with all and every their Rights, Privileges, and
25 Appurtenances thereunto belonging, to have, hold, receive, take, and enjoy the said Premisses, with their and every of their Appurtenances, unto the said
his Executors, Administrators, and Assigns, from henceforth, for and during the Term of   Years, fully to be compleat and ended, in as full, ample, and beneficial Manner, and with such Remedies and Powers for obtaining and recovering the same, and every Part thereof, to all Intents and Purposes, as the said
                    his Successors, Rectors, Vicars, &c. (as the Case shall be) of the said Church, could, or might, or ought to have held, enjoyed, received, taken, or recovered the same, if these Presents had not been made. And the said *A. B.* for himself, his Heirs, Executors, and Administrators, doth hereby covenant, promise, and agree, to and with the said   his Executors, Administrators, and Assigns, That he the said *A. B.* during
the

[15]

the Time he shall continue Rector, Vicar, &c. of the said Parish and Parish Church, shall and will well and truly pay, or cause to be paid, unto the said   his Executors, Administrators, or Assigns, Interest for the said Sum of   or so much thereof as shall remain due at the End of every Year, to be computed from the Day of the Date of these Presents, after the Rate of   *per Centum per Annum*, by Two equal Half Yearly Payments, the First of the said Payments to begin and be made on the   Day of   next; and also, at the several Times before mentioned for Payment of the Interest, as aforesaid, shall and will well and truly pay, or cause to be paid, the Sum of   *per Centum per Annum* of the Principal which remained due at the Beginning of the Year in which every such Payment is to be paid, in case the said *A. B.* shall be resident upon the said Living for the Time mentioned in, and according to the true Intent and Meaning of, the said Act; and in case the said *A. B.* shall not reside upon the said Living during the Time mentioned in, and according to the true Intent and Meaning of, the said Act, he shall pay, or cause to be paid, the Sum of   *per Centum per Annum* of the said Principal Money, by such Half Yearly Payments as aforesaid, instead of the said Sum of   *per Centum per Annum*, and shall and will continue such respective Payments of the said Interest, and on Account of the said Principal Money, so long as he shall continue Rector, Vicar, &c. (as the Case shall be) of the said Parish and Parish Church, unless all the said Principal Money, and Interest for the same, shall be sooner paid and discharged.   Provided always, and these Presents are upon this Condition, That if the said *A. B.* and his Successors, shall well and truly pay, or cause to be paid, the said Principal Money, and Interest for the same, in Manner and at the Times aforesaid, according to the true Intent and Meaning of the said Act, and of these Presents, and also all Costs and Charges which shall have been occasioned by the Non-payment thereof, these Presents, and every Thing herein contained, shall cease and be void.   Provided also, That it shall and may be lawful for the said *A. B.* and his Successors, peaceably and quietly to hold, occupy, possess, and enjoy, all and singular the said Glebe Lands, Tythes,

Rents,

Rents, Modufes, Compofition for Tythes, Stipends, Fees, Gratuities, and other Emoluments and Profits whatfoever, arifing, or to arife, from or in refpect of the faid Living, until Default fhall be made by him or them refpectively in the Payment of the Intereft and Principal, or fome Part thereof, at the Times and in the Manner aforefaid.

28 NOMINATION *of a Clergyman by the Bifhop, to fettle any Difpute about the Proportion of the Payments within the Year in which any Avoidance fhall happen.*

I The Right Reverend   Bifhop of   purfuant to the Authority of an Act, paffed in the Seventeenth Year of the Reign of His Majefty King *George* the Third, intituled, " An Act to promote the Refidence " of the Parochial Clergy, by making Provifion for the " more fpeedy and effectual building, re-building, re- " pairing, or purchafing, Houfes, and other neceffary " Buildings and Tenements, for the Ufe of their Benefices," do hereby nominate the Reverend   being a Clergyman within my faid Diocefe, to adjuft and determine the Matter in Difpute between the Reverend   Clerk, the prefent Incumbent of the Rectory, Vicarage, &c. of   within my Diocefe, and the Reprefentatives of the   the laft Incumbent
29 (in cafe of his Death) or the faid   (in cafe of his Refignation or Promotion) concerning the due Proportion to be paid by each of the faid Parties of the Principal and Intereft which accrued due within the Year in which fuch Death or other Avoidance happened, according to the Direction, true Intent, and Meaning of the faid Act.

AWARD *and* DETERMINATION *of the Clergyman nominated by the Bifhop.*

I The Reverend *A. B.* of   in the County of   and Diocefe of the Bifhop of   Clerk, having been nominated by the faid Bifhop, purfuant to the faid Power given by an Act, paffed in the Seventeenth

Seventeenth Year of the Reign of His Majesty King *George* the Third, intituled, " An Act to promote the
" Residence of the Parochial Clergy, by making Provi-
" sion for the more speedy and effectual building, re-
" building, repairing, or purchasing, Houses, and other
" necessary Buildings and Tenements, for the Use of their
" Benefices," to adjust and determine the Matter in
Dispute between the Reverend
Clerk, the present Incumbent of the Rectory, Vicarage,
&c. of   within the said Diocese, and
                          the Representatives of the last In-
cumbent (in case of his Death) or the said
                          (in case of his Resignation or Promotion)
concerning the due Proportion to be paid by each of
the said Parties, of the Principal and Interest which accrued due within the Year in which such (Death or
Avoidance) happened, according to the Direction and
true Intent and Meaning of the said Act; and having
heard and duly considered the said Matters so referred
to me as aforesaid, do award, adjudge, and determine,
That the said   shall pay, in respect
of the Interest and Principal which became due within
the Year aforesaid, the Sum of
and that the said   shall pay, in
respect of the same, the Sum of
being the Remainder thereof, according to the Provision
and Direction of the said Act.

APPOINTMENT *of the* NOMINEE,
to be wrote on Parchment.

WE whose Names are subscribed, being the Ordinary,
Patron, and Incumbent, of the Rectory, Vicarage,
&c. of   within the County of
and Diocese of the Bishop of   do hereby
nominate and appoint   of
to receive the Money authorized to be raised by an Act,
passed in the Seventeenth Year of the Reign of His Majesty King *George* the Third, intituled, " An Act to pro-
" mote the Residence of the Parochial Clergy, by making
" Provision for the more speedy and effectual building,
" re-building, repairing, or purchasing, Houses, and other
" necessary

"necessary Buildings and Tenements, for the Use of their
"Benefices," for the Purpose of building, re-building,
repairing, or purchasing, the Parsonage House, &c. (as
the Case shall be) to the said Rectory, Vicarage, &c. belonging, and to pay and apply the same, and to enter
into Contracts with proper Persons for such Buildings
or Repairs, and to inspect and take Care of the Execution of such Contracts, and to take such Receipts and
Vouchers, keep such Accounts, and do and perform all
such other Matters and Things, which Nominees are authorized and required to do and perform in and by the
said Act, the said   having given Security for the due Application thereof, according to the
Direction of the said Act.

FORM *of* ORDER *of the Ordinary, Patron, and Incumbent, for laying out or applying the Surplus Money.*

WE whose Names are subscribed, being the Ordinary,
Patron, and Incumbent, of the Rectory, Vicarage,
&c. of   in the County of
and Diocese of the Bishop of   do hereby
order, That the Sum of   now remaining in the Hands of   the Person
nominated and appointed to receive and apply the Money
raised for building, repairing, &c. the Parsonage House,
&c. belonging to the said Rectory, Vicarage, &c. under
the Act of Parliament, passed in the Seventeenth Year of
the Reign of His Majesty King *George* the Third, intituled, "An Act to promote the Residence of the Pa-
"rochial Clergy, by making Provision for the more speedy
"and effectual building, re-building, repairing, or pur-
"chasing, Houses, and other necessary Buildings and Te-
"nements, for the Use of their Benefices," shall be
[paid to   being the Person entitled
to receive the Money now remaining due on the Mortgage made of the Glebe Lands, Tythes, and other Profits
and Emoluments of the said Living, and applied in Part
of Payment thereof, pursuant to the Direction of the said
Act] or [applied in building or repairing, &c. (describing the same) upon the Glebe belonging to the said
Living.]

FORM

FORM of CERTIFICATE from the Two Clergymen.

WE the Reverend *A. B.* of   in the County of   Clerk, and *C. D.* of   Clerk, being Two Clergymen within the Diocese of the Bishop of   do hereby certify to the said Bishop, pursuant to the Directions and Instructions sent by him to us, That we have made Enquiry into the State and Condition of the Buildings upon the Glebe belonging to the Rectory, Vicarage, &c. of   within the said Diocese, at the Time the Reverend   Clerk, the present Incumbent thereof, entered upon the said Living, which was in or about the Year of our Lord   and do find [That the same have been kept in due and common Repair, without any wilful Neglect (if the Case is so)] or [That the same have, by wilful Negligence, been suffered to go to Decay, and that they have sustained Damage from a Want of common and ordinary Repair, to the Amount of   Pounds] and we have also enquired into the Money received by the said   for Dilapidations, from the Representatives of the former Incumbent, and do find, That he hath received the Sum of   for such Dilapidations; and [that he hath expended the Whole, or   thereof (as the Case may be) in the necessary Repairs of the Buildings] or [that the same hath not been laid out or expended in repairing the Buildings] upon the Glebe belonging to the said Living.

A

BILL

TO

Promote the Refidence of the Parochial Clergy, by making Provifion for the more fpeedy and effectual building, re-building, repairing, or purchafing, Houfes, and other neceffary Buildings and Tenements, for the Ufe of their Benefices.

1777.

A

B I L L

[With the Amendments]

FOR

Further reftraining the Negotiation of Promifory Notes, and Inland Bills of Exchange, under a limited Sum, within that Part of *Great Britain* called *England*.

WHEREAS by a certain Act of Parliament, paffed in the Fifteenth Year of the Reign of His prefent Majefty, intituled, "An Act to re-
" ftrain the Negotiation of Promifory Notes,
" and Inland Bills of Exchange, under a li-
" mited Sum, within that Part of *Great*
" *Britain* called *England*," all negotiable Promifory or other Notes, Bills of Exchange, or Draughts, or Undertakings in Writing, for any Sum of Money lefs than the Sum of Twenty Shillings in the Whole, and iffued after the Twenty-fourth Day of *June*, One thoufand Seven hundred and

A   Seventy-

Seventy-five, were made void, and the publishing or uttering, and negotiating, of any such Notes, Bills, Draughts, or Undertakings, for a less Sum than Twenty Shillings, or on which less than that Sum should be due, was by the said Act restrained, under certain Penalties or Forfeitures therein mentioned; and all such Notes, Bills of Exchange, Draughts, or Undertakings in Writing, as had issued before the said Twenty-fourth Day of *June*, were made payable upon Demand, and were directed to be recovered in such Manner as is therein also mentioned:

And whereas the said Act hath been attended with very salutary Effects, and in case the Provisions therein contained were extended to a further Sum, but yet without Prejudice to the Convenience arising to the Public from the Negotiation of Promisory Notes and Inland Bills of Exchange for the Remittance of Money in Discharge of any Balance of Account or other Debt, the good Purposes of the said Act would be further advanced:

Be it therefore Enacted by the KING's Most Excellent MAJESTY, by and with the Advice and Consent of the Lords Spiritual and Temporal, and Commons, in this present Parliament assembled, and by the Authority of the same, That all Promisory or other Notes, Bills of Exchange, or Draughts, or Undertakings in Writing, being negotiable or transferrable for the Payment of Twenty Shillings, or any Sum of Money above that Sum, and less than Five Pounds, or on which Twenty Shillings, or above that Sum, and less than Five Pounds, shall remain undischarged, and which shall be issued in that Part of *Great Britain* called *England*, at any Time after the First Day of *January*, One thousand Seven hundred and Seventy-eight, shall specify the Names and Places of Abode of the Persons respectively to whom or to whose Order the same shall be made payable, and shall bear Date before or at the Time of drawing or issuing thereof, and not on any Day subsequent thereto, and shall be made payable within the Space of Twenty-one Days next after the Day of the Date thereof, and shall not be transferrable or negotiable after the Time thereby limited for Payment thereof; and that every Indorsement to be made thereon shall be made before the Expiration of that Time, and to bear Date at or not before the Time of making thereof, and shall specify the Name and Place of Abode of the Person

son or Persons to whom or to whose Order the Money contained in every such Note, Bill, Draught, or Undertaking, is to be paid; and that the signing of every such Note, Bill, Draught, or Undertaking, and also of every such Indorsement, shall be attested by One subscribing Witness at the least; and which said Notes, Bills of Exchange, or Draughts, or Undertakings in Writing, may be made or drawn in Words to the Purport or Effect as set out in the Schedule hereunto annexed, No. 1 and 2; and that all Promisory or other Notes, Bills of Exchange, or Draughts, or Undertakings in Writing, being negotiable or transferrable for the Payment of Twenty Shillings, or any Sum of Money above that Sum, and less than Five Pounds, or on which Twenty Shillings, or above that Sum, and less than Five Pounds, shall remain undischarged, and which shall be issued within that Part of *Great Britain* called *England*, at any Time after the said First Day of *January*, One thousand Seven hundred and Seventy-eight, in any other Manner than as aforesaid, and also every Indorsement on any such Note, Bill, Draught, or Undertaking, to be negotiated under this Act, other than as aforesaid, shall, and the same are hereby declared to be absolutely void, any Law, Statute, Usage, or Custom, to the contrary thereof in any wise notwithstanding.

And be it further Enacted by the Authority aforesaid, That the Publishing, Uttering, or Negotiating, within that Part of *Great Britain* called *England*, of any Promisory or other Note, Bill of Exchange, Draught, or Undertaking in Writing, being negotiable or transferrable for Twenty Shillings, or above that Sum, and less than Five Pounds, or on which Twenty Shillings, or above that Sum, and less than Five Pounds, shall remain undischarged, and issued or made in any other Manner than Notes, Bills, Draughts, or Undertakings hereby permitted to be published or negotiated as aforesaid; and also the Negotiating of any of such last-mentioned Notes, Bills, Draughts, or Undertakings, after the Time appointed for Payment thereof, or before that Time in any other Manner than as aforesaid, by any Art, Contrivance, or Means whatsoever; from and after the said First Day of *January*, One thousand Seven hundred and Seventy-eight, shall be, and the same is hereby declared to be, prohibited or restrained, under the like Penalties or Forfeitures, and to be recovered and applied in like Manner, as by the said Act is directed with respect to the Uttering or Publishing, or Negotiating, of Notes, Bills of Exchange, Draughts, or Undertakings in Writing, for any Sum of Money less than the Sum of Twenty Shillings, or on which less than that Sum should be due.

And be it further Enacted by the Authority aforesaid, That from and immediately after the passing of this Act, all Promisory or other Notes, Bills of Exchange, Draughts, or Undertakings in Writing, for the Payment of any greater Sum of Money than Twenty Shillings, and less than the Sum of Five Pounds, or on which Twenty Shillings, and less than the Sum of Five Pounds, shall remain undischarged, and being negotiable or transferrable, as shall be issued before the said First Day of *January*, One thousand Seven hundred and Seventy-eight, shall be, and the same are hereby declared and adjudged payable, within that Part of *Great Britain* called *England*, on Demand, any Terms, Restrictions, or Conditions, therein contained to the contrary thereof notwithstanding, and shall be recoverable in such Manner, or by the like Means, as is or are directed in or by the said Act, with respect to Notes, Bills of Exchange, or Draughts, or Undertakings in Writing, therein mentioned to have issued previous to the said Twenty-fourth Day of *June*, One thousand Seven hundred and Seventy-five; and that all and every other the Powers, Provisoes, Limitations, Restrictions, Penalties, Clauses, Matters, and Things whatsoever, in the said former Act contained, with respect thereto, and also with respect to all such Notes, Bills of Exchange, Draughts, or Undertakings in Writing, issued after the said Twenty-fourth Day of *June*, One thousand Seven hundred and Seventy-five, shall be, and the same are hereby, declared to be in force, within that Part of *Great Britain* called *England*, as to all Notes, Bills of Exchange, or Draughts or Undertakings in Writing, for Twenty Shillings or any greater Sum, and less than the Sum of Five Pounds, or on which Twenty Shillings or above that Sum, and less than Five Pounds, shall remain undischarged, issued after the said First Day of *January*, One thousand Seven hundred and Seventy-eight, and previous thereto, respectively, and in like Manner as if the same respectively had been the Object of the said Act at the Time of making thereof, save so far as the same, or any of them, are altered or varied by this present Act.

And

And be it further Enacted by the Authority aforesaid, That the said former, and also this present Act, shall continue in force, not only for the Residue of the Term of Five Years, in the said former Act mentioned, and from thence to the End of the then next Session of Parliament, but also for the further Term of Five Years, and from thence to the End of the then next Session of Parliament.

SCHEDULE.

No. 1.

Place.   Day.   Month.   Year.
───── ───── of ───── ─────

Twenty-one Days after Date, I promise to pay to *A. B.* of
Place.   Sum.
──── or his Order, the Sum of ──── for Value received
by
                                            C. D.
Witness *E. F.*

And the Indorsement, *toties quoties.*

Day.   Month.   Year.
──── of ───── ─────

Pay the Contents
              Place.
to *G. H.* of ────

or his Order.
                    A. B.
Witness
I. K.

No. 2.

No. 2.

    Place. Day.   Month. Year.
    ―――― ――― of ――― ―――

                 Place.
Twenty-one Days after Date, pay to *A. B.* of ―――
          Sum.
or his Order, the Sum of ――― Value received, as advised by

              C. D.

     Place.
To *E. F.* of ―――

    Witness *G. H.*

  And the Indorsement, *toties quoties.*

      Day.   Month. Year.
      ――― of ――― ―――

    Pay the Contents
        Place.
    to *I. K.* of ―――

     his Order.
        A. B.

A

B I L L

[With the Amendments]

FOR

Further restraining the Negotiation of Promissory Notes, and Inland Bills of Exchange, under a limited Sum, within that Part of *Great Britain* called *England*.

1777.

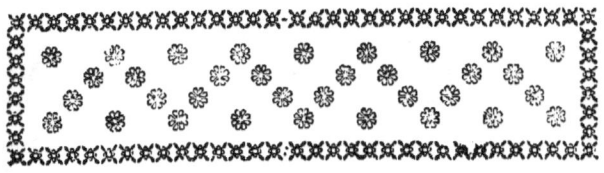

A

B I L L

FOR

Keeping the Militia Forces of this Kingdom compleat, during the Time therein to be mentioned.

Note.— *The Figures in the Margin denote the Number of the Folios in the written Copy.*

WHEREAS it is highly expedient for the Public Service, that the several Regiments and Corps of Militia should be made and kept as complete as possible during the Course of the ensuing Campaign:

And whereas the Time of balloting for many Regiments and Corps, or Parts of Regiments and Corps, will happen between the Months of *May* and *November* next ensuing, whereby such Regiments and Corps will, during that Period, be very much weakened, and rendered unfit for Service:

And whereas the Provisions in Two Acts of Parliament, One made in the Eighteenth Year of His present Majesty, intituled, " An Act to amend and render more effectual the Laws relating " to the raising and training the Militia within that Part of *Great* " *Britain* called *England*, and to establish certain Regulations

" with

"with respect to Officers serving in the Corps of Fencible Men,
"directed to be raised in that Part of *Great Britain* called *Scot-*
"*land*, and certain other Corps therein mentioned;" and the
other, made in the Nineteenth Year of His present Majesty,
intituled, "An Act to explain, amend, and render more effectual,
"the several Laws now in being relative to the Militia Forces
"of this Kingdom, and for making certain Provisions relative to
"the Fencible Men in that Part of *Great Britain* called *Scotland*;"
which were intended to prevent this Inconvenience, have been
found insufficient for that Purpose:

For Remedy thereof, Be it Enacted by the KING's Most
Excellent MAJESTY, by and with the Advice and Consent of the
Lords Spiritual and Temporal, and Commons, in this present
Parliament assembled, and by the Authority of the same, That
from and immediately after
the Colonels and
Commandants of the several Regiments and Corps of Militia, in
which Regiments or Corps the Time of Service of any private
Militia Man will expire between the   Day of
and the   Day of   next ensuing, shall, and
they are hereby respectively required forthwith to apply in the
Manner directed by the said Act of the Eighteenth Year of His
present Majesty, to every such private Man, and to enquire if
he is willing to continue his Service for a further Term of Three
Years, and for what Sum or Price he shall be so willing to continue it, if required.

And be it further Enacted by the Authority aforesaid, That
every such Colonel and Commandant of every such Regiment
and Corps of Militia shall, and he is hereby required forthwith to return a List, as well of such private Militia Men as
are willing to continue so to serve, as of all others whose
Times of Service will expire between the   Day of
and the   Day of   next
ensuing to the Clerk of the General Meeting of the County or
Riding to which such Regiment or Corps shall respectively belong, in like Manner as is directed by the said recited Acts, or
either of them: And all Clerks of General Meetings, Clerks of
Subdivision Meetings, Deputy Lieutenants, Justices of the Peace,
and all other Persons concerned, are hereby respectively authorized and required, upon the Receipt of such Lists, forthwith to
proceed to ballot for proper Men to serve in the Militia, in the
Place of those whose Times will expire as aforesaid, and for that
Purpose

Purpose to execute all the Powers and Directions given by the said recited Acts, or any other Act or Acts of Parliament, respecting the Militia Forces of this Kingdom, as if all the Clauses, Provisions, Powers, Matters, and Things contained in any of the said Acts, relating to the Premises, were repeated and re-enacted in the Body of this present Act.

And be it further Enacted by the Authority aforesaid, That when and as often as any Militia Men shall be ballotted for and sworn in, in the Manner hereinbefore directed, the Clerks of the Subdivision Meetings, respectively, shall forthwith give Notice thereof, and transmit a List of the Names and Places of Abode of such Militia Men, to the Colonel or Commandant of the Regiment or Corps of Militia to which they shall belong; and every Colonel or Commandant of such Regiment or Corps of Militia is and are hereby authorized and required, from Time to Time, to discharge, of those Men whose Times will soonest expire, a Number equal to those who are ballotted for and sworn in, and in Readiness to join his Regiment or Corps, so as to keep his Regiment or Corps as complete as may be, during the Period before mentioned.

4.

A BILL

FOR

Keeping the Militia Forces of this Kingdom compleat, during the Time therein to be mentioned.

1781.

A

BILL

FOR

Finally regulating the Intercourse and Commerce between *Great Britain* and *Ireland*, on permanent and equitable Principles, for the mutual Benefit of both Kingdoms.

Note.—*The Figures in the Margin denote the Number of the Folios in the written Copy.*

WHEREAS it is highly important to the general Interests of the *British* Empire, that the Intercourse and Commerce between *Great Britain* and *Ireland* should be finally regulated, on permanent and equitable Principles, for the mutual Benefit of both Countries:

And whereas, for that Purpose, it is expedient that the Trade between the said Countries, as well in Articles of the Growth, Produce, or Manufacture of either of them, as in those of Foreign
Countries,

Countries, should be encouraged and extended as much as possible, and that a full Participation of the Commercial Advantages which this Kingdom may derive from any of its Foreign Settlements, Colonies, or Plantations, and from the exclusive
2 Privileges enjoyed by the Ships and Seamen thereof, should be secured to *Ireland* on the same Terms as the said Advantages are, or shall be, from Time to Time, enjoyed by the Inhabitants of this Kingdom:

Be it therefore Declared by the KING's Most Excellent MAJESTY, by and with the Advice and Consent of the Lords Spiritual and Temporal, and Commons, in this present Parliament assembled, and by the Authority of the same, That it shall be held and adjudged to be a fundamental and essential Condition of the present Settlement, that no Prohibitions shall exist, in either of the Kingdoms of *Great Britain* or *Ireland*, against the Importation, Use, or Sale of any Article of the Growth, Produce, or Manufacture of the other of the said Kingdoms, except such as are hereinafter excepted:

3 And be it therefore Enacted by the Authority aforesaid, That no Prohibition shall exist in this Kingdom, after the on the Importation, Use, or Sale of any Article, the Growth, Produce, or Manufacture of *Ireland*, except such as now exist, or may hereafter exist, against the Importation of Corn, Meal, Malt, Flour, and Biscuit, and also except such qualified Prohibitions which are now, or may hereafter be, in Force, as do not absolutely prevent the Importation of Goods or Manufactures, or the Materials of Manufactures, but only regulate or prescribe the Tonnage, or Dimensions, or Built, or Country of the Ships or Vessels in which the same may be imported, or regulate or prescribe the Weight, Size, or Quantity of the Article to be therein imported, or the Packages in which the same may be contained, or regulate or prescribe other Cir-
4 cumstances relative thereto; and also except Prohibitions restraining the Importation, for Sale, of Ammunition, Arms, Gunpowder, and other Utensils of War, unless by virtue of His Majesty's Licence; and also except such Prohibitions as may be necessary for protecting the Copy Rights of Authors and Booksellers, the engraved Property of Engravers, and of the Venders of Prints and Maps, and all other exclusive Rights and Privileges which are or may be secured in this Kingdom, for the Encouragement of new Inventions, to Bodies Corporate or Individuals, by Acts of Parliament, Grants from the Crown, or otherwise.

And

And be it further Declared by the Authority aforesaid, That it shall be held and adjudged to be a fundamental and essential Condition of the present Settlement, that in all Cases in which there is a Difference between the Duties on Articles of the Growth, Produce, or Manufacture of *Great Britain*, when imported into *Ireland*, and the Duties on the same Articles, of the Growth, Produce, or Manufacture of *Ireland*, when imported into *Great Britain*, the Duties on such Articles should be reduced, in the Kingdom where they are highest, to an Amount not exceeding the Duties which were payable in the other on the Seventeenth Day of *May* One thousand Seven hundred and Eighty-two; so that in every Case in which any Article was charged with a Duty on Importation into *Ireland* of Ten Pounds Ten Shillings *per Centum*, or upwards, on the Seventeenth Day of *May* One thousand Seven hundred and Eighty-two, the Amount of the said Duties so reduced shall not be less than the said Duty of Ten Pounds Ten Shillings *per Centum*; and that all Articles which are now importable Duty-free into either Kingdom from the other, shall hereafter be imported Duty-free into each Kingdom from the other, respectively: **Be it therefore Enacted** by the Authority aforesaid, That it shall be lawful to import into this Kingdom, all Goods of the Growth, Produce, or Manufacture of *Ireland* (except as herein excepted) subject to such Rates and Duties as aforesaid, to be fixed and ascertained in the Manner to be hereinafter directed.

And be it Declared by the Authority aforesaid, That it shall be held and adjudged to be a fundamental and essential Condition of the present Settlement, that in all Cases in which the Articles of the Consumption of either Kingdom shall be charged with an internal Duty on the Manufacture, such Manufacture, when imported from the other, may be charged with a further Duty on the Importation, adequate to countervail the Duty on the Manufacture; and that in all Cases in which there shall be a Duty in either Kingdom on the Raw Material of any Manufacture, such Manufacture may, on its Importation from the other Kingdom, be charged with such a countervailing Duty as may be sufficient to subject the same to Burthens adequate to those to which such Manufacture is subject, in consequence of such Duties on such Raw Materials, in the Kingdom into which such Manufacture may be so imported; and that in all Cases in which a Bounty shall be given, in either Kingdom, on any Articles manufactured therein, which shall remain on such Articles when exported to the other, such Articles may be charged with a further

ther Duty, in the Kingdom into which they shall be imported, sufficient to countervail such Bounty remaining thereon: Provided always, That the Duty to be imposed upon manufactured Salt, imported into any Part of *Great Britain*, in order to countervail the internal Duty thereon, shall be computed according to the Rate of the internal Duty payable thereon in *England*.

9 And be it Declared by the Authority aforesaid, That it shall be held and adjudged to be a fundamental and essential Condition of the present Settlement, that no new or additional Duty or Duties shall be hereafter imposed, in either Kingdom, on the Importation of any Article of the Growth, Produce, or Manufacture of the other, except such countervailing Duties as may from Time to Time be imposed, as hereinbefore provided, in consequence of any internal Duty on the Manufacture, or of any Duty on the Raw Material of which such Manufacture is com-
10 posed, or of any Bounty given on any Goods manufactured in the other Kingdom, and remaining on such Goods when exported therefrom; and that such countervailing Duties to be imposed as aforesaid, shall continue so long only as the internal Consumption shall be charged with the Duty or Duties on the Manufacture or Raw Material which such Duty so imposed shall have been intended to countervail, or as such Article shall retain, on Exportation from the other Kingdom, the Bounty which such Duty so imposed shall have been intended to countervail.

11 And be it Declared by the Authority aforesaid, That it shall be held and adjudged to be a fundamental and essential Condition of the present Settlement, that no new Prohibition, or new or additional Duties, shall hereafter be imposed, in either Kingdom, on the Exportation of any Article of Native Growth, Produce, or Manufacture, from one Kingdom to the other, except such as either Kingdom may deem expedient, from Time to Time, upon Corn, Meal, Malt, Flour, and Biscuit.

12 Provided always, and it is hereby Declared by the Authority aforesaid, to be a fundamental and essential Condition of the present Settlement, that when any Article of the Growth, Produce, or Manufacture of either Kingdom, shall be prohibited by the Laws of the said Kingdom to be exported to Foreign Countries, the same Articles, when exported to the other Kingdom,
shall

shall be prohibited to be re-exported from thence to any Foreign Country.

And be it Declared by the Authority aforesaid, That it shall 13 be held and adjudged to be a fundamental and essential Condition of the present Settlement, that no Bounties whatever should be paid or payable, in either Kingdom, on the Exportation of any Article to the other, except such as relate to Corn, Malt, Meal, Flour, and Biscuit; and except also the Bounties at present given on Beer, and Spirits distilled from Corn; and such as are in the 14 Nature of Drawbacks or Compensations for Duties paid: **Be it therefore Enacted** by the Authority aforesaid, That all Bounties now payable in *Great Britain*, by virtue of any Act or Acts of Parliament, on the Exportation of any Articles to *Ireland*, shall cease and determine, and be no longer paid or payable, from and after   except the Bounties now payable on Beer, and Spirits distilled from Corn; and except any Bounties which relate to Corn, Meal, Malt, Flour, and Biscuits; and except such as are in the Nature of Drawbacks or Compensations for Duties paid.

And be it Declared by the Authority aforesaid, That it shall 15 be held and adjudged to be a fundamental and essential Condition of the present Settlement, that all Articles of the Growth, Produce, or Manufacture of *Great Britain* or *Ireland* should be exportable, from the Kingdom into which they shall be imported from the other, as free from Duties as similar Commodities of the same Kingdom; and that all Manufactures of either Kingdom, imported into the other, shall be entitled to such Drawbacks or Bounties, on Exportation from the Kingdom into which they shall have been so imported, as may leave the same subject to no heavier Burthens than the Home-made Manufactures of such Kingdom; and that when any such Articles shall be liable, in either Kingdom, to any Duty on being exported to any Foreign Country, the same Articles, if they shall have been imported from such Kingdom into the other, shall, on Exportation from such other Kingdom to any Foreign Countries, pay the same Duties as they would have been liable to on Exportation from the Kingdom of their Growth, Produce, or Manufacture, to such Foreign Country or Countries:

And be it therefore Enacted by the Authority aforesaid, 16 That all Articles of the Growth, Produce, or Manufacture of *Ireland*, imported into *Great Britain*, shall be entitled to such Freedom or Exemption from Duty, and to such Drawbacks, or Bounties in the Nature of Drawbacks, on Exportation from *Great Britain* to any Place or Country whatever, as

B   may

may render them subject, on such Exportation, to no heavier Burthen than the like Articles, of the Growth, Produce, or Manufacture of *Great Britain*, are or may be subject to on Exportation therefrom to the same Countries or Places respectively; and that all Articles of the Growth, Produce, or Manufacture of *Ireland* shall, on being exported from this Kingdom to any Foreign Country, be subject to the same Duty or Duties to which they would have been subject on being exported directly from *Ireland* to such Foreign Country.

17 **And whereas**, in order to ascertain the Duties, Bounties, and Drawbacks, which may take place as aforesaid, on the Importation of the Articles of the Growth, Produce, or Manufacture of either Kingdom into the other, or on the Exportation of the Articles of the Growth, Produce, or Manufacture of either Kingdom from thence to the other, or on the Exportation of the Articles of the Growth, Produce, or Manufacture of either Kingdom from the other to any Foreign Countries, it is expedient that proper Persons be appointed, in each Kingdom, to prepare a Schedule or Schedules thereof, to be laid before the Parliaments of both Kingdoms, for their Consideration and Approbation; **Be it Enacted** by the Authority aforesaid, That

shall, and they are hereby authorized and impowered to meet, confer, and consult touching the Formation of such Schedule or Schedules as aforesaid, or any Particulars relative thereto, with any Person or Persons who may be appointed for the like Purpose by virtue of any Act of the Parliament of *Ireland*.

18 **And be it Enacted** by the Authority aforesaid, That the said

shall, and they are hereby required to lay, with all convenient Speed, such Schedule or Schedules, and a Report of their Proceedings relative to the Formation thereof, before the House of Commons of *Great Britain*.

And be it Enacted by the Authority aforesaid, That the said

shall, and they are hereby authorized and impowered to examine upon Oath any Persons whatever, who shall be willing to be so examined, touching any Matters relative to the Formation of the said Schedules.

And

And be it further Enacted, That the said

the shall, on or before take and subscribe the following Oath, before the Chancellor of His Majesty's Exchequer, or before any One of the Barons of the Court of Exchequer:

" I *A. B.* do swear, That, as a Commissioner appointed
" by virtue of an Act, intituled
"
"
"   I will, to the best of my
" Judgment and Ability, faithfully and impartially dis-
" charge the Trust thereby reposed in me, without Fa-
" vour or Affection to any Person or Persons whatever,
           " So help me G O D."

And be it Declared by the Authority aforesaid, That it shall be held and adjudged to be a fundamental and essential Condition of the present Settlement, that all Articles, not the Growth, Produce, or Manufacture of *Great Britain* or *Ireland* (except those of the Growth, Produce, or Manufacture of any Countries beyond the *Cape of Good Hope* to the *Streights of Magellan*, during such Time as the Trade to the said Countries shall continue to be carried on by an exclusive Company, having Liberty to import into the Port of *London* only) shall be imported into each Kingdom from the other, reciprocally, under the same Regulations, and at the same Duties (if subject to Duties) to which they would be liable when imported directly from the Country or Place from whence the same may have been imported into *Great Britain* or *Ireland* respectively, as the Case may be: **Be it therefore Enacted** by the Authority aforesaid, That it shall and may be lawful to import from *Ireland* into *Great Britain*, in Ships navigated according to Law, all Goods, not the Growth, Produce, or Manufacture of *Great Britain* or *Ireland* (except those of the Growth, Produce, or Manufacture of the Countries beyond the *Cape of Good Hope* to the *Streights of Magellan*, during such Time as the Trade shall continue to be carried on by an exclusive Company, having Liberty to import into the Port of *London* only) under the same Regulations, and at the same Duties, to which such Goods would be liable when imported directly from the Country or Place from whence the same may have been imported into *Ireland*.

And

22 **And be it Declared** by the Authority aforesaid, That it shall be held and adjudged to be a fundamental and essential Condition of the present Settlement, that all Duties originally paid on the Importation of such Goods into either Kingdom respectively, shall be fully drawn back, within a Time to be limited, on the Exportation thereof from one Kingdom to the other, except on the Exportation to *Ireland* from *Great Britain* of Arrack, Foreign Brandy, and Foreign Rum, and all Sorts of Strong Waters not imported from the *British* Colonies in the *West Indies*, and except the Duties to be retained, as hereinafter directed, on Articles exported to *Ireland*, being the Growth,
23 Produce, or Manufacture of Countries beyond the *Cape of Good Hope* to the *Streights of Magellan*: **Be it therefore Enacted** by the Authority aforesaid, That all Duties originally paid or secured, on the Importation into this Kingdom of any Goods or Commodities, not being the Growth, Produce, or Manufacture of *Ireland*, except Arrack, Foreign Brandy, Foreign Rum, and all Sorts of Strong Waters not imported from the *British* Colonies in the *West Indies*, and except the Duties to be retained, as hereinafter directed, on Articles exported to *Ireland*, being the Growth, Produce, or Manufacture of Countries beyond the *Cape of Good Hope* to the *Streights of Magellan*, shall be fully drawn back, or the Security for the same discharged, on Exportation thereof to *Ireland*, within   Years after the Importation thereof into this Kingdom.

24 **Provided always, and be it Enacted** by the Authority aforesaid, That no such Drawback shall be paid, or Security discharged, until a Certificate from the proper Officer of the Revenue in *Ireland*, stating the due Entry and Landing of such Articles, shall be returned and delivered to the proper Officer of the Port from whence the same shall have been exported, and until the several other Particulars by Law required in the Case of Drawbacks shall have been duly observed.

And whereas it is highly and equally important to the Interests both of *Great Britain* and *Ireland*, and essential to the Objects of the present Settlement, that the Laws for regulating Trade and Navigation, so far as relates to the securing exclusive Privileges to the Ships and Mariners of *Great Britain* and *Ireland*, and the *British* Colonies and Plantations, and so far as relates to
25 the regulating and restraining the Trade of the *British* Colonies and Plantations, should be the same in *Great Britain* and *Ireland*, and that all such Laws in both Kingdoms should impose the

same

same Restraints, and confer the same Benefits, on the Subjects of both, which can only be effected by Laws to be passed in the Parliaments of both Kingdoms (the Parliament of *Great Britain* being alone competent to bind the People of *Great Britain* in any Case whatever, and the Parliament of *Ireland* being alone competent to bind the People of *Ireland* in any Case whatever); **Therefore be it Declared** by the Authority aforesaid, That it shall be held and adjudged to be a fundamental and essential Condition of the present Settlement, that the Laws for regulating Trade and Navigation, so far as the said Laws relate to the securing exclusive Privileges to the Ships and Mariners of *Great Britain*, *Ireland*, and the *British* Colonies and Plantations, and to the regulating and restraining the Trade of the *British* Colonies and Plantations, shall be the same in *Great Britain* and *Ireland*, and shall impose the same Restraints, and confer the same Benefits, on the Subjects of both Kingdoms:

And be it therefore Declared and Enacted by the Authority aforesaid, That all Privileges, Advantages, and Immunities, which are now granted, or shall, by any Law to be passed by the Parliament of *Great Britain*, be hereafter granted, to Ships built in *Great Britain*, or to Ships belonging to any of His Majesty's Subjects residing in *Great Britain*, or to Ships manned by *British* Seamen, or to Ships manned by certain Proportions of *British* Seamen, shall, to all Intents and Purposes whatever, be enjoyed in the same Manner, and under the same Regulations and Restrictions, respectively, by Ships built in *Ireland*, or by Ships belonging to any of His Majesty's Subjects residing in *Ireland*, or by Ships manned by *Irish* Seamen, or by Ships manned by certain Proportions of *Irish* Seamen. 26

Provided always, and be it Declared by the Authority aforesaid, That it shall be held and adjudged to be a fundamental and essential Condition of the present Settlement, that such Regulations as are now, or hereafter shall be, in Force, by Laws passed or to be passed in the Parliament of *Great Britain*, for securing exclusive Privileges, Advantages, and Immunities as aforesaid to the Ships and Mariners of *Great Britain*, *Ireland*, and the *British* Colonies and Plantations, shall be established in *Ireland*, for the same Time and in the same Manner as in *Great Britain*, by Laws to be passed in the Parliament of *Ireland* within   Months, if the Parliament of *Ireland* shall be then sitting, and shall continue to sit for   Months next ensuing without being prorogued or dissolved, or, in case 27

the

the Parliament of *Ireland* shall not be then sitting, or shall not continue to sit for   Months without being prorogued or dissolved, then within   Months after the Commencement of the next ensuing Session of Parliament: Provided nevertheless, That the Laws so to be passed in the Parliament of *Great Britain*, for the Purposes aforesaid, shall impose the same Restraints, and confer the same Benefits, on the Subjects of *Great Britain* and *Ireland*.

28. **And be it Declared** by the Authority aforesaid, That it shall be held and adjudged to be a fundamental and essential Condition of the present Settlement, that *Irish* Sail Cloth shall be deemed *British* Sail Cloth, within the Meaning of an Act of the Nineteenth Year of his late Majesty King *George* the Second, or any other Act or Acts of the Parliament of this Kingdom respecting the furnishing of Ships with *British* Sail Cloth; and that *Irish* Sail Cloth shall be entitled to equal Preference and Advantage as *British* for the Use of the *British* Navy.

29. **And be it further Declared** by the Authority aforesaid, That it shall be held and adjudged to be a fundamental and essential Condition of the present Settlement, that the People of *Ireland* now, and at all Times to come, shall have the Benefit of trading to and from the *British* Colonies and Plantations in the *West Indies* and *America*, and to and from the *British* Settlements on the Coast of *Africa*, and in all Articles of their Growth, Produce, or Manufacture, in as full and ample Manner as the People of this Kingdom, and shall likewise have the Benefit of trading in the like ample Manner to and from all such Colonies, Settlements, and Plantations, which this Kingdom may hereafter acquire or establish, and to and from such *British* Settlements as may exist in the Countries beyond the *Cape of Good Hope* to the *Streights of Magellan*, whenever the Trade with those Countries shall cease to be carried on by an exclusive Company having Liberty to import into the Port of *London* only.

30. **And be it Enacted** by the Authority aforesaid, That all Goods and Commodities whatever, which may at any Time be legally imported from *Great Britain* into any *British* Colonies or Plantations in the *West Indies* or *America*, or into any *British* Settlements on the Coast of *Africa*, or into any such Colonies, Settlements, or Plantations, which this Kingdom may hereafter acquire or establish, or into any *British* Settlements which may exist in the Countries beyond the *Cape of Good Hope* to the *Streights of Magellan*,

Magellan, whenever the Commerce to the said Countries shall cease to be carried on by an exclusive Company having Liberty to import into the Port of *London* only, may in like Manner be imported into the said Colonies, Settlements, or Plantations, from *Ireland*, subject only to the same Duties and Regulations as the like Goods shall be subject to on Importation into any of the said Colonies, Settlements, or Plantations respectively from *Great Britain*.

Provided always, and be it Declared by the Authority aforesaid, That it shall be held and adjudged to be a fundamental and essential Condition of the present Settlement, that all such Regulations or Restrictions as relate to the Trade with the *British* Colonies or Plantations, which are now, or shall hereafter be, in Force by Laws passed by the Parliament of this Kingdom, shall be from Time to Time established in *Ireland*, by Laws to be passed in the Parliament of *Ireland* within   Months, if the Parliament of *Ireland* shall be then sitting, and shall continue to sit for   Months next ensuing without being prorogued or dissolved; or, in case the Parliament of *Ireland* shall not be then sitting, or shall not continue to sit for   Months without being prorogued or dissolved, then within   Months after the Commencement of the next ensuing Session of Parliament: Provided nevertheless, That the Laws so to be passed in the Parliament of this Kingdom, for the Purposes aforesaid, shall impose the same Restraints, and confer the same Benefits, on the Subjects of *Great Britain* and *Ireland*.

Provided also, and be it Declared by the Authority aforesaid, That it shall be held and adjudged to be a fundamental and essential Condition of the present Settlement, that all Goods of the Growth, Produce, or Manufacture of any *British*, or of any Foreign Colony, in *America* or in the *West Indies*, or of any of the *British* or Foreign Settlements on the Coast of *Africa*, and all Peltry, Rum, Train Oil, and Whale Fins, being the Growth, Produce, or Manufacture of the Countries belonging to the United States of *America*, or being the Produce of the Fisheries carried on by the Subjects of the said United States, shall, on Importation into *Ireland*, be made subject to the same Duties and Regulations as the like Goods are, or from Time to Time shall be, subject to on Importation into *Great Britain*; or if prohibited from being imported into *Great Britain*, shall in like Manner be prohibited from being imported into *Ireland*.

Provided

Provided always, and be it Declared, That Rum, being of the Produce or Manufacture of the *British* Plantations in the *West Indies*, may be importable into *Ireland* at no higher Duties than are now payable thereon; and also, that all Goods exported from *Ireland* to the *British* Colonies or Plantations in the *West Indies*, or in *America*, or to the *British* Settlements on the Coast of *Africa*, or to any of the Countries beyond the Cape of *Good Hope* to the *Streights of Magellan*, so long as the Commerce to the said Countries shall continue to be carried on by an exclusive Company, having Liberty to import into the Port of *London* only, or to any of the *British* Settlements

34 in the *East Indies*, whenever such Commerce shall cease to be carried on by such exclusive Company, shall from Time to Time be made liable to such Duties, and be entitled to such Drawbacks, only, and be put under such Regulations as may be necessary, in order that the same may not be exported with less Duties or Impositions than the like Goods shall be burthened with when exported from *Great Britain:* Provided always, That Linen and Provisions may continue to be exported from *Ireland* to any *British* Colony, Plantation, or Settlement, Duty free.

35 **Provided also, and be it further Declared** by the Authority aforesaid, That it shall be held and adjudged to be a fundamental and essential Condition of the present Settlement, that no Bounties should be payable in *Ireland* on the Exportation of any Article to any *British* Colonies or Plantations in *America*, or in the *West Indies*, or to the *British* Settlements on the Coast of *Africa*, or in the *East Indies*, or on the Exportation of any Article imported from the *British* Colonies or Plantations in *America*, or in the *West Indies*, or from the *British* Settlements on the Coast of *Africa*, or in the *East Indies*, or of any Manufacture made of such Article, unless in Cases where a similar Bounty is payable in *Great Britain* on Exportation from thence, or where such Bounty is merely in the Nature of a Drawback or Compensation of or for Duties paid, over and above any Duties paid in *Great Britain*.

36 **And be it Declared** by the Authority aforesaid, That it shall be held and adjudged to be a fundamental and essential Condition of the present Settlement, that when any Goods of the Growth, Produce, or Manufacture of the *British West India* Islands, or any other of the *British* Colonies or Plantations, shall be shipped from *Ireland* for *Great Britain*, they shall be accompanied with such original Certificates of the Revenue Officers of the said Colonies, as shall be required by Law on Importation

into

into *Great Britain*; and that, when the whole Quantity included in One Certificate shall not be shipped at any One Time, the original Certificate, properly indorsed as to Quantity, shall be sent with the First Parcel, and to identify the Remainder, if shipped within   new Certificates shall be granted by the proper Officers of the Ports in *Ireland*, extracted from a Register of the original Documents, specifying the Quantities before shipped from thence, by what Vessels, and to what Ports; 𝕭𝖊 𝖎𝖙 𝖙𝖍𝖊𝖗𝖊𝖋𝖔𝖗𝖊 𝕰𝖓𝖆𝖈𝖙𝖊𝖉 by the Authority aforesaid, That when any Ship or Vessel shall arrive from any Port or Place in *Ireland*, at any Port in this Kingdom, laden with any Goods the Growth, Produce, or Manufacture of the *British West India* Islands, or any other of the *British* Colonies or Plantations, no such Goods shall be admitted to be imported into this Kingdom, unless accompanied with such original Certificates of the Revenue Officers in the said Colonies, as shall be required by Law on Importation into *Great Britain* from the said Colonies or Plantations respectively, under such Regulations, Restrictions, Penalties, and Forfeitures, as the like Goods are subject to on Importation into *Great Britain* from the said Colonies and Plantations respectively, or unless, when the whole Quantity included in One Certificate shall not be shipped at any One Time, the original Certificate, properly indorsed as to Quantity, shall have been sent with the First Parcel, and the Remainder shall have been shipped within   and shall be accompanied with new Certificates, granted by the proper Officers of the Ports in *Ireland*, extracted from a Register of the original Documents, specifying the Quantities before shipped from thence, by what Vessel, and to what Port.

37

38

𝕬𝖓𝖉 𝖇𝖊 𝖎𝖙 𝕯𝖊𝖈𝖑𝖆𝖗𝖊𝖉 by the Authority aforesaid, to be a fundamental and essential Condition of the present Settlement, That so long as the Commerce to the Countries beyond the *Cape of Good Hope* to the *Streights of Magellan* shall continue to be carried on by an exclusive Company having Liberty to import into the Port of *London* only, all Ships freighted by the said Company, and which shall have cleared out from the Port of *London* for any of the said Countries, shall be at Liberty to touch at any of the Ports of *Ireland*, and to take on board there any Goods which they might take on board in *Great Britain*, any Act or Acts to the contrary notwithstanding; and that any Goods of the Growth, Produce, or Manufacture of *Ireland*, exported by the *East India* Company to any of the said Countries beyond the *Cape of Good Hope*, shall be considered as *British* Goods within the

39

D   Meaning

Meaning of any Obligation which may at any Time exist upon
40 the said Company to send out to those Countries certain Quantities of the Goods of the Growth, Produce, or Manufacture of *Great Britain*; and that no Ships shall be allowed to clear out from any Port in *Ireland* for any of the said Countries, except such as shall be freighted by the said Company, and shall have sailed from the Port of *London*, and except such Foreign Ships as might, by any Law now or hereafter to be in force, clear out for Foreign Settlements in the said Countries, from *Great Britain*, which Ships shall be allowed to clear out from *Ireland*
41 in the same Manner as from *Great Britain*; and that whenever the Commerce to the said Countries shall cease to be carried on by an exclusive Company having Liberty to import into the Port of *London* only, the Growth, Produce, or Manufacture of the said Countries beyond the *Cape of Good Hope* to the *Streights of Magellan*, shall be importable into *Ireland* from the *British* or Foreign Settlements in the *East Indies*, subject to the same Duties and Regulations as the like Goods shall from Time to Time be subject to on Importation into *Great Britain*, and if prohibited to be imported into *Great Britain*, shall in like Manner be prohibited from being imported into *Ireland*.

42 '**And be it Declared** by the Authority aforesaid, That it shall be held and adjudged to be a fundamental and essential Condition of the present Settlement, that so long as the Commerce to the Countries beyond the *Cape of Good Hope* to the *Streights of Magellan* shall be carried on solely by an exclusive Company having Liberty to import into the Port of *London* only, no Goods of the Growth, Produce, or Manufacture of the said Countries shall be allowed to be imported into *Ireland* but through *Great Britain*, except Dye Stuffs, Drugs, Cotton or other Wool, and Spiceries, and such other Articles as are or hereafter may be importable into *Great Britain* from Foreign *European* Countries; which Articles may be imported into *Ireland*
43 from Foreign *European* Countries, so long as the same are importable from Foreign *European* Countries into *Great Britain*; and that it shall be lawful to export any Goods of the Growth, Produce, or Manufacture of any of the said Countries, from *Great Britain* to *Ireland*; and that such Duties as may now by Law be retained thereon on such Exportation shall continue to be so retained, but that an Account shall be kept thereof, and that the Amount thereof shall be remitted, by the Receiver General of His Majesty's Customs in *Great Britain*, to the proper Officer of His Majesty's Revenue in *Ireland*, to be placed to the

Account

Account of His Majesty's Revenue there, subject to the Disposal of the Parliament of that Kingdom.

And be it Declared by the Authority aforesaid, That it shall be held and adjudged to be a fundamental and essential Condition of the present Settlement, that all Goods and Commodities whatever, which shall hereafter be imported into this Kingdom from *Ireland*, or into *Ireland* from *Great Britain*, should be put, by Laws to be passed in the Parliaments of the Two Kingdoms, under the same Regulations, with respect to Bonds, Cockets, and other Instruments, to which the like Goods are subject in passing from one Port of this Kingdom to another: Be it therefore Enacted by the Authority aforesaid, That all Goods, which shall be shipped or put on board in any Port, Creek, or Member of any Port, in this Kingdom, to be carried to any Port or Place in the Kingdom of *Ireland*, shall be accompanied with the like Sufferance and Cocket, and subject to the like Bond and Security, as are required by any Law in *Great Britain* for the like Goods passing from one Port in *Great Britain* to another; and that no Goods brought from any Port or Place in the Kingdom of *Ireland* shall be permitted to be imported into any Port, Creek, or Member of any Port, in this Kingdom, without a Sufferance and Cocket signed by the proper Officer or Officers of the Revenue in *Ireland*, nor shall be landed in this Kingdom, until the Sufferance and Cocket shall have been produced to the proper Officer of the Customs here, and a Sufferance granted for landing the same, under the like Restrictions, Regulations, Penalties, and Forfeitures, to which Goods carried from one Port of *Great Britain* to another are liable.

And be it Declared by the Authority aforesaid, That it shall be held and adjudged to be a fundamental and essential Condition of the present Settlement, that the Inhabitants of both Kingdoms shall have an equal Right to carry on Fisheries on every Part of the Coasts of the *British* Dominions: Be it therefore Enacted by the Authority aforesaid, That the Subjects of His Majesty residing in *Ireland* shall have equal Privileges and Advantages with His Majesty's Subjects residing in *Great Britain*, in fishing on the Coasts of *Great Britain*, and the Territories belonging thereto.

And be it Declared by the Authority aforesaid, That it shall be held and adjudged to be a fundamental and essential Condition of the present Settlement, that the Importation of Articles from

Foreign Countries shall be regulated from Time to Time, in each Kingdom, on such Terms as may effectually favour the Importation of similar Articles of the Growth, Produce, or Manufacture of the other, except in the Case of Materials of Manufacture which are, or hereafter may be, allowed to be imported from Foreign Countries Duty free.

47. **And be it Declared and Enacted** by the Authority aforesaid, That this Act, and every Part thereof, shall commence and be in Force on the   provided that before the said   an Act shall have been passed in the Parliament of *Ireland*, which shall appropriate whatever Sum the Gross Produce of the Hereditary Revenue shall amount to, after deducting all Drawbacks, Re-payments, and Bounties in the Nature of Drawbacks, over and above the Sum of Six hundred and Fifty-six Thousand Pounds in each Year, towards the Support of the Naval Force of the Empire, to be applied in such Manner as the Parliament of that Kingdom shall direct in the said Act, and which shall also provide that it shall be held and adjudged to be a fundamental and essential Condition of the present Settlement, that the due Collection of the Duties com-

48. posing the said Hereditary Revenue shall be at all Times effectually secured; and provided that before the said an Act or Acts shall have been passed in the Parliament of *Ireland*, for carrying into Effect, on the Part of that Kingdom, the present Settlement, and all Matters, Provisions, and Regulations herein declared to be fundamental and essential Conditions thereof; and provided also, that before the said an Act shall have been passed in the Parliament of *Great Britain*, declaring such Act or Acts of the Parliament of *Ireland* to contain satisfactory Provisions for carrying into Effect the present Settlement.

And be it also Declared, That the Continuance of the present Settlement, and the Duration of this Act, and of every Thing herein contained, shall depend on the due Observance, in the

49. Kingdom of *Ireland*, of the several Matters herein declared to be fundamental and essential Conditions of the said Settlement, according to the true Intent, Meaning, and Spirit thereof.

Provided nevertheless, That all the said fundamental and essential Conditions shall, in all Times, be held and deemed to be, and to have been, duly observed in the Kingdom of *Ireland*, unless it shall have been expressly declared, by an Act of the Parliament of this Kingdom, that the same have not been duly observed.

A BILL

FOR

Finally regulating the Intercourfe and Commerce between *Great Britain* and *Ireland*, on permanent and equitable Principles, for the mutual Benefit of both Kingdoms.

25 Geo. III.
1785.

A

BILL

FOR

Authorizing the Prize Agents, appointed by the Officers of the Garrison of *Gibraltar*, to pay to the Agents of the Corps composing the said Garrison, all such Sums as shall remain or come to their Hands, of the Bounty allowed for the Destruction of certain *Spanish* Ships of War.

N. B. *The Figures in the Margin denote the Number of the Folios in the written Copy.*

 WHEREAS, by an Act made in the Twenty-third Year of the Reign of His present Majesty, intituled, " An Act for authorizing the Treasurer of the Navy " to pay to the Garrison and Naval Department at " *Gibraltar*, the like Bounty for destroying certain " *Spanish* Ships of War, as is allowed to the Officers and Men " on board any of His Majesty's Ships of War, taking or de- " stroying Ships of War belonging to the Enemy," it is among other Things Enacted, That the Commissioners of His Majesty's Navy shall, and they are thereby authorized and required (upon Proof made, to the Satisfaction of the said Commissioners,

A   by

1

by Certificates, or otherwise, of the Number of Men living on board the said *Spanish* Ships of War, at the Time of the Attack and Surrender of them respectively) to make out Bills for the Amount of the said Bounty, directed to the Treasurer of His Majesty's Navy, to be divided amongst the Officers, Soldiers, Seamen, and Marines, within and belonging to the said Garrison and Naval Department, at the respective Times aforesaid, in such Manner, and in such Proportions, as His Majesty should graciously please to order, direct, and appoint; and the Treasurer of the Navy was thereby authorized and required to pay all such Bills, according to the Course of the Navy, to the said Officers, Soldiers, Seamen, and Marines, or to such Agent or Agents as they should authorize or appoint to receive the same:

And whereas great Inconveniences and Difficulties have arisen in the Mode of Payment of the Bounty Money directed to be paid by the said Act to the Officers, Soldiers, Seamen, and Marines, within and belonging to the said Garrison of *Gibraltar*, by the Prize Agents, on Account of their limiting their Attendance to the First *Friday* in every Month; which Inconveniences and Difficulties might be obviated, if the said Bounty Money and Prize Money was to be paid by the Regimental or other Agents to the different Corps belonging to the said Garrison, who are or may be in constant Attendance:

May it therefore please Your MAJESTY,

That it may be Enacted; And be it Enacted by the KING's Most Excellent MAJESTY, by and with the Advice and Consent of the Lords Spiritual and Temporal, and Commons, in this present Parliament assembled, and by the Authority of the same, That

shall be, and they are hereby appointed Commissioners for the examining, stating, and settling all Accounts of such Bounty Money and Prize Money, with the Prize Agents who have received, or shall hereafter receive, all or any Part of the said Bounty Money and Prize Money, or any other Sums which shall be remitted to them from *Gibraltar*, in consequence of the Destruction of the Floating Batteries, or otherwise.

And,

And, for the better enabling the said Commissioners to examine, state, and settle such Accounts, Be it further Enacted by the Authority aforesaid, That it shall and may be lawful to and for the said Commissioners, or any   or more of them, by Writing under their Hands, to summon before them, at such Time and Place as in and by the said Writing shall be expressed, any Agent or Agents, or other Person concerned in the Receipt of such Prize Money, and other Monies as aforesaid, and to order such respective Agents to produce upon Oath all Books, Accounts, and Vouchers, necessary for the Information of the said Commissioners; and if any Agent, or other Person, shall refuse to comply with such Summons, or to produce such respective Books, Accounts, or Vouchers as aforesaid, and to give the Commissioners such Information upon Oath as he is able, every such Agent, or such other Person, shall for every such Offence forfeit and pay the Sum of   to be recovered and applied in Manner hereinafter mentioned.

And be it further Enacted by the Authority aforesaid, That the said Commissioners, on settling the said Accounts, shall allow to the said Agents Five Pounds *per Centum* upon all such Sums as they shall have received and paid by virtue of the said Act: And the said Prize Agents are hereby directed and required to pay over such remaining Balance, and such Sums as they may hereafter receive, into the Hands of the said Commissioners, or such other Person or Persons required so to do, as they, or any   or more of them, shall order and direct; and also to produce and deliver over, when required, all Books of Accounts and Vouchers in their Hands respecting the same; and the said Prize Agents shall be, and are hereby acquitted, exonerated, and discharged from all Claims and Demands whatsoever, that hereafter shall be made upon them, or any of them, for all such Sums as they shall so pay by virtue of or in pursuance of this Act.

And be it further Enacted by the Authority aforesaid, That the said Commissioners, or any   or more of them, shall and may, upon Application being made to them for that Purpose, appoint the Regimental Agents, or other Agent or Agents, who shall distribute the said Balance to the respective Claimants of the respective Corps so entitled, in their due and proper Proportions, as settled by a Board of General Officers, if they have not already received the same.

7 And whereas it appears, by the Distribution made by the Board of General Officers, that there is a Surplus of Four hundred Twenty-three Pounds Eleven Shillings and Four Pence; Be it further Enacted, That the said Commissioners may direct, that all the Expences attending the passing this Act, and such other contingent Expences as may arise in the carrying the same into Execution, may be paid out of that Sum, if not already disposed of, otherwise such Expences to be defrayed from the Monies now in the Prize Agents Hands, over and above the Thirty thousand Pounds already allotted for Distribution.

And be it further Enacted, That at the Expiration of   Years from the passing of this Act, all the unclaimed Shares shall be disposed of in such Manner as His Majesty shall graciously please to direct.

8 And be it further Enacted by the Authority aforesaid, That all Penalties and Forfeitures incurred by this Act, may be sued for and recovered in any of His Majesty's Courts of Record at *Westminster*, wherein no Essoign, Privilege, Protection, or Wager of Law, nor more than One Imparlance, shall be allowed; and such Penalties and Forfeitures, when recovered, shall be applied   to the Use of His Majesty, His Heirs and Successors, and   to be disposed of as His Majesty shall be graciously pleased to direct.

And be it further Enacted by the Authority aforesaid, That no such Claim of any Prize Money shall be admitted or allowed after the   or such further Day as the said Commissioners, or any   or more of them, shall appoint.

BILL

FOR

Authorizing the Prize Agents, appointed by the Officers of the Garrison of *Gibraltar*, to pay to the Agents of the Corps composing the said Garrison, all such Sums as shall remain or come to their Hands, of the Bounty allowed for the Destruction of certain *Spanish* Ships of War.

25 *Geo.* III.
1785.

A

BILL

TO

Explain, Amend, and Reduce into One Act of Parliament, all the Laws now in being for preventing Bribery and Expence in Elections of Members to serve in Parliament.

Note.—*The Figures in the Margin denote the Number of the Folios in the written Copy.*

WHEREAS Bribery in Elections of Members to serve in Parliament may be destructive to the Constitution:

And whereas all Elections should be made freely, without Charge or Expence:

And whereas the Practices hereinafter mentioned have been productive of various bad Effects:

A

[2]

Be it therefore Enacted, and it is hereby Enacted, by the KING's Most Excellent MAJESTY, by and with the Advice and Consent of the Lords Spiritual and Temporal, and Commons, in this present Parliament assembled, and by the Authority of the same, That from and after the
Day of   One thousand Seven hundred and
2 Eighty-   it shall not be lawful for any Person, by himself or herself, or by any Person or Persons employed by him or her, to give or to offer, or to cause to be given or offered, or to make any Agreement, Engagement, or Promise to give, or to cause to be given, to any Person (or to any one whomsoever for his Use, Benefit, Profit, or Advantage) any Money, or any Bond, Note, Draft, Order, Bill, or Ticket for Money, or any Place, Pension, Contract, Office, or Appointment, or any Reward by way of Gratuity, Purchase, Employment, Loan, or other Device, to corrupt, or to procure such Person to vote, or to forbear to give his Vote, at any Election of any Member or Members to serve in Parliament for any County, City, Borough, or Place, or for having voted, or for having forborn
3 to give his Vote, at such Election; and it shall not be lawful for any Person, by himself or herself, or by any Person or Persons employed by him or her, to give or to offer, or to cause to be given or offered, or to make any Agreement, Engagement, or promise to give, or to cause to be given, to any Person who shall have, or claim to have, a Right to vote at any such Election as aforesaid (or to any one whomsoever for his Use, Benefit, Profit, or Advantage) any Money, or any Bond, Note, Draft, Order, Bill, or Ticket for Money, or any Place, Pension, Contract, Office, or Appointment, or any Compensation or Reward, by way of Gratuity, Purchase, Employment, Loan, or other Device, for or under Pretence or Colour
4 of any Loss of Time, or any Expence or Expences incurred, or to be incurred, at or for such Election, by such Person in or by his travelling or going to or from the Place of Election or the Place of Polling, or in or by his staying at such Place of Election or such Place of Polling, or anywise incurred, or to be incurred, by such Person on Account of his voting at such Election; and every Person who shall be found guilty of any of the said Offences shall, for each and every such Offence, forfeit the Sum of   of lawful Money of *Great Britain*, to any Person or Persons who shall sue for the same.

And

And be it further Enacted by the Authority aforesaid, That it shall not be lawful for any Person, directly or indirectly, or by any Ways or Means on his Behalf, to give or to offer, or to cause to be given or offered, or to make any Agreement, Engagement, or Promise to give, or to cause to be given, any Present, Gift, or Reward whatsoever, to or for the Use, Benefit, Profit, or Advantage of any County, City, Borough, or Place, in order to be elected, or for being or having been elected to serve in Parliament for such County, City, Borough, or Place, or in order that any Person whomsoever be elected, or for his being or his having been elected to serve in Parliament for such County, City, Borough, or Place; and every Person who shall be found guilty of any such Offence shall, for each and every such Offence, forfeit the Sum of   of lawful Money of *Great Britain*, to any Person or Persons who shall sue for the same.

And be it further Enacted by the Authority aforesaid, That if a Petition be duly presented to the House of Commons, on the Merits of any such Election as aforesaid, and if any Person who shall have been returned at any such Election to serve in Parliament, or who shall have been a Candidate at any such Election, shall have been guilty of any of the Offences aforesaid, every such Person (shall not only be liable to be sued in due Course of Law for such respective Offence or Offences, but) shall be, and shall, by the Select Committee of the House of Commons duly appointed to try and determine the Merits of such Election, be declared to be incapable to serve in Parliament for such County, City, Borough, or Place upon such Election, or upon any Vacancy which shall or may be occasioned by any Determination of such Select Committee on the Merits of such Election, if such Select Committee shall find that such Person shall have been guilty of any of the said Offences for or at such Election, or for or at any former Election of any Member or Members to serve in that same Parliament for such County, City, Borough, or Place, or shall find that such Person shall have been guilty of any of the said Offences for or at any Election of any Member or Members to serve in any former Parliament for such County, City, Borough, or Place, and that such illegal Act or Acts committed or done during any such former Parliament has or have had any Effect or Operation at or in the Election the Merits of which are to be tried by such Select Committee; and the Determination of such Select Committee upon such Incapacity shall, in each and every of the Cases aforesaid,

said, be final and conclusive to all Intents and Purposes; and such Select Committee shall annex the Declaration of such Guilt and Incapacity to the Report which they shall make to the House of Commons on the Merits of such Election.

9   And be it further Enacted by the Authority aforesaid, That it shall not be lawful for any Person to agree or contract for, or to ask for or demand, or to accept, take, or receive any Money, or any Bond, Note, Draft, Order, Bill, or Ticket for Money, or any Place, Pension, Contract, Office, or Appointment, or any Reward, by way of Gratuity, Purchase, Employment, Loan, or other Device, to vote, or to forbear to give his Vote, at any Election of any Member or Members to serve in Parliament for any County, City, Borough, or Place; and it shall not be lawful for any Person to accept, take, or receive any Money, or any Bond, Note, Draft, Order, Bill, or Ticket for Money, or any Place, Pension, Contract, Office, or Appointment, or any Reward by way of Gratuity, Purchase, Employment, Loan, or other Device, for having voted, or for having forborn to give his Vote at any such Election; and it shall not be lawful for any Person who shall have, or claim to have, a Right to vote at any such Election, to accept, take, or receive any Money, or any Bond, Note, Draft, Order, Bill, or Ticket for Money, or any Place, Pension, Contract, Office,

10   or Appointment, or any Compensation or Reward, by way of Gratuity, Purchase, Employment, Loan, or other Device, for or under Pretence or Colour of any Loss of Time, or any Expence or Expences incurred or to be incurred at or for such Election, by such Person, in or by his travelling or going to or from the Place of Election, or the Place of Polling, or in or by his staying at such Place of Election or such Place of Polling, or anywise incurred or to be incurred on Account of his voting at such Election; and every Person who shall be found guilty of any of the said Offences shall, for each and every such Offence, forfeit the Sum of   of lawful Money of *Great Britain*, to any Person or Persons who shall sue for the same.

11   And be it further Enacted by the Authority aforesaid, That if a Petition be duly presented to the House of Commons upon the Merits of any such Election as aforesaid, the Select Committee of the House of Commons which shall be appointed to try and determine the Merits of such Election, shall deem and consider as null and void all and every Vote or Votes which
shall

shall or may have been given at such Election, by any Person or Persons who shall, by such Select Committee, be found to have been guilty of any of the Offences aforesaid, for or at such Election.

And be it further Enacted by the Authority aforesaid, That every Person who shall (on being sued in due Course of Law) be found guilty of any of the Offences aforesaid, shall be for ever disabled to vote at any Election of any Member or Members to serve in Parliament for any County, City, Borough, or Place.

And be it further Enacted by the Authority aforesaid, That every Person who shall (on being sued in due Course of Law) be found guilty of any of the Offences aforesaid, shall be for ever disabled to hold, execute, or enjoy any Office or Franchise to which he shall, or at any Time afterwards may be entitled, as a Member of any City, Borough, Town Corporate, or Cinque Port, as if such Person were naturally dead.

And be it further Enacted by the Authority aforesaid, That if any Person shall have been guilty of any of the aforesaid Offences, for or at any such Election as aforesaid, and (not having been convicted in due Course of Law of any of the said Offences) shall, within   Calendar Months next after such Offence committed, discover any other Person or Persons who shall have been guilty of any of the Offences aforesaid for or at such Election, so that any such Person so discovered be thereupon convicted, the Person so discovering shall be indemnified from all Penalties and Disabilities which such Person shall then have incurred by having been guilty of such Offence for or at such Election: Provided always, That no Person shall be so indemnified who shall have been guilty of having given or offered, or of having caused to be given or offered, or of having made any Agreement, Engagement, or Promise to give, or to cause to be given, any Money, or any Bond, Note, Draft, Order, Bill, or Ticket for Money, or any Place, Pension, Contract, Office, or Appointment, or any Compensation or Reward, by way of Gratuity, Purchase, Employment, Loan, or other Device, in Manner aforesaid, or any other Present or Gift in Manner aforesaid, contrary to the true Intent and Meaning of this Act, unless the Person claiming such Indemnity shall be or shall have been employed to commit or do any such Act or Acts, and shall discover,

B

cover, in the Manner aforesaid, the Person or Persons by whom he or she shall be or shall have been so employed.

And be it further Enacted by the Authority aforesaid, That it shall not be lawful for any Person, at any Time, to pay or defray, or to cause to be paid or defrayed, or to agree, engage, or promise to pay or defray, or to cause to be paid or defrayed, or by any Device whatsoever to pay or defray, or to cause to be paid or defrayed, any Expence incurred or to be incurred
15 at or for any such Election as aforesaid, for or by any Person who shall have, or claim to have, a Right to vote at such Election, in or by such Person's travelling or going to or from the Place of Election, or the Place of Polling, or any Expence incurred or to be incurred by the Hire, Keep, or Reception of any Horse or Carriage, or other Conveyance, carrying or conveying such Person to or from such Place of Election, or such Place of Polling (whether such Person be so carried or conveyed singly, or together with any other Person or Persons); and every Person who shall be found guilty of any One or more of the said Offences shall, for each and every such Offence, forfeit the Sum of   of lawful Money of *Great Britain*, to any Person or Persons who shall sue for the same: Provided always,
16 That nothing herein contained shall extend, or be construed to extend, to prohibit any Person from paying or defraying any such Expence or Expences incurred or to be incurred at or for any such Election as aforesaid, for any Voter who shall be the Son or menial Servant of such Person.

And be it further Enacted by the Authority aforesaid, That at any Time after any County, City, Borough, or Place shall hereafter have become vacant by any Dissolution of Parliament, or otherwise, and before the   Day after the Election of any Member or Members to represent such County, City, Borough, or Place in Parliament, it shall not be lawful for any Person to give, or to cause to be given, or to agree, engage, or promise to give, or to cause to be given, or by any Device whatsoever to give, or to cause to be given, any Meat, Drink, Treat, Provision, or Entertainment, to any Person hav-
17 ing, or claiming to have, a Right to vote at such Election, for such Person to vote, or for having voted at such Election, or in order to be elected, or for being or having been elected to serve in Parliament for such County, City, Borough, or Place, or in order that any Person whomsoever be elected, or for his

being

being or having been elected to serve in Parliament for such County, City, Borough, or Place; and it shall not be lawful for any Person at any Time to pay or defray, or to cause to be paid or defrayed, or to agree, engage, or promise to pay or defray, or to cause to be paid or defrayed, or by any Device whatsoever to pay or defray, or to cause to be paid or defrayed, any Expence incurred or to be incurred by the giving of any such Meat, Drink, Treat, Provision, or Entertainment; and every Person who shall be found guilty of any One or more of the said Offences shall, for each and every such Offence, forfeit the Sum of   of lawful Money of *Great Britain*, to any Person or Persons who shall sue for the same.

And be it further Enacted by the Authority aforesaid, That if a Petition be duly presented to the House of Commons on the Merits of any such Election as aforesaid, and if any Person who shall have been returned at any such Election to serve in Parliament, or who shall have been a Candidate at any such Election, shall have been guilty of any of the Offences aforesaid, every such Person (shall not only be liable to be sued in due Course of Law for such respective Offence or Offences, but) upon being found guilty of any of the said Offences by the Select Committee of the House of Commons duly appointed to try and determine the Merits of such Election, shall be, and shall by such Select Committee be declared to be, incapable to serve in Parliament for such County, City, Borough, or Place, upon such Election, or upon any Vacancy which shall or may be occasioned by any Determination of such Select Committee on the Merits of such Election; and the Determination of such Select Committee upon such Incapacity shall, in each and every of the Cases aforesaid, be final and conclusive to all Intents and Purposes; and such Select Committee shall annex the Declaration of such Guilt and Incapacity to the Report which they shall make to the House of Commons on the Merits of such Election.

And be it further Enacted by the Authority aforesaid, That if any Person who shall be or shall have been licensed to keep any Inn, Tavern, Victualling House, or Ale House, or to sell any Spirituous Liquors, shall be convicted in due Course of Law of having, during the Time of such Person's being so licensed, wilfully committed any of the Offences aforesaid, such Person

Person (shall not only be liable to the Penalties and Disabilities aforesaid, but) shall, from the Time of such Conviction, and during the Continuance of the then Parliament, and for the Space of   Calendar Months afterwards, be disabled to have any such Licence as aforesaid, and if at the Time of such Conviction such Person shall have any such Licence, the same shall be null and void.

And be it further Enacted by the Authority aforesaid, That if any Person shall, for or at any such Election as aforesaid, give or cause to be given, to any Person whomsoever, any Cockade, or other Mark of Distinction, or shall at any Time pay or defray, or cause to be paid or defrayed, or shall by any Device whatsoever pay or defray, or cause to be paid or defrayed, the Expence of the same, such Person shall forfeit, for every such Mark of Distinction so given or paid for, the Sum of
            of lawful Money of *Great Britain*, to any Person or Persons who shall sue for the same.

And be it further Enacted by the Authority aforesaid, That if any Person shall be or shall have been employed to pay or defray, or to cause to be paid or defrayed, or to agree, engage, or promise to pay or defray, or to cause to be paid or defrayed, or by any Device whatsoever to pay or defray, or to cause to be paid or defrayed, any Expence incurred or to be incurred at or for any such Election as aforesaid, for or by any Person who shall have, or claim to have, a Right to vote at such Election, in or by such Person's travelling or going to or from the Place of Election, or the Place of Polling, or any Expence incurred or to be incurred by the Hire, Keep, or Reception of any Horse or Carriage, or other Conveyance, contrary to the true Intent and Meaning of this Act; or shall be or shall have been employed to give, or to cause to be given, or to agree, engage, or promise to give, or to cause to be given, or by any Device whatsoever to give, or to cause to be given, any Meat, Drink, Treat, Provision, or Entertainment, contrary to the true Intent and Meaning of this Act, or to pay or defray, or to cause to be paid or defrayed, or to agree, engage, or promise to pay or defray, or to cause to be paid or defrayed, or by any Device whatsoever to pay or defray, or to cause to be paid or defrayed, any Expence incurred or to be incurred by the giving of any such Meat, Drink, Treat, Provision, or Entertainment, contrary to the true Intent and Meaning of this Act; or shall be or shall have

have been employed to give, or to cause to be given, any Cockade, or other Mark of Distinction, or to pay or defray, or to cause to be paid or defrayed, or by any Device whatsoever to pay or defray, or to cause to be paid or defrayed, the Expence of the same, contrary to the true Intent and Meaning of this Act; and if such Person shall discover the Person or Persons by whom he or she shall be or shall have been employed to commit any One or more of the said Offences, so that any such Person or Persons, so discovered, be thereupon convicted, the Person making such Discovery shall be indemnified from all Penalties and Disabilities which such Person shall then have incurred by having been guilty of the respective Offence or respective Offences concerning which such Discovery shall have been made as aforesaid: Provided always, That no Person shall be indemnified, as herein last mentioned, who shall have been convicted in due Course of Law of any Offence whatsoever against this Act.

𝕬𝖓𝖉 𝖇𝖊 𝖎𝖙 𝖋𝖚𝖗𝖙𝖍𝖊𝖗 𝕰𝖓𝖆𝖈𝖙𝖊𝖉 by the Authority aforesaid, That all Forfeitures by this Act to be incurred shall and may be sued for and recovered, by Action of Debt, Bill, Plaint, or Information, in any of His Majesty's Courts of Record at *Westminster*, wherein no Essoign, Protection, Wager of Law, or more than One Imparlance, shall be allowed; or shall and may be recovered by summary Action or Complaint before the Court of Session, in that Part of *Great Britain* called *Scotland*, if the Offence shall have been committed in that Part of *Great Britain* called *Scotland*; and in every such Action the Party against whom Judgment shall be given (whether Plaintiff or Defendant) shall pay the   of Suit.

𝕻𝖗𝖔𝖛𝖎𝖉𝖊𝖉 𝖆𝖑𝖜𝖆𝖞𝖘, 𝖆𝖓𝖉 𝖇𝖊 𝖎𝖙 𝖋𝖚𝖗𝖙𝖍𝖊𝖗 𝕰𝖓𝖆𝖈𝖙𝖊𝖉 by the Authority aforesaid, That every such Action or Prosecution shall be brought or commenced within   after the Offence committed, and not afterwards; and the Person against whom any such Action or Prosecution shall be brought or commenced, in any of His Majesty's Courts of Record at *Westminster* as aforesaid, shall be legally served, within the Time aforesaid, with the Writ or Process by which such Action or Prosecution shall be intended to be commenced, unless the Service of such Writ or Process shall have been prevented by such Person's absconding or withdrawing out of this Kingdom; and with respect to that Part of *Great Britain* called *Scotland*, the Petition shall be served within the Time aforesaid, and not after: And provided also, that every Action or Prosecution which shall be brought or commenced

menced as aforesaid shall be carried on without wilful Delay.

And be it further Enacted by the Authority aforesaid, That from and after the said   Day of   One thousand Seven hundred and Eighty   the Act of Parliament made in the Seventh and Eighth Year of the Reign of King *William* the Third, intituled, " An Act for preventing Charge and " Expence in Elections of Members to serve in Parliament," and also the Act of Parliament made in the Second Year of the Reign of King *George* the Second, intituled, " An Act for the more " effectual preventing Bribery and Corruption in the Elections " of Members to serve in Parliament," shall be and are hereby   save and except such Part of the said last-recited Act, which enacts, " That such Votes shall be deemed to be legal " which have been so declared by the last Determination in the " House of Commons; which last Determination, concerning " any County, Shire, City, Borough, Cinque Port, or Place, " shall be final to all Intents and Purposes whatsoever, any " Usage to the contrary notwithstanding."

And be it further Enacted by the Authority aforesaid, That this present Act shall be publicly read at every Election for any Member or Members to serve in Parliament for any County, City, Borough, or Place, previous to such Election; and every Sheriff, Under Sheriff, Mayor, Bailiff, or other Officer presiding at any such Election, who shall neglect to read this Act, or to cause the same to be read, shall forfeit the Sum of   of lawful Money of *Great Britain*, to any Person or Persons who shall sue for the same.

BILL

TO

Explain, Amend, and Reduce into One Act of Parliament, all the Laws now in being for preventing Bribery and Expence in Elections of Members to serve in Parliament.

25 *Geo.* III.
1785.

A

BILL

T O

Prevent Occafional Voters from voting in the Election of Members to ferve in Parliament, for Cities and Boroughs, in that Part of *Great Britain* called *England*.

Note.—*The Figures in the Margin denote the Number of the Folios in the written Copy.*

 𝔥 𝔈 𝔕 𝔈 𝔄 𝔖 it frequently happens, in Cities and Boroughs where the Right of Election of Members to ferve in Parliament is in the Inhabitants Houfe-holders, Houfekeepers, or Pot-wallers, that much Trouble, Expence, and Litigation, is created by Occafional Voters, to the great Prejudice of the real Inhabitants, who bear the Burdens of fuch Cities and Boroughs, and to whom the Right of fending Members to Parliament belongs:

1

For

For Remedy whereof, Be it Enacted by the KING's Most Excellent MAJESTY, by and with the Advice and Consent of the Lords Spiritual and Temporal, and Commons, in this present Parliament assembled, and by the Authority of the same, That from and after the   Day of   no Person shall vote at any Election of a Member or Members to serve in Parliament for any City or Borough of that Part of *Great Britain* called *England*, or the Dominion of *Wales*, as an Inhabitant Householder, Housekeeper, or Pot-waller of such City or Borough, whether there be or be not any other superadded Qualification, unless he shall have been actually and *bonâ fide* resident, and a Householder, Housekeeper, or Pot-waller, within such City or Borough   Calendar Months previous to the Day of the Election at which he shall tender his Vote; and if any Person shall vote at any such Election, contrary to the true Intent and Meaning of this Act, he shall forfeit, to any Person who shall sue for the same, the Sum of   to be recovered by him or her, by Action of Debt, in any of His Majesty's Courts of Record at *Westminster*, wherein no Essoin, Protection, Wager of Law, Privilege, or Imparlance, shall be admitted or allowed; and in every such Action the Proof shall lie upon the Person against whom the same shall be brought: Provided nevertheless, That such Action be commenced within   Calendar Months after the Cause of Action accrued: Provided also, That nothing in this Act contained shall extend, or be construed to extend, to any Person acquiring the Possession of any House, in any City or Borough, by Descent, Devise, Marriage, or Marriage Settlement, or Promotion to any Office or Benefice.

Provided

Provided also, and be it further Enacted, That where there are different Rights of voting in the same City or Borough, depending partly upon Inhabitancy, this Act shall relate only to that Class of Voters who claim to exercise the Franchise of voting as Inhabitants, and shall not extend to any other Description of Persons, who may have an equal Right to vote in such Cities or Boroughs.

A

BILL

TO

Prevent Occasional Voters from voting in the Election of Members to serve in Parliament, for Cities and Boroughs, in that Part of *Great Britain* called *England*.

26 *Geo.* III.
1786.

A

BILL

TO

Repeal so much of an Act, made in the last Session of Parliament, intituled, "An Act for granting to His Majesty additional Duties on Hawkers, Pedlars, and Petty Chapmen, and for regulating their Trade," as restrains Hawkers and Pedlars from exposing to Sale Goods in Market Towns, and as enables Justices of the Peace of any County to prohibit such Hawkers and Pedlars from vending their Goods within the same; and for further regulating their Trade.

Note.—*The Figures in the Margin denote the Number of the Folios in the written Copy.*

WHEREAS, by an Act passed in the last Session of Parliament, intituled, "An Act for granting to His Majesty additional Duties on Hawkers, Pedlars, and Petty Chapman, and for regulating their Trade," it was amongst other Things Enacted, that no Hawker, Pedlar, Petty Chapman, or any other trading Person or Persons, going from Town to Town, or to other Men's Houses, or travelling, either on Foot, or with Horse

A or

or Horses, or opening a Room or Shop, and exposing to Sale any Goods, Wares, or Merchandizes by Retail, in any Town, Parish, or Place, such Person not being a Householder there, or the same not being an usual Place of his or her Abode, or of his or her carrying on Business, should vend, sell, or expose to Sale, any Goods, Wares, or Merchandizes whatsoever, in any City or Market Town in *England*, *Wales*, or the Town of *Berwick* upon *Tweed*, or within the Distance of Two Miles from the Middle of the most central Market Place, by the usual or most common Road, of any such City or Market Town; and in case any such Person or Persons should vend, sell, or expose to Sale, any Goods, Wares, or Merchandizes whatsoever, in any City or Market Town in *England*, *Wales*, or the Town of *Berwick* upon *Tweed* (except as before excepted) every such Person should forfeit and pay for every such Offence the Sum of Ten Pounds, to be recovered and applied as thereinafter is mentioned: And it was by the said Act further Enacted, that it should not be lawful for any Hawker, Pedlar, Petty Chapman, or other trading Person travelling as aforesaid, to vend his or her Goods or Wares in any County, or City being a County of itself, or Town being a County of itself, in *England* or *Wales*, by virtue of any such Licence as aforesaid, in case the Justices assembled at the General Quarter Sessions of the Peace should have made an Order that Hawkers, Pedlars, Petty Chapmen, and other trading Persons as aforesaid, should not have Liberty to vend their Goods and Wares in such County, City, or Town, upon Pain of forfeiting for every such Offence the Sum of Ten Pounds; and that no such Order should at any Time be made, except at the Quarter Sessions next after *Michaelmas*, to be holden for such County, City, or Town, and should not be in Force until Nine Months after Notice should have been given of the same in some public News-paper published or circulated in such County, City, or Town, respectively:

And whereas it is deemed expedient to repeal the above-recited Clauses, contained in the Act above mentioned:

Be it therefore Enacted by the KING's Most Excellent MAJESTY, by and with the Advice and Consent of the Lords Spiritual and Temporal, and Commons, in this present Parliament assembled, and by the Authority of the same, That from and after the   the above-recited Clauses, contained in the said Act of the Twenty-fifth Year of His present Majesty's Reign, shall be, and the same are hereby repealed.

And

And be it Enacted by the Authority aforesaid, That every Person or Persons applying for a Licence to trade as a Hawker, Pedlar, or Petty Chapman, shall, at the Time of his making such Application, and before such Licence is granted to him, deliver to the Commissioners appointed for licencing Hawkers, Pedlars, and Petty Chapmen, or to their Riding Surveyor of the District, or to his Deputy, a Certificate, signed by   reputable Householders of the Place where the Person making such Application usually resides, to the satisfaction of the said Commissioners, or their Riding Surveyor, or his Deputy, certifying that he or she are of good Character, and fit to be licenced as a Hawker, Pedlar, or Petty Chapman; and the Words of such Certificate shall be indorsed on the said Licence, together with the Names of the Persons who subscribe the said Certificate; and no Licence whatsoever shall be granted but upon Delivery of such Certificate, and the Indorsement of the said Certificate on such Licence in Manner abovementioned.

And be it further Enacted by the Authority aforesaid, That no Hawker, Pedlar, or Petty Chapman, or any other trading Person or Persons going from Town to Town, or to other Men's Houses, or travelling, either on Foot or with Horse or Horses, or opening a Room or Shop, and exposing to Sale any Goods, Wares, or Merchandizes by Retail, in any Town, Parish, or Place, such Person not being a Householder there or the same not being the chief Place of his or her Abode, or of his or her carrying on Business, shall vend, sell, or expose to Sale any Goods, Wares, or Merchandizes whatsoever, in any City, Borough, or Corporate Town in *England*, *Wales*, or the Town of *Berwick upon Tweed*, or within the Suburbs thereof, except upon Market or Fair Days, every such Person offending herein shall forfeit and pay for every such Offence the Sum of   to be recovered before   or more of His Majesty's Justices of the Peace of the County, City, Town, or Place wherein the Offence shall be committed, on Proof thereof, either by the voluntary Confession of the Party or Parties accused, or by the Oath of   or more credible Witnesses; and   of every such Penalty shall belong to His Majesty, His Heirs and Successors, and   to the Informer or Informers prosecuting for the same; and in case of Non-payment shall be levied by   of the Offender's Goods and Chattels, by Warrant under the Hands and Seals of such Justices; and the Overplus of the Money raised, after deducting the Penalty, and the

B   Expence

[4]

7   Expence of the   shall be rendered to the Owner; and for want of sufficient   the Offender shall be sent by such Justices to the Prison of such County, City, Borough, Town, or Place, for such Time, not exceeding nor less than   as such Justices shall think most proper.

And be it further Enacted by the Authority aforesaid, That if any Hawker, Pedlar, or Petty Chapman shall be found or detected in trading, vending, or exposing to Sale any smuggled or contraband Goods, and shall be found guilty of the same, on the Oath of   or more credible Witnesses, before   or more of His Majesty's Justices of the Peace of the County, City, Town, or Place where such Offence or Offences shall be committed, such Person or Persons shall for ever thereafter be rendered incapable of being licenced to trade as a
8   Hawker and Pedlar; and the said Justices are hereby directed and required to transmit forthwith to the Office of the Commissioners for licencing Hawkers and Pedlars, the Name or Names of such Hawker, Pedlar, or Petty Chapman as shall be found guilty of such Offence or Offences; and if any Hawker, Pedlar, or Petty Chapman, after being so convicted, shall change his or her Name, and apply for a Licence under a new or different Name; or if any Hawker, Pedlar, or Petty Chapman shall change, erase, or deface, or cause to be changed, erased, or defaced, his or her Name, or the Name of any Persons whatsoever, in any Licence, or use and trade under such Licence knowing the same to be changed, erased, or defaced, every such Hawker, Pedlar, or Petty Chapman shall be deemed and adjudged to be

And be it Enacted by the Authority aforesaid, That from and after   it shall not be lawful to or for any Person or Persons, not being a Hawker or Pedlar,
9   to open any Room or Shop, or Place of Sale, or to sell or expose to Sale in any Manner of Way whatsoever, any Goods, Wares, or Merchandizes by Retail, except the Manufacturer of such Goods, Wares, or Merchandizes, in any Town, Parish, or Place, such Person not being a Householder there, or the same not being the usual Place of his or her Abode, or of his or her carrying on Business, except at any public Market or Fair, under the Penalty of   to be recovered before One of His Majesty's Justices of the Peace of the County, Riding, Shire, Division, City, Liberty, Town, or Place wherein the Offence shall be committed, on Proof of

the

the Offence, either by voluntary Confeſſion of the Party or Parties accuſed, or by the Oath of One or more credible Witneſs or Witneſſes; and   of every ſuch Penalty ſhall belong to His Majeſty, His Heirs and Succeſſors, and   to the Informer or Informers proſecuting for the ſame, and in Caſe of Non-payment ſhall be levied by   of the Offender's Goods and Chattels, by Warrant under the Hands and Seals of ſuch Juſtice; and the Overplus of the Money raiſed, after deducting the Penalty, and the Expence of the   ſhall be rendered to the Owner; and for want of ſufficient   the Offender ſhall be ſent by ſuch Juſtice to the Priſon of ſuch County, Shire, Diviſion, Liberty, Town, or Place, for ſuch Time, not exceeding   nor leſs than   as ſuch Juſtice ſhall think moſt proper.

And be it further Enacted, That if any Perſon or Perſons ſhall find himſelf or themſelves aggrieved by the Judgment of any ſuch Juſtice or Juſtices, then he and they ſhall and may, upon giving Security to the Amount of the Value of ſuch Penalty and Forfeiture, together with ſuch Coſts as ſhall be awarded in caſe ſuch Judgment ſhall be affirmed, appeal to the Juſtices of the Peace at the next General Quarter Seſſions for the County, Riding, or Place; who are hereby impowered to ſummon and examine Witneſſes upon Oath, and finally to hear and determine the ſame; and in caſe the Judgment of ſuch Juſtice or Juſtices ſhall be affirmed, it ſhall be lawful for ſuch Juſtices to award the Perſon or Perſons appealing to pay ſuch Coſts, occaſioned by ſuch Appeal; as to them ſhall ſeem meet.

A

BILL

TO

Repeal so much of an Act, made in the last Session of Parliament, intituled, "An Act "for granting to His Majesty additional "Duties on Hawkers, Pedlars, and Petty "Chapmen, and for regulating their "Trade," as restrains Hawkers and Pedlars from exposing to Sale Goods in Market Towns, and as enables Justices of the Peace of any County to prohibit such Hawkers and Pedlars from vending their Goods within the same; and for further regulating their Trade.

26 Geo. III.
1786.

A

B I L L

[WITH THE AMENDMENTS]

FOR

More effectual Relief of the Poor, and ascertaining the Settlement of Bastard Children.

N. B. *The Words printed in* Italic, *and the Clause marked* (A), *were inserted by the Committee; and the Words printed in* 𝕭𝖑𝖆𝖈𝖐 𝕷𝖊𝖙𝖙𝖊𝖗, *at the Bottom of the Pages, were left out by the Committee.*

Note.—*The Figures in the Margin denote the Number of the Folios in the written Copy.*

WHEREAS the Laws now in being relating to the Poor have not only become very burthensome, but are found to be ineffectual to answer the good Purposes for which they were enacted:

And whereas it might tend greatly toward the Comfort of the Poor, as well as lessen the present Burthen on the Rich, if One General Fund were to be established, to which the Rich should be obliged to become Contributors, for the Benefit of the Poor, and to which also the Poor, while young and in Health, should

A   be

be obliged by small Savings to contribute towards their own Support, when disabled by Sickness, Accident, or Age:

May it therefore please Your MAJESTY,

That it may be Enacted; And be it Enacted by the KING's Most Excellent MAJESTY, by and with the Advice and Consent of the Lords Spiritual and Temporal, and Commons, in this present Parliament assembled, and by the Authority of the same, That from and after *the Twenty-ninth Day of September One thousand Seven hundred and Eighty-seven*, there be established within every Parish throughout England, Wales, and the Town of Berwick upon Tweed, One General Club, or Society, for the Purpose of entitling the Members thereof, on Payment of a certain Sum or Sums Weekly, to a certain Weekly Receipt, under such Provisoes, Limitations, and Conditions as are hereinafter mentioned, specified, and declared, of and concerning the same, and that every Person within England, Wales, and the Town of Berwick upon Tweed (excepting such as are hereinafter excepted) shall be obliged to enter himself or herself a Member of such General Club or Society, and pay into the Hands of such Person or Persons as shall be lawfully appointed to receive the same, all such Sum and Sums Weekly and every Week as shall be hereinafter specified; that is to say, every Male Person on his attaining the Age of Twenty-one Years, or who shall receive to and for his own Use and Benefit the Daily Hire of or more than Ten Pence by the Day, or being a domestic Servant, shall receive the clear Wages of One Shilling and Six Pence by the Week, or Four Pounds by the Year, shall pay, or cause to be paid, into the common Fund of the said Club or Society the Sum of *Two Pence* Weekly, and every Female Person on her attaining the Age of Twenty-one Years, or who shall receive to and for her own Use and Benefit the Daily Hire of or more than ' *Five Pence* by the Day, or being a domestic Servant, shall receive the clear Wages of One Shilling and Three Pence by the Week, or the Sum of Three Pounds by the Year, shall pay, or cause to be paid, into the common Fund of the said Club or Society, the Sum of *Three Halfpence* Weekly, under ' *such* Penalty ' *or Penalties as hereinafter mentioned:* Provided always, That such Persons, whether Male or Female, as shall through Sickness or Accident

' Six Pence ' the ' of.
be

be incapable of maintaining themselves, and such as shall be above the Age of *Thirty*, or being married, shall have One or more Children, shall not be compellable to become Subscribers to the said Fund: Provided nevertheless, That such married Persons as shall have a Child or Children may become voluntary Subscribers to the said Fund, but shall not be entitled to any Allowance in respect of their Child or Children, in Manner as hereinafter mentioned, excepting for such Child or Children, as shall have been born in lawful Wedlock *Nine Months* at least after the Commencement of his or her Subscription: Provided also, that every Person, whether Male or Female, who shall be of the Age of *Thirty Years*, and under *Fifty Years*, and in a sound and perfect State of Health, may and shall be permitted to become a voluntary Subscriber to the said Club or Society upon the Payment of *One Year's* Subscription by Way of Entrance Money, together with *an additional Shilling* for every Year which such Person shall have attained beyond the Age of *Thirty Years* at the Time of such Entrance.

And, in order to guard as much as may be against the Admission of improper Persons into the said Club or Society, as such voluntary Subscribers as aforesaid, Be it Enacted by the Authority aforesaid, That all Persons who shall be desirous of becoming such voluntary Subscribers shall apply for such Admission to the Minister, Churchwardens, and Overseers of their respective Parishes, who shall and may, and are hereby impowered and authorized to admit, or to refuse to admit, all such Persons so applying, as they in their Discretion and Judgment shall think right and fit, the said Ministers, Churchwardens, and Overseers respectively, having been first duly sworn (and which Oath any neighbouring Justice of the Peace is hereby impowered to administer) " to act in the Discharge of this public Trust according " to the best of their Skill and Judgment, without Favour or " Affection, Prejudice or Malice:" Provided always, That no Person shall be admitted as such voluntary Subscriber as aforesaid, unless with the unanimous Approbation and Consent of the said Minister and Parish Officers.

And be it also Enacted by the Authority aforesaid, That all Persons whether Male, or Female, *who shall be seised or possessed of any Freehold or Leasehold Estate of or above the Value of Ten Pounds a Year*, or *who shall be possessed of* Property of the Value of One thousand Pounds Sterling or upwards, shall be compellable to
contribute

contribute the Sum of *Three Pence* per Week, and to increase that Contribution by *One Penny* by the Week for every Thousand Pounds Sterling of which he or she shall be possessed, provided that the Whole of such Contribution or Subscription do not amount to more than the Sum of *One Shilling* by the Week; and also, that no Parish Officer whose proper Business it may be to make a Valuation of such Personal Property, shall rate any
7 Person or Persons any higher, in respect of the same, than such Officer shall be ready to declare (upon Oath, if required) he in his Conscience and bonâ fide believes them to be worth.

And be it further Enacted by the Authority aforesaid, That in Consideration of the several and respective Subscriptions hereby made payable, the several and respective Subscribers shall be entitled to receive, and shall be paid, the several and respective Allowances hereinafter mentioned, according to the Table marked (N° 1.) in the Schedule hereto annexed, which Schedule is hereby declared to be a Part of this Act (that is to say) every Female Subscriber of Three Halfpence by the Week, for and during so long a Time as she shall by Sickness or Accident, not brought on by any unlawful Action, be confined to her Room, and be incapable of Labour, shall be entitled to, and be paid the Weekly Sum of *Three Shillings*; and for and during any subsequent Time that she shall, through the same, or any other Sickness, Accident, or Infirmity, be rendered incapable of earning the
8 Sum of Three Pence by the Day, in the Opinion of the Minister, Churchwardens, and Overseers, or the Majority of them (and who, assisted by the Advice and Opinion of the Parish Apothecary hereinafter mentioned, shall, in these, and in all Cases of the like Nature, judge of and determine the same) be entitled to the Weekly Allowance of *Two Shillings*, so long as that Incapacity shall continue; and also immediately from and after she shall have arrived at the Age of Sixty-five Years, shall be entitled to the Weekly Sum of *Ten Pence Halfpenny*; and from and after the Age of Seventy (or at any Time before, when she shall, in the Opinion of the Persons before mentioned, be rendered incapable, through any Accident or Infirmity, of earning more than Three Pence by the Day) be entitled to the Weekly Sum of *One Shilling and Four Pence Halfpenny*; and from and after the Age of Seventy-five, shall be entitled to the Weekly Sum of *Three Shillings* during Life, and also to the like Sum of *Three Shillings* by the
9 Week, at any Time before the Age of Seventy-five, in case she shall, through Sickness or Infirmity, be deemed and adjudged, by the

the Perſons before mentioned, to be wholly incapable of Labour; and ſuch Subſcriber, under the Reſtrictions before mentioned, ſhall alſo be entitled to receive, for every Child more than *Two*, who ſhall be living at the ſame Time, and ſhall have been born in lawful Wedlock, and be under *Eight* Years of Age, the Weekly Sum of *One Shilling* in her own Right.

And be it further Enacted by the Authority aforeſaid, That every Subſcriber of *Two Pence* by the Week, whether Male or Female, ſhall be entitled to receive in the Firſt Inſtance, as above mentioned, the Weekly Sum of *Six Shillings*, and in the Second Inſtance, during ſuch Male Subſcriber's Incapacity of earning by his Labour the Daily Sum of *Six Pence*, or during ſuch Female Subſcriber's Incapacity of earning by her Labour the Daily Sum of *Three Pence*, ſuch Male and Female Subſcribers ſhall be reſpectively entitled to receive the Weekly Sum of *Three Shillings*, and for every Child more than *Two*, who ſhall be living at the ſame Time, ſuch reſpective Subſcriber ſhall be entitled, under the Reſtrictions before mentioned, to *One Shilling and Four Pence Halfpenny* by the Week, in his or her own Right; and from and after the Age of Sixty-five, ſuch Subſcriber, whether Male or Female, ſhall be entitled to receive *One Shilling* a Week; and from and after the Age of Seventy, *One Shilling and Seven Pence Halfpenny* by the Week, or at any earlier Period of Life during ſuch Male Subſcriber's Inability to earn the Weekly Sum of *Six Pence*, and during ſuch Female Subſcriber's Incapacity to earn the Weekly Sum of *Three Pence*; and from and after the Age of Seventy-five, or at any earlier Period, upon ſuch Male or Female Subſcriber's becoming, in the Judgment of the Perſons before mentioned, incapable of any Labour, ſuch Male or Female Subſcriber ſhall be entitled to *Three Shillings and Six Pence* by the Week during Life.

And be it Enacted by the Authority aforeſaid, That in caſe of the Death of either of the Parents of ſuch Children as aforeſaid, the Survivor, whether Father or Mother, ſhall be entitled to receive the Allowance allotted for and in reſpect of Children, in like Manner as if both the Parents were ſtill living; and in caſe of the Death of both Parents, all Orphan Children of ſuch ſubſcribing Parents, as ſhall be left unprovided for, ſhall be entitled to the Pay allotted to their Parents Subſcription, until they ſhall have attained the Age of *Eight* Years reſpectively, deducting, in each of the Two next before-mentioned Caſes, ſuch Sum or Sums as the Parent or Parents muſt have continued to ſubſcribe

B Weekly,

Weekly, had such Parent or Parents been still living; and if it shall so happen that the said Allowances shall be more than sufficient for the Purposes of Nurture of the said Orphan Children, the same shall be applied for the Benefit of such Orphan Children, in such Manner as the Minister, Churchwardens, and Overseers for the Time being of each Parish respectively, with the Consent and Allowance of One or more neighbouring Justice or Justices of the Peace shall think fit, to order and direct: Provided always, That no Person or Persons shall be entitled to any Allowance in any of the above-mentioned Instances, excepting in the Third relating to Children, unless such Person or Persons shall make it appear, to the Satisfaction of the Minister, Churchwardens, and Overseers of the Parish where he or she may reside, that he or she is not worth the Sum of *One thousand Pounds*, nor has an Income, arising from any other Source whatever, amounting in the Whole to the Sum of *Fifty Pounds* a Year; nor shall any Person or Persons in the Fourth and Fifth Instances be entitled to any Allowance on Account of Age, who shall not in like Manner make it appear, to the Satisfaction of the Persons above-mentioned, that he or she is not possessed of the Sum of *Five hundred Pounds*, nor has an Income, arising from any Source whatever, of *Twenty-five Pounds* a Year: Provided nevertheless, That it shall and may be lawful for the Justices of the Peace assembled at any Quarter Sessions, on the unanimous Application of the Minister, Churchwardens, and Overseers of the Parish where any Person or Persons of either of the Descriptions above mentioned may reside, to order such Payment or Payments to be made out of the Funds as such Person or Persons Weekly Subscriptions would otherwise have entitled him, her, or them to receive: Provided also, That no Man, except he shall have *Two* Children to maintain, and that no Woman, except she shall have One Child to maintain, shall, in the First Instance above mentioned, receive full Pay for any longer Time than *Four Months* on Account of any One Fit of Sickness, but from and after the Expiration of the said *Four Months* shall receive such Pay only as is provided in the Second Instance, and denominated Walking Pay.

And be it further Enacted, That in case any Man, having *Two* Children to maintain, or any Woman, having One Child to maintain, shall become or be made an In Patient of any Hospital or Infirmary, he or she shall be still entitled to receive his or her full Pay during such Confinement; but in case any Man having

ing One Child only to maintain, or any Woman having no Child to maintain, should become or be made such In Patient of any Hospital or Infirmary as aforesaid, then he or she shall be entitled to receive, during his or her Confinement, such Pay only as is denominated Walking Pay.

And be it Enacted by the Authority aforesaid, That in case the Widow of any Subscriber, being herself a Subscriber, should be left with any Number of Children less than *Three*, such Widow shall be entitled to receive *One Shilling* by the Week for One Child, and *Two Shillings* by the Week for Two Children, and if such Widow shall be left with the Number of *Three* or more Children, she shall be entitled to *Six Pence* by the Week for each of *Two* Children out of that Number, and for each Child above *Two* she shall be entitled to the Allowance appropriated to the Parents Subscription, that is to say, where both Parents shall have been Subscribers of *Two Pence* by the Week each, the Widow shall be entitled to receive *Three Shillings and Nine Pence* by the Week for *Three* Children, *Six Shillings and Six Pence* by the Week for *Four* Children, and a proportionate Increase of *Two Shillings and Nine Pence* by the Week for every Child; but in case One of the Parents should have been a Subscriber of *Two Pence*, and the other only *Three Halfpence* by the Week, then such Widow shall be entitled to receive only *Three Shillings and Four Pence Halfpenny* by the Week for *Three* Children, *Five Shillings and Nine Pence* for *Four* Children, and a proportionate Increase of *Two Shillings and Four Pence Half-penny* for every Child, as long as such Child or Children shall respectively be under *Eight* Years of Age.

And be it also Enacted, That it shall and may be lawful for the several Parish Officers, in their respective Parishes, to lay out and expend, from the Stock of the said Club or Society, the Sum of *Twenty Shillings*, for and towards the Expence of the Funeral of every Subscriber, whether Male or Female, who shall be entitled to receive any Allowance by virtue of his or her Subscription.

And whereas it may tend greatly to the public Advantage to have able and proper Persons appointed to take Care of the Sick Poor, and supply them with such Medicines as may be necessary; Be it also Enacted by the Authority aforesaid, That from and after the *Twenty-ninth Day of September One thousand Seven hundred and Eighty-seven* it shall and may be lawful for the Minister, Churchwardens, and Overseers of each respective Parish, to agree

with

with some Apothecary, upon such Terms as may be thought fit and reasonable, who shall, in pursuance of such Agreement be always obliged, upon proper Notice, to attend, take Care of, and supply with necessary Medicines and Dressings, all such Poor of his respective Parish as shall require his Assistance, and also all such Subscribers to the said Club or Society, who, in the Opinion of the Minister, Churchwardens, and Overseers, or a Majority of them, shall be deemed to be not well able to pay for such Assistance; and that *One Moiety* of the Annual Salary of the said Apothecary shall be discharged out of the Poor Rate of the Parish where such Agreement shall be made, and *the other Moiety* out of the Fund arising from the Weekly Subscriptions of the Members of the said Club or Society.

18. And be it Enacted by the Authority aforesaid, That upon any Subscriber's being taken ill, or meeting with any Accident whatsoever, and notifying the same to the Minister, or, in his Absence, to one of the Parish Officers of the Parish to which such Subscriber shall belong, One of such Parish Officers, on such Notice being given, shall, as soon as conveniently may be * after receiving such Notice (under the Penalty of *any Sum not exceeding Ten Shillings*, to be forfeited to the Use of the Poor of the said Parish) be obliged to attend, or to find some proper Person to attend for him, and examine the Situation and Condition of such Subscriber, and give such Directions for his or her Relief as the Case may require; and, if Need be, the said Minister or Parish Officer, or such proper Person appointed by the Minister and Parish Officer as above-mentioned, shall and may, and is hereby authorized to send for and require the Attendance and Assistance of the Parish Apothecary, in taking Care of and providing proper
19. Medicines and Dressings for such Subscriber, the Expence of sending for which Parish Apothecary shall be defrayed out of the Fund belonging to the said Club or Society.

And, for the Purpose of making effectual Provision for the regular and successive Receipts and Payments of all such Subscriptions and Allowances as are by this Act appointed to be received and paid, Be it further Enacted by the Authority aforesaid, That on every Sunday immediately after Evening Service, the several Parish Officers who by virtue of their said Office shall be considered as, and are hereby appointed to be, Treasurers of the said

---

* but within the Space of ,

Club

Club or Society, shall attend at their respective Parish Churches for the Purpose of receiving all such Subscriptions and Contributions as aforesaid (which the Subscribers and Contributors above mentioned shall be and are hereby accordingly obliged to pay to the said Treasurers) which shall be due, and of paying all Allowances, and discharging all Claims that shall be due from the said Club or Society, and shall then and there enter into a Folio Parchment Book or Books, to be purchased at the Expence of each Parish respectively, and marked and ruled in such Manner as is described in the Table marked (N° 2) in the Schedule hereunto annexed, which Schedule is hereby declared to be a Part of this Act, all such Sums as shall have been received or paid, with the Names of the several Subscribers so paying or receiving the same.

And be it further Enacted by the Authority aforesaid, That in case any or either of the said Parish Officers shall be called out of his or their respective Parish or Parishes upon any necessary Business to be done for or on Account of the said Club or Society, he or they shall receive such reasonable Compensation for the Trouble and Expence attending the same, as One or more neighbouring Justice or Justices shall order and direct, the said Compensation to be made out of the Money collected for the Poor Rate of such Parish or Parishes respectively, at such Times and by such Persons as are hereinafter mentioned.

And forasmuch as it may happen that the Person or Persons appointed to be Parish Officers may be unfit and not qualified to discharge the Duties of the Trust hereby intended to be reposed in them; Be it Enacted by the Authority aforesaid, That the Parishioners of every Parish respectively, in Vestry duly assembled, may and are hereby required to judge and determine of the proper Capacity or Incapacity of any Churchwarden or Overseer of the said Parish to discharge the Duties of the Office hereby created; and in case of such Vestry having determined that any or all of such Parish Officers is or are incapable, it shall and may be lawful for the said Vestry to nominate and appoint some other fit and proper Person or Persons to execute the said Office, and to make him or them such Compensation for the same, out of the Poor Rates of the said Parish, as any One or more Justice or Justices shall order and direct: Provided always, That subsequent to the Nomination of such Vestry, and previous to the Appointment of such Officers, the Minister shall

C

shall declare his Approbation or Disapprobation of such Appointment, in Writing under his Hand, in the Words following, or to the like Effect :

" I   Minister of the Parish of
"   do declare, That I sincerely believe that A. B. is
" [or is not, as the Case may be] a fit Person to discharge
" the Office of Treasurer of the Fund for the Use of the
" Poor."

And in case of his Disapprobation, the Matter shall be enquired into, and the Propriety of his Conduct determined, by any Two or more neighbouring Justices of the Peace.

And whereas it is just and reasonable that some Compensation should be made for the Execution of a new and troublesome Office; Be it Enacted, That every Person who shall be duly appointed to, and faithfully discharge, the Office of Treasurer as aforesaid (excepting such Person or Persons as shall execute the same for Hire, and in that Case then the Person hiring) shall be entitled to an Exemption from a certain Portion of Statute Labour for the Repair of the Highways in the Parish where such Officer shall reside, according to the Number of Subscribers within such Parish; that is to say, where the Number of Subscribers shall not amount to *Two hundred*, the Parish Officer or Officers attending and executing the Duty of the said Office shall not be entitled to any Exemption, but where the Subscribers shall amount to the Number of *Two hundred* or more, and be less than *Four hundred*, the said Attendance and Performance shall exempt the said Officer or Officers from One Year's Statute Labour on the Highways of the said Parish for One Plough Land, and where the said Subscribers shall amount to or exceed *Four hundred*, and be fewer than *Six Hundred*, such Officer or Officers shall be exempt from One Year's Statute Labour on the Highways for Two Plough Lands for such Attendance and Performance, and where the said Subscribers shall amount to or exceed *Six hundred*, and be fewer than *Eight hundred*, such Officer or Officers shall be exempt from One Year's Statute Labour on the Highways of the said Parish for Three Plough Lands, and shall be entitled to a proportionate Exemption of One Year's Statute Labour on the Highways of the said Parish, for every additional Number of *Two hundred* Subscribers therein; and in case One Parish Officer shall perform the Whole of the Duty, such Parish Officer shall be entitled to the Whole of the said Exemption, and where Two

Officers

Officers or more shall perform the Duty, the Benefit of the Exemption shall be equally divided between them.

And be it further Enacted, That any Person not above the Condition of a Day Labourer, who, under the Provisions of this Act, shall become a Subscriber to the said Club or Society of a Weekly Sum not exceeding *Two Pence*, shall be wholly exempt from the Performance of Statute Labour on the Highways in any Parish whatsoever, and from any Composition in lieu thereof, so long as such Person shall continue to be such Subscriber of a Weekly Sum not exceeding *Two Pence*.

And be it further Enacted, That Yearly and every Year, at the Petty Sessions of the Justices of the Peace, which shall be held in Easter Week for the Purpose of granting Nomination Warrants to the several Parish Officers then newly appointed and chosen, the several Parish Officers who shall have discharged the Office of Treasurer or Treasurers of the Fund of the said Society shall exhibit their respective Accounts, and shall then and there, before the said Justices, be severally sworn to their respective Receipts, Allowances, and Payments, and the said Accounts, being duly examined, and found by the said Justices to be true and just, shall be signed and allowed by them accordingly.

And whereas it is probable that, for some considerable Time from and after the passing of this Act, the Weekly Receipts of the several Sums subscribed will greatly exceed the several Allowances to be made in Consideration of such Subscriptions; Be it further Enacted, That the several Parish Officers, whose Business it may be as Treasurers to receive the Weekly Contributions of the several Subscribers, shall pay into the Hands of the Parochial Collectors of the Land Tax, at least *Four Times* in the Year, or as often as the said Collectors shall be called upon to pay in their respective Collections, all such Sums as shall be in their Hands respectively, over and above the Subscriptions and Contributions for and in respect of *One Month*, which Sum shall always be and remain in the Hands of the said Treasurers, as and for a Provision for accidental and contingent Expences.

And be it further Enacted, That the said Collectors of the Land Tax, or any One or more of them, whom the said Parish Officers may think fit to intrust with the same, shall pay over the said Surplus, without Fee or Reward, into the Hands of the
Treasurer

Treasurer of each respective County, and take his Receipt for the same, which Receipt shall be put into and kept in the Chest belonging to each respective Parish.

And be it further Enacted by the Authority aforesaid, That the said County Treasurer shall, within *Twenty Days* after the Receipt of the said Surplus Money as aforesaid, cause the same to be invested in and paid into the Hands of the Governor and
27 Company of the Bank of England, in the Name or Names of the Representative or Representatives in Parliament of each respective County for the Time being, and the said County Treasurer shall, and he is hereby likewise required forthwith to publish in some One or more of the public News-papers within the said County, a true and just Account of all such Surplus Monies so by him received and paid as aforesaid, and as soon as it may be conveniently done, after each Quarter Day, the several aggregate Sums of the respective Counties throughout England shall be published, by the Treasurers of each respective County, in the London Gazette.

And, forasmuch as it is probable, that for a considerable Time from and after the passing of this Act there will be a continual Accumulation of such Surplus Monies as are above mentioned; for the better Security and improving the said Surplus Monies, Be it Enacted, That the several Persons who shall be Representatives in Parliament for the several Counties in England
28 and Wales, and Town of Berwick upon Tweed, shall be, and they are hereby appointed to be Commissioners for the Purpose of receiving the said Surplus Monies, and the Interest which shall from Time to Time accrue from the same and of laying out and investing the same, or so much of the same as shall not be required by their respective Counties for the Support of the Subscribers thereunto belonging, in such one or more of the public Funds as may appear to them to be most proper and advantageous, and the said Commissioners are hereby required to lay out and invest in such one or more of the public Funds as aforesaid the Produce of such Accumulation as aforesaid, Once at least in every Quarter of the Year; and the said Commissioners are hereby further impowered and required, as often as Need shall be, to draw out from the said Bank or public Funds such Sums of Money as shall from Time to Time be necessary for the Purposes of supplying the Exigencies of the said Clubs within their respective Counties; and in case it shall at any Time happen,
29 that the Disbursements of the Parish Officers shall exceed their

Receipts,

[13]

Receipts, it shall and may be lawful to and for any *Two* or more Justices of the Peace of the Division, at any Petty Sessions to be held within any County, upon a Representation made by any Parochial Treasurer or Treasurers of each respective Parish within the said Division, to order the Treasurer of the County wherein such Division shall lie to advance and pay unto the said Parochial Treasurer or Treasurers such Sum or Sums of Money as shall be wanting to supply the Deficiency of the said Subscription Fund within the said Parish, and the said County Treasurer is hereby impowered and required to apply to the respective Representative or Representatives of the said County for Monies suitable to such Exigencies, which Representative and Representatives is and are hereby impowered and required to issue the same accordingly. '

And

' And whereas, in the Cities of London and Westminster, and also in several other Cities and great Trading Towns, 30 namely,

House Rent, and almost all the Necessaries of Life, are at a much higher Rate than in other Parts of the Kingdom; for the better and more effectual Relief of the Poor belonging to such Cities and Towns, Be it Enacted by the Authority aforesaid, That every Female Subscriber belonging to the City of London or Westminster, or to any Parish within the Distance of   Miles from the same, shall, in Right of her Weekly Subscription of
    be entitled to receive, over and above the Allowances hereinbefore mentioned, the Weekly Addition in the First Instance of   in the Second Instance of   in the Third of
    in the Fourth of
        in the Fifth of   in the 31
Sixth of   and also every Subscriber of   by the Week shall be entitled to receive the same additional Sums Weekly, in each of the several

And be it Enacted by the Authority aforesaid, That in case any Subscriber shall refuse, or wilfully neglect to pay his or her Subscription, for any longer Time than *Two Months* after the same shall become due, such Subscriber shall not, under any Sickness or Accident, be entitled to any Allowance or Benefit out of the said Fund for that Time, nor at any Time after, until he or she shall have first paid up and discharged all the Arrears of his or her Subscription; and in case any Subscriber shall wilfully neglect or refuse to pay his or her Subscription or Arrears as aforesaid, for more than *Twelve Months*, such Subscriber shall be forthwith considered and put on a Footing with a Non Subscriber. '

And

ral Instances; and every other Class of Subscribers (under such as shall subscribe the Sum of Seven Pence by the Week) shall be entitled to receive the same additional Sums Weekly in each of the several Instances as above mentioned; and every Subscriber belonging to any or either of the other Cities or great Trading Towns above specified shall, in Right of her Weekly Subscription of   be entitled to receive, over and above the Allowances hereinbefore mentioned, the Weekly Addition, in the First Instance, of
            in the Second Instance of
            in the Third of   in the Fourth and Fifth of   each, and in the Sixth of   and so also every other Class of Subscribers (below such as shall subscribe the Sum of Seven Pence by the Week) shall be entitled to receive the same additional Sums Weekly in each of the several Instances as above mentioned.

' and moreover it shall and may be lawful for the Parish Officer, or such Person as may be properly and duly appointed to receive the Weekly Subscriptions, and he is hereby authorized and required to call upon the Employer of any such Subscriber for any Sum that he or she may be in Arrear as aforesaid, and from and immediately after the making of such Demand the said Employer shall be answerable for the same, provided he or she shall be indebted so much to such Subscriber; and upon Complaint to One or more Justice or Justices of the Peace, of the wilful Neglect or Refusal of any Person hereby made compellable to subscribe to the said Fund, to pay his said Subscription Money, or of his or her Employer to pay

And be it further Enacted, That no Person, whether Male or Female, who shall refuse or neglect to subscribe as soon as he or she shall become competent thereto, shall be admitted afterwards into the said Club or Society, until he or she shall first have paid, by way of Entrance Money, ⁷ *One Half* of his or her Annual Subscription for every Year that he or she shall have refused or neglected to subscribe, from the Time of his or her Competency to become a Subscriber; but as it may often happen that idle and improvident Persons may not have Money sufficient to discharge at once the Whole of the Sum required for their Entrance Money as above mentioned, though willing to become Subscribers, it shall and may be lawful for the Minister, Churchwardens, and Overseers of the said Parish, to admit any such Person to become a Subscriber, on his or her advancing the Sum of *One Penny* by the Week over and above their Weekly Subscriptions, until such Entrance Money shall be paid up.

And forasmuch as nothing but ⁸ *an improper* Reliance on Parish Pay can render any Persons (not excempted as before mentioned)⁹ obstinate in refusing or neglecting to subscribe; Be it Enacted by the Authority aforesaid, That all such Persons as shall obstinately refuse or neglect to subscribe, being competent thereto, shall be excluded from all Parochial Relief, and

pay the same, on the Behalf of such Person, the Sum so neglected or refused to be paid as aforesaid shall be recoverable of the Party so neglecting or refusing, by Warrant of Distress, under the Hand and Seal, or Hands and Seals, of the said Justice or Justices, to be issued for that Purpose, and likewise for the Purpose of recovering the Amount of the Sum so neglected or refused to be paid, as a Penalty for such Neglect or Refusal, together with the Costs procured, by Means of preferring, hearing, and determining the said Complaint, and of executing the said Warrant of Distress; and the said Justice or Justices is and are hereby authorized and required to administer the Oaths that may be requisite for the Attainment of Justice between the Parties to the Proceeding, without Fee or Reward: Provided always, that it shall and may be lawful to and for such Employer as aforesaid to deduct out of the Wages due to the Person employed the Money which shall have been paid on his or her Behalf, by such Employer, on Demand as aforesaid.

⁷ the Sum of , ⁸ a profligate

either

either be left to the casual Support of voluntary Beneficence, or
36 shall, on the first Application for Relief, be sent to the Workhouse of the Parish or District (if there be any) and if not, then to the Workhouse of some neighbouring Parish or District where he or she can be received, the Master or Mistress of which is hereby required to admit him or her on such Terms as any neighbouring Justice of the Peace, on Application made to him for ascertaining the same, may think reasonable, and the Person so to be placed in such Workhouse shall not be permitted to depart thence until, by the Profits of his or her Labour, he or she shall have reimbursed his or her respective Parish for the Expence and Charges that may have been incurred by placing and keeping him or her in such Workhouse as aforesaid.

And whereas it may tend to promote the general Good of the Community, and to encourage Persons to become Subscribers to the Fund of the said Club or Society, to permit all such Persons as shall be Subscribers to the said Fund to reside in such Parishes as
37 they may think proper, under certain Restrictions; Be it Enacted, That from and after *the Twenty-ninth Day of September One thousand Seven hundred and Eighty-seven*, it shall and may be lawful for every such Subscriber to go to and reside in any Parish where it may be most convenient to such Subscriber so to do, and such Subscriber shall be irremoveable therefrom by any Order of Justices, so long as he or she shall continue to pay his or her said Subscription Money in such Parish or Place, according to the Regulations herein contained: Provided always, that such Subscriber, on changing his or her Residence, shall take with him or her a Certificate, signifying that he or she is a Subscriber to the said Fund, in the said Parish from whence he or she shall so remove, and specifying the Amount of his or her Subscription, and the latest Period at which it shall have been paid, to the Intent that from the Date thereof such Subscriber may continue his or her Subscription in the Parish to which he or she may go
38 to reside, and may there have the same Benefit, in Consequence thereof, as Occasion may require, that he or she would have derived from a Continuance of Subscription in the Parish from whence he or she came.

And, in order to prevent all Fraud and Imposition in the granting such Certificates as aforesaid, Be it further Enacted, That all such Certificates shall be signed by the Minister and Two of the Parish Officers of each Parish respectively, with all convenient Dispatch, after Request made by such Subscriber as aforesaid,

aforesaid, for the Purpose of enabling him or her to change his or her Residence as aforesaid, and that all and every Person who shall wilfully and fraudulently grant such Certificate, or who shall wilfully forge the Signature or Signatures of the Minister or Parish Officer or Officers to any such Certificate, shall be deemed and adjudged to be an incorrigible Rogue, and shall be punishable as such by virtue of any Law now in being, or which shall hereafter be in Force for the Restraint of Vagrancy, and that any Person who is hereby required to obtain such Certificate as aforesaid shall be compellable to produce the same to the Constable of any Place where such Person shall happen to be, on reasonable Demand made thereof by such Constable; and in case such Person as aforesaid shall refuse to produce to the said Constable such Certificate as aforesaid, on reasonable Demand by him made for that Purpose, the Party so refusing shall be deemed, and is hereby declared to be, in the first Instance, an idle and disorderly Person, and shall for every successive Refusal be deemed to be guilty of a repeated Act of Vagrancy, and shall be punishable accordingly by virtue of any Law now in being, or shall hereafter be in Force for the Restraint of Vagrancy. 39

And be it further Enacted, That in case such Certificate as aforesaid shall not be granted with all convenient Dispatch, after Request made as aforesaid, it shall and may be lawful for such Subscriber, whose said Request shall not have been complied with, to apply to One or more neighbouring Justice or Justices, who is and are hereby impowered and required to order the Person withholding such Certificate forthwith to grant the same. 40

And, to guard as much as possible against Impositions on the Fund belonging to the said Club or Society, from such Subscribers as might claim such Allowance, as is termed Walking Pay, without any Necessity for their so doing, Be it Enacted by the Authority aforesaid, That all such Subscribers as shall refuse to work at any such Employments as they shall be deemed capable of without Injury to their Health, in the Judgment of the Parish Officers of the Parishes where they may respectively reside, or to which they shall respectively belong, shall be liable to have ⁹ *One Half* of what they may be offered by the Day for their Labour in such Employments as they shall, without sufficient Reason, refuse to

⁹ the 𝔖um of

E be

be employed in, deducted from their Weekly Allowance of Walking Pay: Provided always, That it shall and may be
41 lawful for every Subscriber who shall think himself or herself aggrieved by the Offer of [10] *any or of any* improper Employment, to apply to any One or more neighbouring Justice or Justices of the Peace, who is and are hereby authorized and impowered to hear and determine all such Differences and Disputes as may arise between the several and respective Parish Officers, and the Subscribers to the said Club or Society.

CLAUSE (A) *Provided always, and be it Enacted, That no Relief to be given to any such Subscriber as aforesaid shall be deemed or taken to be Alms, for the Purpose of disqualifying such Person from voting at any Election of Members to serve in Parliament.*

And, forasmuch as it may tend to prevent much Fraud and Injustice, if Bastard Children were to follow the Settlement of their respective Mothers, and not be settled in the Parish where they may happen to be born; Be it further Enacted by the Authority aforesaid, That every Bastard Child which shall be born from and after the *Twenty-ninth Day of September One thousand Seven hundred and Eighty-seven* shall be deemed and adjudged to be settled in that Parish where the Mother of such Bastard Child shall have gained her last legal Settlement.

And, for making a more effectual Provision for the proper Employment of the Poor, Be it Enacted, That from and after the *Twenty-ninth Day of September One thousand Seven hundred and*
42 *Eighty-seven,* when and as often as any Poor Person, whether Male or Female, shall apply to the said Churchwardens, Overseers, or any of them, for Employment, they shall be, and are hereby required to provide such Employment as may be fitting and proper for such Poor Person, upon the Terms and in the Manner hereinafter mentioned; that is to say, That in case any Poor Man *or Woman,* who is accustomed to earn the Sum of *One Shilling* or more by the Day (over and above the usual Allowance for Liquor) shall apply to a Churchwarden or Overseer at a seasonable Hour on the Evening, and declare that he *or she* is in Want of Employment for the succeeding Day, and that he *or she* is willing and ready to work at any Employment,

[10] an

that

[19]

according to the Direction of the said Parish Officer, for the Consideration of *such Daily or Weekly Pay as his or her ordinary Labour and Industry were wont to earn, and as he or she is able at the Time of such Application to earn* by the Day, then and in such Case the said Parish Officer is hereby authorized and required to procure him *or her* such Employment, or for Want thereof to pay him *or her a certain Daily or Weekly Subsistence, either in Provisions or in Money, not to exceed Six Pence per Diem*, until such Employment can be procured "; and also, in case any Poor Man usually earning less than *One Shilling* by the Day, or any poor Woman usually earning less than *Six Pence* by the Day, shall apply in Manner as above mentioned, and shall declare his or her Readiness to work for the Consideration of *Two Thirds* of the Sum which they usually earn, in such Case the said Parish Officer shall be, and hereby is required to provide proper Employment for him or her, or pay him or her a Sum daily, which shall be equal to *One Half* of their usual Earnings, the several Sums so to be paid on the Occasions aforesaid to be taken out of the Monies which shall be raised in each Parish respectively for the Use of the Poor: Provided always, That if any Person or Persons shall find himself, herself, or themselves aggrieved, by any Matter or Thing done or omitted to be done in the Execution of this Act, it shall and may be lawful for the Party so aggrieved to appeal to the next General Quarter Sessions of the Peace to be held for the County, City, or Place where such Grievance shall have arisen, giving reasonable Notice to the Party or Parties to be appealed against of his, her, or their Intention to appeal, specifying in the said Notice the Cause of such Appeal ; and the Justices at the said General Quarter Sessions shall have full Power to hear and determine the same, and to award such Costs to the Party or Parties appealing, or appealed against, as the said Justices shall think

44

" in like Manner also, in case any Poor Woman who is accustomed to earn the Sum of   or more by the Day shall apply for Employment in Manner as above mentioned, and declare that she is ready and willing to be employed for the Consideration of   by the Day, in such Case the said Parish Officer is hereby authorized and required to procure her some proper Employment, or in Default thereof to pay her   Daily, until he shall have procured her such proper Employment.

43

fit;

fit; and the Determination of the said Justices shall be final and conclusive to all Intents and Purposes whatsoever, and the Order made therein shall not be removeable by Writ of Certiorari.

And be it further Enacted, That where any Distress shall be made for any Sum or Sums of Money to be levied by virtue of this Act, the Distress itself shall not be deemed unlawful, nor the Party or Parties making the same be deemed a Trespasser or Trespassers, on Account of any Default or Want of Form in any Proceedings relating thereto; nor shall the Party or Parties distraining be deemed a Trespasser or Trespassers, ab initio, on Account of any Irregularity which shall be afterwards done by the Party or Parties distraining; but the Person or Persons aggrieved by such Irregularity may recover full Satisfaction for the special Damage in an Action on the Case: Provided always, that no Plaintiff or Plaintiffs shall recover in any Action for such Irregularity, if sufficient Tender of Amends shall have been made to him, her, or them, by or on Behalf of the Defendant or Defendants, before such Action brought.

46 And be it further Enacted by the Authority aforesaid, That if any Action or Suit shall be commenced or prosecuted against any Person or Persons, for any Matter or Thing to be done in pursuance of this Act, every such Action or Suit shall be commenced within *Six Calendar Months* next after the Cause of Action shall have arisen, and not afterwards, and shall be laid and tried in the County, City, or Place where the same shall arise, and not elsewhere, and the Defendant or Defendants in such Action or Suit may plead the General Issue, and give this Act and the special Matter in Evidence at any Trial to be had thereupon, and that the Matter or Thing for which such Action or Suit shall be commenced was done in pursuance and by the Authority of this Act; and if the same shall appear to have been so done, or if any such Action or Suit shall be brought or commenced after the Time before limited for bringing the same, or shall be laid in any other County or Place than as aforesaid, then and in every

47 such Case the Jury shall find for the Defendant or Defendants, and upon such Verdict, or if the Plaintiff or Plaintiffs shall be nonsuited, or suffer a Discontinuance of his, her, or their Action or Suit, after the Defendants or Defendants shall have appeared, or if upon Demurrer Judgment shall be given against the Plaintiff or Plaintiffs, the Defendant or Defendants shall have *Treble* Costs, and shall have such Remedy for the same as any Defendant or Defendants hath or have for Costs of Suit in any other Cases by Law.

SCHEDULE,

[21]

SCHEDULE, Nº I.

Shall be entitled to receive Weekly;

The Weekly Subscribers of	In the First Instance, viz. Bed-lying Pay.	In the Second Instance, viz. Walking Pay.	In the Third Instance, viz. For Children more than Two.	In the Fourth Instance, viz. For 65 Years of Age.	In the Fifth Instance, viz. For 70 Years of Age. *	In the Sixth Instance, viz. For 75 Years of Age. †
S. D.	S. D.	S. D.	S. D.	S. D.	S. D.	S. D.
— 1½	4 —	2 —	1 —	— 10½	1 4½	3 —
— 2	6 —	3 —	1 4½	1 —	1 7½	3 6
— 3	7 6	3 6	1 7½	1 1¾	1 9	4 —
— 4	8 6	3 9	1 9	1 3	1 10	4 4½
— 5	9 —	4 —	1 10	1 4	1 11	4 9
— 6	9 4½	4 3	1 11	1 5	2 —	5 —
— 7	9 9	4 6	2 —	1 6	2 1	5 3
— 8	10 —	4 7½	2 1	1 7	2 2	5 6
— 9	10 3	4 9	2 2	1 8	2 3	5 9
— 10	10 6	4 10½	2 3	1 9	2 4	6 —
— 11	10 9	4 11	2 4½	1 10	2 5	6 3
1 —	11 —	5 —	2 5	1 11	2 6	6 6

* Or at any Time before, in case the Subscriber shall not be able to earn, the Man   or the Woman

† Or at any Time before, that a Subscriber shall be rendered incapable of all Labour.

F   SCHEDULE,

SCHEDULE, N° 2.

FORM of the Parish Accounts for Receipts.

Number of Weeks received.	1	2	3	4	and so on to 52.
	S. D.				
A. B.	2				
C. D.	1½				
E. F.	4				
G. H.	1				

Weekly Subscribers.

FORM of the Parish Accounts for Payments.

Number of Weeks paid.	1	2	3	4	and so on to 52.
	S.D.	S.D.	S.D.	S.D.	
A. B.					
C. D.					
E. F.					
G. H.					

A

B I L L

[WITH THE AMENDMENTS]

FOR

More effectual Relief of the Poor, and ascertaining the Settlement of Bastard Children.

27 *Geo.* III.
1787.

A

BILL

INTITULED

An Act to regulate The General Penitentiary for Convicts, at *Millbank*, in the County of *Middlesex*.

Note.—*The Figures in the Margin denote the Number of Presses in the Ingrossment.*

1   WHEREAS under and by virtue of an Act passed in the Fifty-second Year of His present Majesty, for the Erection of a Penitentiary House for the Confinement of Offenders convicted within the City of *London* and County of *Middlesex*, and which Act, by the Provisions thereof, was extended also to Offenders convicted in other Parts of *England* and *Wales*, a Penitentiary has been erected at *Millbank*, in the County of *Middlesex*, for the Confinement and Employment of Male and Female Convicts; and the same is now completed for the Reception of a Part of the Number intended to be confined therein : And whereas under and by virtue of the Powers contained in the said Act, His Majesty in Council has been pleased to appoint a Committee to superintend the said Penitentiary: And whereas the Number of Convicts who may be confined in the said Penitentiary may conveniently be increased, without any Enlargement of the Building ; and it is therefore expedient that Provision should be made for that Purpose: And whereas it is also expedient that other and further Provisions should be made, for the due Regulation of
2   the said Penitentiary, and of the Convicts to be confined therein ; be it
(75.)   A   therefore

therefore enacted by the King's most Excellent Majesty, by and with the Advice and Consent of the Lords Spiritual and Temporal, and Commons, in this present Parliament assembled, and by the Authority of the same, That all the Provisions in the said Act contained, so far as they relate to the Number of Convicts who may be confined in the said Penitentiary, and to the Confinement, Employment, and Management of the Convicts in the said Penitentiary, and the Establishment and Duties of Officers belonging to the same, shall be and the same are hereby repealed.

Repeal of certain Provisions of Act 52 G. 3.

And be further enacted, That it shall be lawful for the Supervisors under the said recited Act, and they are hereby empowered, to make Accommodation in the said Penitentiary for the Confinement and Employment of Four Hundred Male and a like Number of Female Convicts, making in the whole Eight Hundred Convicts, any Thing in the said Act to the contrary notwithstanding; and that any Number of Convicts, not exceeding Four Hundred Male and Four Hundred Female Convicts, may, with the Approbation of His Majesty's Principal Secretary of State for the Home Department for the Time being, be imprisoned at one and the same Time in the said Prison or Penitentiary, and confined, employed, and managed therein, under the Provisions of this Act.

Supervisors may make Accommodation for 400 Male and 400 Female Convicts, who may be confined in the said Penitentiary at the same Time.

And be it further enacted, That the Committee which has been nominated and appointed by His Majesty in His Privy Council to superintend the said Penitentiary, shall remain and continue the Committee for that Purpose until a new Nomination or Appointment shall take place; and that it shall be lawful for His Majesty in His Privy Council from Time to Time to remove all or any of the Persons composing the said Committee, and to appoint others in their Stead, or in the Stead of any such as shall die or resign: Provided always, that such Committee shall not at any Time consist of less than Ten nor more than Twenty Persons in Number at the same Time.

Committee to remain until any other appointed.

And be it further enacted, That it shall and may be lawful for such Committee, or any Three of them, to hold Meetings, and to make Bye Laws, Rules, Orders, and Regulations, for the assembling of the said Committee, and for all Matters relating to the Meetings of the same, as well as for the Government of the said Penitentiary, and for receiving, separating, classing, dieting, clothing, maintaining, employing, reforming, managing, treating, and watching the Convicts during their respective Confinement therein, as to the said Committee shall seem just and proper; provided however that such Bye Laws, Rules and Orders, shall not

Committee to make Bye Laws, Rules, &c.

not have force until they shall have been submitted to the Justices of the Court of King's Bench, and until such Justices shall have subscribed a Declaration, that they do not see any Thing contrary to Law in the said Bye Laws, Rules and Orders, so to be made as aforesaid; and all such Bye Laws, Rules and Orders, shall be afterwards added to or altered, from Time to Time, as often as the said Committee shall think necessary; and such Additions and Alterations, so far as the same relate to the employing, reforming, managing, treating, and watching the Convicts in the said Penitentiary, shall also in like Manner be submitted to the Justices of the Court of King's Bench, and confirmed in Manner aforesaid.

And be it further enacted, That it shall and may be lawful for such Committee, or any Three of them, at any of their said Meetings, to appoint any One or more of their said Members to visit the said Penitentiary, during the Intervals between the Meetings of the said Committee, and to delegate, if they shall think fit, Power to such Visitors, or any of them, to make any Order or give any Directions in Cases of pressing Emergency within the said Penitentiary, which might be made or given by the said Committee if they were sitting; provided that every such Order or Direction, together with the Circumstances by which the same was occasioned, shall be reported to the said Committee at their next Meeting. *Appointment of Visitors.*

And be it further enacted, That for the Regulation and Management of such Penitentiary, and previously to the Opening thereof for the Reception of Convicts, there shall be elected and appointed by the said Committee, a Governor, a Chaplain, a Secretary and Examiner of Accounts, a Surgeon or Apothecary, a Master Manufacturer, a Steward, and also for that Portion of the Penitentiary set apart for Female Convicts, a Matron, together with such Taskmasters and other Officers and Servants, as the said Committee, with the Approbation of the said Principal Secretary of State for the Home Department, shall judge necessary; and every Person elected and appointed by the said Committee to any of such Offices, shall from Time to Time be removable by any Order of the said Committee, and when any Vacancies shall happen in any of the said Offices other Persons shall be elected thereto by the same Authority; and such Salaries and other Allowances shall be annexed to the said Offices, as the said Committee, with such Approbation as aforesaid, shall direct. *Appointment of Officers, &c.*

Provided nevertheless, and be it further enacted, That it shall be lawful for the said Committee from Time to Time, with such Approbation as aforesaid, to increase, diminish, discontinue, or vary the Number of *Committee may vary the Number of Officers.*

Officers

(4)

Officers and Servants to be appointed by the said Penitentiary in pursuance of the Directions aforesaid; except by taking away or discontinuing any of the Offices of Governor, Matron, Chaplain, and Surgeon or Apothecary, to the same.

Committee may require Security from any Officer, &c. and in case of any Officer, &c. refusing to quit Possession, a Justice of Peace for the County of Middlesex may by Warrant direct Sheriff to remove him.

And be it further enacted, That it shall be lawful for the said Committee, if they shall deem it necessary, to require any Officers or Persons employed in the said Penitentiary to give such Security to the Governor of the said Penitentiary, for the due Performance of their respective Duties, in such Sums, and with such Sureties, and in such Form or Forms as they shall direct; and if any Person appointed to any Office or Duty in the said Penitentiary, who shall be removed by the said Committee from such his Office or Employment, shall refuse or neglect to quit the said Penitentiary, or to give up the Possession of any House, Building, Premises, or Apartment therein or belonging thereto, within such Period as shall be fixed by the Committee in any Order or Notice in Writing given for that Purpose, not being less than Forty-eight Hours after the Delivery to such Person of any such Order or Notice, then and in such Case it shall be lawful for any Justice of the Peace acting for the County of *Middlesex*, on Application from any Three or more of the said Committee by any Warrant under his Hand and Seal, to direct the Sheriff of the County to remove such Officer or Person out of the said Penitentiary, and the said Sheriff shall thereupon clear the Possession thereof, so far as relates to any Part of the Penitentiary, or any House, Building, Premises, or Apartments therein or belonging thereto, occupied by or in Possession of such Officer, in like Manner as upon a Writ of *Habere facias possessionem*.

Governor to be a Body Corporate.

And be it further enacted, That the Governor of such Penitentiary shall be a Body Corporate, and shall sue and be sued by the Name of " The Governor of the General Penitentiary at *Millbank*, in the County of *Middlesex*."

Governor empowered to contract for Clothing, Diet, &c. necessary for the Convicts, with the Approbation of the Committee.

And be it further enacted, That the said Governor shall have Power to make Contracts with any Persons whomsoever, for the Clothing, Diet, and all other Necessaries for the Maintenance and Support of the Convicts confined in such Penitentiary, and for Implements or Materials of any Kind of Manufacture, Trade, or Mystery, in which Convicts confined in such Penitentiary shall be employed, such Contracts being previously approved by the Committee; and also to carry on such Manufacture and Mystery in such Penitentiary, and to sell such Goods, Wares, and Merchandize as shall be there wrought and manufactured.

And

And be it further enacted, That all Books and Accounts shall be kept by the Governor or other Officers in such Manner as the said Committee may direct from Time to Time; and the several Entries therein shall be examined by the said Committee, or by such of their Members as may be appointed a Sub-Committee for that Purpose, and shall be by them compared with the several Receipts and other Vouchers relating thereto, and shall be verified by such Governor and Officers upon Oath, if required, before such Committee, and shall, if approved of by such Committee, be allowed and signed by any Three of them; and if such Committee shall disapprove of any Articles in such Accounts, they shall disallow the same.

Committee to direct how Books shall be kept, &c.

And be it further enacted, That if the said Committee shall suspect any fraudulent or improper Charges in any Accounts of the said Governor, or other Officer, or Servant, or any Omission therein, they may examine upon Oath the said Governor, or any other Officer or Servant belonging to such Penitentiary, or any of the Persons employed about the same, or any Persons of whom any Necessaries, Stock, Materials, or other Things, have been purchased for the Use of such Penitentiary, or any Persons to whom any Stock or Materials wrought, or manufactured therein, have been sold, or any of the Convicts confined in such Penitentiary, or any other Persons, touching any of the Articles contained in such Accounts, or any Omission therein, or any Thing relative thereto; and in case there shall appear in any such Accounts, any false Entry knowingly or wilfully made, or any fraudulent Omission therein, or any other Fraud whatsoever, or any Collusion between any Officer or Officers, Servant or Servants, belonging to such Penitentiary, or between any such Officer or Officers, Servant or Servants, and any other Person or Persons, in any Matter relative thereto, then besides the private Satisfaction in Damages which the Parties or Party injured may be entitled to recover by Law, the said Committee may dismiss any such Officer or Officers, Servant or Servants, who shall to them appear to have been guilty of any such false Entry, Omission, Fraud, or Collusion, and appoint another or others in his, her, or their stead; and if the said Committee shall see fit, they shall cause an Indictment or Indictments to be preferred against the Officer or Officers, Servant or Servants, or other Person or Persons, so offending, at the next Quarter or other General Session of the Peace to be holden for the County wherein the said Penitentiary is situated, or for any other adjoining County; and in case such Person or Persons so indicted shall be found guilty of such Offence or Offences, he, she, or they shall be punished by Fine and Imprisonment, or either of them, at the Discretion of the Court.

Committee may examine Officers and Servants, &c. upon Oath, and may dismiss and prosecute for Fraud or Collusion.

(6)

Committee to certify to the Principal Secretary of State for the Home Department, when said Penitentiary shall be fit for the Reception of Convicts.

And be it further enacted, That when the said Penitentiary, or a sufficient Part thereof shall be fitted and completed for the Reception of Convicts, and proper Officers shall be appointed for the Care and Management thereof, the said Committee shall certify, under their Hands and Seals, to His Majesty, through the said Principal Secretary of State for the Home Department, that such Penitentiary is so fitted and completed, and that such Officers have been appointed; and after the making of such Certificate, it shall and may be lawful for His Majesty, by an Order in Writing, to be notified by the said Secretary of State, to direct, that any Person who may be under Sentence or Order of Transportation, for any Offence committed within that Part of the United Kingdom called *England* and *Wales*, and who, having been examined by an experienced Surgeon or Apothecary, shall appear to be free from any putrid or infectious Distemper, and fit to be removed from the Gaol or Prison in which such Person may be confined, shall be removed to the said Penitentiary there to remain and continue for and during the Term of Five Years, in case such Convict shall be under Sentence or Order of Transportation for Seven Years only, for and during the Term of Seven Years, in case such Convict shall be under such Sentence or Order for Fourteen Years; and for and during the Term of Ten Years, in case such Convict shall be under such Sentence or Order for Life, or shall have been capitally convicted and pardoned as aforesaid.

Regulations as to the Time of Confinement of Convicts sentenced to Transportation, and removed to the Penitentiary.

Provided always, and be it further enacted, That in case any Convict shall be removed to the said Penitentiary, who, having been under Sentence or Order of Transportation for the Term of Seven Years, shall previously to his or her being removed to the said Penitentiary, have been kept confined in some other Gaol or Prison, during a Part of such Term, such Convict shall be confined in the said Penitentiary under this Act, for Five Seventh Parts of the Residue of his or her Term of Seven Years Transportation, remaining unexpired, when he or she shall be received into the said Penitentiary; and in case any Convict shall be removed to the said Penitentiary, who, having been under Sentence or Order of Transportation for the Term of Fourteen Years, shall, previously to his or her being so removed, have been kept confined in some other Gaol or Prison during a Part of such Term, such Convict shall be confined in the said Penitentiary under this Act for One Half of the Residue of his or her Term of Fourteen Years Transportation remaining unexpired, when he or she shall be received into the said Penitentiary; and in the Case of any Convict who, having been under Sentence or Order of Transportation for Life, or having been capitally convicted, shall be removed to the said Penitentiary for the Term of Ten Years as aforesaid, such Term of Ten

Years

Years shall be computed from the Time of his or her being received into the said Penitentiary.

And be it further enacted, That the Sheriff or Gaoler having the Custody of any Convict, whose Removal shall be ordered in Manner aforesaid, shall, with all convenient Speed after the Receipt of the Notification of any such Order, convey or cause to be conveyed every such Convict to the said Penitentiary, and there deliver him to the Governor thereof, together with a true Copy, attested by such Sheriff or Gaoler, of the Caption and Order of the Court before which such Convict was tried, containing the Sentence of Transportation of such Convict, by virtue whereof he shall be in the Custody of such Sheriff or Gaoler, and also a Certificate containing his or her Age, and an Account of his or her Behaviour in Prison, before and after Trial, and the Gaoler's Observations on his or her Temper and Disposition, and such Information concerning his or her Connections and former Course of Life, as may have come to the Knowledge of such Gaoler; and the Governor of the said Penitentiary shall give a proper Receipt in Writing to the Sheriff or Gaoler, for the Discharge of such Sheriff or Gaoler. *Sheriffs or Gaolers to deliver Convicts to the Penitentiary without Delay.*

And be it further enacted, That all reasonable Expences which the Sheriff or Gaoler shall incur in every such Removal, shall be paid by the County, Riding, Division, City, Borough, Liberty, or Place, for which the Court in which the Party was convicted shall have been held; and the Sheriff or Gaoler shall receive the Money due for such Expences from the Treasurer of such County, Riding, Division, City, Borough, Liberty, or Place, such Expences being first allowed by the Order of the Justices of the Peace at their Quarter or other General Sessions of the Peace, who are hereby required to make such Order as shall be just in that Behalf. *Expences of such Removal to be paid by the County, &c.*

And be it further enacted, That after Delivery of any such Convict as aforesaid into the Custody to which he or she shall be so ordered as aforesaid, such Governor, or other Person having the Custody of Convicts under his Direction, shall, during the Term for which such Convict shall be ordered to remain in his Custody, have the same Powers over such Convict as are incident to the Office of a Sheriff or Gaoler; and in case of any Abuse of such Custody, or other Misbehaviour or Negligence in the Discharge of his Office, shall be liable to the same Punishment as a Gaoler is now liable to by Law. *Governor to have the same Power over Convicts in his Custody as a Sheriff or Gaoler.*

(8)

Infane Convicts may be removed from and returned to Penitentiary after Recovery, as in cafes of other Prifoners in Gaols.

And be it further enacted, That if any Convict confined in the said Penitentiary shall become infane during such Confinement, and be so reported by the Committee to His Majesty's Principal Secretary of State for the Home Department, it shall be lawful for such Secretary of State to order and caufe such infane Convict to be immediately removed to some proper Place of Confinement; and upon Recovery to be returned to such Penitentiary, in the same Manner as in the Cafe of any Prifoner becoming infane, after and while under Sentence, in any other Gaol or Prifon.

17

Convicts, when brought, to be feparately lodged and wafhed, and examined by the Surgeon.

And be it further enacted, That when any Convict who shall be ordered to be confined in the said Penitentiary shall be brought thither in pursuance of the Powers contained in this Act, he or she shall be separately lodged and wafhed, cleanfed and purified, and shall then be examined by the Surgeon or Apothecary, and shall continue in such feparate Lodging until it be certified, by such Surgeon or Apothecary, that he or she is fit to be received among the other Convicts, or until he or she shall be removed to the Infirmary; and the Clothes in which he or she shall then be clothed shall be burnt, if neceffary, or otherwife shall be fold and difpofed of, at the Difcretion of the Governor, and the Produce thereof shall be accounted for to the Committee aforefaid, and shall be by them directed to be carried by the said Governor to the Account of the said Convict in the Books of the said Penitentiary; and such Convict shall not be difmiffed at the End or other Determination of his or her Term, if he or she shall then labour under any acute or dangerous Diftemper, unlefs at his or her Requeft; and when such Convict shall be finally difcharged, such other decent Clothing, as shall be judged neceffary and proper by the Committee aforefaid, shall be delivered to such Convict; and alfo such Sum of Money for his or her immediate Subfiftence, as the said Committee shall think proper, so as such Sum shall not exceed Three Pounds; and if such Convict, at the End or other Determination of his or her Term, shall procure any fubftantial Houfekeeper or other refpectable Perfon, to take him or her into Service, or provide him or her with proper Employment for One Year then next enfuing, the same to be approved by the Committee aforefaid, he or she, having served accordingly, shall be entitled at the End of the Year to such other Sum of Money, not exceeding the like Sum of Three Pounds, as the said Committee shall think fit.

18

When difcharged to be furnifhed with decent Clothing. Allowances.

19

Keeping Convicts to Labour.

And be it further enacted, That every such Governor of the said Penitentiary shall, during the Term for which such Convict shall remain in such Cuftody, keep him or her to Labour of such Kind as the Committee

mittee before mentioned shall direct and appoint; and if the Work to be performed by any such Convicts shall be of such a Nature as may require previous Instruction, proper Persons shall be provided to give the same, by Order of the said Committee, to whom a suitable Allowance shall be made.

And be it further enacted, That such Convicts as shall be sent to the said Penitentiary shall, during the Hours of Labour, be separated from each other, or shall work together in Companies composed of more or fewer Persons in Number, in such Manner as the Bye Laws, established as aforesaid by the Committee, shall prescribe; and that all Convicts, not confined in the Infirmary, shall during their Hours of Rest be kept entirely separate and apart from each other, and be lodged in separate Rooms or Cells; except in Cases in which it may be deemed expedient to place Two or more Prisoners together on account of the Health or State of Mind of One of such Prisoners. *Convicts, how to be lodged.*

And be it further enacted, That such Convicts shall be employed in Work at the said Penitentiary, every Day in the Year, except *Sundays*, *Christmas Day*, *Good Friday*, *Ascension Day*, and any Day appointed for a General Fast or Thanksgiving, and also except such Days when ill Health will not allow of their working; and the Hours of work in each Day shall not exceed Eight Hours in the Months of *November*, *December*, and *January*, Nine Hours in the Months of *February* and *October*, and Ten Hours and a Half in the Rest of the Year (exclusive of the Hours provided for Meals): Provided always, that it shall and may be lawful for the said Committee, by a written Order, to permit any Convict to labour voluntarily for a longer Time than is herein mentioned, upon such Conditions as shall in the said Order be expressed. *Hours of Work.*

And be it further enacted, That it shall be lawful for the said Committee to allow to any of the Convicts confined in the said Penitentiary, as a Reward and Encouragement, any Part or Portion of the Profits arising from their Labour, not exceeding such Proportion thereof as shall be approved of and allowed by the said Principal Secretary of State for the Home Department; subject to such Conditions and Regulations as the said Committee shall direct and appoint. *Granting Rewards.*

Provided always, and be it further enacted, That the several Convicts to be sent to the said Penitentiary shall be divided into Two Classes, which shall be called the First and Second Classes; for which Purpose, the Time for which such Convicts shall be severally ordered to be confined, shall be divided *Dividing Convicts into Classes.*

(75.) C

(10)

divided into Two equal Parts, and during the firſt Part of the Time of the Impriſonment, he or ſhe ſhall be ranked in the Firſt Claſs, and during the Second Part of ſuch Time, he or ſhe ſhall be ranked in the Second Claſs; and the Confinement of ſuch Convicts as ſhall from Time to Time be ranked in the Firſt Claſs ſhall be more ſtrict, and the Confinement of the Convicts in the Second Claſs ſhall be more moderate; which ſeveral Degrees of Confinement for each Claſs ſhall be ſettled by the ſaid Committee, by Orders of Regulation to be approved of in Manner aforeſaid: Provided always, that if the ſaid Committee ſhall at any Time obſerve, or be ſatisfactorily informed of any extraordinary Diligence or Merit in any of the ſaid Convicts who are ranked in the ſaid Firſt Claſs, it ſhall be lawful for the ſaid Committee to order ſuch Convict to be transferred to the Second Claſs, for the Remainder of the Term for which he or ſhe was ordered to be confined in the ſaid Penitentiary, although ſuch Convict may not have completed the Period of his or her Impriſonment in the ſaid Firſt Claſs.

Committee to report Convicts, who ſhall manifeſt extraordinary Diligence.

And be it further enacted, That if the ſaid Committee ſhall at any Time obſerve or be ſatisfactorily informed of any extraordinary Diligence or Merit in any of the Convicts under their Inſpection, who ſhall be ranked in the ſaid Second Claſs of Convicts, the Committee ſhall report the ſame in Writing to the Principal Secretary of State for the Home Department, in order that he may recommend ſuch Convict to His Majeſty as an Object of the Royal Mercy, on ſuch Conditions as to Him ſhall ſeem meet.

How the Convicts ſhall be fed and clothed.

And be it further enacted, That every Convict who ſhall be ordered to ſuch Penitentiary, ſhall, during the Time of his or her Confinement therein, be fed and ſuſtained with a ſufficient Quantity of coarſe but wholeſome Food, and alſo be clothed with a coarſe and uniform Apparel, with any diſtinguiſhing Marks which may be deemed uſeful to facilitate Diſcovery in caſe of Eſcape, the Whole to be ordered in ſuch Manner as the Committee aforeſaid ſhall from Time to Time appoint; and no ſuch Convict ſhall during the Time of his or her Confinement be permitted to have any other Food, Drink, or Clothing, than ſuch as ſhall be ſo appointed.

And be it further enacted, That no Perſon except the Officers, or Servants of the Penitentiary, or ſuch Perſon or Perſons as ſhall be authorized according to the Regulations eſtabliſhed by the ſaid Committee, ſhall be permitted at any Time to enter any of the Apartments or Court Yards allotted to the Convicts, or to hold Converſation or Communication with any of them.

Provided

Provided also, and be it enacted, That it shall and may be lawful to for the Governor of the said Penitentiary to employ, with the Consent of the said Committee, any of the Convicts aforesaid, who shall be ranked in the Second Class, as Overseers, or Assistants, in the Management of the Works, and the Care of their Fellow Convicts, instead of their being confined to such their Daily Labour as aforesaid. *And Governor may employ Convicts as Servants.*

And be it further enacted, That no Officer or Servant of such Penitentiary shall supply any of the Convicts therein with any Money, Clothing, Provisions, or Diet, or with any Spirituous or other Liquors whatsoever, except such Money, Clothing, Provisions, or Diet, or such Water and Milk, as the Governor of the Penitentiary shall from Time to Time permit or direct, and except such Diet and Liquors as the Surgeon or Apothecary attending such Penitentiary shall think proper to order for any such Convict, in case of Illness; and in case any such Officer or Servant shall be found guilty of carrying to any such Convict, or of knowingly permitting to be carried to any such Convict, any Money, Clothing, Provisions, or Diet, or Liquors whatsoever, contrary to the Intent of this Act, such Officer or Servant shall immediately be suspended by the said Governor, who shall report the same to the Committee at their next Meeting; and such Committee shall inquire thereof upon Oath, and shall punish such Officer or Servant by Forfeiture of Office, and by any Fine not exceeding Ten Pounds, or by either of such Punishments, as the said Committee shall in their Discretion think proper; and if any other Person or Persons shall wilfully supply any such Convict, at any Time during the Term of his or her Confinement with any Food, Drink, or Clothing, other than such as shall have been appointed by the Committee as aforesaid, or with any Money, he or she so supplying such Convict shall, for every such Offence, forfeit a Sum not exceeding Five Pounds, nor less than Forty Shillings, at the Discretion of the said Committee. *Punishing Officers or Servants supplying any Convict with Money, Provisions, or Liquor, contrary to this Act.*

And be it further enacted, That the Chaplain shall read Prayers and preach a Sermon both Morning and Evening, in the Chapel of such Penitentiary, on every *Sunday* in the Year, and also on every *Christmas Day, Good Friday,* and *Ascension Day,* and on every Day appointed for a General Fast or Thanksgiving; and all the Convicts confined in such Penitentiary, who shall not be disabled by Illness, or whose Attendance shall not be dispensed with by the Committee, shall attend the said Prayers and Sermons, which shall also be attended by the Resident Officers and by the Servants of such Penitentiary, or such of them as can be spared from their several Employments, and shall not be prevented by Illness; and the said Chaplain shall visit such Convicts, under such Regulations as may hereafter *Chaplain to read Morning and Evening Prayers, and preach Two Sermons on Sundays, &c.*

(12)

after be prescribed by the said Committee, for their moral and religious Education.

Chaplain may baptize and bury in the Penitentiary, and shall keep Registers and transmit Copy monthly to the Incumbent of the Parish, who is to enter the same in Register, and may have Allowance for so doing.

And be it further enacted, That it shall be lawful for the Chaplain of the said Penitentiary, or such other Person as shall act for or assist him, and no other, to baptize all Children born, and bury all Persons who shall die therein, or in any Buildings or Premises belonging to or making Part of the said Penitentiary, and to perform Divine Service and administer the Sacrament according to the Liturgy of the Church of *England*, within the said Penitentiary; and such Chaplain shall keep an accurate Register of all such Christenings and of all such Burials, and shall Once in each Month transmit a Copy thereof to the Incumbent of the Church of *Saint John the Evangelist* in *Westminster*, or his Curate, in the Absence of such Incumbent, who shall, as soon after the Receipt thereof as can conveniently be, enter the same in the Register of the said Parish; and it shall be lawful for the said Committee to order and direct that an Allowance shall be made to such Incumbent for making each such Entry, according to the Custom in like Cases in the said Parish. 27

Convicts to walk and air themselves.

And be it further enacted, That the Convicts ordered to be confined in such Penitentiary shall be permitted to walk and air themselves in the airing Yards or Grounds belonging thereto, for such stated Time as their Health may require, and the Regulations of such Penitentiary shall permit. 28

Convicts, when sick, to be visited by the Surgeon; and if necessary, be sent to the Infirmary.

And be it further enacted, That in case any such Convict shall appear to be sick, he or she shall be visited by the Surgeon or Apothecary attending such Penitentiary, and if the Sickness be found to be real, the said Surgeon or Apothecary shall report the same to the Governor, who shall, if the Sickness be of such a Nature as to require it, order such Convict to be sent to the Infirmary belonging to such Penitentiary, and his or her Name to be entered in a Book, to be kept for that Purpose; and when such Convict shall have so far recovered his or her Health as that the said Surgeon or Apothecary shall judge him or her to be in a proper Condition to quit the Infirmary, and to return to his or her Employment, and the said Surgeon or Apothecary shall so report, the said Governor shall order such Convict to be brought back to his or her Cell, and to be again employed in labour, so far as shall be consistent with the Health of such Convict. 29

Committee to examine into the State of

And be it further enacted, That the said Committee, at every Meeting at which Three of them at the least shall be present, shall inquire into

into the State of such Penitentiary, and occasionally see every Convict confined therein; and shall inspect the Accounts of the Governor and other Officers, and also examine into their Conduct, into the Management of such Penitentiary, and into the Behaviour of the Convicts confined therein. *the Penitentiary, and inspect the Accounts.*

And be it further enacted, That the Governor of such Penitentiary shall have Power to hear all Complaints touching any of the following Offences committed by any of the Convicts confined therein; (that is to say), Disobedience of any of the Orders established for the said Penitentiary; Assaults by one Person confined in such Penitentiary upon another, when no dangerous Wound or Bruise is given; profane Cursing and Swearing, or indecent Behaviour; Absence from Chapel, or irreverent Behaviour there; and Idleness or Negligence in Work, or wilful Mismanagement of it, or wanton Damage or Injury to the Prison or Furniture thereof; all which are declared to be Offences by this Act; and the said Governor may examine any Persons touching such Offences, and may determine thereupon, and may punish such Offences by ordering the Offender or Offenders to close Confinement in a dark Cell, or by keeping him or her upon Bread and Water only, or by both such Punishments, for any Term not exceeding Three Days. *Governor empowered to hear Complaints.*

And be it further enacted, That if any Convict who shall be confined in any such Penitentiary shall, during the Term for which he shall be so confined, be guilty of any Offence which the Governor of such Penitentiary is not hereby authorized to punish, or for which the Punishment which such Governor is hereby authorized to inflict, shall by such Governor be deemed not sufficient, by reason of the Enormity of the Offence, or the Repetition thereof, such Governor may confine such Offender either in his or her own Cell, or in a dark Cell belonging to such Penitentiary, till the next Meeting of the said Committee, and shall in such Case report such Offence, with the Time and particular Circumstances thereof, and the Name of the Offender, to the said Committee; and such Committee shall have Power to inquire of, upon Oath, and determine, concerning all such Offences so reported to them as aforesaid, and may order any such Offender to be punished by close Confinement in a dark Cell, with Bread and Water only for Sustenance, for any Term not exceeding One Month, or by removing such Offenders, if ranked in the Second Class, into the First Class, or by both such Punishments; and in case of Removal into the First Class, the Offender shall, from the Time of making such Order of Removal, remain in such First Class, unless he or she be restored to the Second Class *Enormous Offenders to be confined by the Governor, and reported to the Committee.*

by Order of the Committee, or until the Term of his or her Confinement shall be completed.

Committee may administer Oaths.
And be it further enacted, That whenever by this Act the said Committee, or any Three of them, are empowered or directed to make any Inquiry or receive any Proof upon Oath, any One of the said Committee is hereby authorized to tender and administer such Oath; and any Three of the said Committee may summon or cause to be summoned such Witnesses, as they shall think meet, to appear and give Evidence before them; and if any Person, being duly summoned, shall refuse or neglect to appear, or being present and competent to be a Witness shall refuse to be sworn, or being sworn shall refuse to give Evidence, such Person shall forfeit any Sum not less than Twenty Shillings, nor more than Ten Pounds, at the Discretion of the said Committee. 32

Governor to keep regular Books, and Returns to be made therefrom.
And be it further enacted, That the Governor of the said Penitentiary shall keep a regular Book or Books, in which shall be entered the Names of all and every the Person or Persons who shall be in his Custody, the Offences of which they shall have been guilty, the Court before which each Person was convicted, the Sentence of the Court, the Age, Bodily Estate, and Behaviour of every such Convict while in Custody; and also the Names of all and every the Person or Persons who shall have died under such Custody, or shall have escaped from such Place of Confinement, or shall have been discharged from thence by Order from One of His Majesty's Principal Secretaries of State, or otherwise; from which Books Returns shall be made of the Particulars mentioned above, on the First Day of every Term, to His Majesty's Court of King's Bench, and shall be verified on the Oath of the Person making the same.

Reports to be laid before the King in Council, and both Houses of Parliament.
And be it further enacted, That the said Committee shall at the Beginning of every Session make a faithful Report to the King in Council, and to both Houses of Parliament, specifying the State of the Buildings, the Behaviour and Conduct of the respective Officers, the Treatment and Condition of the Convicts, the Amount of their Earnings, and the Expences of such Penitentiary, and also in Matters of extreme or pressing Necessity, shall and may make a Special Report thereof to the Justices of His Majesty's Court of King's Bench. 33

Bye Laws, Rules, &c. to be reported to the King in Council, and to both
And be it further enacted, That the said Committee shall report to His Majesty in Council, and to both Houses of Parliament, all Bye Laws, Rules, or Regulations, made under the Authority of this Act, and all Aterations therein or Additions thereto, within Thirty-one Days after the

Commencement

(15)

Commencement of the next Session of Parliament after such Bye Laws, Rules, and Regulations, or Alterations or Additions, shall have been confirmed by the Justices of the Court of King's Bench, as herein-before is directed.

Houses of Parliament.

And be it further enacted, That the said Penitentiary, and all the Buildings and inclosed Area and Appurtenances belonging thereto and making Part thereof, shall be and they are hereby declared to be wholly freed and exempt from all Public and Parochial Taxes, Rates, Assessments, and Charges whatsoever, any Thing in any Act or Acts of Parliament now in force, or which may hereafter be passed in relation to any Public or Parochial Taxes, Rates, or Assessments, to the contrary notwithstanding: Provided always, that no Person belonging to or employed in the said Penitentiary, and no Child born therein, shall thereby gain a Settlement in the Parish in which the said Penitentiary is situate.

Penitentiary to be exempt from Public and Parochial Taxes.

34

And be it further enacted, That an Account of the Expences of carrying this Act into Execution shall be annually laid before the House of Commons, and after deducting therefrom such Profit as may have arisen from the Earnings of the Convicts, over and above the Expences occasioned by their Labour, and any Allowances which shall have been made to such Convicts, or to the Officers superintending such Labour, by Order of the Committee, the Remainder shall be provided for in the next Supplies to be granted to His Majesty by Parliament.

Expences of executing the Act, to be laid before the House of Commons.

And be it further enacted, That if any Convict who shall be ordered to be confined in the said Penitentiary shall at any Time during the Term of such Confinement break Prison, or escape from the Place of his or her Confinement, or in his or her Conveyance to such Place of Confinement, or from the Person or Persons having the lawful Custody of such Convict, he or she so breaking Prison or escaping shall be punished by an Addition of Three Years to the Term for which he or she at the Time of his or her Breach of Prison or Escape was subject to be confined; and if such Convict so punished by such Addition to the Term of Confinement shall afterwards be convicted of a Second Escape or Breach of Prison, he or she shall be adjudged guilty of Felony, without Benefit of Clergy.

Punishment of Convicts breaking Prison or escaping.

35

And be it further enacted, That if any Person shall rescue any Convict who shall be ordered to be confined within the said Penitentiary, either during the Time of his or her Conveyance to the said Penitentiary, or whilst such Convict shall be in the Custody of the Person or Persons under

Punishing Persons rescuing or attempting to rescue Convicts.

whose

whose Care and Charge he or shall be so confined; or if any Person shall be aiding or assisting in any such Rescue, every such Person so rescuing, aiding, or assisting, shall be guilty of Felony, and may be ordered to be confined to the said Penitentiary for any Term not less than One Year, nor exceeding Five Years; and if any Person having the Custody of any such Convict as aforesaid, or being employed by the Person having such Custody as a Keeper, Underkeeper, Turnkey, Assistant, or Guard, shall voluntarily permit such Convict to escape; or if any Person whatsoever shall, by supplying Arms, Tools, or Instruments of Disguise, or otherwise be in any Manner aiding and assisting to any such Convict in any Escape, or in any Attempt to make an Escape, though no Escape be actually made, or shall attempt to rescue any such Convict, or be aiding and assisting in any such Attempt, though no Rescue be actually made, every such Person so permitting, attempting, aiding, or assisting, shall be guilty of Felony; and if any Person having such Custody, or being so employed by the Person having such Custody as aforesaid, shall negligently permit any such Convict to escape, such Person so permitting shall be guilty of a Misdemeanor, and being lawfully convicted of the same, shall be liable to Fine or Imprisonment, or to both, at the Discretion of the Court.

Mode of Trial and Conviction.

And to the Intent that the Prosecutions for Escapes, Breaches of Prison, and Rescues, may be carried on with as little Trouble and Expence as possible, be it further enacted, That any Convict escaping, breaking Prison, or being rescued in Manner aforesaid, may and shall be tried before the Justices of Oyer and Terminer or Gaol Delivery, or at the Great Sessions, either for the County where he or she shall be apprehended and retaken, or for the County in which the said Offence shall have been committed; and in case of any Prosecution for any such Escape, Attempt to Escape, Breach of Prison, or Rescue, either against the Convict escaping or attempting to escape, or having broke Prison, or being rescued, or against any other Person or Persons concerned therein, or aiding, abetting, or assisting the same, a Copy properly attested, of the Order of Commitment to such Penitentiary shall, after Proof made that the Person then in question before the Court is the same that was delivered with such Order, be sufficient Evidence to the Court and Jury that the Person then in question was so ordered to such Confinement.

The Committee or Visitors may direct any Person not being Offi-

And be it further enacted, That in case it shall appear to the said Committee, or to any Member thereof, who shall be appointed a Visitor as aforesaid, that the Continuance within the said Penitentiary, of any Person, not being an Officer or Servant of the said Penitentiary or a

Convict

(17)

Convict confined therein, is inexpedient or objectionable, it shall and may be lawful for such Committee or Visitor, by an Order in Writing to direct such Person to quit such Penitentiary; and in case such Person shall refuse or neglect so to do within Six Hours after the Receipt of such Order, it shall and may be lawful for any One of His Majesty's Justices of the Peace, acting in and for the County of *Middlesex*, on Application from such Committee or such Visitor, by Warrant under his Hand and Seal, to authorize and empower any Person to whom such Warrant shall be directed, forthwith to remove such Person from and out of the said Penitentiary. *cers, Servants, or Convicts, to quit the Penitentiary.*

39 And be it further enacted, That the said Penitentiary shall be regulated by the Provisions in this Act contained; and no other Act or Acts of Parliament relating to Gaols, Prisons, or Houses of Correction, or any Clauses, Provisions, Regulations, Penalties, or Forfeitures, contained in any such Act or Acts, shall extend or be construed to extend to the said Penitentiary, except so far as any such Acts, Clauses, Provisions, or Regulations are by this Act referred to and made applicable to the Purposes of this Act, or to the said Penitentiary, or to any Persons belonging to or confined as Convicts therein. *Other Acts relating to Gaols, &c. not to apply to the Penitentiary.*

And be it further enacted, That any pecuniary Penalties created by this Act, for the Recovery of which no Mode is herein-before prescribed, shall be recoverable before Two or more Justices of the Peace in the County in which the Offence shall be committed, on Proof of the Offence by the Oath or Oaths of One or more credible Witness or Witnesses, or on Confession of the Offender; and One Moiety thereof shall be paid to the Use of the Penitentiary, and the other Moiety to the Informer or Informers prosecuting for the same, and in case of Non-payment, the same shall be
40 levied by Distress and Sale of the Offender's Goods and Chattels, by Warrant under the Hands and Seals of such Justices; and the Overplus of the Money raised, after deducting the Penalty and Expences of the Distress and Sale, shall be rendered to the Owner; and for want of sufficient Distress, the Offender shall be sent by such Justices to the Prison of such County, for such Term not exceeding Six Months, nor less than One Month, as such Justices shall think most proper. *Recovery of Penalties.*

And be it further enacted, That the Provisions of an Act of Parliament passed in the Twenty-fourth Year of the Reign of His present Majesty, and of all other Acts of Parliament for the rendering Justices of Peace more safe in the Execution of their Offices, shall extend and be construed to extend to all Persons nominated to form Part of the said Committee *General Issue to be pleaded.*

(75.)   E

mittee for superintending the said Penitentiary, and to the Governor thereof, so as that no Action shall be brought against any such Person or Persons for any Thing done under this Act, without Notice, to enable him or them to tender Amends; and if any Suit or Action shall be prosecuted against any Person or Persons for any Thing done in pursuance of this Act, such Person or Persons may plead the General Issue, and give this Act or the Special Matter in Evidence at any Trial to be had thereupon, and that the same was done by the Authority of this Act; and if a Verdict shall pass for the Defendant or Defendants, or the Plaintiff or Plaintiffs shall become Nonsuit, or discontinue his, her, or their Action or Actions after Issue joined, or if on Demurrer or otherwise, Judgment shall be given against the Plaintiff or Plaintiffs, the Defendant or Defendants shall recover Treble Costs, and have the like Remedy for the same as any Defendants have by Law in other Cases; and though a Verdict shall be given for any Plaintiff in any such Action or Suit as aforesaid, such Plaintiff shall not have Costs against the Defendant, unless the Judge, before whom the Trial shall be, shall certify his Approbation of the Verdict.

Treble Costs.

Limitation of Actions. And be it further enacted, That all Actions, Suits, and Prosecutions to be commenced against any Person or Persons for any Thing done in pursuance of this Act, shall be laid and tried in the County or Place where the Fact was committed, and shall be commenced within Six Months after the Fact committed, and not otherwise.

Act may be altered this Session. And be it further enacted, That this Act may be altered or amended by any Act or Acts to be passed in the present Session of Parliament.

A

BILL

INTITULED

An Act to regulate The General Penitentiary for Convicts, at *Millbank*, in the County of *Middlesex*.

8 *May* 1818.

A BILL

For the more effectual Prevention of Frauds and Abuses in the Manufacture, Exportation, and Importation of sundry Wares, and for the Relief of distressed Workmen brought up to practise the Manufacture of Clocks and Watches.

Note.—*The Figures in the Margin denote the Number of the Folios in the written Copy.*

𝔚𝔥𝔢𝔯𝔢𝔞𝔰 the Arts, Manufactures, and Trades, of making exporting, importing and dealing in divers wares of Gold and Silver, as also Watches, Clocks, Timepieces, Clock and Watchwork, Mathematical Instruments, and Engraving, have been and are of considerable extent and importance; and very few persons, having occasion to purchase such wares and manufactures, being able to detect any imposition or deficiency therein, until it is too late to obtain any remedy, although there remain and stand in force a great number of Acts and Statutes on this behalf, yet partly for the variety and number of them, and chiefly that many of the said Laws are not answerable to this time, and cannot conveniently be put in due execution for the prevention of forgeries, frauds and abuses, committed by evil disposed persons carrying on or using the said arts, manufactures and trades, especially in secret places, it is expedient that some more adequate provision should be enacted, for the protection of His Majesty's subjects, and other persons having occasion at home or abroad to purchase use or depend upon such wares and manufactures, particularly in and for the navigation of Ships at Sea: AND to the end that poor labouring Workmen and other Persons using the same arts, manufactures and trades, as their avocation hereafter may, by their labour therein, obtain, both in the time of scarcity and in the time of plenty, a portion of Wages meet and convenient for the sustenance of themselves and their families, and neither depend upon Parochial Rates or Charities, nor on the labour of other Persons to make up any deficiency thereof;

Preamble.

(2)

Be it therefore Enacted, by The KING's Most Excellent MAJESTY, by and with the Advice and Consent of the Lords Spiritual and Temporal, and Commons, in this present Parliament assembled, and by the Authority of the same, THAT from and after the   day of   no Person or Persons whatsoever shall make up, or cause to be made up, any Clock, Watch or Mathematical Instrument or other production of the said arts or manufactures, or either of them; in which there shall be any false jewelling of the pivot holes, or external appearance of jewelling, the same not being really jewelled, or external appearance of shewing seconds, or the day of the month, or of the moon's age, or any object or motion exhibited or to be exhibited by or in the said art, manufacture or otherwise, nor in which there shall be any deficiency of the several appropriate parts, internal mechanism, work and works, duly to give motion and otherwise unto and for all such works, motions and objects whatsoever, apparently or pretended, or purporting to be shewn exhibited or set forth by such Clock, Watch, Mathematical Instrument and Production respectively; nor shall any Person whatsoever make up any Clock or Watch or Mathematical Instrument, without engraving or putting on one or more principal and permanent part or parts of the main Frame, Plate or Plates, and in a conspicuous manner and visible situation upon every such Clock and Watch, and in an equally permanent, conspicuous and visible manner and situation, upon every such Mathematical Instrument, his or her and each of their own proper christian and surnames and place of abode, in words at full length, and a distinct number in numerical figures upon each, by which each and every such Clock, Watch and Mathematical Instrument may be described and identified, and no other name or place whatsoever; nor shall the names or place of abode of the maker of any Clock or Watch or Mathematical Instrument, be placed upon any moveable Namepiece, Barrel-piece or Dial, only thereon, but shall be in all cases so permanently engraven and affixed on some principal part of the body of such work ware or manufacture, and in the manner aforesaid, that such name and place of abode may not be easily removed therefrom, or admit the substitution of any other name or place instead of those of the Person who made the same work or ware; nor shall any Person change, alter, obliterate, conceal or take away, the inscription of the name or place of abode of the maker, upon off or from any Clock, Watch, Mathematical Instrument or Engraving, nor cause nor procure such offence to be done or committed by any other Person; nor shall any Person forge, engrave, enamel, paint or put, nor cause nor procure to be forged, engraven, enamelled, painted or put, the name or place of abode of any Clockmaker, Watchmaker, Mathematical Instrument Maker, or Engraver who made it not, upon any Clock, Watch, Mathematical Instrument, or Engraving; nor shall any Person put use or apply the name or place of abode of any such Clock, Watch, or Mathematical Instrument Maker or Engraver, upon any work ware or manufacture, without his or her express order respectively, whose name shall be so put used or applied; nor shall any Person or Persons export or send, or endeavour to export or send out of this United Kingdom, any outward

or

Marginalia:
- Frauds in the manufacture and deceptive works and practices in the arts and trades prohibited.
- No Clock or Watch or Mathematical Instrument to be made without its bearing the names and place of abode of the Maker;
- and no other name or place whatsoever.
- Names, &c. not to be put upon moveable peices, but on some permanent part of the work or ware.
- Name, &c. not to be changed, altered, or obliterated.
- Name, &c. of Makers not to be forged.
- Nor any Maker's Name used without his order.
- Unfinished work not to be exported;

4

5

6

7

er inward box, case, dialplate, movement, or other prepared material, of any nature or kind whatsoever, for Clock, Watch or Mathematical Instrument, without the movement and proper parts and appurtenances in and with every such box, case, dialplate, movement and prepared material, made up complete and fit for use, and with the names and place of abode of the certified Clock Watch or Mathematical Instrument Maker, and a distinct number engraven on each and every of them as aforesaid, and no other name or place, upon the penalty of forfeiting to the *nor finished wares without the names, &c. of the Maker thereon.*

proper use of the Person or Persons who will seize and convey the same before any one or more of His Majesty's Justice or Justices of the Peace acting in or for the County City or Place wherein any such Offence as aforesaid shall be done or committed, and also the further Penalty of forfeiting the sum of   of lawful money for each and every such Offence.

Penalty.

Provided always, and be it Enacted, That nothing in this Act, or in any other Act contained or expressed, shall be taken or construed to extend to prohibit or prevent the free sale and exportation, without penalty or forfeiture, of any Clock, Watch, or Mathematical Instrument whatsoever, which shall have been made or engraven on or before the   day of

All Clocks, Watches, &c. made before a certain day, to be freely sold and exported.

And provided always, and be it Enacted, That all and every the forfeitures and penalties in and by a certain Act made in the Ninth and Tenth years of the Reign of his late Majesty King *William* the Third, chapter twenty-eight, intituled "An Act for the Exportation of Watches, "Sword-Hilts, &c." directed and appointed, shall cease and determine, as to all and every offence before the   day of   done or committed; and all and every the said forfeiture and penalties are hereby repealed, made void, and of no effect, and the persons who have so offended, indemnified from and against the same.

Indemnity for Persons who have offended against the Act 9 and 10 William III. c. 28.

And provided always, and be it Enacted, That nothing in this Act contained shall be taken or construed to extend to prevent any Clock, Watch or Mathematical Instrument maker, who is duly registered and certified in the manner and form as in this present Act is required and mentioned, from ordering or procuring to be made up any Clock, Watch, or Mathematical Instrument, and causing to be engraven or otherwise lawfully placed thereon, his or her own proper names and place of abode, in manner aforesaid.

One certified Workmaster may make up work for another certified Workmaster.

AND for the more effectual prevention of such Forgeries, Frauds and Abuses as aforesaid, BE it further Enacted, That from and after the said   day of   no person whatsoever engaged in or carrying on the art trade and mystery of a Clockmaker, Watchmaker, Mathematical Instrument maker, or Engraver, shall exercise, use, follow or practice the said art, trade or mystery, or either of them, except as an Apprentice lawfully bound unto some known workmaster, until his or her proper christian and surnames, place of abode, and particular profession

All Persons who use the Arts and Trades mentioned, to be registered.

(4)

and to take out a Certificate of such Registry.
sion or avocation as aforesaid, shall first have been truly registered and enrolled in the public register hereinafter in that behalf mentioned and appointed; nor until he or she shall have taken out and obtained a Certificate of such enrollment and registry, in the manner and form as in this Act hereinafter is mentioned;

No Person to use the Trades, &c. that is not registered, nor any Alien.
nor shall any person whatsoever, that has not lawfully obtained such Certificate as aforesaid, or that is not a natural free-born subject, or having been naturalized, employ or set to work any journeyman, workman, or other person, in the manufactoring of any Watch or Clock, Mathematical Instrument or Engraving, upon the penalty of

Penalty.
                    contrary to the true intent and meaning of this Act, and the sum of   of lawful money for each and every such offence.

Public Register, by whom and where to be kept.
And be it further Enacted, That the said public Register of the names, qualifications, and place of abode of persons using or practising the said arts, manufactures and trade of Clockmaking, Watchmaking, Mathematical Instrument making and engraving respectively, shall be kept by the Company of the Master, Wardens, and Fellowship of the art and mystery of Clockmaking, at their Common Hall or Office by them for that purpose from time to time to be appointed within the City of *London*; and in the said Register by the proper officer of the said Company in that behalf to be appointed, shall be enrolled the proper christian and surnames and place of residence and particular profession of all such persons, being natural free-born subjects, or having been naturalized as at this day are engaged in or practise the said art, manufacture and trades of making Clocks, Watches, Mathematical Instruments, and Engraving respectively, or any part or branch thereof, and who shall on or before the   day of   apply or desire to practise and be registered as Clockmakers, Watchmakers, Mathematical Instrument makers or Engravers respectively as aforesaid;

All Persons now using any part or branch of the Arts or Trades, may be registered as Clock, Watch and Mathematical Instrument Makers, or as Engravers, except Aliens.
and in like manner henceforth shall be enrolled in the said register the proper christian and surnames, place of abode, and professions of all such person and persons, being natural free-born subjects, or having been naturalized, who shall apply and desire to be so registered as aforesaid, having first duly served as apprentice to a Clock, Watch or Mathematical Instrument maker, or to an Engraver respectively, or in or to some one or more of the parts or branches of the

Persons registered hereafter must first have served as Apprentice in the arts mentioned, or some of the branches set forth.
said arts or trades hereinafter mentioned, that is to say, a Clock-movement maker, or a Watch-movement maker, or a Clock finisher, or a Watch finisher, or a Watch-escapement maker, or a Repeating-motion maker, and no other person or persons whatsoever.

Retainings and covenants made before this Statute good and effectual for all purposes.
Provided always, and be it also Enacted, That this Act or any thing therein contained, shall not extend to invalidate any lawful Retainings, Covenants or Indentures of Apprenticeship, had made or entered into before the passing of this Act, but all and every the Parties to such indentures, retainings or covenants, shall and may have the full advantages of such indentures, retainings and covenants; and every such person shall by virtue of the same indentures, retainings and covenants, when the terms thereof shall have been duly performed, be admitted, enrolled and certified

certified as a Clock or Watch or Mathematical Instrument maker, or as an Engraver in manner aforesaid.

And Provided always, and be it Enacted, That every Person whatsoever now using the said arts or trades, or any part thereof, and who before the said   day of   shall not apply to be registered and certified as a Clockmaker, Watchmaker, Mathematical Instrument maker, or Engraver, in manner and form as aforesaid, may nevertheless work as a journeyman or workman to with and for any lawfully registered and certified Workmaster in the said arts, manufactures and trades, or either of them.

Persons now using the Arts and Trades who do not apply to be registered and certified as Master Tradesmen, may work as Journeyman or Workman.

And Provided always, and be it Enacted, That it shall and may be lawful to and for the Widow and Widows of any and every such lawfully enrolled and certified Clock or Watchmaker, Mathematical Instrument maker, or Engraver, deceased, to produce the Certificate of registry of her deceased husband to the Registrar of the said Company; and upon the surrender of the said certificate, the said widow shall by virtue thereof, be enrolled and certified as of and in her own proper names and place of residence, and may thenceforth continue, use, practice and carry on the art or trade which her deceased husband did use; any thing in this Act contained to the contrary thereof in anywise notwithstanding.

Widows may use the Trades, &c. of their deceased husbands, being first duly registered and certified.

And be it further Enacted, That the said Certificates of registry and qualification to use and practice the art and trade of a Clock and Watchmaker, Mathematical Instrument maker, or Engraver respectively, hereinbefore directed to be taken out and obtained by all Persons previous to their practising the said arts or trades, or either of them, shall be issued by the said Company of the Master, Wardens and Fellowship of the art and mystery of Clockmaking, who are hereby empowered and required to issue the same, under the hands and seals of the Master and Wardens of the said Company of Clockmakers, and countersign of their Clerk, on the   day of   and afterwards to all such Persons duly qualified and registered as aforesaid, being natural free-born Subjects, or having been naturalized, and being at this day engaged in using or practising the said arts and trades, or any part or branch thereof, or who shall have served as apprentice in the manner aforesaid, as shall apply for the same Certificate, being first duly registered and inrolled as aforesaid.

By whom the Certificates shall be issued.

To whom Certificates shall be granted.

And be it further Enacted, That every Person who shall desire or apply to be registered and certified as such Clock and Watchmaker, Mathematical Instrument maker, or Engraver as aforesaid, shall produce and exhibit to the said Company of Clockmakers, or to their Registrar in that behalf appointed, his or her indenture of apprenticeship, and reasonable proof of his or her having served and fulfilled the same accordingly; or the testimony to be given before one or more of his Majesty's Justice or Justices of Peace acting in or for the County, City or Place nearest unto and in which such Applicant resided at the time of such using the said arts or trades or servitude of apprenticeship,

Proofs to be exhibited by Persons desiring to be registered and certified.

Indenture of Apprenticeship, or in default, proof upon oath, stating the servitude in or using the Trades.

(6)

ship, whereupon the said Person claims to be registered, inrolled, admitted and certified as aforesaid; such testimony being given upon the oath of such Applicant, and of Two competent Witnesses, having knowledge of the Facts alledged, and that such Applicant has used or been employed in, or has duly served as apprentice in the said arts and trades, or in the said branches thereof, and in the manner aforesaid, and thereby is entitled to such Registry or Inrolment and Certificate as aforesaid, every such Applicant paying the sum of

<small>Sum to be paid for each Certificate,</small>

for each and every such Inrolment or Certificate; and every Person so inrolled and certified shall thenceforth be entitled and at full liberty to exercise and follow the art and trade of a Clock and Watchmaker, Mathematical Instrument maker, or Engraver, as his or her case shall respectively be, or be certified as aforesaid; and which said sum of   shall be taken and applied by the said Company of Clockmakers, in aid of or towards the expenses of executing the provisions of this Act.

<small>and to be applied towards the Expenses of executing this Act.</small>

<small>Lists of the registered Persons to be prepared annually.</small>

And be it also Enacted, That on or before the   day of   in every year the said Company of Clockmakers shall cause to be printed or otherwise prepared a true and corrected List, in alphabetical order, of the surnames arranged, and which List shall contain the christian and surname and place of abode of all and every Person and Persons registered in the books of the said Company, and admitted and certified as qualified in the manner aforesaid, to practise, use, follow and carry on the said art and trade of a Clock and Watchmaker, a Mathematical Instrument maker, or Engraver respectively as aforesaid, any or either of them; and in case of any such Person removing his or her place of residence, he and she shall, within one month thereafter, notify such removal, by or in writing to the Clerk of the same Company, that the Register may be corrected accordingly, upon pain that he or she shall forfeit and pay the sum of   for every such offence.

<small>Removals of registered Persons to be notified to the Registrar.</small>

<small>Penalty.</small>

<small>Copies of the Lists to be had on paying a reasonable price to the Registrar.</small>

Provided always, and be it Enacted, That the Clerk of the said Company shall, in all usual hours of business, furnish a copy of the said corrected list of registered Persons, upon the application of any Person desiring the same, such Person paying to the said Clerk a reasonable price or compensation for the said List; and provided also, that upon the payment of the sum of   to the said Clerk, he shall exhibit or cause to be exhibited, in the office of the said Company, to all such Person and Persons having reasonable cause in that behalf, all and every book and books, register and registers, enrolment and enrolments, touching or in anywise concerning this Act, and the provisions thereof; and also the said Clerk shall suffer and permit such Person and Persons to view and examine, copy and make copies or extracts of and from the same, in writing, upon pain that for every refusal and time of refusing, act and default by the said Clerk refused, omitted, done or committed, contrary to the true intent and meaning of this Act, he shall forfeit and pay the sum of   of lawful money.

<small>Registers and Books to be viewed, and Copies or Extracts taken by Persons, on paying for such search.</small>

<small>Penalty on the Clerk refusing, &c.</small>

And

And be it also Enacted, That no Clockmaker, Watchmaker or Mathematical Instrument maker, being duly registered and certified as aforesaid, shall, by reason or on account of making or selling Clocks or Watches, Watch Chains, Seals or Keys, or Mathematical Instruments, of any metal or material whatsoever, be construed or deemed to be a manufacturer of or dealer in wrought Gold or Silver Plate; nor shall any such Person as aforesaid be deemed liable or required to take out the Licence required to be annually taken out by workers of and dealers in Gold and Silver Plate, under or by virtue of an Act passed in the thirty-first year of King *George* the Second, chapter the thirty-second, or any other or subsequent Act to enforce or increase the said Plate Licence Duty; nor shall any Stamp Duty whatsoever be paid or payable on the enrolling, certifying or admission of any Person to be a Clock or Watchmaker, Mathematical Instrument maker or Engraver as aforesaid, the said Act of the Thirty-first year of King *George* the Second, chapter the thirty-second, or any other Act, Law or Usage to the contrary hereof in anywise notwithstanding.

Persons making or selling Clocks, Watches, &c. are not workers of nor dealers in Gold or Silver Plate,

and are not liable to take out a Plate Licence.

No Stamp Duty payable on enrolling or registering any Person pursuant to this Act.

And be it further Enacted, That from and after the   day of   no Person or Persons whatsoever, that is not at this day a professed workman in the said several arts or trades of Clockmaking, Watchmaking, Mathematical Instrument making or Engraving respectively, shall set to work entertain or retain any Person whatsoever as Apprentice, or by any other name whatsoever, in the said arts or trades, or in any part or branch thereof; nor shall any Clock and Watchmaker, Mathematical Instrument maker or Engraver, take entertain or retain any Apprentice in the said arts or trades respectively, or in any part or branch thereof whatsoever, for less term and time than Seven whole years, to be fully compleat and ended, and according to the custom of apprentices in the City of *London*; and provided also, that every such Apprentice shall be bound and retained upon and according to the form of Indenture in the Schedule to this Act hereinafter mentioned and set forth, and not otherwise nor contrary thereto; nor shall any person whatsoever take unto him or herself as Apprentice in the said arts or trades or either of them, any person that is not a natural free-born subject, or who has not been naturalized; nor shall any Person who is not a natural free-born subject, or having been naturalized, take any apprentice whatsoever in the said arts or trades or either of them; nor shall any Person or Persons take have or retain any Apprentice whatsoever in the said arts or trades or either of them, without enrolling or causing to be enrolled each and every such apprentice and apprentices in the registry to be kept by the Company of the art and mystery of Clockmaking in the City of *London* the indenture of such apprenticeship, within twelve calendar months from the date of every such indenture, and the time of retaining such apprentice; nor shall any Person or Partnership of Persons jointly trading in or using the same arts or trades or either of them, take have or entertain any greater number than One Apprentice at one and the same time, other than his or her own child or children, in the said arts or trades, unless such Person or Partnership of Persons shall have given full and entire employ for Two whole years then next preceding to one able journeyman

No Person that is not a professed Workmaster to take any Apprentice.

No Apprentice to be taken for less term than Seven years.

Form of the Indenture of Apprenticeships in these Arts and Trades.

No Alien to be taken as Apprentice therein.

No Alien to take an Apprentice.

All Apprentices to be enrolled in the Register of the Clockmaking Company.

No Person to have more than One Apprentice, unless they have employed a Journeyman, and then only Two Apprentices at one time.

282.

(8)

journeyman at the least in the said arts or trades, and in the house or workshop of such Person or Partnership; and in such case such Person or Partnership may lawfully take entertain and retain a second apprentice and no more at one and the same time in his or their service, upon any plea or pretence whatsoever; nor shall any person have take or retain upon approbation any person who is desirous or willing to become an apprentice in the said arts or trades, or either of them, for any period of approval exceeding Three calendar months, but such person shall within the said period of Three months be bound as apprentice as aforesaid, or absolutely and for ever dismissed by such his said master or mistress; nor shall any person take or entertain in the said arts or trades or either of them any apprentice without teaching such apprentice or causing him or her to be taught the whole art of making the several parts and interior pieces of mechanism of Clocks Watches and Mathematical Instruments, or of Engraving, which his said master practises respectively as the case shall be, whereby every such Person having duly served as apprentice henceforth on the expiration of his or her term of servitude, shall nothing lack of a sufficiency of knowledge and mechanical skill to execute and fulfil such work and wares, productions of the said arts and trades, to his and her own credit and the profit of the Nation at large, and no deficiency or fraud therein upon the penalty of forfeiting and paying

of lawful money for each and every such offence.

Persons coming upon approval, to be bound Apprentice within Three months, or dismissed.

Masters to teach, or cause to be taught, their Art to their Apprentices

Penalty.

And be it also Enacted, That from and after the day of   no Pawnbroker shall receive in pledge nor purchase any unfinished Clock or Watch or Mathematical Instrument, or part or prepared Material for the same, nor any Tool nor Implements used or for the use of or in the arts manufactures or trades aforesaid, or any part thereof; nor shall any Person whatsoever carry on the trade avocation or business of a Pawnbroker and of a Clockmaker or a Watchmaker, or a Mathematical Instrument maker, and *vice versa*, at one and the same time; nor shall any Workman or other Person whatsoever to whom any Clock or Watch, Mathematical Instrument or Engraving, or any Work, Materials, Tool or Tools, used in or for the same arts or trades or either of them, shall be entrusted to work upon or with, or to repair or otherwise detain the same or any part or portion thereof, but he she and they shall forthwith upon demand made, and without covin or fraud, return the same Clock, Watch, Mathematical Instrument, Engraving, Work, Material, Tool and Tools, and every part thereof, to the Owner thereof, or to the Person who so intrusted the same to him or her respectively; and if any Pawnbroker or other Person shall be found and adjudged to have acted or done otherwise, every such Pawnbroker and other Person so offending shall forfeit

contrary to the true intent and meaning of this Act, and the sum of   of lawful Money for each and every such offence, refusal and time of offending as aforesaid.

Pawnbrokers not to take in pledge nor purchase unfinished Work or Wares, nor Tools.

Pawnbrokers not to be Clockmakers, nor Watchmakers, nor Mathematical Instrument makers.

Workmen to return, upon demand, all Work, Materials and Tools to them entrusted.

Penalty.

Workmen, &c. may retain Clocks, &c. until Work and Repair done thereon are paid for.

Provided always, and be it further Enacted, That it shall and may be lawful for any Workman or Person employed as aforesaid to retain possession of such Clock, Watch, Mathematical Instrument, Engraving, Work,

(9)

Work, Material, Tool and Tools, entrusted to him or her to work upon or repair as aforesaid, until the work done thereon or therewith by such Workman or other Person shall be duly paid for and lawfully discharged in the current Coin of the Realm; and if any person shall pay or offer to pay to any Workman, or for any work done or to be done or executed in the said art or trades of Clockmaking, Watchmaking, Mathematical
35 Instrument making, or Engraving, or in any part or branch thereof, in any commodity, or in any other manner or way whatsoever than in the current Coin of the Realm only, and not otherwise, every Person so offending, and for each and every time he and she shall so offend shall forfeit and pay the sum of   of lawful money. *Workmen not to be paid in Commodities, but Money only.* *Penalty.*

And be it also Enacted, That from and after the day of   no person or persons whatsoever shall export or endeavour to export, any Clock or Watch without first making true entry thereof at His Majesty's Custom House, and previous to shipping the same endorsing on the cocket of the said entry a specific declaration of the description, mark and number of every package in which any such
36 Clock or Watch shall be contained, together with a particular account of the number and description of the Clock and Watches therein contained, upon the Penalty of forfeiting
and the sum of   of lawful money for every offence to the contrary thereof; nor shall any Shipmaster or Owner or other person, at any time after the passing of this Act, take or receive on board any ship or vessel, by the way of trade or for sale, or upon freight or for exportation to parts or places beyond the seas, any Clock or Watch, until a distinct and true entry of every such Clock and Watch, and the description thereof, and of the mark and number of the package, if any such there be, in which the same is contained, shall first have been duly made at His Majesty's Custom House as aforesaid, upon the penalty of
37 forfeiting   for each and every such offence and time of offending; and the like Penalties and Forfeitures shall also be paid and borne by the Shipmaster or Owner of every vessel in which any Clock or Watch shall have been clandestinely exported, or in which any such Clock or Watch shall be found, not having been, previous to the shipping thereof, duly entered for exportation as aforesaid. *How Clocks, Watches, &c. shall be entered for exportation.* *Penalty.* *Ship Masters, &c. not to receive any such on board without due entry, &c.* *Penalty.*

Provided always, and be it Enacted, That any Shipowner or Master
38 against whom any such Penalties shall have been levied for such clandestine shipping of such Clock or Watch, not having been privy to the contents of the Package in which the same shall be or have been contained as aforesaid, shall have his or her remedy against the proprietor or other shipper of such Clock or Watch, Clocks or Watches, so clandestinely exported or endeavoured so to be as aforesaid, and shall recover his or her damages and full costs of suit in the recovery thereof. *Remedy for the Ship Master, &c. suffering any penalty, and not being party to such contraband Shipping.*

And be it also Enacted, That all and every the Penalties, Punishments and Forfeitures, in and by the several Acts and Laws now in force, touching and concerning the manufacture working and making of wares of *Penalties on Persons transposing Marks, &c. on or from Gold and Silver Wares, repealed.*

282.   C

of wrought Gold and Silver, directed to be inflicted upon Persons adjudged to have been guilty of removing the Goldsmith's Hall Mark or Marks from one piece or ware of wrought Gold or Silver that has been lawfully assayed and marked, and transposing or attaching the same to any other piece of Gold or Silver work or ware that has not been so lawfully assayed and marked, shall cease and determine, and all such Penalties Punishments and Forfeitures are hereby repealed, made void, and of no effect.

39

Wrought Gold Wares to be assayed and marked in London, Edinburgh, or Dublin only.

And be it also Enacted, That from and after the   day of   no Manufacture, Work or Ware of wrought Gold, which by any Act or Law now in force shall, previous to the sale or exchange of the same by the maker thereof, be required to be touched, assayed and marked, shall not be so touched, assayed, or marked, but at one or other the Assay Office of the respective Companies of Goldsmiths or Wardens of the Touch in *London*, *Edinburgh* or *Dublin* respectively, where the same Manufactures, Works and Wares shall be tried and assayed, touched and marked, with the Marks, and by, under, and subject to such rules and regulations as by the Acts and Laws now in force are appointed; nor shall any such Wares as aforesaid be assayed for the purpose of being marked, nor any such Hall-marked, in any other Assay Office, City, Town or Place whatsoever, any law, usage or custom to the contrary hereof in anywise notwithstanding.

40

Against transposing the Marks on or from one ware or piece of work to another.

And be it also Enacted, That from and after the   day of   no person or persons whatsoever shall exchange or remove the marks of any Goldsmith's Hall or Assay Office, on, off or from any piece of work or ware, or from any part of any such piece of work or ware of wrought Gold or Silver, that has been lawfully assayed and marked, nor transpose, put or attach the same marks or marked piece of Gold or Silver work or ware, to any other piece of Gold or Silver work or ware, that has not been so lawfully assayed and marked as aforesaid; nor shall any person or persons put or attach the same marks, or Hall-marked piece of work or ware, to any other piece of work or ware of Gold or Silver than the proper work and ware which was or shall have been lawfully assayed and Hall-marked, as and for part of the same work, ware and manufacture, other than and excepting only needful repairs to any old or worn work, ware or manufacture; nor shall any person or persons increase the weight of any piece of work or ware of wrought Gold or Silver, at any time after the same shall have been assayed and Hall-marked as aforesaid, by adding or attaching thereto any other Gold and Silver that has not been so assayed and hall-marked, other than and excepting any needful repairs to any old or worn work, ware or manufacture as aforesaid; upon pain that each and every such person being upon the oath or oaths of any one or more competent witness or witnesses, before any one of His Majesty's justices of the peace as aforesaid, lawfully convicted of any such offence, he or she shall forfeit and pay the sum of   for each and every such piece of work and ware, in or upon which or in respect whereof any such transposition or offence as aforesaid shall have been done or committed; and also

41

42

(11)

also shall by such justice of peace, by warrant under his hand and seal, be committed to the common gaol of the same county, city or place, there to remain the full space and time of

And be it also Enacted, That from and after the   day of no person or persons whatsoever shall add, put or attach any solder or stuffing to any such plate work or ware of Gold or Silver, after the same shall have been produced at the Assay Office, and examined, assayed and hall-marked, and previous to the sale or exchange thereof; nor shall any person make up or cause to be made up or wrought, any work or ware whatsoever of Gold or Silver inferior to one or other the standards for wrought Gold and Silver respectively, as by the laws now in force are appointed; nor shall any person make up or cause to be wrought, any work or ware, or part or piece of or for any work or ware of Gold or Silver, that by reason of the smallness or delicacy of the workmanship thereof, cannot without damage be assayed and receive the touch and the hall-marks thereon, but he or she shall duly put therein and in every piece and part thereof, a full and lawful proportion of fine Gold or of fine Silver respectively, as the said ware or manufacture shall purport to be, and according to one or other of the standards respectively by law appointed and required to be used in manufactures of wrought Gold and Silver respectively; nor omit to put or stamp upon each and every such piece of work or small Gold and Silver wares as aforesaid, a proper distinguishing mark of the initial letters of the christian and surnames of the maker of such small wares and work, and which distinguishing mark shall be duly entered at and in the Assay Office or Goldsmith's Hall nearest unto the place of residence of such maker or worker of small wares as aforesaid; nor shall any person use any fraud or deceit, nor conceal in the internal or other part or parts of any ware of Gold or Silver, any Gold or Silver inferior to the lawful standard for such work or ware; nor any base metal, nor any stuffing, nor more than a proper quantity of solder to attach together the pieces and parts of such work or ware; and which proper quantity of solder shall be judged of and determined by the Wardens of the Company of Goldsmiths respectively nearest unto whose Assay Office any dispute or cause of dispute touching the premises shall be or arise, such Wardens respectively at all times hereafter previous to taking upon them or either of them the said office of Warden, being or having been practical working Goldsmiths or Silversmiths, and being duly elected, appointed and sworn to the lawful exercise of his and their said office and offices respectively, upon the Penalty of forfeiting   to and for the proper use of the person who will seize, convey and sue for the same, before any one or more of His Majesty's Justice or Justices of the Peace acting in or for the County, City or Place where such Offence shall have been committed, and the sum of   of lawful Money for each and every such Offence.

No Gold or Silver inferior to the standard to be wrought into any ware

Small wares to be wrought of the lawful Standards.

Makers Mark to be put upon all small wares.

Against concealed frauds in Gold and Silver wares.

Wardens to determine the quantity of solder.

Penalty.

And be it also Enacted, That from and after the twenty-ninth day of May next ensuing, no person whatsoever shall work or make or cause to be made

To prevent the making of Pendants in quality inferior to the Standards appointed for Gold and Silver.

282.

made or wrought, any Gold or Silver Pendant, or pendant Bow for a Watch-case, less in fineness than one of the standards by the laws now in force appointed for wrought plate, or sell exchange or expose to sale any such Gold or Silver Pendant, or export the same out of this United Kingdom, or solder or otherwise attach the same to any Watchcase of Gold or Silver (such Watchcase Pendant and pendant Bow respectively having been made after the said twenty-ninth day of May) until such Pendant and Bow shall have been lawfully marked with the mark of the worker or maker thereof, together with some one or more of the marks by the laws now in force required to be used for the marking of Watchcases of Gold and Silver respectively, upon pain that every such person or persons for every such offence shall forfeit and pay the sum of

And to prevent the same from being used to Watch cases until duly Hall marked.

Penalty.

All Pendants made before the 29th day of May next, to be freely sold or exported, whether marked or not.

Provided always, and be it Enacted, That nothing in this Act contained shall be construed or taken to prohibit the free sale or exportation of any Watch with a Pendant attached thereto, the cases of which Watch and which Pendant respectively shall have been made before the said twenty-ninth day of May, notwithstanding such Pendant may not have received any of the marks by this Act or any other law now in force directed to be impressed on Pendants of Gold or Silver for Watchcases.

Work found upon Assay worse than Standard, to be broken and re-delivered to the Owner without other penalty.

And provided always, and be it further Enacted, That whensoever any work, ware or manufacture of wrought Gold or Silver shall be sent to or delivered at any Goldsmith's Hall or Assay Office by law established for the purpose of such ware being assayed and touched, and upon assay and trial thereof upon three succeeding working days duly made, the said work, ware or manufacture shall be found and adjudged worse in fineness than one or other of the standards for work and wares of wrought Gold and Silver respectively lawfully appointed, every such insufficient work, ware and manufacture shall be broken cut or otherwise utterly defaced, and the materials thereof shall by the warden or officer of such Assay Office be re-delivered to the Owner or Owners thereof, or the person by him her or them, by writing under his her or their hand or hands, authorized to demand and receive the same; and such delivery shall be made without any further or other pain penalty let or hinderance whatsoever, to or upon the maker or proprietor thereof, other than such breaking and defacing of the workmanship as aforesaid.

Gold and Silver in which any concealed fraud is suspected may be cut and assayed.

Provided also, and be it Enacted, That it shall and may be lawful to and for the Assayer or other chief officer of the several Companies of Goldsmiths, Wardens of the Touch, and Assayers respectively, at the several Assay offices by law appointed and established for the purpose of assaying and marking of wares and manufactures of wrought Gold and Silver respectively, to cut and examine, or cause to be cut and examined, any piece or parcel of work, ware and manufacture, brought to be assayed as aforesaid, wherein or in the construction whereof such Assayer or other officer shall suspect any concealed fraud, covin or deceit, either in the interior or other parts or construction of such work, ware or manu-

If any fraud is found therein

facture; and if upon trial and assay lawfully made, any concealed fraud shall be found or discovered in such work, ware or manufacture, the maker

maker thereof shall forfeit and pay the sum of   for   *Penalty.*
every such piece of work, ware or manufacture, so found to be fraudulently
or deceitfully wrought.

52   Provided always, and be it Enacted, That if no fraud or deception be found in such work, ware or manufacture, so cut and examined as aforesaid, the Assayer or other Officer as aforesaid shall, out of the public funds and monies received in the said Assay Office, immediately pay unto the Workman aggrieved, the full value of the workmanship, and all loss and damage by such Workman sustained from and by reason of the cutting and defacing of his said work, ware or manufacture as aforesaid.   *If no fraud is found in such work or ware, the Workman to be paid his damage and costs.*

53   And provided always, and be it Enacted, That if any Assayer or other Officer or Person shall act or do contrary to the true intent and meaning of this Act, or shall unlawfully spoil or unnecessarily deface or injure any work, ware or manufacture brought to be assayed at the public Assay Office as aforesaid, there being no fraud or deficiency in the Gold or Silver thereof, such Assay Officer or other Person shall pay to the Person or Workman thereby aggrieved, his or her especial damage sustained, and all Costs of Suits in recovering the same, before any one or more of His Majesty's Justice or Justices of Peace acting in or for the County, City or Place wherein such offence shall have been committed.   *Assay officers doing unnecessary damage to work sent to be assayed, shall pay the especial damage to the Person injured*

54   And be it further Enacted, That if any Person or Persons whatsoever from and after the   day of   shall enter at His Majesty's Custom House, for the purpose of exporting to Foreign parts, by way of merchandize, any work, ware or manufacture of wrought Gold or Silver made within this realm, and upon the making whereof the several duties by law appointed have been duly paid and satisfied, and such Person shall desire to draw back and have repaid to him or her such portions of the said duties on such work or wares as by law are allowed to be drawn back on the exportation thereof, that in every such case the Customer, Searcher or other chief Officer of His Majesty's Customs, at the Port in which such Gold or Silver wares shall be so entered for exportation, shall put his seal upon every Package containing such Gold or Silver ware, and shall, at the expense and risk of the   *To prevent frauds in drawing back the duties on Gold and Silver Plate exported, and re-importing and selling the same without duty.*

55   intending exporter, transmit such package to the Goldsmiths Hall or Assay Office wherein the said work or ware was marked, and paid the duty on the manufacture thereof, where the same work or ware being capable to receive a mark, shall be again marked with a mark by the Wardens of the Company of Goldsmiths in *London*, to be from time to time appointed and ordained, to testify by such mark that the same work and ware has been entered and marked for exportation ; and the drawing back of the duties thereon as aforesaid, and being so marked, the same work and wares shall in like manner be sealed up in a package by the

56   Assay officer, and by him at the cost, expense and risk of the intending exporter, re-conveyed to His Majesty's warehouse of the Custom House from whence the package so came to be marked as aforesaid, and such work and ware of wrought Gold and Silver may then lawfully be exported, and the duties thereon drawn back and repaid, subject to such provisions as

Penalty.	as by the laws in force are shall or may be appointed, touching or concerning the exportation of and drawing back the duties on wrought Gold and Silver plate; and if any plate, work or ware of wrought Gold or Silver, that has been so marked for exportation as aforesaid, shall afterwards be found in the possession of any Person or Persons whatsoever, and shall not have been previously re-entered, and the duties thereon repaid and satisfied, and re-marked on the importation thereof, he or she shall forfeit and the sum of for every piece thereof.
Wardens, together with the Chief Assayer, may search for fraudulent wares. 3d of Edward IV, cap. 4. re enacted for Gold and Silver wares.	AND for the more effectual suppression of frauds and abuses in the manufacture, working, alteration, trading, dealing in and sale of Gold and Silver wares, committed in secret places and shops; BE it also Enacted, by the authority aforesaid, That from and after the day of it shall and may be lawful to and for the Wardens, together with the Chief or Head Assay-master of the several Companies of Goldsmiths and Guardians of the Touch respectively, or of either of them, (such Wardens respectively at all times hereafter, and previous to taking upon either of them the said office of Warden, being or having been practical working Goldsmiths or Silversmiths, and being duly elected, appointed and sworn to the lawful exercise of his and their said Office and Offices respectively) with whom or in whose public Assay Office, lawfully appointed, the mark of any maker or worker for dealer in Gold or Silver wares shall be entered, or nearest unto whose public Assay Office as aforesaid, any dealer in Gold or Silver wares shall be dwelling, or any two of such Wardens, together with their chief Assayer as aforesaid, at any and all working time and times, as to the said Wardens shall seem meet, to enter into the several and respective workshops, shops, warehouses, place and places of business, of every such Gold or Silver worker and dealer in Gold or Silver wares, and there to search and search for, inspect and take view of, and if the said Wardens shall see it fitting, to touch, assay, and by their best means and ability, try and ascertain the lawful quality and sufficiency of any or every the work, wares and materials of Gold and Silver, there found and wrought or in progress to be wrought, by or for any such workmaster or dealer as aforesaid; or, if the said Wardens shall so think fit, to convey the same wares, works and prepared materials of Gold and Silver, to the public Assay Office of the said Company of Goldsmiths, or Guardians of the Touch,
Fraudulent or deceitful wares, work, &c. Penalty.	and there to touch, try and assay the same; and if any fraud or deceit shall be found therein, such of the said wares, works and prepared materials, so unlawfully wrought, shall be and broken, and the sale price or value of the broken materials thereof, shall be appropriated to and in aid of a fund, by the same Company of Goldsmiths to be applied and used in, to and towards the prosecution of Offenders
Refusing the wardens, &c. entrance to search for frauds.	against the provisions of this Act; and if any Person or Persons whatsoever shall refuse admittance to, or shall impede the said Wardens and Assayer, or either of them, in the execution or performance of the duties so assigned to them as aforesaid, he she and every of them so offending, and so often and for every time that he she or they shall so refuse or impede

(15)

impede the said Wardens and Assayer as aforesaid, shall forfeit and pay the sum of — *Penalty.*

62 Provided always, and be it Enacted, That such work, ware and materials, in which no fraud or deceit shall be found, shall be returned to the owner thereof, within one working day from the day on which the same was so conveyed to the Assay Office to be examined as aforesaid. *Time for returning unobjectionable work.*

63 Provided always, and be it Enacted, That if any Shopkeeper or Dealer in Plate or wares of wrought Gold or Silver, or other Person not being privy or party to the working or making of any such unlawful or deceitful wares or manufactures as aforesaid, shall suffer or sustain any penalty loss or damage by reason of any such fraud or deceit, such Shopkeeper Dealer and other Person shall recover double Damages and Costs of Suit and recovery from the Workman, Worker or Maker who wrought or sold such deceitful work or ware; and which damages and costs shall be determined awarded, and the payment thereof enforced, by such Justice or Justices of Peace as aforesaid. *Remedy for Shopkeepers and other Persons aggrieved by any fraud in Gold or Silver wares*

64 And be it also Enacted, That so much and such part of a certain Act made in the Twelfth year of the reign of his late Majesty King *George* the Second, chapter the twenty-sixth, as enacts, " that no Action or Suit at Law shall be had commenced or prosecuted, against any of the Wardens or other Officers of the several Companies of Goldsmiths or Guardians of the Touch, and the respective Assay Officers, for any act matter or thing by him or them in their said Offices done, in the touching assaying or marking of work or wares of wrought Gold or Silver, or otherwise touching the premises, unless such Action or Suit shall be brought or commenced before the end of the next term after the fact committed, and not afterwards," shall be and it is hereby repealed. *Part of the Act 12th Geo. II, cap. 26, repealed.*

65 Provided always, and be it Enacted, That such Action or Suits as aforesaid, touching or concerning the premises aforesaid, shall and may be had brought and commenced at any time within one year next ensuing the expiration of the usage or change of the variable Mark or Letter of the said Company of Goldsmiths or Assay Office for the year within which cause of Action or Suit shall be discovered by the Person aggrieved, and not afterwards. *Time for commencing Actions and Suits against Assay Officers, &c. limited.*

66 And be it Enacted, That from and after the   day of   no unfinished Clock or Watch, nor prepared material of or for a Clock or Watch, or of or for a Musical Piece, Snuff Box or Machine, to be moved by Clock or Watchwork, nor any Musical Box, Snuff Box or other Box or Jewellery, Clock or Watch, in or upon which is represented placed or attached any print, painting or figure, movement or motion, of an immoral or obscene description or tendency whatsoever, shall be imported into these Realms from foreign parts or places, under any plea or pretence whatsoever; and all such unfinished foreign made Clocks and Watches, prepared Materials, Musical Pieces, *The importation of foreign unfinished Clock and Watchwork, &c. prohibited.* *Seizable wheresoever found, and to be destroyed.*

282.

Pieces, Snuff Boxes, Clock and Watchwork and Jewellery as aforesaid, which after the said   day of
shall be found or discovered, shall and may be seized by the Person who shall discover and will convey the same before any one or more of His Majesty's Justice or Justices of the Peace acting in or for the County City or Place where such prohibited articles goods and wares as aforesaid shall be found or discovered; and upon proof being made on the oath of one or more credible Witness or Witnesses, that the same are such prohibited articles goods and wares as aforesaid, they and every of

Penalty. them shall be
for the proper use of the Person who seized the same articles goods and wares as aforesaid; and the Person or Persons in whose possession any such prohibited articles goods or wares as aforesaid shall be found or discovered, shall also feifeit and pay the Sum of
for each and every time that any such prohibited articles goods or wares shall be found or discovered in his or her possession.

Foreign-made Clocks, Watches, &c. to be allowed to entry in the Port of London only;

And be it also Enacted, That from and after the said   day of   no finished and complete Clock or Watch, Musical Snuff Box or other Box or Jewellery, in which any motion, sound or music is produced on bells, wires, musical springs or organ pipes, operated upon by Clock or Watchwork, wheels, springs or other machinery, shall be imported from foreign parts, and allowed to entry but at His Majesty's Custom-house in the port of London only, where such foreign-made wares shall be liable to, and the owner or owners thereof shall pay and satisfy such duties of customs thereon which by any law now in force, or which hereafter shall be enacted, may and lawfully ought to be levied and paid on the importation of such foreign-made goods and wares as aforesaid; nor shall any such foreign-made goods or ware as aforesaid be entered or admitted at or in any other port or place than the said port of *London*; nor unless every such foreign-made Clock and Watch, Musical Box or Piece as aforesaid, shall be compleat

and none to be admitted, unless they bear the names, &c. of the maker thereon.

and fit for use, and shall have thereon engraven, or otherwise permanently put placed and affixed, the christian and surnames and place of abode of the maker, together with a distinct number upon each, by which such Clock and Watch, Musical Box and Piece, may be known, described and identified, upon the penalty of forfeiting

Penalty.

upon which the christian and surnames and place of abode of the maker, and a distinct number on each and every thereof, shall not be duly engraven, or otherwise permanently and conspicuously put or placed, or which shall not have been entered in the port of *London* for the payment of the duties thereon as aforesaid; and the same penalty and forfeiture shall be to the proper use of the Person who will seize and convey such Clock and Watch ware, Musical Box and Piece, to His Majesty's warehouse of the Customs in the said port of *London*.

No British name, either of Person or Place, to be put upon foreign work.

And be it further Enacted, That from and after the   day of   no person whatsoever shall engrave, paint or otherwise place put or attach, upon any foreign-made Clock or Watch, any name or names, being or purporting to be the name or names

(17)

72 names of any British person or place; nor by any other way or means whatsoever, alter or disguise the name or appearance of any Clock or Watch of foreign make, so that the same may appear, or be mistaken or sold as or for British manufacture; nor shall any person sell, exchange or expose to sale, or exchange as or for British manufacture, any Clock or Watch of foreign make or any Clock or Watch whereof the movements or internal parts are of foreign make and the cases British, or whereof the movements or internal parts are British and the cases foreign made; but all such Clocks and Watches shall be sold as and for the mixed workmanship, as the fact shall be, and not otherwise; nor shall any foreign made Clock or Watch, or any Clock or Watch having thereon any forged
73 name, or imitation of a name of a British person or place, or any forged imitation of marks impressed on Watches or Watchcases, in at or by any public Office or otherwise in *Great Britain*, be imported, sold, exchanged, repaired, altered or exported by any person whatsoever, upon the penalty of forfeiting   and the sum of   of lawful money, for each and every of such Clocks and Watches as aforesaid, to the use of the Person who will seize and convey the same Clocks and Watches before any one or more of His Majesty's Justices of Peace as aforesaid, and upon proof upon the oath of any one or more competent witness
74 or witnesses, every such unlawful Clock and Watch shall be broken and utterly destroyed, and the broken materials thereof shall be to the use of the Person who seized the same as aforesaid; nor shall any Person whatsoever, after the   day of   import, purchase, deal in, or vend or expose to sale as a dealer in, any Clock or Watch, or any piece of Clock or Watchwork, Mechanism or Machinery, or Jewellery wares, of foreign make, until he and she shall, in the manner hereinafter mentioned, be duly authorized and licensed to trade or deal in the said foreign made wares and manufacutures, upon the penalty of
75 forfeiting   and the sum of   for each and every such foreign Clock and Watch, piece of Clock or Watchwork, Mechanism, and Machinery, and Jewellery ware, which shall be found in the possession of any Person so importing, purchasing, vending or exposing to sale the same goods or wares, such person not having been previously thereto duly licensed to import and deal in such goods and wares as aforesaid; and which forfeitures and penalties shall be to the use of the Person who will seize the said goods and wares, and will sue for the same before any one of His Majesty's Justices of the Peace as aforesaid.

And be it further Enacted, That such license and licenses to import and deal in foreign-made Clocks and Watches, Clock and Watchwork,
76 Mechanism or Machinery and Jewellery of foreign make, shall be granted issued and distributed on or before the   day of   next ensuing, and afterwards on or before the   day of   in every year, by the Commissioners for managing the receipt of His Majesty's duties of Excise, at their head office in *London*, who are hereby empowered and required to enroll and issue such licenses, under the hands and seals of the said Commissioners, or of any two of them

Foreign-made work not to be altered or disguised so as to appear as British.

Foreign-made work not to be sold as British manufacture.

All Clocks and Watches, partly of foreign and partly British manufacture, to be sold as such mixed work.

Foreign-made work, and all Clocks and Watches, having or bearing thereon any forged name or forged marks, not to be repaired, sold, &c.

Penalty.

None to import or deal in foreign Clocks, &c. until duly licensed.

Penalty.

Foreign Clock and Watch dealers Licence to be annually renewed.

By whom and in what manner such Licences shall be granted.

Sum to be paid for each Licence.	them, upon the payment of the sum of by the Person requiring such license, for each and every such license to import and deal in such foreign-made goods and wares as aforesaid.
Foreign Clocks, Watches, &c. imported after paying the duties, are, previous to sale, to be marked by the Clockmakers Company, pursuant to patent granted 22d August 1631.	And be it also Enacted, That each and every foreign-made Clock and Watch, and all other the productions of the said arts and manufactures of Clock and Watchmaking, already imported, and which hereafter shall or may be imported from parts and places beyond the seas, shall, after the duties payable on the importation thereof shall have been paid and satisfied, be delivered by the Officer and Officers of His Majesty's Customs, or other Persons having the custody thereof, unto the proper Officer in that behalf appointed of the Company of the Master, Wardens and Fellowship of the art and mystery of Clockmaking of the City of *London*, taking his receipt for the same ; and each and every the foreign-made Clocks and Watches, works and productions aforesaid, shall, by the said Company or their proper Officer, be properly and sufficiently marked according to the provisions in the Charter granted to the said Company on the twenty-second day of August in the year one thousand six hundred and thirty-one, for that purpose mentioned and expressed, and by the marks so impressed or otherwise put thereon by the said Company, to notify that each and every the same Clock and Watchwork and production has been duly examined, and also that the duties thereon as by law is required have been duly paid, before the same is or shall be permitted or allowed to pass into the possession of the importer or owner thereof ; and the said
Price to be taken by the Company for marking.	Master, Wardens and Fellowship, or their proper Officer, shall and may lawfully ask demand and receive, for the marking and allowing of such foreign-made Clocks and Watches, works productions and wares of the arts and trades aforesaid, as lawful fit and proper to be imported and sold, such sum of Money as to the said Company of Clockmakers shall appear reasonable to defray the expense of examining and marking the same as aforesaid, not exceeding in the whole pence in the pound sterling of the value of the Clocks, Watches, works and productions so imported and brought to the office of the said Company to be examined and marked as aforesaid.
No Person shall work upon or finish any foreign Clock or Watchwork,	And be it further Enacted, That from and after the day of no Clockmaker or Watchmaker, or other Person, shall make up or complete, or employ any workman to make up, work upon or complete any unfinished foreign work, or part or prepared
nor repair any such, that is not duly marked.	material of or for a Clock or Watch ; nor shall any person work upon or repair any foreign-made Clock or Watch, that is not duly marked with the marks hereinbefore directed to be impressed or put thereon by the Company of Clockmakers as aforesaid, without first sending every such Clock or Watch to the proper officer of the said Company to be marked, and
Penalty.	the duties thereon duly paid and satisfied, upon the penalty of for every such offence, and upon pain of forfeiting to the use of the person who will seize and sue for the same as aforesaid.

Provided

(19)

Provided always, and be it Enacted, That nothing in this Act contained shall be taken or construed to extend, to prevent any person from repairing any Clock or Watch of foreign make, that has been lawfully marked in pursuance of the provisions of this Act. *Not to prevent the repairing of Clocks and Watches lawfully marked.*

§2. And be it further Enacted, That on or before the   day of   all and every such foreign-made Clocks and Watches as shall be in the possession of any person whatsoever, whether as a dealer therein or otherwise, shall be brought to His Majesty's Custom House in the port of London, for the purpose of being examined, and the duties payable on the importation thereof satisfied, or proof given that the said duties have already been answered and paid, and then to be delivered to or at the office of the said Company of Clockmakers in London, to be examined and marked as aforesaid; and every such foreign made Clock and Watch, which after the said   day of   shall be exposed to sale by or which shall be found in possession of any person whatsoever, which shall not have been entered at §3. the Custom House, and marked as aforesaid, or on which the duties payable on the importation thereof shall not have been duly answered and satisfied, shall be   and conveyed to His Majesty's Custom House, and being first duly marked by the said Company of Clockmakers, as aforesaid, shall be delivered thence to and for the proper use of the person who did so seize and convey the same to the Custom House as aforesaid; and the proof, if any, to the contrary of such forfeiture, shall be upon the owner of or person claiming restitution of the said goods before the nearest Justice or Justices of the Peace, as aforesaid. *Foreign Clocks and Watches now imported to be brought to the Custom-house, to ascertain the payment of duties thereon; and then to be delivered to the Company of Clockmakers to be marked. Foreign Clocks and Watches not marked conformable to this Act, to be seized, &c. Proof to the contrary to lie upon the owner.*

§4. Provided always, and be it Enacted, That all and every the finished Clocks and Watches of foreign make, which shall be seized or taken by the officers of His Majesty's Customs, for under valuation by the importer thereof, and condemned, shall be sold for exportation only, in the same manner as prohibited goods. *Foreign Clocks and Watches seized to be sold for exportation only.*

And provided always, and be it Enacted, That all such foreign-made Clocks and Watches as aforesaid, which at this day are in the possession of any Person bonâ fide using the same Clocks and Watches, and not being dealer therein, shall be brought to the Custom House in London, and shall be marked as aforesaid, and delivered to the Owner, without any duty, charge, or expense whatsoever thereon. *All foreign-made Clocks and Watches now in possession of Persons bona fide using the same, to be marked duty-free.*

§5. AND, for the better execution of the provisions of this Act, BE it further Enacted, by the Authority aforesaid, That from and after the   day of   every Person whatsoever who shall use as his or her calling or avocation the art, trade or mystery of Clockmaking, Watchmaking, Mathematical Instrument-making, or Engraving, or any part or branch thereof, shall and may become a Freeman and Member of the said Company of the Master, Wardens and Fellowship of the art and mystery of Clockmaking of the City of London, and shall not be refused to be admitted accordingly; upon pain that every Person that shall be found offending to the contrary hereof, shall forfeit and pay the sum of *For the prevention of frauds and abuses, all persons who use the arts and trades shall or may become freemen of the Company of Clockmakers. Penalty.*

282.   Provided

(20)

Marginal note	Text
All Persons now using the arts and trades to be admitted to the freedom of the Company, on paying the usual duties and fees, as by apprenticeship.	Provided always, and be it further Enacted, That every such Person as aforesaid, who shall make application to be admitted as Freemen and Members of the said Company, shall be so admitted, upon paying the same Stamp to His Majesty, and also the like Fees and Charges to the said Company for such their admission, as shall from time to time be paid and payable by Persons entitled to be admitted to the Freedom of the said Company by apprenticeship, such Person and Persons first taking and subscribing such Oath and Oaths as shall be usually and lawfully administered, taken and subscribed by Persons admitted to the Freedom of the said Company;
Persons residing in the country, how to be admitted and enrolled.	and in case such Person shall dwell or reside at any distance more than ten miles from the City of *London*, such Applicant shall be sworn by and before any one of His Majesty's Justices of the Peace acting in or for the County City or Place wherein such Applicant shall reside or be dwelling; and the said Applicant and the said Justice of Peace shall sign the same upon the form of Oath, to be previously for that purpose furnished by the Clerk of the said Company, and which said Subscription and Oath being transmitted to the said Clerk, shall be inrolled in the Registers of the said Company, and the said Applicant shall from thenceforth be admitted free and a Freeman of the said Company, to all intents and purposes whatsoever.
Company to stand and be incorporated as in the Charter is mentioned.	And be it further Enacted, That the said Company of the Master Wardens and Fellowship of the art and mystery of Clockmaking, shall stand and be incorporated in such sort and with the Powers and Authorities, as in the Charter for the Incorporation of the said Company is mentioned.
Of whom the Company shall consist.	Provided always, and be it also Enacted, That there shall henceforth be one Master and three Wardens and twenty-four Assistants, three Auditors of Accounts, one Clerk and Registrar, and so many Persons as shall be and become Free and Freemen of the said Company; and that shall be the said Master, and
Master and Wardens named.	shall be the said Wardens of the said Company, to hold and exercise the said Offices of Master and Wardens respectively until the first Monday which shall be in the month of January next ensuing, and from thence until such time as they and each of them respectively shall be succeeded by some other Person and Persons lawfully elected and sworn, in his their and each of their said office and offices respectively; and that
Assistants named.	shall be the present Assistants of the said Company, to continue and hold the said office and offices as Assistants, for and during their and each of their natural lives, unless they or either of them shall for any good cause be removed by four parts in five in number upon the ballott, in any General Assembly of the said Company for such purpose duly convened; and that after the death or removal as aforesaid of any one or more of the said Assistants, that then there shall be, in the manner and form hereinafter mentioned and appointed, an election of one other Person in the place and stead of each and every
Auditors named.	of the said Assistants so dying or being removed as aforesaid; and that shall be the Auditors of the

the said Company, to hold and exercise the said office and offices respectively, as to one Auditor, until the first Monday which shall be in the month of January now next ensuing, and as to one other Auditor until the like day following one year from the day last mentioned, and as to the remaining one Auditor, to continue in his said office until the like day following two whole years from the day last mentioned; and for avoiding disputes amongst the said Auditors respectively, they shall determine by the ballot amongst themselves which of them respectively
91 shall go out of office on the three several days aforesaid.

And provided always, and be it Enacted, That all future Masters Wardens and Assistants shall be or have been practical Clockmakers, Watchmakers, Mathematical Instrument-makers or Mathematicians, and Engravers, at all times composing the whole number of persons, by seven persons of each of the said four branches of the said incorporation respectively, and also being or becoming Freemen of the said Company, and of the Livery of the City of *London*, and being duly sworn to a just impartial and lawful exercise of the duties of the said offices respectively, previous to taking upon themselves or either of them the said offices or either of them; and that   shall be the Clerk and Registrar of
92 the said Company of Clockmakers, to hold the said office, and exercise the duties of the same from henceforth during the good will and pleasure of the said Company, and subject to be removed by and by the order of any especial general Assembly of the said Master Wardens Assistants and Freemen of the same Company, and so on as to any and every future Clerk and Registrar, Clerks and Registrars of the same Company; and so often as any vacancy shall be occasioned or happen by the death or removal of the Clerk and Registrar for the time being, the said office shall, within thirty days thereafter, be filled up by a new election of a fit and proper person, to be determined by the ballot in an especial general Assembly of the Master Wardens Assistants and Freemen of the said Company, for that purpose to be convened and holden.

Masters, Wardens and Assistants to be composed of Persons of the several incorporated arts, and to be duly sworn.

Clerk and Registrar how to be elected, &c.

And provided always, and be it also Enacted, That at the hour of eleven of the clock before noon, on the first Monday in the month of
93 October in every year, there shall be, at the Common Hall or usual place of meeting of the said Company, a General Court and Assembly of the said Master, Wardens, Assistants and Fellowship, to nominate and elect four fit and proper persons, from among the Freemen of the said Company, who at the time being are not any of the Assistants of the said Company, to fill and exercise the office and offices of Master and Wardens respectively for one year, and one fit and able person to be one of the Auditors of Accounts of the said Company for three years; and after the death or removal of the present Assistants, to elect eight other fit and able persons, or such other part of the said number, to replace vacancies occasioned by death, removal or resignation in the said number of Twenty-four Assistants, to hold the said office of Assistants, for three years next following the first Monday in the month of January then next ensuing such election as aforesaid.

General assembly of the Company annually for elections.

How long the Persons newly elected are to serve in their respective offices.

All elections to be determined by the ballot.	And provided also, and be it Enacted, That all and every Election and Elections of Officers shall be by Ballot, which Ballot shall be taken between the hours of twelve of the clock at noon and five of the clock
What Persons must be present to form a Court able for business, and to prevent adjournment.	in the afternoon of the same day: Provided always, That if the Master and the more part of the Wardens and Assistants, and at least thirty Freemen of the said Company, shall not be in attendance at and within one hour of the time appointed for the assembling of any General Court of or for Elections or otherwise as aforesaid, or that the said number having been present, any of them shall have departed, so that the quorum as aforesaid be not present during the whole of the business of such Assembly, that in every such case the said Court shall be adjourned until the Monday then next ensuing, and so on from Monday to Monday, until the election and acceptance of Office, by writing under the hand and hands respectively of the persons who shall be or have been chosen
Notice to be given of adjourned General Courts.	to be such Officers as aforesaid, due notice of every such adjournment, when any such shall happen or take place, being given at their places of residence to the Freemen of the said Company residing within three miles of the said Common Hall, and to all others by advertisement in the London Gazette and one public daily newspaper, stating the object and business of such adjourned Court, so to be holden as aforesaid.
In case of the death, removal or resignation of the Master or Wardens, what shall be done to replace the Head of the Company.	And provided always, and be it Enacted, That in case of the death, removal or resignation, with consent of any General Assembly, of the Master for the time being of the said Company, then the senior Warden for the time being shall immediately thereupon become *ipso facto* Master of the said Company in his place or stead, who so died, was removed, or resigned as aforesaid, and the Wardens remaining shall also advance in their offices, and so on as to either of the Wardens of the said Company: and within thirty days after any such death, removal or resignation, there shall be a General Assembly of the said Company as aforesaid, to elect by the ballot a fit and proper person to be junior Warden of the said
New election, in case of the death or resignation of Assistants.	Company for the remainder of the then current year of service; and in case of the death or resignation of any Assistant of the said Company, the vacancy thereby occasioned shall be filled up by a new election of one or other fit person as aforesaid in his place or stead, and so on, so often as and for so many as shall have died or been removed from the said office of Assistant, such election to be decided by the ballot as aforesaid, in the Quarterly Court and General Assembly next ensuing
How long to serve in office.	the death, removal or resignation of such Assistant respectively; and the person and persons so elected shall have and hold the said office of Assistant until the first Monday in the month of January next ensuing
After the death or resignation of the present Assistants, one-third of the Assistants for the time being to go out of office every year.	such election: Provided always, That after the death or resignation respectively of the Assistants hereinbefore named, one third part in number of the Assistants for the time being shall yearly and every year quit and go out of the office of Assistant on the first Monday in the month of January, and shall be replaced in the said office of Assistant, by eight fit and proper persons to be for that purpose elected at the General Court for elections then next preceding, as aforesaid.

And

(25)

98 And be it further Enacted, That on the first Monday in the months of January, April and July, and the third Monday in October, yearly and every year, and oftener, when the Master and Wardens shall cause the same to be convened, and so often as the holding of such General Assembly shall be demanded on the requisition of thirty Freemen of the said Company, by writing under their hands addressed to the Master, or to the Clerk for the time being of the said Company, as to the requirers shall seem fitting, there shall be held at their Common Hall or usual place of meeting, a General Assembly of the said Company, for the dispatch and ordering of such business and affairs of the said Company, and touching or concerning the arts and manufactures aforesaid, as shall then and there be, by any Freeman whatsoever, produced, proposed and submitted to the decision and order of the same General Assembly, wherein every Freeman of the said Company shall and may attend, and
99 freely express his sentiments, and assent or dissent, vote and ballot, to and upon all and every such propositions, matters, affairs and business whatsoever; and further, that any Freeman whatsoever shall and may be at full liberty to orignate and propose the enactment or repeal of any bye law, order, business or question as aforesaid; and every question in the said General Assembly, and in every General Assembly of the said Company, shall be decided by the ballots of three parts in four in number of the ballots of the Freemen present at or in such General Assembly and balloting as aforesaid.

General assemblies of the Company to be held four times in every year, and oftener, when the Master and Wardens shall think fit; and upon requisition of thirty freemen.

Every freeman may originate any business and vote thereon in such Courts.

All questions to be decided by the ballot of three parts in four of the number of freemen balloting.

100 Provided always, and be it further Enacted, That it shall and may be lawful to and for the said Company of the Master Wardens and Fellowship of the art and mystery of Clockmaking, in General Court, by and upon seven days previous notice and advertisement in the London Gazette, and in one public daily newspaper, for that purpose especially assembled, to make such good and wholesome Laws, Orders and Ordinances, as to the same General Assembly, and which being confirmed by a subsequent General Assembly, to be in like manner convened as aforesaid, shall appear fitting and proper for the good rule and government of all person and persons using and employed in the said arts, manufactures and trades of Clockmaking, Watchmaking, Mathematical Instrument-making, and Engraving, and the several parts, branches, works and wares thereof whatsoever, and for the prevention of Frauds and Abuses therein;
101 and for apportioning, raising and collecting from the several Persons using or employed in the said arts, manufactures and trades as aforesaid, as well Freemen as others, such reasonable and rateable contributions in money, from time to time, as may be and be deemed necessary for and to defray the expenses attendant on the due execution of this Act, and the several provisions herein mentioned; and in every such law, order and ordinance, shall assign such penalties and forfeitures to enforce obedience to the same laws, orders and ordinances, as to the said General Assemblies shall seem meet and reasonable: Provided always, That no such penalty or forfeiture shall exceed the sum of
for any one offence, or any one time of offending; and that the same shall be sued for, prosecuted and recovered, in such and the like manner

General assemblies to make laws for touching and concerning the arts, manufactures and trades, and for prevention of frauds and abuses therein.

How the Monies shall be raised to defray the Expenses of executing this Act.

Penalties to be assigned for breach of any law made by the Company in pursuance of this Act, not to exceed £. for any one offence.

How such penalties shall be prosecuted for and recovered.

282. and

(24)

and form as for the forfeitures and penalties in this Act hereinafter is mentioned, directed and appointed.

General assemblies may alter, amend or repeal any such law as aforesaid.

And provided always, and be it also Enacted, That such General Assembly duly convened and holden as aforesaid, shall and may from time to time, and at all times hereafter, alter, amend, repeal and make anew, all any and every Law and Order, Laws and Orders of the said Company whatsoever, any law usage or custom to the contrary hereof in anywise notwithstanding.

Forgery of certificates, marks, &c. or perjury touching the premises.

And be it further Enacted, That if any Person whatsoever shall forge, alter, transpose or falsely use any Certificate, or any Stamp, Mark, or Device, or the Signature, or any writing purporting to be the Signature or Certificate of or by any Justice of the Peace, Clerk or Registrar, or other Officer by this Act appointed, allowed or required to be used, applied, issued or given, or shall falsely swear or give false testimony or evidence touching or concerning the provisions or directions of this Act, by any manner or means, he or she for each and every such offence shall

Penalty.

forfeit and pay   and shall be committed to and suffer imprisonment for the space and time of
in the common Gaol of the County, City or Place, wherein such offence shall have been done or committed.

Workmen and other Persons concerned may give evidence against offenders, and be themselves indemnified from penalties.

Provided always, and be it also Enacted, That if any workman employed upon or in the manufactures aforesaid, or either of them, or any other person being party to or concerned in the doing or committing of any offence contrary to the true intent and meaning of this Act, or any part thereof, and shall give information thereof, so that any one or more such offender or offenders shall be lawfully convicted of such offence, such workman and other person shall be for ever released from all and every pain, penalty and forfeiture whatsoever, for touching and consequent to the said offence, had such information as aforesaid not been given; and his or her testimony shall be good and valid, and shall be received as such in the adjudication and determination of the offence charged to have been done or committed.

Application of the penalties, and where they may be sued for, and offenders prosecuted.

And be it further Enacted, That all Forfeitures and pecuniary Penalties hereby imposed, shall (if sued for within   from the time of the discovery of the offence committed, for which any such forfeiture or penalty shall have been incurred) be to the use of the person that shall seize such unlawful and prohibited Clocks, Watches and wares as aforesaid, or who will sue for the same; and the same forfeitures and penalties, together with all costs of suing for and recovering the same, shall be delivered and paid accordingly.

Justices may determine offences, &c.

Provided always, and be it further Enacted, That it shall and may be lawful to and for any Justice of Peace residing near the place where the offence shall be committed, to hear and determine any offence against this Act, which subjects the offender to any pain penalty or forfeiture, pecuniary or otherwise, which said Justice of Peace is hereby authorized

and

106 and required upon any information exhibited, or complaint made in that behalf, within one year after the time of the discovery of the offence committed, to summon the party accused, giving to each party three days notice, to appear before such Justice of Peace, and also the witnesses on either side, and to examine into the matter of fact; and upon proof made thereof either by voluntary confession of the party accused, or by the oath of one or more competent witness or witnesses, to give judgment or sentence accordingly, and for the forfeiture and penalty as in and by this Act is directed to be delivered and paid to the informer, and to award Application of the penalties, &c. which may be levied by distress, &c.
107 and issue out his Warrant, under his hand and seal, for committing to prison such offenders, and for the time and times aforesaid, and for the levying the said forfeitures and penalties so adjudged on the goods of the offender, and to cause sale to be made thereof in case they shall not be redeemed within six days, rendering to the party the overplus, (if any,) and where the goods of such offender cannot be found sufficient to answer the penalty, to commit such offender to prison, there to remain for any space of time not exceeding   nor less than   unless such pecuniary penalty shall be sooner paid and satisfied; and if any party shall find himself or themselves aggrieved by the judgment of Persons aggrieved by such decision, may appeal to the Quarter Sessions.
108 any such Justice, then he or they shall and may, upon giving security to the satisfaction of such Justice, and to the amount and value of such forfeiture and penalty, together with such costs as shall be awarded in case such judgment shall be affirmed, appeal to the Justices of the Peace at the next General or Quarter Sessions for the County, Riding, Division, Shire, City or Place, which shall happen after fourteen days next after such Conviction shall have been made, and of which Appeal reasonable notice shall be given, who are hereby empowered to summon and examine witnesses upon oath, and finally to hear and determine the same; and in case judgment shall be affirmed, it shall be lawful for such Justices to award the Person or Persons appealing to pay such costs occasioned
109 by such Appeal as to them shall seem meet.

And be it further Enacted, That if any Person or Persons shall be summoned as a witness or witnesses to give evidence before such Justice or Justices, touching any of the matters relative to this Act, and shall neglect or refuse to appear at the time and place to be for that purpose appointed, without reasonable excuse for such neglect or refusal, to be allowed of by such Justice or Justices of Peace, or appearing shall refuse to be examined on oath (or being of the people called Quakers, upon solemn affirmation) and give evidence before whom the prosecution shall be depending, that then every such Person shall forfeit for any and every Witnesses not appearing, or not giving evidence.
110 such offence the sum of   to be levied, paid recovered Penalty. and appropriated in such manner as is hereinbefore directed, and so on so often as he or she shall offend as aforesaid.

And be it further Enacted, That the Justice or Justices of the Peace before whom any offender shall be convicted as aforesaid, shall cause the said Conviction to be made out in the manner and form following, or in Form of Conviction.

any other form of words to the same effect, *mutatis mutandis*; that is to say:—

" BE it Remembered, That on the   day of
"   in the year of our Lord   in the
" County of   of   was convicted
" before me [*or*, us]   [one *or*, two] of His
" Majesty's Justices of Peace for
" residing near the Place where the offence was committed; for
" that the said   since the
" day of   one thousand eight hundred and
" now past, did, contrary to the form of the Statute in that case
" made and provided [*here state the Offence against the Act,*]
"   and I [*or*, we] do declare and adjudge, That
" the said   hath [*here state the pain or
" penalty incurred, and the goods and wares forfeited, if any,*] and
" the sum of   lawful money of Great Britain,
" for the offence aforesaid, to be applied to such uses as the
" Law directs. Given under   [my *or*, our] hand
" and seal the   day of   one thousand eight
" hundred and

Convictions to be kept among the County Records, and not removeable into any Court.

Which Conviction the said Justice or Justices shall cause to be wrote fairly upon parchment, and returned to the next General or Quarter Sessions of the Peace for the County, Riding, Division, Shire, City or Place where such Conviction was made, to be filed by the proper Officer there, and there to remain and be kept among the Records of the same County, Riding, Division, Shire, City or Place; and no such Conviction shall be removed by Certiorari or other Process, into any Court whatsoever, any thing herein contained, or any Law or Statute to the contrary thereof in anywise notwithstanding.

SCHEDULE

SCHEDULE.

113   The Covenants of INDENTURE of APPRENTICESHIP, in this Act before mentioned and directed to be used.

T HIS INDENTURE Witnesseth, That   son of   late of   doth put himself Apprentice to   of   citizen and   of   to learn his art of   and with him (after the manner of an Apprentice,) to serve from the day of the date hereof, until the full end and term of Seven Years from thence next following, to be fully compleat and ended; during which term the said Apprentice his said Master faithfully shall serve; his secrets keep; his lawful commands every where gladly do. He shall do no damage to his said Master, nor see it to be done of others;

114   but that he to his power shall let or forthwith give warning to his said Master of the same. He shall not waste the goods of his said Master, nor lend them unlawfully to any. He shall not commit fornication, nor contract matrimony, within the said term. He shall not play at cards, dice, tables, or any other unlawful games, whereby his said Master may have any loss. With his own goods or others, during the said term, without license of his said Master, he shall neither buy nor sell. He shall not haunt taverns nor playhouses, nor absent himself from his said Master's house and service, day or night unlawfully, but in all things, as a faithful Apprentice, he shall behave himself towards his said Master, and all his, during the said term. And the said Master in consideration of   his said Apprentice, in the same art which he useth, by the best means that he can, shall teach and instruct, or cause to be taught and instructed, finding unto the said Apprentice (in the dwelling house of his said Master,) meat, drink, apparel, lodging, and all other necessaries, according to the custom of the City of *London*, during the said term. And for the true performance of all and every the said Covenants and Agreements, either of the said Parties bindeth himself unto the other by these Presents. In witness whereof the Parties above named to these Indentures interchangeably have set their hands and seals, the   day of   in the   year of the reign of our Sovereign Lord   by the grace of God of the United Kingdom of *Great Britain* and *Ireland*, King, Defender of the Faith, and in the year of our Lord one thousand   hundred and

Sess. 1818.

A

BILL

For the more effectual Prevention of Frauds and Abuses in the Manufacture, Exportation, and Importation of sundry Wares, and for the relief of distressed Workmen brought up to practise the Manufacture of Clocks and Watches.

Ordered, by The House of Commons, to be Printed,
8 *May* 1818.

www.ingramcontent.com/pod-product-compliance
Lightning Source LLC
Chambersburg PA
CBHW022106300426
44117CB00007B/606